LETTERS
— from a —
PRINCE

LETTERS
— from a —
PRINCE

EDWARD, PRINCE OF WALES
to
MRS FREDA DUDLEY WARD
MARCH 1918 – JANUARY 1921

Edited by
RUPERT GODFREY

LITTLE, BROWN AND COMPANY

A *Little, Brown* Book

First published in Great Britain in 1998
by Little, Brown and Company

A CIP catalogue record for this book is
available from the British Library.

ISBN 0 316 64677 6

Typeset in Garamond by M Rules
Printed and bound in Great Britain by
The Bath Press, Bath

Little, Brown and Company (UK)
Brettenham House
Lancaster Place
London WC2E 7EN

CONTENTS

EDITOR'S NOTE

The discovery of these letters is a story in itself – the result of a series of co-incidences: in November 1996, my wife and I were on holiday, visiting friends abroad. Our host, an avid collector all his life – particularly of stamps, envelopes and postcards – was recovering from an illness, and had decided that the time had come to sort out some of the material he had accumulated over the previous fifty years.

He was in the process of doing this during our visit, and quite by chance I was with him when he opened an old trunk filled with bundles of letters – some loose, some in envelopes – and bulging cardboard boxes, stuffed full of more letters, postcards and the odd photograph. He told me that he had not looked in this trunk for probably twenty years, but part of it was a collection he had bought from a Canadian work colleague back in the early 1950s. At that time he had been interested in a few of the envelopes for their early Canadian stamps, and some of the postmarks.

I began examining some of the envelopes, and, in particular, one dated 1918. I glanced at the letter inside, which appeared to be from a soldier in Italy writing to his wife. Mildly interested, I looked at more, and, with mounting excitement, started to suspect who had written them. Digging deeper into the trunk, I found another fading envelope full of old photographs which confirmed these suspicions: the writer was Edward, Prince of Wales.

Again, coincidentally, I had recently been rereading Philip Ziegler's biography of Edward VIII, and knew who 'Mrs Dudley Ward' was. My host had no such knowledge, and had never given more than a cursory glance to the actual letters in the envelopes. How his work colleague had acquired them was impossible to find out, as he had been dead some thirty years, though subsequent research showed that William Dudley Ward, Freda's husband, had settled in Alberta, Canada, after their divorce, and had died there.

Virtually the whole of the next few days were spent sorting out the contents of the trunk, separating this correspondence from all the other material, and matching up letters with their envelopes. At the end of this time, we had collected 263 letters written by the Prince, together with speeches, newspaper cuttings, odd cards and over 100 photographs, mostly signed or annotated by him. Also found in the same trunk were letters written by two of Freda's other admirers – Major Reginald Seymour and Michael Herbert.

After spending the next few days laboriously making what turned out to be 1,200 pages of photocopied material, I was able to give the correspondence my full attention.

Reading the letters for the first time, and then transcribing and editing them, became a truly fascinating experience, as, because of Edward VIII's key role in twentieth-century British history, any fresh information about his formative years is of great importance where it leads to a better understanding of his later actions.

It is sometimes hard to believe that the writer of these letters was the heir to the greatest throne in the world: his immaturity and insecurity show themselves constantly, and, even without the benefit of Freda Dudley Ward's replies to him, it is clear what a tremendous support she was to him. She must have had extraordinary patience and tolerance to be able to put up with his unceasing self-pity and unhappiness with his lot.

After his return from the war in 1919, her increasing influence in his life made any separation from her harder and harder for him to bear, and he relied on her letters to see him through his long tours abroad. How his staff must have dreaded any mail delivery which did not include a letter from her!

As well as his constant need for reassurance, however, what shines through the letters is the Prince's all-consuming love for his 'Fredie darling': a devotion which lasted for sixteen years, surviving other affairs – some brief, some longer-lasting – until it was abruptly transferred to Wallis Simpson in 1934, where it once again dominated his life, this time leading to his abdication.

What happened to Freda's correspondence to the Prince is unknown, although it is unlikely it survived long after their break-up. One of her letters to him, however, was found in the same trunk, and, while the words are tender, they do not remotely match the adoration and worship expressed by him.

As to the letters themselves: written in pencil, they are full of spelling, punctuation and grammatical errors, together with words omitted and gaps left. They were often written in the small hours of the morning, after a gruelling day's activities on a hectic schedule, so these faults are understandable, and their frequency or otherwise perhaps show his state of mind at the time.

For the most part the letters have been reproduced as they were written. However, except where the Prince spells particular words incorrectly on purpose, and they form part of his personal language with Freda, spelling errors have been corrected as their frequency would have been an irritation to the reader. For the same reason, and in order to ensure that interpreting the meaning of the many long, unpunctuated sentences does not become too wearing, simple punctuation has been added and the occasional grammatical mistake has been corrected. The addition of [*sic*] to indicate that the original material has been faithfully reproduced would have necessitated so many such insertions that this convention has been laid aside, but my own observations or explanations within the text of the letters are given in italics in square brackets.

The Prince's language was sometimes colourful: where he has used blanks, I have copied them; sometimes, however, he was not so polite, although, after an admonishment from Freda, the use of swear words diminished.

All of the photographs, newspaper cuttings and other material used to illustrate the book have been selected from the collection discovered with the letters, and many are referred to by the Prince in his correspondence. Not all of them are previously unseen: some are copies of pictures widely published elsewhere, others are personal mementos, but a good deal of them bear handwritten captions especially for Freda and they all complement the letters with which they were found.

By definition the editing process has necessitated the omission of some passages and some complete letters: there is such a wealth of correspondence that it would not have been possible to include it all. The two principal features which recur constantly throughout the entire correspondence are the Prince's outpourings of love for Freda and the expression of his misery at his lot in life.

Many such passages have been condensed or omitted entirely, as have others dealing with minor domestic or social matters. Cuts are indicated by ellipses.

Yet we are extraordinarily lucky that the Prince was such a prolific writer, and so frank with his own feelings. It is fascinating to read these letters in conjunction with his autobiography, *A King's Story*, written in 1951, to see how time, and writer's licence, changed his view of himself, these years and the people who shared them with him. Not surprisingly, but sadly, there is no mention of Freda in his book, which makes these letters all the more valuable.

Rupert Godfrey
Blandford Forum
September 1998

ACKNOWLEDGEMENTS

My first 'thank you' must be to the owner of the letters, who allowed me the opportunity to produce this book. My second is to my wife, Julie, for her support and patience throughout, especially while I learned to use a word-processor.

My agents, Mike Shaw and Andrew Best, were always helpful and encouraging, as were Alan Samson and Caroline North at Little, Brown.

Special thanks go to the Earl of Rosslyn for his permission to read, and to quote from, the unpublished autobiography of his grandmother, the Lady Loughborough of these letters.

I am grateful to L'Institut Pasteur, Paris, to which the late Duchess of Windsor bequeathed her late husband's literary estate, for its collaboration in seeing this collection through to publication.

Finally, thanks to the staff of Blandford Forum Public Library, who were always quick and efficient in meeting my requests.

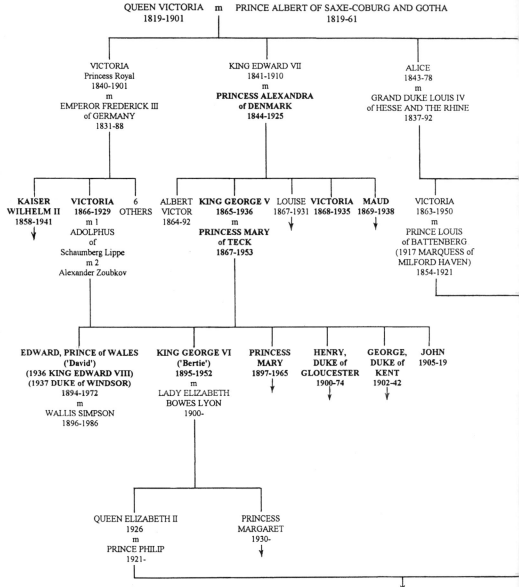

QUEEN VICTORIA **m** PRINCE ALBERT OF SAXE-COBURG AND GOTHA
1819-1901   1819-61

VICTORIA
Princess Royal
1840-1901
m
EMPEROR FREDERICK III
of GERMANY
1831-88

KING EDWARD VII
1841-1910
m
PRINCESS ALEXANDRA
of DENMARK
1844-1925

ALICE
1843-78
m
GRAND DUKE LOUIS IV
of HESSE AND THE RHINE
1837-92

KAISER
WILHELM II
1858-1941

VICTORIA
1866-1929
m 1
ADOLPHUS
of
Schaumberg Lippe
m 2
Alexander Zoubkov

6
OTHERS

ALBERT
VICTOR
1864-92

KING GEORGE V
1865-1936
m
PRINCESS MARY
of TECK
1867-1953

LOUISE
1867-1931

VICTORIA
1868-1935

MAUD
1869-1938

VICTORIA
1863-1950
m
PRINCE LOUIS
of BATTENBERG
(1917 MARQUESS of
MILFORD HAVEN)
1854-1921

EDWARD, PRINCE of WALES
('David')
(1936 KING EDWARD VIII)
(1937 DUKE of WINDSOR)
1894-1972
m
WALLIS SIMPSON
1896-1986

KING GEORGE VI
('Bertie')
1895-1952
m
LADY ELIZABETH
BOWES LYON
1900-

PRINCESS
MARY
1897-1965

HENRY,
DUKE of
GLOUCESTER
1900-74

GEORGE,
DUKE of
KENT
1902-42

JOHN
1905-19

QUEEN ELIZABETH II
1926
m
PRINCE PHILIP
1921-

PRINCESS
MARGARET
1930-

Family members featured in this book appear in bold type

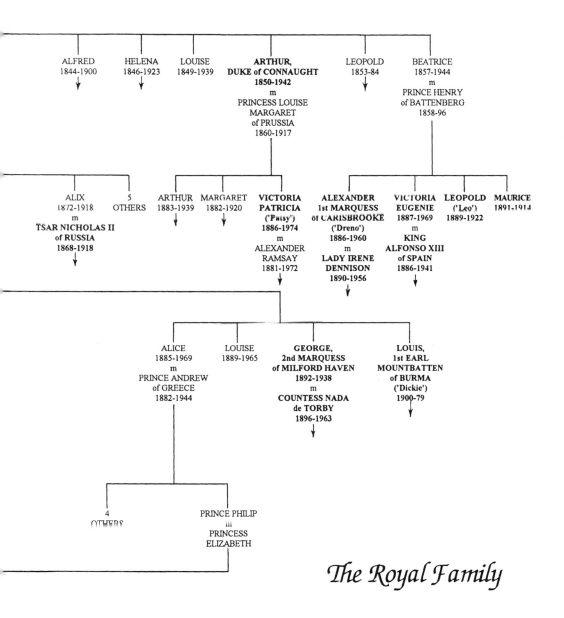

| ALFRED 1844-1900 | HELENA 1846-1923 | LOUISE 1849-1939 | **ARTHUR, DUKE of CONNAUGHT 1850-1942** m PRINCESS LOUISE MARGARET of PRUSSIA 1860-1917 | | LEOPOLD 1853-84 | BEATRICE 1857-1944 m PRINCE HENRY of BATTENBERG 1858-96 |

| ALIX 1872-1918 m **TSAR NICHOLAS II of RUSSIA 1868-1918** | 5 OTHERS | ARTHUR 1883-1939 | MARGARET 1882-1920 | **VICTORIA PATRICIA ('Patsy') 1886-1974** m **ALEXANDER RAMSAY 1881-1972** | **ALEXANDER 1st MARQUESS of CARISBROOKE ('Dreno') 1886-1960** m **LADY IRENE DENNISON 1890-1956** | **VICTORIA EUGENIE 1887-1969** m **KING ALFONSO XIII of SPAIN 1886-1941** | LEOPOLD ('Leo') 1889-1922 | MAURICE 1891-1914 |

| ALICE 1885-1969 m PRINCE ANDREW of GREECE 1882-1944 | LOUISE 1889-1965 | **GEORGE, 2nd MARQUESS of MILFORD HAVEN 1892-1938** m **COUNTESS NADA de TORBY 1896-1963** | **LOUIS, 1st EARL MOUNTBATTEN of BURMA ('Dickie') 1900-79** |

| 4 OTHERS | PRINCE PHILIP m PRINCESS ELIZABETH |

The Royal Family

CAST OF CHARACTERS

THE PRINCE'S FAMILY

George V (1865–1936): second son of Edward VII (the eldest son, Albert Victor, died in 1892); succeeded his father in 1910. A stickler for discipline, he found it difficult to communicate with his children, who were frightened of him well into adulthood. His favourite was his daughter, Mary.

He was moody and easy to anger; it is likely that some of his irascibility stemmed from the incessant pain he felt from a severe injury to his pelvis, sustained in October 1915, when, during a visit to troops on the Western Front, his horse reared up and fell on him.

He was a shy man, too, and his irritation with his eldest son has been put down by several observers to the jealousy he felt at the Prince's popularity, and the apparent ease with which his heir carried out his duties.

He had a passion for punctuality, and a fussiness about clothes. He was happiest when either shooting, or poring over his stamp albums. He did not enjoy socialising, and usually dined at home with his family around him, which his growing sons naturally found boring and repressive.

Blinkered by his narrow outlook, and surrounded by old-style courtiers, he did not begin to appreciate the changes in society being wrought by the Great War.

Queen Mary (1867–1953). Princess Mary of Teck was to have married Prince Albert

Victor before his unexpected death. Instead, she married Prince George a year later. She was dedicated to her husband and to the monarchy, and had a keen sense of duty. She adored her eldest son, though she, too, found it difficult to show her affection for her children.

During the Great War she had organised women's war work, and set an example by stopping all luxuries at the royal table with a code of rationing for the Royal Family and their guests. The cellars were locked and no alcohol was served.

Like her husband, however, she failed to move with the times: although she lived during the reigns of six British monarchs, she never in her life used the telephone, or flew in a plane, or tasted a cocktail.

They had six children:

Edward Albert Christian George Andrew Patrick David (known as David to family and very close friends), born 23 June 1894, died 28 May 1972. Created Prince of Wales on his sixteenth birthday, he was educated privately; then at Osborne Naval College; then Dartmouth; and, finally, at Magdalen College, Oxford. He joined the Grenadier Guards in August 1914, despite being five inches under the regulation height of six feet.

His boyish good looks and his radiant smile made him one of the first 'pin-ups', and, even before his tours of the Empire, he was an immensely popular figure. Despite the adoration of the masses around the world, however, he lacked confidence and generally hated what he saw as the role he had to play as Prince of Wales.

He was addicted to strenuous exercise, and he ate little, being concerned about getting fat. These two characteristics, especially when combined with the rigours and stress of his tours – when he often smoked and drank too much, and stayed up late at night – contributed to both physical and mental problems, as seen especially in the middle of his Australian tour programme.

His relationship with his father was never good: whereas King George loved everything old, his eldest son was completely the opposite, relishing the new, and realising the great changes to society and the old order that the war had wrought.

Albert (1895–1952), known as Bertie, later to become George VI. Bertie suffered from ill health as a child, and always had a weak stomach. He had knock knees and had been forced to wear splints on his legs, which, together with his being forced to be right-handed against his natural inclination, probably contributed towards the stammer which plagued his life.

His ill health made his life in the Royal Navy a difficult one; he served at Jutland, but after a long-overdue operation in November 1917 for a stomach ulcer, and a lengthy convalescence, he went to Cranwell and joined the RAF.

Mary (1897–1965), who later married Lord Lascelles, the future 6th Earl of Harewood. Her father's favourite, she led a cloistered life with her parents at whichever royal residence they were staying. Her eldest brother was very fond of her, and did what he could to help her lead a normal life, without great success.

Henry (1900–74), later Duke of Gloucester. After education at Eton, he attended Sandhurst. Amiable but highly strung, he never overcame the nervous strain caused by his fear of his father. Soon after the war, so a story goes, aged about nineteen, he came down late for breakfast one morning and before his father had time for a rebuke, he fainted.

George (1902–42), later Duke of Kent. A naval cadet at Dartmouth. He was the only one of the four brothers who remained uncowed by his father's discipline.

John (1905–19). He developed epilepsy at the age of four, after which he was separated from his brothers and sister. From then on, he lived a secluded life, latterly at Wood Farm, Wolferton, on the Sandringham estate, looked after by the royal nanny, Lala Bill.

The Royal Family spent their time at Buckingham Palace, Windsor Castle, Balmoral, and York Cottage on the Sandringham estate (the main house was still used by Queen Alexandra, widow of Edward VII).

The Prince's Entourage:

Lord Claud Hamilton (often referred to as 'the Lord Claud'). Son of the 2nd Duke of Abercorn. Captain in the Grenadier Guards, and awarded the DSO, he joined the Prince in 1915.

Piers 'Joey' Legh: son of Lord Newton, he joined the Prince in 1916.

Godfrey Thomas, the Prince's part-time Equerry, and later his private secretary. He left the Foreign Office to join him as his 'minder', in an attempt to get him to eat more and exercise less.

Lord Louis Mountbatten, known to the Prince as 'Dickie'. The son of Prince Louis of Battenberg (the First Sea Lord forced to resign in 1914 because of his German birth) and cousin to the Prince, whose entourage he joined for the tour to New Zealand and Australia in 1920.

KEY CHARACTERS

Freda Dudley Ward, born 28 July 1894, elder daughter of Colonel Charles Birkin, a prosperous lace manufacturer, of Lamcote, Radcliffe-on-Trent, Nottinghamshire, and his American wife, Claire. In 1913, she married William Dudley Ward. They had two children: Penelope and Angela. Freda had a sister called Vera.

Freda epitomised the changes in society which had taken place during the war, being fun-loving and sociable, though never superficial. She was petite, elegant and pretty, and seems to have been liked by all who met her, from all classes. Her charm was matched by her tact and discretion, and her influence on the Prince was seen by all who knew them as almost entirely for his good. Her most individual characteristic was her voice, which was rather thin and high, though oddly attractive.

Her great friend, Sheila, Lady Loughborough (see next page), described her: 'She was absolutely fascinating to look at, she had a good mind, a tremendous character, great loyalty and a wonderful sense of humour. She built one up and made one feel amusing and attractive. She had a strong influence on us all.'

Freda clearly liked the attentions of the men who clustered around her – the 'barrage' as she called them – and she was not averse to encouraging the attentions of more than one admirer at the same time.

William Dudley Ward ('Duddie'), nephew of the 1st Earl of Dudley, and grandson of the 1st Viscount Esher. Educated at Eton, he was a distinguished 'wet bob' (an Etonian who goes in for rowing), and rowed in the Cambridge Eight for three years. Sixteen years older than his wife, he was Liberal MP for Southampton 1906–22 and Vice-Chamberlain to the Royal Household 1917–22. Lady Loughborough described him as 'kind, jolly and vague'.

Rosemary Leveson-Gower, daughter of the 4th Duke of Sutherland, and niece of the Earl of Rosslyn. The Prince was very attracted to her in early 1918, and was considering marriage, but was warned off her by Queen Mary, probably because of an alleged strain of madness in her mother's family.

'Geordie', 5th Duke of Sutherland (Rosemary's brother), and **Eileen**, his Duchess (the daughter of Lord Lanesborough). They had houses in London; at Sutton Place, near Guildford; and Dunrobin in Sutherland.

Sheila, Lady Loughborough ('Sheilie'), née Chisholm, an Australian. Freda described her as the most beautiful girl she had ever seen.

She had married **Lord Loughborough** ('Loughie'), heir to Lord Rosslyn, in Cairo in 1915, as he convalesced after having been wounded at Gallipoli. After returning to England, he was appointed Adjutant of the King's Royal Rifle Corps, and served at the depot in Winchester. They had a house nearby, called Lankhills.

Sheila soon became part of 'the Duchess of Sutherland's set' in London society, spending much of her time with the same friends: Freda, the Sutherlands, 'Poots' Francis (see below), and, soon, the Princes, Edward and Bertie.

Loughie, however, like his father Harry, Earl of Rosslyn, was addicted to gambling and alcohol, and the marriage was a shaky one, held together by the birth in 1917 of a son and heir, Tony.

Gwendolyn Francis, née van Raalte, known as 'Poots'. (Her sister, Margherita, was the great hostess Lady Howard de Walden.) Her husband, Noel, and Loughie were birds of a feather, and Poots became a great friend of Freda, Sheila and the Prince. She lived in a large maisonette at 65 Duke Street, off Grosvenor Square, at which her friends often stayed.

Portia Cadogan (Lady Sybil), a close friend of Princess Mary, who had a mutual attachment to the Prince in 1916–17. Why it was broken off is unknown, but early in 1917, she became engaged to Edward Stanley, one of the Prince's friends from Oxford days, and son of Lord Derby. Bertie had also been very fond of her.

Marion Coke, wife of Viscount Coke, heir to the Earl of Leicester, who lived at Holkham in Norfolk, quite close to Sandringham. Twelve years older than the Prince, she was his first great love, although the relationship was almost certainly uncon-summated. He needed to be mothered, and she may have fulfilled that role for him. Once the 'relationship' was over, however, the Prince turned totally against her, as was to happen to many others.

Major Reginald Seymour ('Reggie'), the son of Sir George Seymour, and great-grandson of the 1st Marquess of Hertford. He had been severely wounded in South

Africa in 1901, and, serving with the King's Royal Rifle Corps, was again badly wounded in 1914.

He had been appointed Equerry to George V in 1916, and was regularly in attendance on the Royal Family at Windsor, Buckingham Palace and Sandringham. Born in 1878, he met Freda in April 1918 and was soon smitten by her. Thirty of his letters to her, written during 1918 and 1919, were also found, and, where relevant, have been quoted.

Michael Herbert, the Earl of Pembroke's younger brother, feared by the Prince, as time passed, as his main rival for Freda's affections. Initially, Michael disliked the Sutherland set, moving in a different circle himself, and was jealous of Freda when she was with them. Some of his letters to Freda, written during 1923, were also discovered, and are interesting in that they show the same insecurity and jealousy prevalent in the Prince's correspondence when his rival is mentioned.

Lord Burghersh ('Burghie'), son of the Earl of Westmorland, a long-standing admirer of Freda's.

Sir Philip Sassoon of the Sassoon dynasty, known as 'the Rothschilds of the East', bankers to successive Ottoman rulers in Baghdad, and cousin of Siegfried Sassoon, the war poet. Extremely wealthy and highly intelligent, Sassoon had become the youngest MP at Westminster when elected for Hythe, and during the war had served as Douglas Haig's secretary in France.

After the war he became Secretary to Lloyd George. He had houses at 25 Park Lane, in London; Trent Park, a 1,000-acre estate near New Barnet; and Port Lympne, in his constituency, near Folkestone in Kent, described by 'Chips' Channon as 'a triumph of beautiful bad taste'. Highly regarded, but also criticised as a sycophant, he moved in the highest social and political circles.

INTRODUCTION

The spring of 1918 was the fourth of the Great War. The conflict, which had begun in August 1914 with British generals confidently predicting victory by Christmas, had slowly ground to a static, trench-dominated stalemate, punctuated by a series of bloody battles as both sides sought to make a significant breakthrough of the opposing lines.

The autumn of 1917 had seen the failure of the British to make any real gains in the Third Battle of Ypres, otherwise known as Passchendaele, at enormous cost. The British generals appeared to have learned little from earlier battles, and had not radically changed any of the tactics that had proved so ineffective before, and the figure of 860,000 British casualties during the year told its own story.

In Italy, the stalemate of the previous two years had been ended with the crushing defeat of the Italian army by a combined German and Austrian force, at Caporetto, in November.

There was, therefore, little to cheer about as 1918 began, little to suggest that the war would be over within the year. The position was changing on both sides, however: the collapse of the Russian Empire had allowed the Germans to transfer large numbers of troops to the Western Front, seriously changing the balance of power in the short term.

By now, too, the Germans knew that their campaign of unrestricted U-boat warfare was in danger of costing them the war. Not only had it failed to starve the Allies into submission, but, more importantly, in April 1917, it had brought America, with its huge resources, into the conflict against them. Although their troops had barely begun to arrive in France in March 1918, the threat was clear.

Having lost the war at sea, therefore, Germany decided to stake all on a last desperate gamble on land: the 'Kaiser's battle', planned for March 1918.

Code-named 'Michael', the German Commander-in-Chief Ludendorff's planned attack aimed to separate the bulk of the British army from the French, and force it back to the Channel. This, he hoped, would also cause the French to collapse, and make the Americans think twice before committing their troops to a lost cause.

At this time, Edward, Prince of Wales, was on leave in London. He had joined the staff of Major-General Lord Cavan in France in 1915. After a scare at the Battle of Loos, when enemy shells burst dangerously close to his party, and another killed his chauffeur, the Prince was kept as far from the action as possible, rarely being allowed to venture close to danger. He had complained to Lord Kitchener, then Secretary of State for War, saying that as he had four brothers, it did not matter if he was killed. Kitchener replied that he was not worried about the Prince being killed, but seriously concerned that he might be captured.

After a visit to the Middle East in early 1916, the Prince rejoined Lord Cavan, now commanding the XIV Army Corps. In 1917, British and French reinforcements were suddenly transferred to the Italian front, to bolster the fragile Italian army after the disaster at Caporetto. Cavan's corps was chosen, with the Prince of Wales playing a morale-boosting role, alternately liaising with the Italians and French armies, and visiting British troops at the front whenever possible.

The Prince's experiences in France had filled him with admiration for the soldiers of both the British and French armies (though he had little confidence in their senior officers), but he had no time for the Italians, or some other allies, like the Portuguese and Belgian contingents in France.

The situation in Italy stabilised almost immediately the reinforcements arrived, so much so that, early in 1918, Edward was called home to make a tour of defence plants, and took advantage of being in London to enjoy some leave as well. The presence in London of the Prince, now aged twenty-three and the most eligible bachelor in the Empire, was the cause of much excitement.

Early in his leave he spent much of his time with Rosemary Leveson-Gower, and going to balls and parties, whenever he could get away from the confines of family life at Buckingham Palace.

Late in February the Prince attended a party in Belgrave Square. During the evening, an air-raid warning sounded, and a couple, Buster Domingues and Freda Dudley Ward, who had been walking through the square, sought refuge in the doorway of the house where the party was taking place. The hostess, Mrs Kerr-Smiley (ironically the sister of Ernest Simpson, who would figure so prominently in the Prince's later life), saw them and invited them in to shelter with her other guests in the cellar.

Edward was immediately attracted to Freda, and when the all-clear sounded, she was persuaded to stay, and they danced together for the rest of the evening. Freda's marriage, by this time, was over in all but name, and she and her husband led largely separate lives, with Freda bringing up their two daughters while at the same time enjoying an active social life.

After the party, the Prince wrote to 'Mrs Dudley Ward' at 70 Lowndes Square, suggesting a further meeting, but the letter was opened in error by Freda's mother-in-law, with whom she was staying. She invited the Prince for what must have been a very surprising tea, but her efforts to thwart him were evidently unsuccessful, as there began a relationship which was to last until 1934, and the arrival of Mrs Simpson on the scene.

The first letter dates from just days after this meeting.

Buckingham Palace,
S.W.

3rd March 1918.

Dear Mrs Ward,

Here is your latch
key which was found in the
electric car after all; but I'm
so glad it has been found !!
It was awfully nice of you
having me to tea yesterday
evening, ~~it~~ & waiting for a
later train; I hope you got
down to Windsor in time for
dinner !! I leave for Glasgow
to-night but hope to get
back early Thursday morning;
will there be any chance of
seeing you that day & can you
suggest any ~~and~~ rendez vous

Buckingham Palace,
S.W.

26th March 1918.

My Angel !!

I can't tell you how I
hated having to say good bye this morning
I hoped against hope that I might get
a note from you to say that you had'nt
gone after all & that we could meet
again !! But alas, no note, ~~it~~ ~~it~~ I suppose
you have gone & I'm sure ~~it~~ in the best
thing for you to do, tho' I do feel so
lonely & miserable, darling !! And my
last night in England too & I'm off
to ITALY not FRANCE, to-morrow
which means I shall be away months
instead of weeks !! ~~It~~ too fearfully sad
& depressing, as is the news & everything
else just now, but we must hope for
the heat !! Just after I left you at 1.0.
I was told to postpone my departure
for French G.H.Q. "till further orders" which
might have meant waiting in London a
week or more, very pleasant ~~as~~ as I
should have stayed over next Sunday, but

England, France and Italy

❧

1918

Buckingham Palace, SW
3rd March 1918

Dear Mrs Ward,

Here is your latch key which was found in the electric car after all; but I am so glad that it has been found!! It was awfully nice of you having me to tea yesterday evening, & waiting for a later train; I hope you got down to Windsor in time for dinner!!

I leave for Glasgow tonight but hope to get back early Tuesday morning; will there be any chance of seeing you that day & can you suggest any rendezvous other than 70, Lowndes Square which house, I must confess rather terrifies me!! But of course it is for you to say whatever you wish me to do!! I'm afraid I'm an awful bore but I can't help it!!!!

Please forgive this fearful scrawl & hoping I may see you somehow, somewhere on Thursday, I remain,

Yours very sincerely

Edward

The Prince was travelling to Glasgow to spend three days touring shipyards on the Clyde.

Freda spent much of her time at Kilbees Farm, Winkfield, near Windsor; the Prince would later refer to Kilbees as 'the Little Cottage', after a popular song of the time.

Electric cars were relatively common in 1918. They could cover between fifty and eighty miles on a single charge, and were particularly popular with ladies, who found starting handles hard work. The introduction of the electric self-starter motor in the 1920s led to the electric car's rapid decline.

> *Buckingham Palace, SW*
> *7th March 1918*

Dear Mrs Ward,

Thank you ever so much for asking me to dinner tomorrow night through Burghie [*Lord Burghersh*]; but alas I can't manage tomorrow, I'm so sorry, if only I had known before!! But we must fix up another evening next week if you would care to; perhaps we may meet at the Pembrokes' dance this evening as I think you told me you were going, & we can have a talk then. But I write in case we shan't meet though I sincerely hope we shall!!

I only arrived back at 9.00 this morning; I suppose you have been away racing today!! I hope you got the key all right. Please forgive my inflicting you with another scrawl & I remain,

yours very sincerely,

Edward

The Earl of Pembroke had houses in London and at Wilton, near Salisbury. Michael Herbert, later the Prince's rival for Freda's affections, was his younger brother.

> *Buckingham Palace, SW*
> *8th March 1918*

Dear Mrs Ward,

Yet another note, only I have been unlucky as regards the telephone as you had just gone out when I rang up this morning!! So please forgive me!!

Now what about this dance this evening? You didn't seem very keen to go last night (or rather this morning) & I can't say I am really unless it's the only chance of seeing you!!

Look here, may I look in about 6.15 or 6.30 this evening if you will be in by then? I told you I have to go to this ⸺ ⸺ tea party at the Farquhars' at 5.00 & shall have to stay there at least an hour I'm afraid!! But I could look in afterwards; could you send me a message to the Bath Club to say Yes or No as I shall be there soon after 6.00 P.M.

But there are several things I want to ask you as regards Sunday & next week, if you will be alone. But a dance is such a rotten place to meet for a talk isn't it?!!

I'm so fearfully sorry about dinner tonight but I was fixed up though I should like to explain about that too!! I do hope that I may look in but only if it suits & you will be alone & please forgive my being such a bore but I can't help it!!!!

Hoping you may get this before 6.00 I remain

yours very sincerely

Edward

Horace, 1st Earl Farquhar, was Master of the Household under Edward VII, and a close friend of George V, to whom he let the shooting on his Norfolk estate, Castle Rising, close to Sandringham. When he died in 1923, he left an estate provisionally valued at £400,000, with many bequests to the Royal Family. However, not only had debts rendered the estate valueless, but also £80,000 had been appropriated from a trust fund, which his co-trustee, Louise, the Princess Royal (George V's sister), had to make good. His London house was in Grosvenor Square, and after his death, it was bought by Maud (later 'Emerald') Cunard.

The Bath Club was a swimming pool, Turkish bath and squash courts in Berkeley Street.

MARCH 1918: THE KAISER'S BATTLE

At 4.40 A.M. on the morning of 21 March, the German artillery opened fire. The attack, which had been expected by the British, and yet who had made few contingency plans to counter it, differed from previous ones, in that instead of a barrage lasting days, or even weeks, as some preceding ones had, the bombardment lasted a mere five hours.

However, it was the most concentrated barrage of the war to date: 7,000 guns fired over one million shells on a front of 30 miles. One in four of the shells was gas, knocking out the infantry opposing them; the others were high explosive, cutting the barbed wire and destroying the trenches and the communication system behind them.

The barrage was followed by another innovation: the infantry attack was made up of small squads of German stormtroopers, who infiltrated the smashed British front line and quickly created breaches through which the German Eighteenth Army poured, virtually unopposed, into the open country beyond.

The success of the attack exceeded all expectations. By midday, Haig's Fifth Army had lost one third of its strength, and in two days the Germans made the sort of advance unheard of in recent battles – a distance of fourteen miles. Only the smashed remnants of Haig's forces stood between the Germans and Amiens, a key strategic rail centre, and the link between the British and French forces.

Field Marshal Sir Douglas Haig had been Commander-in-Chief of the British forces since December 1915, when he had succeeded Sir John French. It has long been debated whether it was his lack of strategic vision, and his blinkered, old-fashioned ideas of warfare (he believed that cavalry were the key to long-term success on the Western Front, and that machine-guns had only a limited use), that led to the costly and ineffectual campaigns of 1916 and 1917; or whether he was hampered in his role by the political demands of the French on the one side, and Lloyd George's interference on the other. The evidence appears to support the former argument, and the performance of some of his generals was little better.

Haig had expected to be able to withstand any German attack on the British sector, but was confounded by the tactics employed, and the speed of the German advance. This confusion and uncertainty in northern France meant that the Prince, who was expecting to join Haig at his headquarters, was instead instructed to return to Italy.

Buckingham Palace, SW
26th March 1918

My Angel!!

I can't tell you how much I hated having to say goodbye this morning. I hoped against hope that I might get a note from you to say that you hadn't gone after all & that we could meet again!!

But alas, no note, so I suppose you have gone & I am sure it is the best thing for you to do, though I feel so lonely & miserable, darling!! And my last night in England too & I'm off to ITALY not FRANCE, tomorrow which means I shall be away months instead of weeks!! It's too fearfully sad and depressing for words as is the news & everything else just now, but we must hope for the best!!

Just after I left you at 1.00 I was told to postpone my departure for French G.H.Q. 'till further orders' which might have meant waiting in London a week or more, very pleasant as I should have stayed over next Sunday, but still hardly politic just now when my father & everybody are anxious for me to go abroad at once!! [*The King was keen that nobody should suggest that the Prince was staying out of danger in England because the situation in France was so poor, especially as Prince Albert was convalescing at home at the same time.*]

So as they don't want me in France, I am just returning to my billet at G.H.Q. ITALY & in many ways I am glad; but of course it means that I shall be away much longer & that we may not meet for ages & I simply hate to think of that, darling!! I will write as soon as I arrive at G.H.Q. ITALY though God knows when that will be & 'the Lord Claud' [*Hamilton*] & I will probably have lots of adventures on the way out, particularly this side of Paris!!!!

Again millions and millions of thanks for all your great kindness to me & everything, darling; I can't possibly write all I want to say to you or thank you properly but I know you will understand!! I'm afraid this is a very indiscreet letter but you said it was safe to write & that it wouldn't be opened; I can't help writing like this (& how much more could I write but dare not!) though please tell me if I have been silly as I expect I have!! I have been careful not to mention names or places or dates or anything like that & I don't think I have said anything very terrible though how I long to, angel!!

Please don't forget the photos as I'm so miserable having to go away without one & please do write often as I will!! It will be so wonderful to hear from you & your letters will cheer me up & do me worlds of good!!!! You know my address & I have all yours!!

I had a hectic afternoon & had to go to the War Office again to find out where I was to 'proceed' (good word) to French G.H.Q. or ITALY!!!! . . .

Again thank you, millions & millions & millions of times for everything my angel; tons & tons of love from

your E.

Hotel Meurice, Paris
28th March 1918

Angel!!

. . . I arrived here this afternoon & leave for Italy tomorrow night; I stayed last night in BOULOGNE as there was no train & motored here today in about 7 hours, a long dusty drive and we passed hundreds of wretched refugees on the road: A very pathetic & depressing sight though the news from our front seems a bit better; it's the French on our immediate right who are being hard-pressed now & the Huns have taken Montdidier & are still advancing South of Amiens!!

But enough war shop; I should reach G.H.Q. ITALY on Sunday with luck!! Paris is actually rather depressed, as bad as London in fact. One can't buy any chocolate or I would have sent you some darling!! . . .

Please forgive such a fearful scrawl but it's all such a rush here as you can imagine!! Dull & cold & beastly weather though it should prevent air raids!!

Tons & tons of my very best love, Freda darling
from your vvvvvvv devoted

E.

The Hotel Meurice was always a favourite of the Prince's. Immediately after his abdication, when he was living in Paris, he had a semi-permanent suite there.

1918: THE WAR IN ITALY

The Kingdom of Italy had only existed since 1860, when most of the country was united, although it was not until 1870 that the Pope was displaced as ruler of Rome, which became the nation's capital.

Although territories with large Italian populations still existed under Austrian rule, Italy had joined a 'Triple Alliance' with Germany and Austria-Hungary in 1882. Despite this alliance, however, Italy had remained neutral in 1914, although under intense German pressure to declare war on the 'Triple Entente' of France, Britain and Russia.

While Austria prevaricated about Italian territorial demands, the Triple Entente promised Italy everything it wanted in the secret Treaty of London of 26 April 1915, with the result that war was declared on Austria-Hungary in May 1915.

The Italian army was led by General Cadorna, who had transformed it by 1915 from an inefficient force into a credible unit, though it was still beset by problems of supply and a poor-quality officer corps. Over the next two years, the front in Italy, in the Isonzo valley, was the scene of a dozen ineffective Italian offensives against the Austrians, which achieved little, at enormous cost to both men and morale.

The Austrians, however, worn down by these repeated battles, decided to gamble on a massive counterattack. On 24 October 1917, the Austro-Hungarian army, reinforced by German troops from the now almost defunct Russian front, broke through the Italian defences at Caporetto, and, over the next two weeks, captured 300,000 prisoners and 3,000 guns.

Strengthened by the British and French, and with Cadorna replaced by General Diaz, the Italians regrouped and set up a new defensive position on the Piave River, just north of Venice.

G.H.Q. British Forces, ITALY
1st April 1918

Angel!!

Just a line to tell you that I arrived at my destination in Italy at 8.00 A.M. this morning . . . I had to leave the train at 6.30 A.M. though I slept all the way in the car during the hour's drive to this spot, in the hills South of Asiago!!

It has been pouring in sheets the whole day which has made my return here all the more depressing & I feel absolutely like death tonight darling!!!! And heaven only knows how long I shall be stuck out here now; months & months I should think though I must hope for the best!! And it's a whole week since we parted; it seems years & years somehow!! Oh!! this — — — — war!!!!

You will be amused to hear that 3 of the famous shells fell & burst in Paris on Friday afternoon & that I heard one of them; & they were shells all right & fired from a long-range gun, there was no mistaking the sound!!!!

The news from France seems to be a little better though the situation is still very serious; how kind fate is to have sent me back to ITALY, so that I am escaping that fearful battle!! It's very unpatriotic of

me to say this but still these are my genuine feelings whatever else I
may say, & I always tell you my feelings; & after all this is the 4th year
of war isn't it? Not that I haven't been a — — 'red tab' [*staff officer*] the
whole time!! . . .

It's too beastly for words back amongst all these generals again, to
whom I am more or less chained; of course the 'Lord Claud' travelled
back with me & we found Legh here [*Piers 'Joey' Legh*] who returned
about a month ago, having only had 2 weeks' leave!! Still my leave
wasn't all roses as you know though the last fortnight was marvellous
somehow, from my point of view!!

But I must stop now, so as to catch the [*King's*] Messenger's bag,
which is really the only way to send letters!!!!

How I am looking forward to getting the photo & snapshots you
have promised me; I hate not having one with me!! And please tell me
if these silly letters of mine bore you or are too hopelessly indiscreet
but I can't help writing like this!!

Good night, Freda darling, tons & tons of all my very best love from
your

E.

P.S. My address is always Buckingham Palace.

A huge German howitzer with a range of 65 miles, nicknamed 'Big Bertha' after the
wife of its manufacturer, Gustav Krupp, had begun to shell Paris on 23 March.

The 'King's Messenger' service dated back to 1199, when it was set up by King
John as a confidential courier system between the monarch and his ambassadors. At
the outbreak of war in 1914, the service had only six Messengers, and these were aug-
mented by naval and military staff, to ensure secure communications between
Generals and Commanders-in-Chief back to the War Office. The Prince used the service for all his mail.

G.H.Q. British Forces, ITALY
4th April 1918

My Angel,

What a joy to get that sweet & wonderful letter from you today . . .
Darling how can you ask me if I love you? What a fearful question

when you know I love you to distraction & you know I mean it too!!
It's such a relief to know that you didn't think my 1st letter frightfully
indiscreet & dangerous; anyhow all my letters will now go to Kilbees
Farm, where they can only fall into the hands of your wonderful maid if
you are away!!!! So I feel quite safe though I didn't like writing to
Nottinghamshire [*Lamcote, Freda's father's house*] so much!!!!

How can you say I was nice to you when I inflicted all those drives
in taxis on you & kept you up so late at dances & other evenings!! It
was too wonderful of you not to mind my weird habits of dining at
home so often & generally neglecting you; but you know now, that it
wasn't my fault & that I longed to spend every minute of each 24 hours
with you, darling!!

How I loved & can never forget that last Sunday afternoon & evening
at the Farm; that was easily our best stunt [*'stunt' was the Prince's
favourite term for describing any official, or private, engagement*] but may it
often be repeated is all I can pray for!! . . .

I'm afraid I have no news for you from here, though our G.H.Q. isn't
such a bad spot considering, being a comfortable 'villa' in the foothills
below the ASIAGO mountains; we have 3 Divisions out here, 2 of which
are in the line, up in the mountains, from opposite ASIAGO to a few
kilometres to the West, an interesting though luckily quiet sector!! I
was up there yesterday & visited 2 O.P.'s [*Observation Posts*] & got
wonderful views which is a pleasant change to sitting in muddy
trenches in FLANDERS!!

Of course the one great drawback to Italy is the leave question
though I think all leave has been stopped for the present while this
great battle rages which seems to have abated somewhat the last day or
two!!

We have I think saved the situation though there is no doubt that
the French have helped us enormously; 2 more French Divisions have
been ordered back to FLANDERS today from this front so that shows how
short of troops they are as well as ourselves!!!!

But I must hope for the best as regards leave & seeing you again,
darling one; you bet that I shan't miss a chance of getting home again
as soon as possible & I only hope my family will be at Windsor then, I
wonder why!!!!

Life is as deadly dull & depressing as ever out here & I am so bored

ITALY. April 1918.

The Prince photographed near Asiago
on his return to Italy.

though this is only my 4th night here; but I suppose I shall get used to it again; you see I've been away about 2 months which is a very long time compared to my previous leave, & the longer one is away, the worse is the return off leave!!!!

But I got a bottle of your scent (Royal Briar) the morning I left & that means a great deal to me though I don't suppose you can realise this!! But I put some on my handkerchief when I go to bed & then I feel happy as it smells of you, angel!! It is too divine for words though of course it has a fearful effect on me & makes me temporarily insane!!!! But I adore feeling like that for you & thinking of you more than ever, though how can I ever stop thinking of you which I do throughout each 24 hours!! . . .

Goodnight Freda my darling & do write again soon as I just live for your letters! Tons & tons of my very best love & des milliers de baisers from your very very devoted adoring

E.

THE BRITISH ARMY

The British Forces in Europe were composed of a number of separate 'armies', made up, on paper, as shown below:

Name	Officer	Numbers of men
Army	General	200,000
4 Corps	Lt-General	50,000
4 Divisions	Major-General	12,000
3 Brigades	Brigadier	4,000
2 Regiments	Colonel	2,000
2 Battalions	Major	1,000
4 Companies	Captain	250
4 Platoons	Lieutenant	60
4 Sections	Lance-Corporal	15

THE PROGRESS OF OPERATION MICHAEL

Ludendorff's offensive against Amiens had ground to a halt: he had made the strategic error of splitting his assault into three, each with different objectives, instead of concentrating on Amiens. Crucially, he also lacked the reserves of men and supplies vital to capitalise on his initial success, which would ultimately lead to the failure of the German offensives.

On 9 April, however, Ludendorff switched his attack to Flanders, across the River Lys, where, after a Portuguese division had given way, Haig issued his famous 'Order of the Day': 'There must be no retirement. With our backs to the wall, and believing in the justice of our cause, each one must fight to the end.' The British troops responded once more, and, again, this German attack came to a halt.

G.H.Q. British Forces, ITALY
7th April 1918

Angel,

Your perfectly sweet letter of last Sunday, 31st March, reached me this morning; how I do love it & thank you millions & millions of times for it!! . . .

You do write me such wonderful letters darling, & they do make me feel so happy, my only ray of light in this fearful existence of boredom & monotony. I'm beginning to feel desperate & I've only been back a week; heavens only knows how many more I shall be doomed to spend here or what I shall get like later on!!

But I really oughtn't to grouse as here I am sitting in comfort at a G.H.Q. & not in France; of course the root of all my troubles is the way I miss you, darling, & I do miss you so so terribly & I can't cure that!! I can't bear to think of a fortnight ago today, that most divine of all afternoons & evenings & how happy you made me, darling; but I mustn't go on lamenting over the past & should on the other hand look forward to let's hope even happier days together next time I am home!! . . .

How can you suggest that your letters might become irksome? I have told you darling that they are the only things that keep me alive, though your plan of only writing when I write is a very good one as then our letters won't cross!! I'm afraid mine are stupid & boring to a degree but still I must write to you, darling, even if I have no news, as I do so love it & feel so much better & happier when I have written!!

8th April

This has been a hectic day as the Duke of Connaught [*Arthur, Edward VII's younger brother, and Edward's great-uncle*] arrived here for lunch & is staying till Friday; he is on his way home from Egypt & Palestine & has come to look at the 'British Forces, ITALY'!! So a general 'flap' & everyone rushing about & heavy meals etc. etc.!!!!

But I had a long walk on Saturday & climbed right up to an O.P. in the mountains which did me worlds of good, as I hadn't had any exercise for months except dancing!!!! There were masses of primroses all the way up on the banks of the mule track & I picked the enclosed for you, darling, & they have squashed [*pressed*] rather well, haven't they?

Then yesterday I had to motor miles to call on the King of Italy [*Victor Emmanuel III, Italy's last king, who was finally to abdicate in 1946*] & afterwards General Diaz, the Italian Commander-in-Chief, which was rather a bore; but I went in my own car (or rather the Lancia lent me by the Italians) which I always drive myself, so that made the trip less monotonous.

These Italians are such terrible people for paying & returning calls & they are altogether far too polite, though I suppose it's their custom!! They are funny people & no mistake, though some of them are quite nice.

Legh went to ROME last Wednesday to meet the Duke of Connaught & had 48 hours there on his own though I don't think he found it such fun as he (& we) expected he would!! I hope to get there some time next month for a few days as I feel I ought to see the place & what there is there though I expect I shall be very disappointed!!

I have to get up at 6.00 A.M. tomorrow to go round some trenches up in the mountains, which is a perfectly loathsome thought; I hate having to shove off before 9.00 as I hate getting up before 8.00 A.M. at the earliest!! 10.00 A.M. is more my style!!

What a lazy brute I am, though I always prefer sitting up late to getting up early & doing all my writing late at night & never go to bed before 2.00 A.M.!!!! But tonight I must, so I shall be finishing this letter now, though it's a great effort to stop writing to you, darling!!

Heavens how I wish you were here as I do feel so fearfully lonely; this villa isn't such a bad spot & the views are divine!! But of course it is completely ruined by being a H.Q. & full of generals & staff officers . . .

. . . Tons & tons of my very best love to my darling from her very very very very devoted E.

Milles et milles baisers, Bébée!!!!

G.H.Q. British Forces, ITALY
11th April 1918

My Angel,

It seems ages since I last wrote so I must just send you a line to say that I'm still alive; the Duke of Connaught leaves us tomorrow & so I'm sending this home with one of his people!!!! . . .

I went up into the mountains early on Tuesday & had a long walk in 'no man's land' in front of our front line trenches though behind our outpost line, which is a long way out!! But we have a very quiet & cushy sector & I wasn't so very frightened though of course I was a bit!! But those sort of walks do me more good than anything in the world & teach me so much more from every point of view, besides making me so grateful to fate that I don't have to live up there!!

I hear my family went to WINDSOR last Saturday; oh!! why am I not there too & it would be so easy to slip over to the farm from there!! I brought a gramophone back with me too & I play 'Have a heart' & 'The Little Cottage' & all our tunes when I'm feeling particularly lonely & it does me good in a way though it's also rather depressing sometimes!!

I suppose you go up to London from time to time, though that must be more depressing than anything else or any other place just now, particularly as we have begun to be attacked & to lose ground from MESSINES to LA BASSEE, which we heard this morning.

Who would have thought that the Huns would attack up North as well; and I'm afraid they won't stop yet awhile & that we are in for a bad summer in FRANCE & probably all leave stopped which alone is a pretty grim & morbid thought!! . . .

Must stop now, & please forgive this silly pencil scrawl but it's very late & I'm very sleepy!!

Good night Freda darling, & don't forget your E who sends tons & tons of love & 'des milliers de baisers les plus tendres'!!!!

G.H.Q. British Forces, ITALY
14th April 1918

My Angel,

What a joy to get another sweet letter from you today dated 7th. Thank you millions & millions of times for it, darling one, & all the lovely things you said in it which have made me so frightfully happy despite the bad news from FRANCE!! . . . If only I could get just a glimpse of you again soon; what a cruel thing this war is, ruining the best years of one's life & banishing one from England!! . . .

I heard a rumour that the King had written personally to Lady Drogheda remonstrating with her for giving that dance though I haven't heard any other details except what you tell me; but I must say that I think it's the worst possible form to give dances during this most desperate & critical period of the war, don't you darling? [*Lady Drogheda's dance made her very unpopular, as not only was the battle raging in France, but it was also Holy Week.*]

I know you do & of course you didn't go to her dance though I hear 3 'embusqué' [*military slang for a 'shirker'*] generals were there, needless to say 'Branker' was one!!!! [*Sefton Branker, later Director of Civil Aviation, who died in the R101 disaster in 1930.*] What a disgusting little man & you remember how he used to 'barge' around at all those parties, rather drunk!!!!

Things are looking pretty black on the Western Front, aren't they, particularly with this Northern Hun advance & we are all fearfully anxious out here as you may imagine though fairly confident!! It's the manpower question which is apparently our real trouble & anxiety, though I suppose & trust we shall come out 'on top', somehow or other as we generally do!! [*Haig had considered that he had adequate troops to withstand any German attack, and plenty of time to reinforce them should it become necessary. These miscalculations, coupled with the government's reluctance to send more troops to the slaughter, had resulted in a critical shortage of manpower to counter the German attack on the British sector of the Western Front.*]

Thank goodness IRELAND has at last been roped in to conscription, though this ought to have been done ages ago!! I don't know where Guards Division is now, though I have seen 2 of their casualty lists though there was nobody I knew well; the cavalry have had some casualties too, though you will know far more about this than I do!! . . .

Tons & tons of love to my Angel from her devoted E.

Conscription in Ireland was a thorny problem, but as Lloyd George had recently raised the age of compulsory military service to fifty, there was a feeling that this should apply to Ireland, too. Others felt that it would be completely counterproductive, and that more soldiers would be needed to enforce conscription than it would bring in. After a General Strike across the whole of Ireland on 23 April, the issue of conscription was dropped.

G.H.Q. British Forces, ITALY
17th April 1918

My own sweet Angel,

I must send just a line to thank you millions & millions of times for another most wonderful letter dated the 10th which arrived by King's Messenger this morning though he was 24 hours late, the silly ass having missed his train at Turin on Monday!! . . .

At last we have had a fine bright day without rain which is more cheerful, though the news from FLANDERS seems to be getting worse & worse & one really does wonder when & where it will all end!!

Our men are having a pretty rotten time up in the mountains really & shelled a certain amount too though of course nothing like the Western Front compared to which it is absolute peace!!

London must be too gloomy & depressing for words nowadays & no place to live in; no-one on leave of course & no parties or practically none!! . . .

Tons & tons of love & everything else that your E can possibly send!!!!

G.H.Q. British Forces, ITALY
19th April 1918

My own Angel,

How bored you must be getting with my eternal letters but I have only missed writing to you by one King's Messenger & have vowed that I will never miss another!!

I haven't been out today; merely office work & thinking of you, darling, though I'm always doing that, even climbing a track or in the front line!!!! But it's when I'm in bed (merely a 'flea bag' [*officer's sleeping bag*]) that I'm really with you & when I can use your scent 'Royal Briar', which thoroughly upsets me!!!! And I more than feel 'all next day (& every day) like little children after play'!!!! [*An early advertising slogan.*] What rot I do write but I do mean it all so sincerely, darling one!! Please forgive me but I can't help it!!

I'm on duty in the beastly office tonight & I've been warned that the —— Austrians may attack early tomorrow morning!! It's only the old Italians who think this & they have always got 'the wind up them' but we have to be on the alert!! . . .

Good night, my own darling little Freda; I will add a P.S. early tomorrow.

20/4/18   7.00 A.M.

Needless to say the Austrians haven't attacked us, not that we ever thought they would, so that I've had a peaceful night on duty!!

Goodbye my own darling one from your v.v. devoted

E.

G.H.Q. British Forces, ITALY
22nd April 1918

Beloved Angel,

Another sweet & wonderful letter from you today; Darling your letters are becoming more & more the only joys of this fearfully dull & boring existence & so I do thank you again for writing so regularly & so divinely!!!! . . .

If only you could come out to ROME & stay with the Erskines; I know I could easily get there though I fear we shouldn't be as much alone as we should want to be darling one!! I must look out for 'Viola' Erskine if I do go there? & particularly if she is a 'divine woman'!! How well I can hear you saying that, & you are a very good judge!!!! [*Viola Erskine is later referred to by the Prince as Freda's sister-in-law, but his ideas on family relationships were not always accurate. 'Divine woman' was a term the Prince copied from Freda to describe any attractive woman*]

How funny that you should have passed the King in an e-normous car; I wonder if he saw you, darling?!! Oh!! this —— war & why has fate ordained that I should spend my life 'au front'? I'm so fearfully bored & getting worse each day & absolutely no chance of leave even in sight!! How depressing & sordid it all is!!!! . . . [*'Sordid' was an all-purpose word the Prince used to describe anything unpleasant, boring or irritating.*]

The news from FRANCE isn't much better; all one can say is that we haven't lost any more ground up North for a few days though I suppose that is merely because those —— Huns haven't really attacked us again though I think a fresh attack South of AMIENS is expected this week!! Some of the staff here have had letters from FRANCE giving a few details; of course it was those —— Portuguese who 'carted' us in the North though the old Belgians surprised us all very much by taking 700 prisoners a few days ago!! [*'Carted' was slang for 'left us in the lurch': Portugal had entered the war in 1916, but its army was poorly trained, with low morale among the troops, and the fear that they would crack under pressure was proved correct.*]

What can have come over them & I should think those 700 Huns must feel pretty small; but enough war shop, as I do so hate that subject, particularly when I'm writing to you darling one!! And then there are plenty of troubles & rows at home, on top of the battles in FRANCE, what with conscription for IRELAND, the R.A.F. resignations [*Lord Trenchard had been removed from the post of Chief of Air Staff after disagreements with Lord Rothermere, the Air Minister*], & worst of all the manpower situation!! But enough of all this though heaven only knows where it will all end!!

I had tea with Edward Stanley yesterday [*the Prince's friend from Oxford days; Portia Cadogan's husband*]; his wife's infant is due any day now though he hasn't heard anything yet!! Must stop now as it's 2.30 A.M.!!

Tons & tons of love from your loving

E.

G.H.Q. British Forces, ITALY
24th April 1918

Beloved Angel,

Please forgive this pencil scrawl but it's 1.00 A.M. & I've got to go out at 7.00 A.M. up to the line in the mountains . . .

I had to attend some sports given by one of our R.A.F. squads this afternoon . . . & we had an Italian General & 2 of his officers to dinner tonight (I sat between 2 Italians!!) so that I've had a hectic day!!

Yesterday I had lunch with a French General: the way we 'cement' the 'Entente'!!!!

The news from France is as depressing as ever really, as, though fighting has eased down, one is beginning to hear of casualties & what has happened to Divisions, Brigades & Battalions! I hear our 4th Battalion has been wiped out; cheerful isn't it!!

You'll have heard that Portia Stanley has 'given birth to a son & heir'; we got a wire from Edward yesterday, a great relief to him, though more of a relief to her!!!! . . .

Tons & tons of love from your ever loving

E.

G.H.Q. British Forces, ITALY
26th April 1918

My beloved Angel,

Both yesterday & today I have been up to the front line, it sounds very wonderful but isn't really as our line is at least 1,000 yards from the Austrians & 2,000 yards away in places!! Yesterday I was at the point of junction of our left DIV. & the Italian DIV. on our left; today I was with the French DIV. on our right & visited the right company of our right DIV. & the left company of the French DIV.!!!! The 'Entente' followed by another e-normous lunch with the G.O.C. [*General Officer Commanding*] French DIV. though the food was excellent as only the French can cook it!! And food is a great factor 'au front' & one thinks about it a lot & looks forward to one's meals; one of the few things one has to look forward to, though I have your sweet letters, darling one.

Today's news from FRANCE is worse again, both in the North, & the South of AMIENS; but I'm afraid we can't expect much else but bad news as long as the Huns attack as they are doing!!

But that ZEEBRUGGE stunt is a real triumph & one of the most wonderful & heroic things ever done in this war!!!! [*The St George's Day raid on the U-boat base, led by Admiral Sir Roger Keyes of the Dover Patrol, was a heroic failure, which, nonetheless, did wonders for morale during a very difficult stage of the war. The plan was to sink three old cruiser blockships in the harbour, preventing the passage of submarines, in or out. In the event, two of*

the blockships missed their targets, and there were 588 casualties in the raiding
force of 900 which tried to storm the harbour mole. Eight VCs were won, but
the Germans had dredged a channel around the blockship within twenty-four
hours, and the base was fully operational again in three weeks.]

But enough war shop; it's still raining & there's 2ft of snow up in the
mountains & this is spring in ITALY!! . . .

Tons & tons of love, my own darling little Freda from your very very
devoted

E.

G.H.Q. British Forces, ITALY
29th April 1918

My beloved Angel,

What a joy it was to get 2 sweet letters from you yesterday, dated
18th & 21st April for which millions & millions of thanks & for all you
say to me!! . . .

Yes, Reggie Seymour is a charming & delightful fellow & I like him
particularly though I don't know him very well!! . . . he was shot in the
heart on the Aisne & so is a complete crock as regards 'active service
abroad' though from what I know of him, his heart is still an easy
target & is often hit in another way!! How funny I'm trying to be!
Though 'entre nous' I think it is the truth!! . . .

Darling, the news from FRANCE seems to get worse & worse & it is
now gradually becoming known that the 2nd debacle in the North was
entirely the fault of those —— Portuguese!! Bad luck to them or what
is left of them & I don't think that is much; & there seems to have been
a Portuguese mutiny in progress at the time of the 1st attack in the
ARMENTIERES area!! What hopeless allies (excepting the French) we
have !!!! . . .

Lots of people here have had & are getting leave to ROME but do you
know, darling one, that I haven't the smallest desire to go there or
anywhere on leave if I can't see you, angel!! I want to & pine to get to
ENGLAND, nothing else; & I think you know that I mean this when I say
it, though I suppose leave to ROME or anywhere in ITALY ('local leave') is
better than sitting here!!

A few days ago I found out that the Duchess of Aosta, a sort of relation of mine, is living near here, & I lunched with her at her villa yesterday; she is a 'divine woman' in her own way & very kind though she is about 50 now, rather old perhaps?!! But it's a great thing to be able to go there occasionally and get back to civilisation, as she has asked me to do!!

She is a sister of Queen Amelie's [*the Queen of Italy*] (consequently French) but she seldom even sees her husband the Duke, who commands an Italian army though he has behaved very badly to her 'et il y a un tas d'histoires' [*and there are a heap of stories*]!! But that's the same all the world over, isn't it? . . .

We have a large room in this villa in which we have been able to mark out a 'Badminton Court' where we play every evening; it's not such a bad game when there is nothing else & anyhow it's a form of exercise, & I can't do without exercise 'au front'!! But it's funny how one can do without it on leave & I wonder why? . . .

On 2 April, Freda had met Captain Reginald Seymour at Kilbees Farm. Aged thirty-nine, and Equerry to George V, he lived at Ascot when 'in waiting' at Windsor Castle. He had served in France at the outbreak of war, and on 31 October 1914 had been shot in the chest, the bullet damaging his lungs and ending up near his heart.

30th April

. . . So Burghie is going to a staff job in South Africa or says he is . . . I like Burghie, he's a delightful creature in his own way, & then he has been very ill & won't be fit again for ages, if he ever is properly!!

My 2nd brother is just the same [*Prince Albert was still recovering from his ulcer operation in November 1917*]; oh!! & then my third brother Henry has passed into Sandhurst, which will give such a good excuse to motor down to the neighbourhood of Ascot when I'm stuck in London, won't it, darling one?!!

You won't work too hard at the hospital, will you darling, & how you must hate scrubbing floors; but still I suppose it is really better to have something to do nowadays though you have been so ill! [*Freda was working as a VAD – Voluntary Aid Detachment – nurse at a hospital in Ascot and later transferred to the King Edward VII Hospital in Windsor.*

Many of the upper classes had set up hospitals, some in France, others in
converted parts of their houses in England, to help the huge numbers of wounded
returning home from the Western Front. It was common for women in Freda's
position to become volunteer nurses to help out.]

I can't help reminding you that you've never sent me any more
photos & I do so so want some more good ones; I know I'm a bore but I
can't help it!!

Tons & tons of love from your E who loves & adores you.

G.H.Q. British Forces, ITALY
1st May 1918

My own beloved angel,

I have yet another sweet letter of 23rd April to thank you millions of
times for & for another wee photo which is far better than the print you
sent me & which I love & adore!!!! Darling one, how could you suggest
my tearing either of your 2 snapshots up when they both live in a little
leather frame which never leaves my pocket!! They are my most
precious possessions; of course that bottle of your scent means a great
deal to me too & what an effect it has on me!!!! . . .

This has been a day of conferences; of course these — — generals
would choose a lovely day like this to sit in a nasty room & talk
nonsense (which I have to listen to!!) with French & Italian
generals!! . . .

Oh!! where and when shall we meet again darling one? I'm hoping it
will be at the 'Little Cottage' even if I am living in London, as no-one
can stop my Rolls, which is a military car. But leave hasn't even opened
yet & won't for the present, alas . . . what a shame it is, though thank
goodness we aren't on the Western Front.

Adoration does not express what I feel towards you; Tons & tons of
all the love I can send from your

E.

G.H.Q., British Forces, ITALY
4th May 1918, 7.00 A.M.

My own beloved Angel,

. . . Have you seen any of my family riding in the Park or anywhere as
they are still at Windsor? My sister [*Mary*] had her 21st birthday there
last week & there was a small dinner party at the Castle that evening & I
see Charlie Marsham [*later 6th Earl of Romney*] went!! But I expect he has
told you all about it, those 2 rather attractive 'Cambridge' cousins of
mine are staying at the Castle too I think!! [*The daughters of Queen Mary's*
brother the Duke of Teck, who had been created Marquess of Cambridge.]

Tons & tons of all my love to my own darling little Freda from her
own E. who loves & adores her!! There's another K.M. in tomorrow so
that I'm getting excited already!!

In 1917, George V had decided that the name of the Royal Family should change.
After three years of war, anti-German feeling was at its height, and the name 'Saxe-
Coburg and Gotha' was felt to be inappropriate. It was Lord Stamfordham, the King's
Private Secretary, who is credited with proposing the name 'Windsor'. The Kaiser
apparently remarked that he was going to the theatre to see *The Merry Wives of Saxe-
Coburg & Gotha*.

At the same time, the Battenbergs anglicised their name, literally, to 'Mountbatten'.
Prince Louis of Battenberg, who had been forced to resign as First Sea Lord in 1914
because he was, by birth, a German, became the first Marquess of Milford Haven.

Alexander, the eldest son of Queen Victoria's youngest daughter, Beatrice (who had
married Prince Henry of Battenberg), was created the first Marquess of Carisbrooke,
and his brother became Lord Leopold Mountbatten.

The Prince, however, had never felt himself to be German, and the war confirmed
his feelings that he was English through and through.

G.H.Q. British Forces, ITALY
6th May 1918

My own beloved Angel,

2 more wonderful letters from you received yesterday & how happy I
was to find them here on my return from a 'joy ride' to VENICE!! Heavens

how I long to see you again & want you & want you more than ever, angel!! I do feel so fearfully naughty tonight; it must be your last photo which is standing up in front of me now on my table in this —— office where I've got to sleep, being 'on duty'!! An office is hardly conducive to 'naughtiness' but your photo makes me so anywhere!!

So you spent last weekend at Sutton [*Place*] & I'm glad you ragged Geordie [*Duke of Sutherland*]; it's so good for him . . . I haven't heard a word about Eileen [*the Duchess*] for ages, though I think she would be returning to England about now; I believe she stayed in Rome with the Rodds in March!! [*The Ambassador to Italy was Sir James Rodd, later the first Baron Rennell of Rodd.*]

You simply mustn't work too hard at that old hospital, though I suppose a little work is good for one; I hate to think of you scrubbing a beastly floor, darling; can't you do some other form of work, less strenuous?!

I feel very 'flattered' (I suppose that's the right thing for me to say) to hear that there's a picture of me hung up in the ward where you work & love to think that you look at it sometimes!!!!

Yesterday I went to VENICE with the 'Lord Claud' & Edward Stanley which made a slight change & was a more pleasant way of spending a day than going up into those —— mountains!! We motored to the coast (over 2 hrs) & then found an Italian naval launch awaiting us (which we had fixed up & kept for the day) & pushed across to that extraordinary city where we lunched & saw some of the sights!! I don't know if you've ever been there darling, but it's supposed to be interesting with St Mark's & the Doge's Palace etc. to visit; personally sightseeing leaves me absolutely stone cold nowadays & I went to Venice one day last December!! We 'launched' across to LIDO Island in the afternoon where we had a stroll on the beach; LIDO is (or rather was) the fashionable place to stay. It is now an aerodrome & the beach is a mass of barbed wire!!

Talking of the Stanleys, you have guessed right; I have been asked to be godfather to the 'son & heir'; She's a 'divine woman' in many ways, but he is rather heavy at times, though I know him well as he was at Oxford with me; but he's rather too heavy for me!!!!

I have the completest confidence in Phoebe [*Freda's maid*] & so write anything I like & I do, don't I, darling, though I do hope you don't think me very silly, though I know you would curse me & 'tell me off' if you wanted to!! . . .

All, all my love is for you alone et tous les baisers que je puisses envoyer!!

Your very very loving & adoring

E.

G.H.Q. British Forces, ITALY
8th May 1918

My beloved Angel,

What a joy to get another sweet letter . . . I'm writing at once (less than 24 hrs from my last letter) as I have to leave very early for a French {*gunnery*} school on the Lake of Garda & shan't get back till Friday evening!! . . .

So Charlie Marsham did tell you about the dinner party at Windsor Castle on my sister's birthday, which must really have been an extraordinary effort on the part of my family, what with games in the dark etc!! It all sounds very seductive though I bet it wasn't so one atom, though perhaps we should have known how to take advantage of the darkness, darling one!! . . .

I saw a great friend of mine off to France, or rather the Western Front, today & I hated it; it's beastly when a fellow one likes & knows well leaves one, & heavens only knows what will happen to him now!! . . . [*One of the few close friends the Prince had made, Lord Desmond Fitzgerald, who was allowed to call him 'Eddie', had been killed while training with his regiment near Calais in early 1916. The padre had a go at throwing a hand grenade, bungled the attempt, and Fitzgerald was fatally injured.*]

Goodbye Freda my own darling angel; your very loving

E.

G.H.Q. British Forces, ITALY
10th May 1918

My beloved Angel,

I returned here from GARDA in time for lunch today after quite a
pleasant 48 hours with the French on the whole, though of course I had
to do the polite & be on my very best behaviour the whole time!! But
GARDA is a divine little place on that great lake & I longed to have you
there with me darling one more than ever!!

But instead of having you I had to attend demonstrations & watch
M.G. [*machine-gun*] barrages & eat huge meals, though I did have a
good trip on the Lake yesterday afternoon in an Italian armed motor
boat. Of course it ended by having to look at a horrible big gun which
spoilt it all!!

I was accompanied by an old French general all the time though he
was a dear old man in his way & I dined with him at VERONA last night
where I slept at a beastly hotel!!

But Wednesday night was the worst when I had to attend a dinner
party of 24 & half of them Italians & the bowing & scraping that went on
was very tedious!! I don't like Italians as a whole, though of course I have
come across a few nice ones; I prefer the French but a few at a time!!!!
But thank heavens I'm an Englishman darling & anyhow not of a Latin
race is what I think the more I live on the continent, though I like the
French very much really!! But their habits & ideas & outlook on life are
so different to ours though it's a good thing to get to know them!! . . .

I enclose 2 silly little snapshots which may amuse you; they were
done by a Frenchman & I have written where they were done on the
back of each, though I have cut out the 'duds' who were standing next
to me!!!! But perhaps you wouldn't have thought them 'duds'!! . . .

Milles et milles baisers les plus tendres de ton petit E qui t'aime et
qui t'adore follement!!

G.H.Q. British Forces, ITALY
13th May 1918

. . . I'm being interrupted the whole time by that —— telephone; we
are rather short-handed in this —— office now as 2 of the staff have

gone & their reliefs haven't yet turned up, curse them!! And then I'm on night duty again!!

Oh!! & I must tell you that I am going to ROME in about 10 days time, but more or less officially, not on leave . . . but I'll tell you all the details & why I'm going in my next letter as I don't know much about the stunt yet & was only told last night!! . . . [*The Italians had decided to celebrate the third anniversary of their declaration of war, and the Prince was invited to represent Britain in the festivities.*]

Must stop now as I'm so sleepy; I can't think how this filthy blot got on the paper but 'c'est la guerre'; bonne nuit et dors bien, ton petit E.

G.H.Q. British Forces, ITALY
15th May 1918

My own beloved angel,

Millions & millions of thanks for your last sweet letter received yesterday; how could I mind you writing in pencil when I often do it myself as I'm doing now!! It's so much less trouble & much quicker, isn't it, darling? Shall we agree always to write to each other in pencil?

I think you are very wise to go to the Windsor hospital instead of the Ascot hospital as 6 miles each day on a pushbike on top of hospital work is enough to kill anyone & a bus is so much more comfortable!! But how energetic you are to have stuck it for so long, though it couldn't have been good for you & I'm very glad to hear you've stopped it, darling!!

What a day you had when you went to London to see your mama & then went to sleep in the train & got to Henley by mistake; you were a silly little baby, though I should have done just the same as I simply can't keep awake in either trains or motors, which has been the cause of more than one awkward situation in my life; only the other day at Garda I went fast asleep when driving with the old French general & he wasn't a bit pleased!!

As usual your sweet letter was the only one I got by yesterday's Messenger, except for a couple of family letters, though I did hear from my mama & I love hearing from her!! But as I've said before, darling, I don't want any letters except yours & I could just murder any

Messenger who brings me letters from other people & none from you!! . . . [*One of Reggie Seymour's letters, at the beginning of June, states: 'I hear the "Capt. Edward" writes to none of his family now, says he's too busy – I wonder why, don't you?*]

The only thing of interest I have done today is to buy a sun helmet from the Ordnance stores; I actually found one to fit me & I long to wear it, though I suppose the sun isn't quite hot enough yet!! I only tell you this, darling, to show you what we consider an interesting event in this deadly existence!! . . .

Do you know Marigold Forbes, who is engaged to Archie Sinclair? She was engaged to Eddie Compton [*grandson of the Marquess of Northampton*] about a year ago & then broke it off; 'quite attractive'!! The engagement epidemic seems to have subsided of late, probably because there are fewer men at home than ever with all leave stopped!!

The fighting seems to have been less strenuous & serious on the Western front the last week, though another terrific Hun attack is expected & the old 'Ice Creams' [*Italians*] have the wind up & think the Austrians are going to attack us & which I now think they may do, though I don't think they'll do much good!! . . .

Good night my own darling from your loving & adoring

E.

G.H.Q. British Forces, ITALY
17th May 1918

My beloved Angel

. . . Yesterday I spent with the French on our right, visiting the French DIV. commander, who took me up to one of his O.P.'s & then I lunched with him; it was some meal & it nearly killed me as we sat down at 1.30 & only arose at 4.00!! Heavens, how foreigners eat, & how they live, though I must say the food was excellent; it was a cheery meal & I'm all for cementing the 'entente', which is stronger than ever it was just now!! . . .

I think my family has returned to London & Windsor Castle is empty again; but I hope it will be inhabited again in August & September & that I may get home again during that time; you bet I'll try very hard darling, though it rather puts one off when one talks to regimental officers who haven't had leave for 14 months, as I did today; I did feel so uncomfortable & one does feel so fearfully sorry for them!!!!

Tons & tons of love from your ever loving & adoring

E.

G.H.Q. British Forces, ITALY
20th May 1918

Millions of thanks beloved angel for your last sweetest of sweet letters giving me all your news & some gossip!! . . .

I have been watching an Italian 'Assault Battalion' do a practice attack this morning & I lunched with one of our R.A.F. Fighting Squadrons on my way back!! The R.A.F. are doing the most marvellous things out here now & often 'crash' ½ dozen Austrians before 8.00 A.M.!!!! They are marvellous people, all those pilots, though somewhat 'moches' [*literally 'shoddy'; but the Prince probably means 'a bit middle-class'*] & hard to talk to off 'flying' etc., though what a —— snob I am!!

21st May

. . . Yes, darling, I do get fits of depression & very bad ones too, sometimes, though not very often & it's generally on account of cold & wet weather, though not always, of course!! And isn't it odd how quickly these fits of depression come & go? . . .

You naughty little baby, how dare you ask me what sort of a French school I went to & what I learnt there?!! If only you knew how far removed I am from what you mean!! Oh!! to get home to you darling is my only desire & all that I can think about . . . I love & adore you to distraction & you know it, sweetheart!!!!

I'm off to ROME tomorrow evening & if only you were going to be there, darling, then I should be looking forward to going instead of dreading it as I am now!! It's going to be a pretty grim 4 or 5 days but anyhow it isn't leave & will make a change, though not a very pleasant one what with these ridiculous Italian celebrations or whatever there is going to be & the various semi-official visits I shall have to pay.

However, it may not all be as bad as I expect . . . I'm sure to see Viola Erskine, your sister-in-law, whom you told me about, & so I shall feel anyhow I am seeing someone connected with YOU!! . . .

Ma toute petite amour je t'embrasse de tout mon coeur et milles et milles fois, ton petit E.

British Embassy, ROME
24th May 1918

My beloved Angel,

Well here I am in ROME & having a pretty strenuous though deadly dull time. Just a long string of official stunts . . . The 'Lord Claud' & I had a very hot train journey South on Wednesday night & my arrival in ROME was a trying one, with crowds of people in the streets, guards of honour, bands, & crowds of terrible old Italians to meet me at the station & I had to drive here in state!! It was all so unexpected & such a shock, though so well meant!!

But the Rodds, with whom I'm staying here, are very nice kind people & are a very great help & making everything as easy for me as they can; I think they are rather sorry for me being let in for all this, though of course I realise it's all necessary & anyhow it's a change from the mountains.

All this must bore you, darling; still, perhaps you would like to hear the sort of stunts I'm having to attend!! Rodd the Ambassador took me out sightseeing yesterday afternoon. We went to St. Peter's & the ruins of ancient ROME & saw the real Colleisium [*sic*] though I'm afraid I was terribly bored & have flatly refused to do any more sightseeing as it's too 'éreintant' [*exhausting*] on top of all these official stunts. I spend my spare time strolling about the streets & in the public gardens, which has been my only form of relaxation up to now!!

There was an official dinner here last night & a sort of reception afterwards, too terrifying for words, though there was a band of sorts & some singing, which helped a little!! This morning I visited the Queen of Italy (who looks like a big unattractive housemaid!!) & this afternoon the Queen Mother & the Duke of Genoa; not that all these names will convey anything to you, darling, as they didn't to me till today!! They all live in separate 'palazzos' so it all took time!!

But I've just returned from the worst stunt of all, the celebrations of the 3rd anniversary of Italy's declaration of war, which took the form of endless speeches in a place like the Albert Hall [*the Augusteum*], when your poor little E had to say a few words & it was very nearly my death, sweetheart!!!! [*Both Sir James Rodd and Claud Hamilton reported that the Prince had spoken extremely well, and he received a rapturous ovation.*]

But it's all over now, though I feel rather a wreck, particularly as we sat in the 'Albert Hall' from 9.00 till 12.30, though thank the Lord it was after dinner!! How these Dagoes do love talking & we had a huge band which played all the Allied national anthems several times over!!

I'm very sleepy as a result of all this & as it's 2.00 A.M. I'll stop though I must tell you I have met Viola Erskine, which was at tea, & then at the reception yesterday; I have hardly had a chance of talking to her yet, but she seems charming & is certainly what you would call a 'divine woman', most attractive!!!! . . .

I really must go to bed now, though I will carry on again tomorrow night & tell you more of my doings in ROME, though I'm afraid they can't be anything but deadly dull while I'm leading this ghastly official existence!!!! How bored I am!!!!

25th May

Today has been as busy as ever; lunch with the old & 'gaga' Duke of Genoa (who is an uncle of the King of Italy's) & then a reception at the Capitol (the Mansion House of ROME), both fearful stunts though Viola Erskine's little party & dance from which I have just returned made up for it!!

It has been quite an amusing evening & most awfully nice & kind of her to give it & there were 2 or 3 quite attractive women not counting her, though of course they were all very out-of-date as regards dancing & the music was only a piano (played by one of the secretaries at the Embassy) helped by a gramophone when he was resting!!!!

But I've missed you more than ever, sweetheart (if that is possible), & longed & longed to have you so that we might at any rate show them how to dance!!!! But it's still more now (after the dance) that I miss my own sweet angel; it seemed so unnatural driving back in a car with the

'Lord Claud' & perhaps he thought the same driving back with me!!!!
Oh!! for my next leave to England & to YOU!!

G.H.Q. British Forces, ITALY, 30th May

I never had another moment to continue this epistle in ROME, darling
one . . . and to think that I haven't written for over a week . . .

I was quite sorry to leave ROME & depressed to find myself back here,
though the mere sight of your 3 envelopes cheered me up at once &
now I don't care, in fact I'm rather glad to be back to peace & quiet
again after that official week in ROME . . . I must tell you of my last 4
days in ROME!!

Sunday I had to go for a 'picnic' with the Queen & her children out
to their chateau & woods on the sea 1 hour in a car from the town . . .
It's a dud family except for the 3rd girl 'Giovanna', who is a little
darling, aged 11, & great fun!!

Monday morning I had an audience with the POPE [*Benedict XV*]
at the Vatican, an interesting experience in its way, though he is a
very unprepossessing little man, a dirty little priest with spectacles
who hadn't shaved for several days, though he did talk French!! The
whole place was 'stiff' with cardinals & I was glad to get out of
it!!!!

A reception at the French Embassy at 5.00 P.M. & then I had to go to
the opera after dinner & a particularly dull one too; needless to say the
audience was much more interesting than the stage!!

Tuesday I lunched at the Excelsior Hotel & had to dine with the
Queen of Italy; & yesterday I lunched at the Grand Hotel with the
Erskines & Viola was in great form & we (she & I) discussed your photo
in last week's 'Tatler'!! I mean the one of you with the 2 children & I
find it also in the 'Sketch': funny that both the office copies of these 2
papers should now each have a page missing!!!! She is indeed a 'divine
woman' & she told me all the gossip & scandal of ROME, which is pretty
choice!! [Tatler *and the* Sketch *were the 'society' magazines – full of articles
and pictures of the upper classes at work and at play.*]

My last 2 days were more or less free as I only had soldiers' clubs etc.
to visit; of course I was still staying at the Embassy & so had to be on
my very best behaviour & my footsteps were dogged by 2 swarthy

detectives whenever I stirred outside, which was only to walk to the Excelsior Hotel with the 'Lord Claud' to drink a cocktail, which we used to twice a day!! So 'j'ai été bien sage' [*I have been very well-behaved*], sweetheart & haven't given Rome any food for talk!!

Do you know anything about a Mrs Wynne who was in ROME when I was & travelled both there & back in the same trains (& carriages!!) as I did!! She runs a motor ambulance convoy of her own & is with 3rd Italian Army though she was in Belgium in 1914 & spent 3 years on the Russian Front; a remarkable woman in her way & very mysterious & très riche!! . . .

So that nasty old 'Rock' [*the Earl of Rocksavage, heir to the Marquess of Cholmondeley*] has been trying to hunt you again & don't please have anything to do with him, sweetheart, though I know you won't & how much he repels you; of course he is amusing in a way but that is only one side of him!! . . .

Des milliers et des milliers de baisers les plus tendres de ton petit

E.

In May 1918, Claud Hamilton and the Prince had a row, with the former threatening to resign, probably relating to an episode with some women from the Voluntary Aid Detachment (VAD). The Prince apparently promised to turn over a new leaf and behave himself, though Hamilton was still gossiping about the occurrence some months later. From the admissions in the later letters of 9 and 11 October 1918, it appears that the Prince was still misbehaving during this Rome Trip.

G.H.Q. British Forces, ITALY
2nd June 1918

My own beloved Angel,

. . . I am writing this sheet on the shores of the Lake of Garda, near a place called SERMIONE where we have taken 2 hotels & turned them into 'Rest Camps' for our officers & men. I motored over from G.H.Q. this morning in the Lancia to look at the place. 'The Lord Claud' & Joey Legh are with me . . .

Leave to England re-opened about a week ago; though I fear it will be stopped again on account of the new offensive against the French, the ——— Huns have made a big hole, having reached the Marne, & are now uncomfortably near Paris & will be able to shell it worse than ever . . .

Ludendorff, having failed in his plan to destroy the British, had turned his attention to the French on 27 May, and, once more, broke through the Allied defences, sweeping across the River Aisne and reaching the River Marne, only thirty-seven miles from Paris, on the 30th. Here, again, the Germans faltered against resolute French and American resistance. By now, 180,000 American troops were in France, helping to prop up the shaky Allied defences.

3rd June

I've been in bed all day with a touch of fever . . . whether it was the effects of bathing I don't know, but anyhow I began to feel seedy at tea at the Club at Sermione & so we motored back here at once & I went to bed with a temperature of 100 degrees!! Today it has been 101 degrees . . . it's the prevalent disease throughout the 'British Forces, ITALY' just now, though it doesn't last long as a rule!!!!

I'm not in very good letter writing form today but I must finish this one . . . every atom of love that I have to you my own beloved little Freda from your own very loving & adoring E.

G.H.Q. British Forces, ITALY
[undated]

My own beloved Angel,

Well, I'm still in bed, sweetheart, though I did sit in a chair in my room this afternoon; it's extraordinary what a limp wreck a fever like that leaves one & I shan't be absolutely fit again for some days . . .

I wonder how you knew about Viola's party in Rome? Or was it in the papers? I hope not as we tried to keep it a secret, anyhow the fact that we danced!!!! But ROME is a hopeless place to try & keep a secret; worse than London if that is possible!!!!

You must be fearfully busy at the hospital just now & it's wonderful of you sticking to it, darling, as I know only too well the ghastly wounds one has to dress, the operations, the ether etc. the mere thought of it all makes me sick!! . . .

There was a great 4th June O.E. [*Old Etonian*] dinner here last night, though luckily not in our mess; it was down in the village so they didn't worry me, though I hear it was as noisy as all 4th June dinners generally are!! [*4 June was the birthday of George III, a great supporter of Eton, and is a day of celebration at the school.*]

I suppose you've seen that Diana Wyndham is engaged to a man called Capel? Though I think it's been on the tapis [*under discussion*] for some months!! I've never heard of him!! [*Diana Wyndham, née Lister, a war widow (her husband, Percy, had been killed in September 1914) and the daughter of the 4th Baron Ribblesdale, married Captain Arthur Edward Capel, known as 'Boy', and, after his death – see letter of 2 January 1920 – married Lord Burghersh. She served at Millicent, Duchess of Sutherland's – Geordie's mother's – hospital in France, and is pictured in Philip Ziegler's biography of Edward VIII with the Prince and Rosemary Leveson-Gower.*]

Have you heard this? (What is the crack corps in France? The WAACs.) [*The WAACs were the Women's Army Auxiliary Corps.*]

Bonne nuit ma toute petite Freda . . . E.

G.H.Q. British Forces, ITALY
7th June 1918

Beloved Angel,

. . . What do you think of P— Billing getting off? I know nothing about the case; I've only read extracts, though I do think that a man who has the face to bring up all that he did in court ought to be punished somehow!!!! . . . [*The trial of Pemberton Billing, an eccentric MP, was notorious for his 'black book', supposedly containing the names of 47,000 persons in high places – including Darling, the judge trying the case – who were being blackmailed by the Germans on account of their sexual perversions.*]

What does anything matter nowadays except stopping the Huns in the West?!! Of course it's only the Americans who are going to pull us through now as regards manpower, but enough war shop!! . . .

I wonder if you were able to fathom that silly little riddle about the WAACs?

Bonne nuit . . . E.

G.H.Q. British Forces, ITALY
10th June 1918

My beloved Angel,

. . . The French seem to have dealt well with yesterday's new Hun push, which seems to have been a really big one & they've hardly gained any ground at all; but it's Paris that I'm still rather frightened about as they are so close now, though I hear that the morale of the Parisians is good!! Anyhow of 'les Parisiennes'!!!!

As regards the air, we've crashed 21 Austrian planes in the last 4 days; I should hate to be an Austrian aviator on this front, as an American with our R.A.F. said: 'It's like taking candy from a kid', it's so easy to 'crash them'!! . . .

All my love to you my own darling Freda from your own E. who loves & adores you more than ever.

G.H.Q. British Forces, ITALY
12th June 1918

Still no letter, though I must be patient I suppose & give you time to receive my first letter after ROME? It's a great strain being patient, darling, though of course you aren't to blame, only rotten me, sweetheart, & it's very wrong of me to go on like this!! . . .

I'm feeling thoroughly peevish tonight, darling, particularly as I had to dine out with a dud French General in a very dull French mess!! But how I do grouse, though all these generals do get on my nerves so; it's such a bore to be so completely at their mercy as I am & they are so full of their own importance, though all this 'entre nous'!!!!

These —— Huns still seem to be making serious progress towards Paris & the situation must really be very serious as they still seem to have masses more fresh DIVS!! . . . I'm so pessimistic tonight, darling; I suppose it's the weather!!!! . . .

Too late for more, darling . . . all, all my love my own darling Freda from your own very very loving & adoring

E.

G.H.Q. British Forces, ITALY
17th June 1918

My own beloved Angel,

What a wonderful K.M. arrived yesterday morning bringing 3 of the sweetest letters from you, my own darling, & how happy they have made me & all you said & that lovely little photo of the V.A.D., though 'woe is me' it was only a proof or whatever it's called, as it's gone quite dark brown & I can hardly make you out, darling!! . . .

I meant to write by Saturday's K.M. but the Austrians had the cheek to attack us early that morning, though we were expecting it 48 hrs before & there was a fearful 'wind' on Friday & I never got a moment to write, darling one, though I was miserable as you know how I loathe missing a K.M.!!

But these last 3 days have been hectic & our 2 DIVS in the line had 30 hrs heavy hand-to-hand fighting & the Austrians had penetrated our line at one place & got as far as 1 km behind it!! However they were all killed or captured or driven back by noon yesterday, though it was a heavy attack & the Austrians meant business!! [*This half-hearted attack was the main activity on the Italian front during 1918, until the Allied advance in October.*]

We have captured over 1,000 prisoners & killed several hundred of them though we have over 1,000 casualties!! But the prisoners are really very glad to be out of it & chez nous & not chez the Italians & many are deserters; they loathe the Huns & use the most frightful language at the mere mention of them!! The French on our right also repulsed the attacks & have taken several hundred prisoners so that the Anglo-French line is completely restored & intact & runs as it did on Friday!!

I visited both DIVS in the line yesterday & 1 of our brigades as well as both French DIVS & they were all very pleased with themselves & in good spirits!! And so was I, having also your 3 letters & the photo in my pocket!! . . .

This attack was a general one from here to the sea & I'm afraid the old 'Ice Creams' haven't done as we & the French have, repulsed the attacks!! They have lost a good deal of ground in places, particularly on the PIAVE, & we are very fed up with them, though I think we have good reason to be, don't you? They are the most hopeless people & not really worth fighting for, though their men are all right, it's their ——— generals & staffs!!

But of course we can't say so & all I've told you is very secret indeed & 'entre toi et moi', though I needn't tell you that, sweetheart!! And the PIAVE situation still isn't too pleasant & anything may happen, though we are hoping that the 'Ice Creams' will stop them all right . . . But we are all glad that at last something has happened on this front & that we've done some good . . .

'Bonne nuit' your very very loving & adoring E.

But all is peace & quiet here again, now almost more so than last week, though I'm afraid not on the PIAVE!!

G.H.Q. British Forces, ITALY
19th June 1918

Beloved Angel,

. . . I was in the front line both yesterday & today, at different points where the Austrians broke through, though of course I found everything normal & as peaceful & quiet as ever, if not more so!! I saw a few Hun corpses but not many as most of them have been buried by now; but all our men are in the best of spirits & have their tails right up. All say they had a great shoot on Saturday, though they got properly shelled in the morning!!

Please forgive my inflicting you with more war shop, darling, but as you can imagine all our minds are obsessed with our more than successful 24 hr battle & repulse of the Austrians, & mine is particularly so, having been to the scene of it all, & talked to so many officers & men who were in the battle & killed Austrians!! I collected a few souvenirs & have one or two for you, sweetheart, in case they would interest you!! But how different it all is from France, & how unpleasant & dangerous a forward area would be there, after such a battle!!

As regards the PIAVE, the situation has improved & the 'Ice Creams' are reported to be fighting well; the river rose a lot after Tuesday's rain & washed all the Austrian bridges away, or anyhow most of them!!!!

But I really must change the subject sweetheart; what a boring & war sodden dud I have become, though that is the result of 'la guerre' & actually you couldn't find anyone less warlike than your E, so I suppose it's all camouflage!! [*The Prince often used 'camouflage' to describe any pretence, role-playing or play-acting that he had to perform.*] But this battle does make one proud of ourselves, & pleased with the French, though more sick than ever of & with these old 'dagoes'!!!! . . .

I wonder if you went to the Sandhurst sports? I have a young brother [*Henry*] there now, quite a good boy I should say, & an Old Etonian, though I've seen so little of him since the war!!

Again all the sweet & angelic things you say make me feel so fearfully naughty, darling one, despite my being in this —— office on night duty again!! Alas the fact of my being a major doesn't get me out of this tedious duty; I've got to be a lieut. colonel for that!!

I've just had all your darling photos out of their frames & have given each one 'un petit baiser bien doux' wishing more than ever I could do so to the original, though it would not be a case of 'un petit baiser'; it would be tous tous mes baisers, ma toute petite amour à moi qu'envoie ton E qui t'aime et qui adore à distraction!!!!

G.H.Q. British Forces, ITALY
21st June 1918

I've only got time for this measly little scrawl tonight, beloved one, as most of my staff have gone sick & I'm fearfully busy . . .

The Italians say that they are slowly pushing the Austrians off the MONTELLO & back across the PIAVE & they do seem to have been fighting better now, but they never tell the truth!!

Now I have a great secret for you, sweetheart. It has been suggested from home that I should return to England for 6th July, which is my family's 'silver wedding day'; that is if all is still peaceful & quiet here, though I'm only to be away from here for a fortnight, journeys included!!

Of course I was fearfully excited at first, darling, but on thinking it over & talking to my general we have both come to the conclusion that just now is hardly the moment to go home, particularly as it's merely for the silver wedding & only 3 or 4 days at home with those 2 fearful long journeys really isn't worth the candle!! So we've 'cut it out' & wired home to say I can't get away!!

I now feel I'm mad to have refused this chance of 3 or 4 days in England & perhaps a glimpse of my own beloved angel, but I'm sure this isn't the moment to go home & it really isn't fair on everybody else; don't you agree darling one?

But having refused this chance I shall now have no hesitation in asking for leave in about 2 months' time & try & get a month or so & do some more visits to munitions factories, though what ages 2 months does seem to have to wait, doesn't it, sweetheart? . . .

. . . The Sandhurst sports seems to have been a great success & my family went to them; I've heard from my brother there who is happy & likes the life, though he says it's very hard work. But then that is very good for him!!

Must stop now angel as I'm so sleepy . . . tous tous les baisers les plus tendres de ton E.

G.H.Q. British Forces, ITALY
24th June 1918

My own beloved angel,

Millions & millions for your last 2 sweet letters received yesterday . . . How you do spoil me with all the sweet & marvellous things you say to me & how your letters do upset me & make me feel so fearfully naughty so that I just can't be sensible!!

What must you have thought of my last letter? That I'm mad; but I'm sure I'm right not to attempt to go home to England now from every point of view & then the Italian news has been better than ever the last 48 hrs & they have chased all the Austrians back across the Piave & off the Montello, so that the Austrian offensive has been a real fiasco for them & a great victory for us. Won't the Huns be sick about it all!!

We heard rumours last night about a revolution in Austria but fear that it's only a usual food riot in Vienna!! But anything might happen on this front now . . .

I was up in the mountains again on Saturday where I saw some horrible sights, the worst of which were 2 or 3 dying Austrian prisoners!! It's fearful to have to see all these horrors when one has to go up the line too; it makes one all the more frightened of shells as if I wasn't sufficiently so already!! . . .

All you tell me about Capel is very interesting; no, I've never met Gabrielle Chanel or 'Coco' though she sounds as if she is worth meeting, darling, another divine woman!!!! . . .

Again millions of thanks . . . your loving & adoring

E

'Coco' Chanel had worked with her sister as a milliner until 1912, when she opened a shop of her own. After serving as a nurse during the war, she opened a couture house in Paris, from where she was to revolutionise women's fashions during the 1920s.

G.H.Q. British Forces, ITALY
26th June 1918

My beloved angel,

. . . Darling one as usual there is no news from here. The 'Ice Creams' have got the wind up again as usual they always have, & some wit said they had the permanent vertical breeze, not very funny, though I wasn't the wit!!!!

But they really are the limit & the way they issue & cancel orders is too maddening for words!! Horrible people, & it's such cheek doing it to us; it just makes me mad, though of course we bow & scrape to them, we are a d—d sight too polite to them!! . . .

Henry Wilson, the C.I.G.S. [*Chief of the Imperial General Staff*] leaves us tomorrow . . . he has got Duncannon with him, his A.D.C. I think he is an effeminate ass, though he married a 'divine' Frenchwoman!! . . ,

Please, darling one, don't go on saying you feel a long way from me sometimes when I've had to be official; it does make me so sad & depressed & you know that the official side of my life is all camouflage!! . . .

Must stop now as it's late . . . Bonne nuit ma tout petite amour tous tous les baisers de ton

E.

Henry Wilson, unusually, got on well with both politicians and the French. His worst quality was his inability to make decisions, followed by a levity which sometimes detracted from the weight of his position. Later MP for North Down in Ulster, he was killed in London in June 1922 when confronted by a Sinn Feiner brandishing a pistol.

G.H.Q. British Forces, ITALY
27th June 1918

My beloved Angel,

Just a mad scrawl to tell you that I am to return home for the 6th July after all; just heard from my family who practically order it so that I've no choice but to leave here next Sunday 30th!! I've done my best to get out of it as you know darling one, so that I've got a clear conscience & of course now I'm too too fearfully excited & delighted at the mere thought of a glimpse of you again, sweetheart!!

Is there any chance of your being in London, darling one? Do try & we will manage to meet somehow & discuss the chances of my perhaps being able to spend the Sunday afternoon & evening with you at the 'Little Cottage'!!!!

Oh!! What a divine thought, but we mustn't build 'castles in the air' darling, must we? It seems as if there is going to be some sort of public celebration for the Silver Wedding on Saturday 6th July; but I ought to manage to get away on Sunday afternoon & I've always got a brother at Sandhurst to go & see as an excuse to get out in your direction!! . . . Do try to be in London on Thursday as talking is so much more satisfactory than the telephone, isn't it? . . .

Tous tous les baisers de ton E qui t'aime et qui t'adore à folie!!

P.S. Do send me a note to Buckingham Palace on Thursday, darling, so that I may find it on arrival, just to say where you are!!

G.H.Q. British Forces, ITALY
28th June 1918

My own beloved Angel,

Another mad scrawl to tell you that my return to England is a 'wash out'; my general has just had a wire from my family to say that on no account am I to return if there is any chance of another attack, or if it interferes with the work!!

As a deserter who came in to our lines today warned us of an impending Austrian attack (how useful these deserters are!!), & as most of our staff are down with fever he has wired tonight to say that he doesn't think I should return to England just now!!

And I'm sure he is right, darling, & I'm very relieved as I didn't at all like the idea of going away for 4 or 5 what I call 'heavy family days'!! At the same time, sweetheart, I'm most fearfully disappointed at missing this chance of a glimpse of you . . . but I'm sure it's better that I should stay here, & 'entre nous' everybody here is very glad I've influenced my general not to let me go & it has made 'une bonne impression'!!!! But this really is 'entre nous' darling, though I suppose it's all camouflage & 'eye wash' really, though I don't say so!! . . .

Tous tous les baisers de ton amant et adorant

E.

VENICE, *30th June 1918*

My own beloved Angel,

. . . I've already asked my sister to let me know when my family are returning to Windsor, though it's generally about 1st week in August I think, so that I shall concentrate on getting my leave then & my chances of getting it are good unless there's a big battle on in France or Italy!! . . .

How funny that people have been cursing you for not writing lately, because, sweetheart, my friends have been asking me why I don't write any more too. I also wonder why my large correspondence has so greatly diminished these last 3 months that I've been back in Italy after my last leave?!!!!

You'll be wondering what on earth I'm doing in VENICE tonight!! Well, I've come here to visit some Italian naval batteries at the mouth of the PIAVE . . .

. . . 'The Lord Claud' & Joey Legh have gone to Milan for the weekend for the races ETC. (the races are camouflage) & I tried to get leave to go too but my general wouldn't let me!! A very strict man about my leave is 'Frederick Rudolph 10th Earl of Cavan', though not a word, & perhaps he is right, though it's a bore sometimes!!

But although very dull as compared to MILAN it's a pleasant change & everything to sleep away from G.H.Q. . . . I'm staying at a small but the only hotel which isn't closed in VENICE which has a restaurant & we had a 'siesta' this afternoon after a heavy lunch, which I'm not used to as I practically never have a sit-down lunch at G.H.Q., being out all day as a rule!!

This evening we had a short cruise in some of the canals in a motorboat & sat in the Piazza S. Marco & listened to a band!! What a wonderful place VENICE must have been in peacetime & if only you were here tonight, darling one, we could have spent such a pleasant 2 or 3 hrs in a gondola full of soft cushions!!!!

But I just daren't think of it, sweetheart, it makes me feel too naughty for words!! I wonder if I know the riddle about the W.A.A.C.s you say you are too shy to tell me; I heard of a notice that has been put up in the Officers' club at G.H.Q. France (which is swarming with W.A.A.C.s) relative to them but I'm too shy to put it on paper too!! However I shall write on when I get back to our G.H.Q. tomorrow night, & if I don't feel too shy then I will put it down on a separate slip of paper, but it is too naughty for words!!

Contrary to Edward's & my expectations of a long lie-in tomorrow morning we've got to leave here at 8.00 A.M. with an old Admiral to visit these —— naval batteries which is a bad shock, so goodnight sweetheart, if only you were here to kiss & hug instead of the photos!!

1st July, G.H.Q., ITALY

I arrived back from VENICE this evening; this morning's trip up the canals & lagoons to the Italian front line at the mouth of the PIAVE was quite interesting though 'un peu long' & it wasn't exactly getting away from the war . . .

'The Lord Claud' & Joey Legh don't seem to have had a particularly amusing weekend in Milan, so I don't think I missed much!! The war seems to be going well on this front, darling, & the situation seems to be improving daily & these old 'Ice Creams' have had several successes this weekend; so that my chances of getting home in August are improving . . .

So Eileen has asked you to go & nurse in her hospital at 39, Portman Square, but I should certainly wait till you return to London for the winter, though I like the way I render my advice!!!! [*The Sutherlands had converted their London house into a naval hospital, and Dunrobin, in Sutherland, into a convalescent home.*]

I won't send you the notice about the W.A.A.C.s in this letter as I must get the wording of it right & I've forgotten it already, I'm so hopeless at remembering these things!! And I've got another worse little joke from Paris for you, darling, only don't be shocked, but I couldn't be shy with you & would tell you anything:– (The big gun that shoots at PARIS is called Rasputin because it comes once every 15 minutes!!!!) After that I think it's nearly time I stopped, sweetheart, but do send me any stories or jokes you hear, I love them . . .

De nouveau tous tous mes baisers . . . et tu est toujours dans mes pensées, ton E qui t'aime et t'adore.

P.S. Please forgive that little Paris joke, darling; it's the limit, but I know you won't mind hearing it from me & I'm sure it will amuse you & I hope you haven't heard it before!!

G.H.Q. British Forces, ITALY
3rd July 1918

My beloved one,

What a hopelessly rotten ending the 2nd sheet of my last letter was darling, though I couldn't write that night somehow. Captain Larking [*the British Naval Attaché in Rome*] was here & we sat up yarning till very late; he only left this evening & I took him up into the forward area today & we visited some O.P.'s!! He's a nice cheery little man & it's nice to have someone like him here for a few days, & it does us all good & gives us fresh ideas as those sort of people who are always living & circulating in the best spots (LONDON, PARIS, ROME etc) always have the latest news & gossip!!!! . . .

I got a few games of Badminton in the evening; I have started playing that game again & it isn't too bad & anyhow gives me some exercise without which I just can't live in this country & climate!! I'm rather mad in that way as the hotter it is the more energetic I feel & the more exercise I want, whereas in winter when it's cold I get quite comatose & prefer sitting in front of a fire to going out!! But then I am rather mad, aren't I, darling? . . .

How I do adore those 2 lovely & divine photos . . . I am the absolute limit as I've never yet made 'the Lord Claud' take a photo of me 'découvert' & with my collar undone which you asked me for; but it isn't so easy as one has to be so frightfully careful about cameras . . .

The 'shocking little notice' that so amused the Prince, and which he enclosed with his letter of 3 July.

The Prince in unusually relaxed pose. Freda had asked for some photographs of him with his collar undone.

I enclose the 'shocking' little notice about the W.A.A.C.s, though it may be the one you meant; I hope you don't mind me sending you these sort of things . . . after all they really are very harmless little jokes & yet amusing!! . . .

G.H.Q. British Forces, ITALY
5th July 1918

My own beloved Angel,

What a divine & sweet letter arrived from you yesterday . . . how happy it has made me & it all seems like a dream; of course I remember our talks, sweetheart, when you gave me such good advice & understood why I wasn't freer when on leave!! But you know as well now that this lack of freedom is only & could only be due to my family, & that despite all you say about my not being tied (which is too angelic of you to say, darling one) I am 'entièrement à TOI' sweetheart, although we only met about 4 months ago & that we didn't see 1/100th as much of each other in March as I longed to, yet I feel somehow that we know each other extraordinarily well & that we have much in common in tastes & ideas!! What do you think, darling?!!

I only hope that you don't catch this 'Spanish Flu', though as half the men in your hospital have it & it's very infectious, I fear that it's more than on the cards!! But please do take the greatest care of yourself, sweetheart, as it's a beastly fever & does pull one down so . . . I should be so miserable & worried if you were ill!! . . . [*The flu outbreak of 1918 vies with the fourteenth-century 'Black Death' as the world's greatest natural disaster. Inaccurately named 'Spanish Flu' at the time, it is now thought to have originated in Kansas. The virulent strain was unlike any other, before or since, killing more of the young and fit than the old and very young – 15 per cent of its victims were aged between fifteen and thirty-five, and 25 per cent under fifteen. A first wave of the epidemic peaked in June and July, but was followed by an even deadlier outbreak in October and November. Worldwide, at least twenty million people died, more than were killed during the war itself. In France 166,000 died; in Britain 228,000; in Germany 225,000; in the USA 550,000. In the US forces in France, 60,000 died of flu, compared to the 50,000 killed during the fighting. India suffered the worst, with over ten million deaths.*]

I have a great secret for you; my general has sent in my name for the next junior staff course at Cambridge which commences about the middle of October I think!! Although I think they keep one pretty hard at it there, I'm sure one could work such things as weekends & anyhow there is a week's leave at ½ time & a whole fortnight at the end!! But I'm afraid I'm building a lot more of those silly 'castles in the air', though my future is looking rosier; I say looking, not that it will be!! . . .

I visited a new advanced operating centre which we have just established up in the mountains on Wednesday where all the very bad head, lung & abdominal cases are operated on & kept as long as 3 weeks if necessary!! You see our C.C.S.s [*casualty clearing stations*] are so far back that these bad cases would probably die going down in the ambulances (as some did during the battle) & so it's a great saving of life; it's very well equipped & has 3 good wards (huts) & there are 5 nursing sisters up there, though they are all very plain, poor dears, as most of them are!! I'm not talking of V.A.D.s, that's quite another matter!!!! But I saw some real bad sights up there as well as an operation in progress; I don't think I could ever work in a hospital, darling, though I suppose one gets used to it in time . . .

I suppose the next Hun attack in France may come any day now, in fact it's overdue!! We may get some Huns on this front later, though I hope not till September as I do want to get some leave to England in August so frightfully badly sweetheart & you know why!!

Must stop now so good night darling one . . . des millions et millions de mes baisers les plus tendres chère petite amour de ton E.

On 25 June, Reggie wrote: 'Can't I see in my evening paper that the P of W is going to marry an Italian princess?' It was rumoured that one of the reasons that the Prince was based in Italy was to facilitate an engagement between him and Princess Yolande of Savoy, eldest daughter of King Victor Emmanuel III of Italy. There is, however, no evidence that this had ever been seriously considered.

Ever since his adolescence, the subject of the Prince's marriage had been preoccupying the King and Queen. Apart from a friendship with Princess May of Schleswig-Holstein in the summer of 1914, ended abruptly by the outbreak of war, the Prince had never given serious thought to marriage with a suitable royal princess. The war deprived him of many further chances as potential brides became enemy aliens overnight.

The Prince never appeared to be anxious to find a wife; he was physically slow to mature, and a serious attack of mumps which afflicted him in 1911, during adolescence, while at Dartmouth Naval College, may have rendered him sterile. It is unlikely that he lost his virginity before the end of 1916, when Claud Hamilton and Piers Legh delivered him into the experienced embraces of a French prostitute called Paulette.

Friendships with Marion Coke and Portia Cadogan were followed by a much more serious relationship with Rosemary Leveson-Gower, with whom the Prince was spending much time during his leave in February 1918, at the time when he met Freda. Queen Mary took it seriously enough to warn him against considering marriage with Rosemary, an act she must have bitterly regretted as the years passed (see letter of 19 February 1919).

Although the King became resigned to his sons marrying non-royal brides (as Prince Albert was to do, with Elizabeth Bowes Lyon), it does not appear that the Prince had ever realised that this option was open to him, despite having seriously considered it with Rosemary. It is hard to believe, however, that the dreadful lack

The eligible young Prince, sporting a sun helmet, in Italy.

of communication that existed between George V and his eldest son had prevented discussion of such a fundamental issue. During a reported conversation with his father in March 1932, when the King asked him if he had considered marrying a well-born English bride, the Prince replied that he had never supposed it would be possible.

G.H.Q. British Forces, ITALY
8th July 1918

My own Darling,

It's been the dullest weekend on record . . . Oh! the monotony of it all & I feel like going mad tonight & I'm so depressed . . . It annoys me so to see so many other people slipping away for a few days, generally camouflage duty when I'm not allowed to go away myself; my general has got me properly tied to him not by string or rope but by a steel cable & he won't let me move from this —— hole!! . . .

Oh! Sweetheart in your past letter you asked me if I was going to marry an Italian princess; it's too sweet of you to say that this matter interests you & I can tell you most emphatically that I'm not, though don't you think I would tell you if I got engaged, darling one? I don't see the slightest chance of my being that for years, though I suppose I shall have to marry some day!!!! But 'sufficient unto the day is the evil thereof' (that's a good bit of quotation!!) & don't let's look so far into the future!! . . .

Too late for more tonight darling . . . All my love et baisers – your own loving & adoring

E.

G.H.Q. British Forces, ITALY
10th July 1918

My own darling,

. . . You seem to have been having rather fun in London lately & quite right too that everybody should get as much enjoyment out of life as possible when there is nothing doing in France!! . . .

So Ali & Leo are off to India. I haven't seen the latter for ages, a curious creature I've always thought & of course he's a permanent invalid, though a very plucky one!! He went out to France in August 1914 in the same battalion of 60th [*King's Royal Rifles*] with his brother Maurice, hoping to get killed, but of course Maurice was!! Ali I know well by sight but I've never met him!!

It made me laugh a lot to hear that Eddie Compton & Sylvia had the room next door to you at the Ritz the 1st night of their honeymoon; did you hear any sounds?!! But I don't think she's the least bit attractive, do you, darling? In fact I've always found her & her sister the other way about, in Italian 'molte brutti' [*very ugly*]! . . .

Ali & Leo's farewell dinner party must have been great fun; so Dreno was there looking as pompous as ever . . . he's such a conceited affected effeminate ass is Dreno, though of course he has very bad health, not that that is any excuse!! Irene his wife is a 'divine woman' & far too good for him!! . . .

Still no Hun attack in France, though I suppose they are waiting till August so as just to stop my getting my leave then!!

The mosquitoes are getting bad & my room is buzzing with the little brutes tonight who are attacking me unmercifully; it must be the light on my table that's attracting them so I think I shall have to put it out or I shall be a nasty spotty sight in the morning, not that there's anybody who matters to see me!! . . .

Tons & tons of love from your loving & adoring E.

Leo, Maurice and 'Dreno' (Alexander, the eldest – elsewhere spelled 'Drino') were the three sons of Queen Victoria's youngest daughter, Beatrice. She had married Prince Henry of Battenberg, who died of fever on a military expedition to Africa in 1896.

Beatrice was Queen Victoria's favoured companion, and had played a major role, with her husband, in bringing the Queen out of her extended mourning after the death of Prince Albert, and her children had been the Queen's favourite grandchildren. When the Battenbergs were anglicised to Mountbatten in May 1917, Dreno was created Marquess of Carisbrooke.

He was serving with the Grenadier Guards in France at the time, but after the war, he abandoned the Battenberg military tradition, and went into commerce, joining Lazard Brothers as a junior clerk. In July 1917 he married Irene Dennison, the only daughter of the second Earl of Londesborough, whom the Prince, at this stage, thought 'divine'. As with so many other women, however, within a couple of years he hated her.

Leo (Leopold), born in 1889, was a haemophiliac – an affliction, passed on by Queen Victoria, that plagued the males of many of the royal families of Europe. A dislocated hip, which deteriorated into chronic lameness, added to his misfortunes. Despite these problems, however, he attended Magdalene College, Cambridge, and travelled extensively. In 1914, despite his disabilities, he managed to persuade the King and Kitchener to let him enlist. He served in France, was mentioned in dispatches and attained the rank of Major. His health problems worsened after the end of the war, and he died in 1922 aged thirty-three.

The reason for Leo's trip to India is unknown, but Reggie wrote on 16 July: 'We could do with him out of England'. Clearly Freda criticised him for being rude about her friend, for on 6 August he wrote that Leo had let him down by giving him misleading information on a subject which Reggie had taken up with the King: 'I fought his battles for him rather strenuously with the All-Highest [*George V*], and I fought them on the strength of his assurance to me of his complete innocence of the charges that were then made against him . . . I had hardly done so before I found out that a lot of what he had told me was not strictly true . . .

'In addition he never said thank you or acknowledged in any way that I had done a certain amount to help him which I may say without conceit that I had as the All-Highest and his Private Secretary [*Stamfordham*] had the father and mother of a down on him at that time and he narrowly escaped being "outed" into civilian life . . .

'I may say that his own mother first opened my eyes and she gave him completely away when I dined there one night to talk over his alleged iniquities . . .'

Maurice, the youngest brother, had held a commission in the 60th (King's Royal) Rifles, and, after the outbreak of war, was soon in action in France, being mentioned in dispatches. On 27 October 1914, however, he was killed by shrapnel.

Princess Beatrice's second child had been a daughter, Victoria Eugenie (Ena), who married King Alfonso XIII of Spain, and lived until 1969, having narrowly escaped death from an assassin's bomb on her wedding day. Her grandson, Juan Carlos, became King of Spain after the death of General Franco.

Leo's companion Ali was Alastair Mackintosh, another member of 'the Duchess of Sutherland's set', described by Lady Loughborough as 'witty, kind, and generous to a fault'.

Eddie Compton was the son of Lord Alwyne Compton, himself the son of the 2nd Marquess of Northampton; Sylvia was the daughter of A.H. Farquharson.

Officers' 'Club' Sermione, Lake of Garda
14th July 1918

My own beloved Angel,

. . . So you sat next to Lady [*Marion*] Coke at the Baseball Match
[*held at Chelsea's Stamford Bridge football ground on 4 July, Independence
Day, the match was between the US Army and the US Navy*]. How small
the world is sweetheart, but old Farquhar's behaviour to you was the
absolute limit the other day; never thought he could be so insulting,
particularly after what he said to Charlie Marsham about you in
March!! Of course I've known him as long as I can remember & he's
always very nice to me when I see him, though I don't know him very
intimately & didn't think he could behave like that; & he's much too
old & ought to know better, which makes it all the worse & anything
to touch the obvious insult of it all!!

But I shouldn't let him worry you, sweetheart, not that I imagine for
a moment that you would & he really can be 'cut out' & he's gone down
feet in my estimation for I always looked upon him as the essence of
civility & as a kind benevolent old man!!

But enough of old Farquhar; it's wonderful to hear you are taking a
house in London for the winter darling, I hope it won't be far from
'Buckhouse' [*Buckingham Palace*]!! . . .

I arrived here in time for lunch & spent most of the afternoon
sleeping, though I had a stroll before tea, merely to get hot before a
good bathe in the lake about 5.00 which was very pleasant & I was able
to stay in a long time as the water is quite warm!! I told you what this
place was darling the last time I came here, only now it's been enlarged
& improved & there are 80 officers & 300 men here; we went to a men's
concert before dinner & after dinner we had a man in to play the piano
& we danced & sang, or rather the 'Lord Claud', Legh & I danced,
hoping the rest of the officers would, but I've never struck such a sticky
crowd of duds in my life as they simply wouldn't budge & we had to
try & make them sing & they didn't do that with much enthusiasm!! A
gunner got up & told a few quite good dirty stories & they went down
quite well so it hasn't been too bad an evening for an officers' club &
we didn't break up till midnight!! . . .

15th July, G.H.Q.

. . . I motored back here after lunch, driving the Lancia myself . . . but it was a very hot drive & it's hotter than ever here . . . but I've discovered an ice factory not very far away & bought 2 huge blocks there on my way back this afternoon which makes a lot of difference to life . . .

There are very strong rumours tonight that the big Hun attack has at least been launched this morning each side of Rheims so we are eagerly awaiting tomorrow's wires!! [*Ludendorff had attacked again, on 9 July, near Montdidier, with limited success. However, he followed up near Rheims and managed to establish a bridgehead across the Marne, and settled to plan the final knock-out blow against the French and British.*]

So the notice about the W.A.A.C.s was the one you meant & I'm so glad you like me to tell you any little good stories or riddles I hear & please tell me some & I'll try not to be shocked!!!! . . .

All all my love is thine . . . your own loving & adoring E.

G.H.Q. British Forces, ITALY
17th July 1918, 1.00 A.M.

My very own beloved angel,

I'm so so distressed to hear that you have at last got that beastly 'Spanish Flu' . . . do stay in bed & don't get up too soon, as I have had it & so know what a complete wreck it leaves one, when the fever has gone!! . . .

I can't help reverting to my — — self at once sweetheart as I've lots of news for you!! First of all my father has approved of the suggestion of my attending the next Cambridge staff course which commences about the middle of October & which means that with any luck I ought to manage to spend most of the winter in England, which is the time of year I dread most of all 'au front'!!!! And secondly my leave to England in August is as good as given, though of course I can't give you any dates yet . . .

11.00 P.M.

. . . One doesn't know what the result of the big Hun push each side of
Rheims will be; although the French & Americans seem to have
stopped them, they have gained more ground South of the Marne,
though I think the news can be called good considering!! . . .

Goodnight my own beloved Freda . . . your own very very loving E.

G.H.Q. British Forces, ITALY

21st July 1918

My own beloved darling one,

. . . I love the rhymes, which are all new to me except 'May you live
as long as you want to'. The best line you sent me is 'If I thought you'd
do it well, I might!!' I suppose they are rather naughty, but that only
makes them all the nicer . . .

I'm afraid my family won't be going to Windsor before the middle
of August, at least that is what my mama tells me in a letter
today!! . . . It's too too sweet of you to say you would like me to spend
every minute of my leave with you, would to heaven that I could, the
mere thought drives me crazy, but I think somehow that you'll see a
good deal of me, anyhow whenever humanly possible . . .

22nd July, 2.00 A.M.

I had settled down for a long night of letter-writing when suddenly
someone produced 3 Italian soldiers, a violin, piccolo & piano & they've
been playing too marvellously for the last 3 hrs & we've been dancing
& singing!! How I've been longing & longing for you in the big gallery
above my room, sweetheart, for it's been such a waste having a good
band with only men to dance with . . .

I do so agree about Ralph Peto, darling, he's a disgusting man the
way he's always tight at parties; if one must get tight do it privately,
not in public!! He was an absolute disgrace several nights in February
& March, though I'm sure he's all right otherwise & very kind!! [*Ralph
Peto had served with the Royal Hussars, and was later in the RAF.*]

How funny if you had met my 3rd brother [*George*] at the Eton &
Harrow match; he's a good boy & I don't think you would have found

him shy, not half as shy as his eldest brother was the 1st time you met him, darling!!!! He was shy, wasn't he?

But sweetheart you just can't think what a difference it makes having you as a real friend in whom I can really confide & say anything to & you know that you can always look upon me in the same light & that I'm 'safe' as regards our secrets!!

It's angelic of you to tell me to let you know if there's anything I want sent out from London; of course I should just love some of the new gramophone records, 'The First Love' & 'For Me & My Girl' being the most up-to-date tunes I have heard & know!! . . .

(Still 22nd July but 11.00 P.M.)

. . . At last I'm enclosing some snapshots of myself sweetheart, the ones the 'Lord Claud' took yesterday & they are as successful as any photos of me could be!! . . . in 2 of them I'm holding a tame leveret (the young of the hare I believe!!) which Claud found a few days ago; it's a sweet little creature & a female, though I'm afraid it will soon grow large & fat!! I tell Claud he must get her a male later on & it would be cruelty if he

Two snapshots sent to Freda from Italy. In the first the tame leveret the Prince described to her can be seen on the windowsill.

didn't!! But I don't know much about hares or if they breed as heavily as rabbits!! What rot I am writing tonight . . .

I've got to do the heavy tomorrow morning & decorate 4 Italian soldiers with the M.M. [*Military Medal*] at an Italian divisional parade; 4 men who saved one of our pilots off an island on the Piave onto which he had to land during the battle in June as he was wounded, a fine show!! . . .

I wonder if you know either of the two enclosed rhymes, one of which is a 'toast'; they are both very naughty, especially the 'toast'!! . . .

Heavens how I'm looking forward to seeing you again, my own precious & beloved one & in less than a month's time I hope . . . tous tous les baisers les plus tendres de ton E.

[*Separate slip of paper*]

A Toast

'Here's to the girl who loves me to rest,
With my arms around her waist & my head on her breast,
Cheek to cheek, & face to face,
And everything else in its proper place!!'

'I love the girls who do,
And I love the girls who don't.
But I hate the girls who say they do
And then you find they won't,
Of all the girls that I love the best
And I think you'll say I'm right;
Is the girl who says she never does
But looks as if she might!!'

H.Q. British Forces, ITALY
25th July 1918

Beloved one,

. . . The Italian parade went off quite well though it was the usual pantomime that Italian parades always are!! I pinned 4 M.M.s & some 'Valore' medals on Italian officers & men though it was rather a strain as I was so afraid of sticking the pins into them!! . . .

I dined with some Frenchmen on Tuesday night, a huge mess at French G.H.Q. 2 villages from here, though they weren't a very young or cheery crowd but in good spirits on account of their recent victory in Champagne!! . . .

This week is decidedly cooler, the actual temperature is still about 80 degrees F but it's more cloudy so we don't get so much of that relentless & scorching sun.

How tragic the wretched Czar being shot. What brutes the Bolshevists are & I don't believe a word about the conspiracy; he was a charming man, though of course hopelessly weak!!

I've got so much more to tell you sweetheart & I hate having to stop but they've already started collecting letters for the K.M.'s bag!! . . .

All all my love, your own very very loving E.

The Czar was George V's cousin, and his friend, and in March 1917 there had been proposals and discussion between the British and Russian Governments that he and his family should take up exile in Britain. The British Government initially approved the idea, but the King became concerned about the effect on his own popularity of the presence of the autocratic Czar's family (especially his wife – a German by birth and in sentiment) in Britain, and the Government's worries grew for its impact on Russia's new rulers, and their continuance as military allies.

After much prevarication, the original offer of asylum fell by the wayside, and as the Bolsheviks grew in strength, the position of the Imperial family weakened, leading ultimately to their execution in Ekaterinburg in the Ural Mountains.

G.H.Q. British Forces, ITALY
26th July 1918

My own beloved Angel,

. . . The 2 enclosed photos of me 'doing the heavy' at that Italian parade last Tuesday may amuse you sweetheart . . . Aren't they an ugly crowd? & isn't that a terrible man with the big black beard!! But I'm sorry to say it's a pretty typical crowd of 'dagoes'!!!! . . .

It's very late so 'bonne nuit' . . . your own very very loving

E.

'Doing the heavy' at the Italian parade. Dark men with beards became a standing joke between the Prince and Freda.

G.H.Q. British Forces, ITALY
28th July 1918

Darling beloved one,

. . . My sister has promised to tell me when my family goes to Windsor as soon as she knows!! Little can she guess why I'm so anxious to know & why I'm so keen to spend my leave at Windsor!! Not a word!!!! But you are quite safe in telling Sheila [*the first mention of Freda's great friend, Lady Loughborough*] that she can go to you the first 10 days in August as I don't expect to even leave here before the 10th, more likely 12th 13th or 14th, though I'm sure to be in England before 20th darling one!! . . .

What a relief it must be to have a safe & confidential maid like Phoebe; I've got a servant just like that, without whom I'm completely lost & perfectly helpless, though I shouldn't think one could ever trust a servant like one can a maid!! . . . [*The Prince's servant was called Finch, and later served as his butler.*]

Mrs Astor's & Jean Kinloch's [*later Mrs Richard Norton*] parties must have been great fun & how I should have enjoyed them; but do you see that 'the Court' has been plunged into mourning for the late ex-Czar?

I'm very sorry for the poor man & he was charming, but I do think it rather far-fetched, particularly when one thinks of the way Russia (either as an empire or republic) has carted us, & the French, & the Yanks, who have had such a ghastly 4 months on the Western Front, as a consequence of it all!! But you can well imagine how much 'entre nous' this all is, though I needn't say so . . .

The C-in-C [*Cavan*] says that all the troops (British, French & American) on the Western Front have all got their tails up, right over their heads, since the last 10 days when we have been driving the Huns North from the Marne . . .

So Sheila is going to have a war baby & I can well imagine someone wanting to get away from Loughie for a bit, as although I don't know him, I've heard the kind of fellow he is & he must indeed be trying to live with!! He was sacked from the R.N. College, Osborne, my 1st term there in the summer of 1907; I've only met Sheila once, I had a dance with her at one of the parties in March though I can't remember which & she certainly seemed a 'divine woman' though we didn't have a long talk: Rosemary introduced me to her!!!! [*Lady Loughborough recalled the meeting. She asked Rosemary Leveson-Gower what she should say or do when presented to the Princes, David and Bertie. Rosemary replied, 'Curtsey to the ground, call them "Sir" and treat them like dirt!'*]

It's awful cheek my referring to Sheila but you won't mind darling & I've got into the way of calling people by whatever name you do!! . . .

I think my family were going to Charlie's wedding [*Charlie Marsham married Marie Keppel*], but didn't on account of the Czar's murder; of course the 'court mourning' would do me in for anything in London, parties, the theatre etc., so I'm glad I'm not going to spend my leave there . . .

Good night Freda my own darling . . . your very very loving & adoring

E.

G.H.Q. British Forces, ITALY
31st July 1918

My own beloved one,

Another sweet letter from you yesterday . . .

Portia Stanley went to Paris last week with Lord Derby to meet

Edward & they were by way of returning to England together yesterday
for his leave!! 'Comme ils vont s'amuser' as she was 'going to have a baby'
the last 2 months he was home & he's been away from her for 4 months so
that means 6 months, as I can corroborate his fidelity!!!! But of course all
this is 'très intime et entre nous' darling one, as I'm fond of them both!!

I played 4 chu   of polo [*the Prince obviously did not know how to spell
'chukkas'*] this evening with our G.H.Q. cavalry, the Northamptonshire
Yeomanry, who play 3 times a week on one of our aerodromes; it was
good exercise though I didn't hit the ball much, not having even tried
to since July 1914; but I was better than some of them!!!!

How I'm looking forward to all your 'baisers' & to giving you more
still, all that I can give, though you have all my 'paper ones' now!!!!

Your own very very loving

E.

Please take the very greatest care of your darling self till I return!!

Lord Derby had been War Minister, but was regarded as a weakling by Lloyd George,
and had been replaced by Milner. He was sent in semi-disgrace to be Ambassador in
Paris. Edward Stanley was his son.

G.H.Q. British Forces, ITALY
3rd August 1918

Darling beloved one,

. . . We've just heard the wonderful news about the French having
retaken Soissons & advancing North towards the Aisne, which the
Huns seem to be going to retire across, let us hope for ever!! . . .

I've just heard rather a nice little riddle sweetheart, & though rather
naughty it's well camouflaged & looks all right on paper; I simply must
tell it to you, so here it is:–

Q. What is the difference between looking into a woman's eyes & into a
horse's eyes?
A. You have to get off the horse!!!!

Not so bad is it? . . .

Goodbye my Freda . . . ton E. qui est entièrement à toi chérie.

G.H.Q. British Forces, ITALY
5th August 1918

My own beloved angel,

. . . Leo & Ali arrived about Noon having had a great week in
Rome . . .

Of course Leo is fearfully lame, but we made Ali play Badminton
after tea & he soon got very good at it too!! Of course I had never
actually met him before today (though often seen him!) but he seems a
delightful man, one might almost say a 'divine' man!! . . .

But you can't think how much 'wind' there has been tonight
sweetheart: 2 Austrian deserters have warned us of an Austrian
retirement in front of us & the French forces & it was 'touch & go'
whether we are to attack or not; we've all been sitting up till midnight
awaiting the decision of a conference which thank heavens has decided
we aren't to push, only raid as usual!! I & several others have been
'sweating blood' the whole evening as of course a 'Push' meant no
leave!!!! What a nightmare . . . what a fearful 3 hours of anxiety I have
spent, darling; I feel quite 'abbrutti' . . . how I'm longing & longing to
see you again & to give you all my 'baisers' that have been
accumulating for nearly 5 months now!!

Your own very very loving E.

G.H.Q. British Forces, ITALY
7th August 1918

My own darling one,

Thank you millions & millions of times for another sweet letter . . .
so you loathe dark men with beards & I'm not surprised, though I'm
glad the photos amused you!! . . .

We had quite good fun yesterday though we didn't do much
sightseeing as you may imagine; we didn't reach Venice till 1.45, as we
had a puncture, & had a couple of cocktails before a heavy lunch which
we didn't arise from till 3.00!! We looked into a couple of shops on our
way back to the motor launch & landed again about 4.30, motoring

back to Padova where Leo & Ali had to catch their train for Rome at 7.30.

Having 'oceans' of time we had more refreshments (iced coffee) & 'The Lord Claud' & I had to leave them about 6.00 to get back here in time to meet [*the Maharajah of*] Pattiala at dinner, such a bore & bad luck too!! Leo & Ali were both in good form yesterday & I'm sorry they couldn't stay longer; I think Ali charming the little I've seen of him & he's such wonderful company, & has a marvellous fund of priceless stories, though I needn't tell you that, darling!!!! I only wish I had got to know him in London in February & March!! It's a pity they are both going out to India & are going to be away so long & you'll miss them!!

Thank goodness Pattiala & 'suite' left this afternoon; it's such a bore having to entertain those sort of parties & worse still having to find sleeping accommodation for them!! And Indians aren't attractive guests to say the least of it, very dark men with beards!! The Lord Mayor of London is the next one, though thank heavens I shall have gone by the time he arrives; but what can he want to come up here for?!! . . .

I've just been smoking one of those 'cigarettes ambrées' [*amber-scented*]. I brought over 2 boxes with me but I haven't touched one for months; it's made me feel so terribly naughty sweetheart & reminds me so much of a certain sofa, in a certain room in a certain house!!!!

Oh!! to be back on that sofa again & with any luck I shall soon!! I wonder if you still smoke any of those cigarettes, darling, & whether you have any left, though I always think they ought to be smoked 'à deux' & not 'tout seul'!!

Au revoir Freda chère petite amour à moi . . . ton E. qui t'aime à la folie

Following the French counterattack in July, British forces followed suit on the Somme on 8 August, which Ludendorff later called 'the black day for the German Army'.

Haig had managed to conceal the build-up of his troops, only allowing them to move forward at night, and had amassed nearly half a million men. Under cover of a 'creeping barrage' from 2,000 guns, his Australian and Canadian shock troops, who had proved themselves the most ferocious and effective attackers, penetrated the German lines, supported by over 400 tanks.

By the end of the day, they had advanced four miles, annihilating the German defenders. Though, like the Germans, the British were unable to exploit fully their initial success, it became clear to Ludendorff that his last gamble had failed.

G.H.Q. British Forces, ITALY
9th August 1918

My own darling one,

. . . I've just returned from dining with the King of Italy so I'm moving in high circles aren't I sweetheart? But he didn't give 'the Lord Claud' & I a regal dinner as we expected, au contraire it was a very nasty one, & it was a 2 hr drive back so I'm feeling rather peevish!

We had some successful little operations last night, several raids which brought in about 400 prisoners & put the wind up the Austrians, & the French are doing the same tonight & evidently hotting them up properly too, as they are making a lot of noise now as I write & I can see the gun flashes from my window!! . . .

But 'goodbye to the war for me' on Thursday I hope . . . I've written to say that my Rolls must be standing by from Saturday onwards!! Only 5 more days of this —— life here though they are going to be 5 very long days!!

It's grand to hear of a British push again, an 8 mile advance, 10,000 prisoners etc was this morning's news from France; it's cheered us all up a lot; if only one could think it meant the war was going to end this year, sweetheart, though alas it can't!! . . .

Bonne nuit Freda . . . ton E. qui t'aime!!!!

G.H.Q. British Forces, ITALY
12th August 1918

My own darling one,

Just a last & final scrawl before I leave . . . I only wish I had asked you before if there was anything you wanted in Paris in the way of clothes; I know that there are things you get in Paris that you can't get anywhere else!! . . .

Yesterday I motored 2 hrs each way to lunch with the Colonel commanding the U.S. Infantry Regiment that arrived in Italy about a

fortnight ago at his regimental headquarters near Verona; they are a
cheery crowd of d—d good fellows & keener than I ever imagined!!
How long it will last is another question but when I asked them what
leave arrangements they had, their reply was the last verse of a very
good one-step tune 'We won't go back till it's over over there'!!!! Made
me feel very small & I don't at all like the idea of waiting till the war is
over before returning to England!! . . . [*'Over There' was a hugely popular
American song, by professional writer George M. Cohan, which was even
recorded by Enrico Caruso. The words ran: 'We're coming over/And we won't
come back/Till it's over/Over there . . .'*]

But the news from France is marvellous & it is so cheering to hear of
a British push again & such a very successful one, in fact a real big
advance though there seems to be the inevitable lull during the
weekend!! . . .

'The Lord Claud' & Piers Legh are going home with me & we are
motoring from here as far as Turin, sleeping Thursday night in
Milan . . . we ought to reach Paris on Saturday . . . & hope to get across
in a destroyer early on Monday morning!! Voilà ma itineraire!

So bonne nuit chère petite amour . . . your own very very loving E.

Leave

❦

1918

The Prince's joy at being on leave at Windsor, with Freda staying nearby at Kilbees Farm, was tempered by the restrictions he felt being back within the confines of his family and the Court, under his father's critical eye. Even after the war, the Prince was still expected to wear a morning coat to visit his father; and to don white tie, tails and the Garter Star at dinner, even if there were no other guests.

Windsor Castle
20th August 1918, 8.00 P.M.

My very own darling beloved one,

What a joy to find your sweet & delicious little letter here where I only arrived 1 hr ago; how it has cheered me up on my depressing entrance into this 'prison' from which I haven't had time to find an escape yet!!

So angel, I'm very much afraid that I shan't be able to get to you tonight; you see I want to make a careful reconnaissance first as it would be such a calamity if I got caught out my first night here!!

Oh!! my beloved, what a dream of a night last night was, only it makes me long to get back to you more & more, sweetheart, & if you say you love me 10 times more it's a case of a million times more with me!!

The only picture discovered of the Prince and Freda together – with, on the right, her husband, Duddie.

This is a mad scrawl written before a terrible dinner party; but you know I'll turn up if I possibly can!! Oh!! why can't I spend my leave 'chez toi petite amour' at the Little Cottage but anyhow tomorrow night!!

I'll telephone somehow tomorrow, darling, & perhaps we might fix something up for the daytime!! . . .

. . . Ton E.

Windsor Castle (Back in Prison!)
22 August 1918, 3.30 A.M.

My very own darling darling beloved one,

I got in here 'sans accident' at 3.15; it was a much easier 'push' back & of course it was cooler!! But I am sleepy & just dread my 8.30 'parade' ride!! But 'c'est la guerre' & what does anything matter, now that I am so so frightfully happy!! And all through you, my own darling little girl, & I did so love our long talk tonight & it has made such a difference for now we really do know each other, don't we sweetheart?!! . . .

It was such a shame waking you up as I did & then arriving 'dans cet stat de nage si dégoutant' [*in such a disgusting sweat*]; you were so sweet not to mind beloved & I only hope it won't have to be a pushbike again & that I'll be able to fix up for the car!!

But how I have enjoyed tonight, it all seems like a dream writing here in my bed & it's such a large double bed too! I'm just dropping off to sleep, darling, so you must forgive the writing; I'll finish this scrawl on my return from the ride!! . . .

10.00 A.M.

'Bonjour', sweetheart!! I woke up fresher than I expected & it wasn't a strenuous ride so that I'm not feeling dead; on the contrary very much alive & so so looking forward to coming over tonight, beloved one!!

I'm going out with my Mama again this afternoon which is very pleasant really, as long as I don't have to do it every day!! What divine weather, though it does make me feel naughtier than ever & as for that moon last night darling, well — — you know!!

I'm going down to Eton with my brother again this morning where I'll post this & only hope you'll get it this afternoon or this evening!!

So 'au revoir' my own darling little girl, how wonderfully happy I am today & just adore Windsor & couldn't spend my leave anywhere else, though how I long to be living with you at the one & only 'Little Cottage' instead of in this prison!! 'A ce soir', I only hope, beloved one, though it's such a shame waking you up!! . . .

. . . Ton E.

Windsor Castle
1st Sept 1918, 8.00 P.M.

My own darling beloved one,

I'm so miserable not even having telephoned you today; I tried very hard but didn't get a chance till 7.00 & then of course I found the Post

Office shut & my Mama wanted to see me ¼ hr later so that I had no time to go to a hotel!! But I know you'll understand darling, & that I did try!!

What was Maidenhead like & how did the lunch party go? I buzzed my sister there in the Rolls after lunch just for a run & I hoped I might just get a glimpse of my angel either in a car or walking!! But no such luck, although I drove very slowly through the town & was on the look-out!! . . .

The Cokes are here but she hasn't asked me any rude questions, though I haven't seen her alone!! [*Viscount Coke was heir to the Earl of Leicester; his wife, Marion, had been the Prince's great friend and confidante, but now, any meeting with her was an embarrassment to him.*]

How this day has dragged but how I'm looking forward to tomorrow evening, darling one . . . I hope to reach the Little Cottage at 7.00. I fear I can't get away before & it may be 7.30, not that this will surprise you!! . . .

Un petit baiser bien sage till tomorrow evening from your own very very loving & adoring

E.

P.S. Yes, I fear we shall have to cut out our mad but divine scheme of motoring up to London together on Tuesday morning!!

The Prince's plans for their last night together were shattered by an unexpected invitation for William Dudley Ward ('Duddie') and Freda to stay at Windsor as guests of the King and Queen. Previous books about the Prince's friendship with Freda have quoted her as saying that she never met the King or Queen, but the events below show that she did, and that the King was initially captivated by her, as everyone was.

'Buckhouse' S.W.
3rd September 1918, 2.00 A.M.

My own beloved darling girl,

Imagine my feelings at this hour, having to write instead —— well ——!!!! I've had a very sordid evening dining at Claridge's with Godfrey Thomas (where we saw Lady Coke & the Lord Claud!) & we

went on to 'Going Up' at the 'Gaiety' after which I went to see the
Carisbrookes, where I sat talking & smoking till about midnight.
[*Going Up was a musical based on the successful play* The Aviator, *about the
author of a fictional book about flying, challenged to a race by an air ace, with
the girl they both love as the prize. Louis Hersch wrote the numbers. The Gaiety
Theatre was London's leading musical theatre, built up by George Edwardes.*]

Irene is charming, though alas he [*Dreno*] was there who thoroughly
gets on my nerves & I longed to hit him!! I got back too late to see her
as I said I was going to do, & she asked me to look in after the
theatre!! . . .

How I've been thinking of you tonight at Windsor; I'm so longing
to hear all about it, sweetheart, though what cruel bad luck it has been
& I've never been so disappointed in my life & you know it!!

To think that our marvellous little planned 'tête-à-tête' etc. had to
be cut out. 'GUD' what I think of life & it's back to those old dagoes at
9.00 A.M. But only for a month, thank God, & I'm looking forward so
madly to seeing you about 12th October, sweetheart!!

You know I shan't think or dream of anyone but you beloved all the
weeks I am away & I'm just living for our next meeting & you know
that I've never meant what I write as much as I do this!!

I still haven't recovered from the shock of you being at Windsor
Castle tonight, but it was too divine being able to get down to see you
this afternoon, darling, though it hardly made up for our 'petit diner
manqué', did it? It was such a rush, though how sweet you were to me,
angel, & sent me away so happy despite the disappointment of tonight!!

Of course this has been quite the most wonderful leave of my life
darling & I've been able to see far more of you than I ever expected I
should, though how little as compared to what I wanted to!! I only
trust all is well as regards 'Duddie' & that he doesn't suspect
anything!! . . .

I hope you were able to talk to my sister [*Mary*] alone; she is such a
darling really, & such a marvellous friend & confidante to me, although
she may not appear to be!! I'm going to ring her up about 8.00 to ask
her the size of her feet so that I may get her some stockings in Paris
when I get yours!! I shall incidentally ask how the dinner went; I do so
wonder what you think of it all though how glad you'll be to get away
again!!

But I'm glad you know what I have to go through so many nights of my leave; pretty grim isn't it, angel? And what did you think of my two young brothers [*Henry and George*]? I can't tell you how I've loathed tonight when I think what it should have been but for the million-to-one chance which 'bitched' it!!

I'm being called at 6.00 so I must stop now, though I'll write again from Paris tomorrow!! . . .

Your very own E.

Hotel Meurice, PARIS
4th September 1918, 2.00 A.M.

My own darling beloved one,

. . . We had a smooth crossing by a destroyer, landing at Boulogne at 1.30, & then we left for Paris by car soon after 2.00 & did the trip in 5 hrs as we had a marvellous run in a G.H.Q. Rolls!! I dined at the Café Henri with the Lord Claud & Legh very late, about 9.00, & then we went on to Concert Mayol, though the priceless revue that I told you about is over & the new thing is a dud!! . . . [*The Concert Mayol was the showpiece of Felix Mayol, a music-hall performer famed for his blond quiff and lily-of-the-valley buttonhole.*]

I've cut the enclosed out of yesterday's Times & must send it to you underlined, it just makes me livid to look at it, sweetheart; I'm so longing to hear all about the dinner from you & I wonder if you saw my sister the next morning!! But I'm glad I wasn't there, darling, as I should have died of it, though I still haven't recovered from you being asked the one night of nights . . .

7.00 P.M.

. . . I'm staying on here another 24 hrs as Lord Derby is very anxious for me to meet two French officials at lunch tomorrow . . . Paris falls very flat just now & I'm not enjoying it at all. The only good I'm getting out of it is learning all about dressmakers & hat shops as Portia Stanley has been trotting me round to a few today!! . . .

Then I lunched at the Embassy with her & old Derby & Rosemary

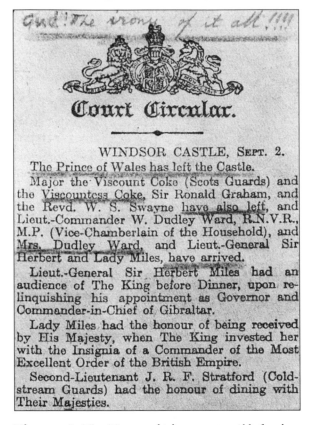

The report in The Times *which was responsible for the Prince's feelings of frustration.*

was there & they both took me to the famous Chanel shop this afternoon which made me think of a certain dress beloved one . . .

I think the Lord Claud & I are going to look in at the Embassy at about 10.00 to meet Lord Reading [*Rufus Isaacs, 1st Marquess of Reading, later Viceroy of India 1921–6*] & an American of high standing, in other words, 'to do the heavy'!! Legh has left for Italy as he didn't feel justified in overstaying his leave, though I did my best to make him stay on, silly boy!! Goodnight angel.

5th September   7.00 P.M.

I've spent a very quiet day going to some more 'modistes' with Portia & Rosemary & then came that terrible luncheon party which was very sticky!! Old Joffre [*Marshal of France, and President of the Allied War*

Council] was there & 2 'Parisian beauties', though I thought them very plain . . .

This afternoon Portia & I went to tea with Diana Capel at her flat & saw her & Rosemary off to Deauville, where they are going for a week . . .

Now, about the stockings, I went to 8 Rue d'Anjou & they only had 4 pairs of the grey ones, so I got 2 more of another colour to make up the ½ dozen!! Then I went to another marvellous stocking shop with Portia later on & couldn't resist getting you another dozen pairs (½ doz thick & ½ doz thin for evening) of the latest & most fashionable tint . . . I think they are good stuff & wear well!!

It all seems so sordid here without you, & I do mean that with all my heart!! What it is to be in love & I am so madly in love with you, my own darling; far more than I ever thought I could be, & I realise it more now that I have left you!! . . .

Au revoir my own darling beloved girl . . . ton E.

On 3 September, Reggie wrote to Freda from Windsor Castle: 'It was very little I saw of you during your stay here . . . but may I congratulate you on achieving a tearing and unqualified success? Everyone loud in your praises with the possible exception of Lady Miles! whom the king hardly addressed during dinner as he was so busy swapping lies with you!' Lady Miles was also a royal guest, with her husband Lt-General Sir Herbert Miles, retiring Governor of Malta.

Freda's need for male company when separated from the Prince is apparent by 6 September, when Reggie is writing of the 'two lovely days' he has spent with Freda, thanking her for saying she 'loved him a little', and adding: 'Our's has been a short little love affair . . . but it has been a very sweet one.'

Reggie realises and admits that the affair cannot go on, but it continues, on and off, into the autumn.

G.H.Q. British Forces, ITALY
7th September 1918

My own darling sweetheart,

. . . Nothing doing out here, everyone & everything just as I left them 3 weeks ago & how those 3 weeks have flown!! . . .

The news from the West seems to get better each day & we really are advancing at an astounding speed; the Parisians are in very good spirits & we are far more popular in Paris than the Americans, not that I want to run them down . . .

All all my love . . . you know how much your E loves & adores you.

While the Prince was on leave, the Allies had attacked again, gaining ground in all sectors. General Pershing, the American C-in-C, had not endeared himself to the French (and particularly to Foch, the overall commander of the Allied forces) through his insistence that the American troops should be used as an independent army, rather than simply as reinforcements for the British and French where required.

G.H.Q. British Forces, ITALY
9th September 1918

My own darling sweetheart,

. . . What a huge joy to find a sweet & marvellous letter! It was too sweet of you to write to me from Windsor Castle. I never thought you would be able to do that, beloved one!! . . . What a fearful shame & how cruel fate was, that my own little angel should have had to sit in that — — old castle on Monday night while I had to spend that night (my last) alone in London at Buckhouse!! . . .

So my father didn't talk any war shop; I'm glad for your sake though I wonder what else he found to talk about; & you say that George reminded you of me; he's a cheery boy as I expect you found; I wonder what you thought of Henry?

Yes, my sister was longing for 'une conversation intime' with you but she told me on the telephone that you never got the chance to talk that night!! Such is court . . . it's very trying darling, but I do feel that I'm breaking away from it a little more now, & that I'm taking more of a line of my own!! And this is all due to my angel's good influence . . .

There is a lot of 'wind' here today as to whether there is something or nothing doing from the Italians; of course the French are fearfully sick with them at their continued inactivity (that's good) but I think it's a case of 'niente' or nothing doing despite Diaz's visit to Paris!! The

result is that we are more fed up with these —— dagoes than ever . . .
[*The French wanted some offensive action on the Italian Front, in order to
distract Ludendorff, and, they hoped, to compel him to send reinforcements taken
out of the line in France.*]

But on the strength of 'nothing doing' Frederick Rudolph, 10th Earl
of Cavan is proceeding to England on Wednesday for one whole
month's leave . . .

We've just been singing 'Wild Thyme' & 'Beautiful Girl' & some of
the other new songs I brought back; one of the gunners here plays well
& needless to say 'Wild Thyme' is the favourite, though it depressed
me to sing it with ½ dozen rather tight officers instead of as a duet
with my own darling girl . . .

I heard a filthy French story in Paris & must give it to you, though
please forgive my depraved mind!! 'Un Boche viola une jeune Française
dans le pays envahi; après il la dit: "Je vous ai torpillé." Elle répond:
"Oui, mais c'est vous qui va couler".'!!!! [*A Boche violated a young French
girl in the occupied territory; afterwards, he says to her: 'I have torpedoed you.'
She replies: 'Yes, but it's you who is going to sink.'*] Pretty disgusting,
darling one . . . Now I must go to bed . . .

10th September

. . . You know darling girl that you've changed my whole life & way of
looking at things; it all seems so different now since this last leave in
England . . . I feel older somehow, but much happier, though as you
know I get fearful fits of depression . . .

All all my love & baisers . . . your very own E.

G.H.Q. *British Forces*, ITALY
12th September 1918

My own darling sweetheart,

. . . I've received an official intimation that the staff course
commences on Saturday 19th October, which is the day I suppose I
shall have to report at Cambridge!! Cavan returns here on 10th October
so that I shan't be able to get away from here till 11th or 12th . . .

I long to be able to dash about a bit more & feel that I would do more good that way than by sitting down here!! Still Cavan doesn't seem to think so & so here I sit . . .

Au revoir my own darling . . . ton petit E.

G.H.Q. British Forces, ITALY
13th September 1918

Darling sweetheart,

. . . Oh!! Why can't we have a month or even a week just to ourselves, just toi et moi, darling girl; how happy we could be . . . but there are e-normous possibilities in the thought of a house or flat of your own in London; no more —— taxis!! . . .

Today I lunched with one of our reserve Brigades . . . no new stories, though the Brigade Major told me he was going on leave to Turin with the excuse of going there on duty to buy 3,000 'capottes' [*condoms*] for the brigade!!!! . . .

Tous tous mes baisers . . . ton petit E.

G.H.Q. British Forces, ITALY
15th September 1918

My own darling sweetheart,

. . . I'm so glad the stockings arrived safely from Paris . . . but you most certainly shan't pay for them, sweetheart; they are mine & I just haven't the vaguest idea what they cost!! . . .

So you've been to or are still at Brighton, though I'm sure you made certain that old 'Rock' wasn't going to be there before you went; what a thoroughly nasty old man, sweetheart, & I just hate to think of my darling girl being bothered by him, not that I don't think she is more than capable of dealing with him even in person!! Ugh!! Almost as bad as dagoes with black beards . . .

It amuses me to hear that you met old Farquhar at dinner & how nice of him to be civil to you, the old ——!! . . . [*Reggie, too, was derogatory about Farquhar, referring to him as the 'dirty old man'.*]

So Reggie says the dinner at Windsor was a succés & he ought to know; but my sister says it was too & she has enough experience, poor darling!! Gud!! If only we could get her married & save her from

complete ruination & get her away from court; but that's easier said
than done & heavens only knows how any man will ever see enough of
her to fall in love with her & take her!!

Of course my sister's future has been a great worry to me for some
time; & don't you think she would be quite attractive if only she was
allowed to dress decently & cultivate a proper chic straight figure
which the poor darling isn't!! . . . I suppose we shall get her off one day,
though Gud only knows when & it won't be easy!! [*Mary eventually
married Viscount Lascelles, fifteen years her senior, in 1922, though it was
unkindly rumoured that he had only proposed in order to win a bet at his club.*]

How small the world is that 'Poots' [*Gwendolyn Francis, a great friend
of Freda's, always referred to by her nickname*] should have had the next
room to mine au Meurice on my way through Paris & caught me at a
bad moment; yes, I remember the incident well sweetheart, & I expect
I did use some pretty filthy language as it is annoying to be locked out
of one's own room when one is in a hurry, though I can't remember
what the hurry was!! But you know how I invariably lose my head
when in difficulties & always do everything but the right thing; I am a
pretty hopeless specimen!! . . .

If only you had the least idea of how madly I'm in love with you &
adore you . . . what you say about 'liking' or in other words being real
friends & knowing each other so well is also marvellous for me,
sweetheart!! Yes, loving & liking are 2 different things but the
combination of both makes perfection!! . . .

16th September

I've had a marvellous 'fly' this evening in a Bristol fighter with a
wonderful Canadian pilot called Baker who has downed about 40 Huns
& Austrians; I went to tea with his Squad & he took me up afterwards
& it was too thrilling for words darling, & we went up to 10,000 ft &
over the mountains & got a marvellous view of the lines & saw miles
into Switzerland & Austria!!

This is only my 2nd fly. I'd only been up once before at Ypres last
year so that I didn't feel very comfortable the first ¼ hr & it took me
that time to get my 'air legs', but then I loved it & am going up again
soon!! . . .

Oh!! Darling you do promise to send me any new snaps that are done of you & then you also promised you wouldn't change your scent till I returned, do you remember? It isn't fair on me if you do as I always like to use my own darling girl's scent (though I only put a little on my handkerchief when I go to bed) which is now that 'Chypre' from Floris!! And it does make me feel so deliciously naughty . . . though it's a fat lot of good feeling naughty here, isn't it!!

I see that photo of Sheila is in last week's 'Sketch' . . . she does look so good doesn't she, & has such a babyish face though a very pretty one!!

Marvellous American news from France, though they seem to have got about as far as they can for the present . . . [*On 12 September, Pershing had launched the first all-American attack of the war, near St Mihiel. Despite its success, it was achieved at great cost, with 'green' troops fighting an experienced, albeit demoralised, enemy. The inexperience of the American forces, and an apparent willingness to take heavy losses, increased their death toll: one American commander estimated that ten Americans died for every German killed. Lloyd George had been concerned by Pershing's lack of experience, and had urged President Wilson to put him in charge of the rear reserves, out of harm's way. Sadly, this advice was not acted upon, and the American troops paid the price.*]

Good night my own sweet darling . . . your own very very loving & adoring E.

G.H.Q. British Forces, ITALY
18th September 1918

My own darling sweetheart,

. . . Today I had to lunch with an Italian DIV general, at 12.00 noon, a huge repast followed by sweet champagne & I feel so ill from it still . . . they are indeed a repulsive nation these dagoes, both the men & the women, & I'm just longing to quit them for good & all!! . . .

19th September

. . . We seem to have made another successful push North of St Quentin, though the Huns are trying to make peace with Belgium!!

That & the Austrian peace note are very encouraging & one really does feel that the war may be over next year, not that I'm betting on it yet!! . . . [*Austria's armistice proposal was the result of both internal problems and external pressure from a successful Allied push in the Balkans against her Bulgarian allies. It was rejected by the UK and US governments.*]

How I'm living for my return to England that I may share a 'Wild Thyme' with my own darling girl again . . . Au revoir petit amour . . . ton amant

E.

G.H.Q. British Forces, ITALY
20th September 1918

Darling Sweetheart,

. . . Today has been 'Italy's Day' or something equally silly & I got stuck for a beastly parade of the Dagoes' 'R.A.F.' or whatever they call it & the King of Italy was there surrounded by Army Commanders & try to picture your poor little E amongst them all!! Gud! how I loathe these brutes & I saw some pretty horrid sights this afternoon + beards!

But it fairly thrilled me to watch 2 of our pilots doing the most marvellous stunts, looping etc. etc. while their rotten machines did d—d all, & all the Dagoes marvelled & couldn't get over it!! Gud!! how English this war is making me, darling . . .

Tous tous les baisers de ton E sont à TOI!!

20 September was the date in 1870 on which Italian troops entered Rome and seized control from the Papacy.

G.H.Q. British Forces, ITALY
22nd September 1918

My very own darling beloved one,

. . . So you spent last week at your mama's hospital [*at Lamcote*], sweetheart . . . I'm sure my little girl made herself very useful though she was absent from King Edward VII Hospital at Windsor when 'Their Majesties accompanied by the Princess Mary & attended by Major Reginald Seymour' visited the hospital on the afternoon of 17th September!! (Extract from that ridiculous paragraph entitled the Court Circular!!) . . .

I do so wonder & am longing to hear what yours & Reggie's long talk was about, though sweetheart, I'm very relieved to hear that it wasn't about your poor little E!! . . . [*Reggie wrote: 'We went to your hospital Wednesday, they all told me about you, said you were such a bright little thing! Swish! So sorry you weren't there, we could have had a giggle.'*]

Gud! how these weeks are dragging, though I've less than 3 now to spend & idle here; I'm afraid I shan't be able to get away till 11th as apparently Cavan expects to find me here on his return off leave on 10th!! The —— ——, as he can't want to see me, he never does, & if he's got any orders for me I could meet him in Turin & he could give me them there!! Gud, these —— —— generals are the curse of my existence & make my life unnecessarily dull, monotonous & wretched . . .

23rd September

. . . As a profound secret sweetheart (though I know I need never call anything I ever tell you a secret when all our letters to each other are greater than secrets) we are exchanging our 3 DIVS out here with 3 tired DIVS from France which is only right . . . they will be a great help in France, having had more or less a year's rest in Italy, & of course they are marvellously well-trained!! . . .

Now I really must stop: marvellous news from Palestine; 25,000 Turk prisoners! [*On 19 September, General Allenby had destroyed the Turkish Army at the Battle of Megiddo.*]

Tous tous mes baisers . . . ton E.

G.H.Q. British Forces, ITALY
24th September 1918

My own darling sweetheart

Such a divine little letter arrived from you by this morning's K.M. . . . They did work you hard at Lamcote & to think of my angel driving 'T.G.s' [*Their Graces: the Duke and Duchess of Rutland from Belvoir*] into Nottingham to go to the theatre!! . . .

25th September

I've been out the whole day visiting the French Corps Cavalry Regt. (21st Chasseurs à Cheval) near Verona; I looked at their horses & watched some jumping, not so bad considering they were French, but then followed an e-normous déjeuner which nearly killed me!! Gud! how these foreigners do eat & they take it as an insult if you refuse a dish with the result that again your poor little E. feels very ill tonight as he just doesn't have the 'carrying capacity'!! . . .

We've made a habit of dancing for ½ hr after dinner every night & it does us all a lot of good, though Gud! how it does make me long for YOU, particularly when the gunner I told you about plays 'Wild Thyme', though some of these nasty-minded fellows have concocted a naughty version of the words & the last line runs; 'Can't I sow a wild oat in you'?!!

Disgusting, I call it . . but it's all merely the result of sitting idle here & you just can't think the amount of filth we talk; in fact we don't talk anything else . . .

Just to show you how we look on Italy, one of my friends (& needless to say he isn't married) returned from Stresa on Lake Maggiore today, after a week's leave there which is THE place in Italy in September, & he said that by far the best moment was arriving back here to find his English letters! . . .

26th September

The worst has happened in the form of a letter from my father today who says he wants me to go straight to France now to be attached to the Canadian & Anzac [*Australia and New Zealand Army Corps*] Corps instead of going to the staff course at Cambridge!! Oh!! it's a real heartbreaker darling girl, but 'c'est la guerre' & I mustn't grouse & I've wired to my father today asking for 3 days' leave in England before reporting myself in France, which I'm sure he'll give me!! . . .

I'm so miserable & depressed at the thought of being done out of my 3 months in England, angel, but you know it is all for the best & I really ought to have returned to France months ago!!

You must forgive this mad scrawl, sweetheart . . . again millions of thanks for your last perfectly divine little letter & for being so sweet & delicious to your E, who is more more madly in love with his own beloved darling little girl every day!!

G.H.Q. British Forces, ITALY
27th September 1918

My own darling sweetheart,

. . . I've started going round to say goodbye to people & had another short fly this evening . . . Another pilot I know took me up & did a few 'stunts' with me which did me worlds of good & have given me confidence in the air though the first one put the wind up me & I was nearly sick after about 4 though of course they were my first stunts & I shall get to love them soon!!

The news from France, Palestine & Macedonia seems to improve every hour & both we & the French & the Yanks have pushed on well in the last 48 hours . . . [*In Macedonia the Allies had made significant advances during the previous week, and on 20 September, Bulgarian forces had begun to mutiny against their treatment by their German allies. On 30 September, Bulgaria surrendered.*]

I do so wonder where I shall find you sweetheart, though I hope at Kilbees . . . anyhow write to me at Buckhouse so that I may know your whereabouts, and give me your telephone number if you aren't at Kilbees (I think somehow that I know 338 Ascot!!) so that I can ring you up . . .

28th September

I've been out all day & have only just got back for tea but find a wire from my father waiting for me, granting me my 3 days leave in England!! . . . I fear I shan't be able to get out of spending the weekend with my family in Norfolk though I see every chance of being able to extend my leave well into the next week . . .

Au revoir ma petite amour adorée . . . your very own E.

There are no letters during the Prince's leave.

Towards Peace

༄

1918

G.H.Q. FRANCE, C-in-C's Train!! (Haig's HQ)
9th October 1918

My own very darling sweetheart,

It is quite impossible for you to imagine how much I loathed having to say goodbye to you this morning . . . you must tell 'Poots' how much I apologise for surprising her in her 'nightie' though it wasn't my fault, I was just shown up into that room!! . . . [*Freda was staying at Poots's house in Duke Street.*]

We've had such marvellous talks & we know each other better than ever; I feel I know my darling girl better than I've ever known anybody before, & just couldn't ever tell you a lie now darling, even if I have done so before!! They were lies, angel, I can't deny it, but they were of absolutely no consequence, & you must forget them, do please, darling, particularly as I've promised, more solemnly than I've ever promised anything before, never to tell you another lie again!!

It was all so different before my August leave; I was merely madly in love with you sweetheart & we didn't really know each other as we do now!! . . . I live for you, beloved one; you are everybody & everything to me . . . though I'm fearfully undemonstrative so perhaps you can't realise it!! If only you could, sweetheart, though I think you do sometimes!!!!

Gud! I'm tired & sleepy tonight so that I must get on with my diary of today . . . I saw my brother Bertie at Dover, though only for 5 mins; he said that Mrs Weigall had asked him to her party on 16th but that he wasn't going; I suppose he's got a 'bit' at Folkestone as he's only going to London on 18th & to France on 20th!! . . . [*Mrs Weigall features later in these letters, when, as Lady Weigall, wife of Sir Archie Weigall, Governor of South Australia, she becomes a great friend of the Prince during his tour.*]

I can't remember the name of this place, but anyway it's a railway siding not far from Arras where Haig's train is, in which he has apparently lived for a whole year; it's marvellously comfortable as a 'logement au front' though one can't call this being 'au front'!! We arrived in time for tea with that man Thompson [*who was to become a thorn in the Prince's side*] I told you about who met us at Boulogne in a Rolls; that long drive was very depressing as it reminded me so much of a drive in another Rolls yesterday evening!!

Haig made himself very pleasant at dinner & I had an interesting talk with him afterwards & he didn't frighten me as much as he used to!! Of course the news is too marvellous & we've taken Cambrai . . . they all seem very optimistic here at G.H.Q. & say the Huns are going back a lot further yet, if they ever stop, though I'm afraid we aren't as near the end as they lead one to imagine!! . . .

Tous tous mes baisers les plus tendres. Bless you!

E.

On 9 October, Reggie wrote to Freda, calling her 'faithless darling . . . I heard that E. P. was at home and gathered that I took a back seat'. He continued: 'How was your young man? Do you like him making love to you better than me? . . . I can't forget how divine you were to me last Thursday, only 6 days ago . . . I fully accept my position of No. 2 . . .'

G.H.Q. FRANCE (C-in-C's Train)
11th October 1918, 10.30 P.M.

My very own darling sweetheart,

. . . What marvellous things you say to me & I just feel happier tonight than I've ever felt before in my life!! Not happier than Friday or Monday or Tuesday nights of course, or any moment I spent with you; but you can imagine what a joy this most marvellous letter of yours is to me here . . .

You are just the greatest & most divine darling little angel in the whole wide world & Gud! I just feel the biggest & foulest brute (& everything else loathsome I can think of) for ever having told you the lies I did after my trip to Rome, & such childish & useless lies when my darling little girl never asked me any questions!!

Beloved one, please forgive your very repentant little E. who promises to be absolutely straight with his idol, for such you are to him!! Gud only knows what possessed me to write you such lies, darling; I can't even try to excuse myself, though of course I didn't know you then as I do now & I suppose I was trying to make you love me!! But what a perfectly foul way to go about it, & I just 'grovel' at my idol's feet asking forgiveness which I don't deserve in the least, though which I hope may be granted when I assure her that I would shoot myself sooner than tell her one more lie!!

What a worm I do feel & not the least worthy of your love, which to me is the most marvellous thing I can possibly imagine & what I crave for far far more than anything else in the whole world!! . . . Anyhow in future, all I do or try to do will be for your sake, darling, as I know you want me to make a success of things & I can promise you that I shall work like a slave for this & for you, my idol!! . . .

I got into Cambrai yesterday afternoon, a ruined town & such a filthy & depressing mess & the East end of it was being lightly shelled; it's no place to live in yet though I had a walk in the town & saw some dead Huns!! I passed 2 DIVS on the march, one going up the line & the other coming out, & both looked marvellously smart & cheery; what a different war to what I knew a year ago & even a greater contrast to the situation 3 months ago.

I had tea with Byng (G.O.C. 3rd Army) & he seemed very pleased &

cheery & Haig was very pleasant again at dinner!! [*Julian Byng was highly regarded by the Canadians, whom he had commanded. He was blessed both with good sense, and also a lack of desire for personal fame – both rare qualities on the Western Front. Later, as Viscount Byng of Vimy, he was Governor-General of Canada.*]

This morning I called on the Canadian Corps which I'm to join on Monday & had tea with one of the Canadian DIVS . . . I must say that I'm very favourably impressed with my first proper introductions to these fine stouthearted fellows & I'm now looking forward to spending a month with them . . . and I'm longing to get away from this G.H.Q. & to be in it all again!! [*Throughout the war, the Canadian forces had proved themselves to be one of the most effective – and ferocious – units in the British Army.*]

You'll be surprised to hear that the 'Lord Claud' is taking this letter to England with him, but the poor boy's sister Phyllis was drowned in that Irish mailboat that was torpedoed off Kingstown yesterday [*the Leinster, in which 587 civilians died*] & I'm sending him to his Mama [*the Duchess of Abercorn*] in London for a few days, as I'm afraid she'll feel it fearfully & I know it's only Claud who can be of any comfort to her!!

It's a real tragedy; I only read of it by chance in this evening's wireless & had to go & tell Claud who hadn't seen it & so didn't know, a very trying task, sweetheart, as you may imagine!! . . .

How I'm looking forward to getting your little disc for my chain, which will be by far my most precious possession . . . [*The Prince was keen on small chains with attachments.*]

Bonne nuit petite amour . . . Ton E est entièrement à TOI et ne vie que pour TOI seulement!!

> G.H.Q. FRANCE (*C-in-C's Train*)
> 13th October 1918

My very own darling sweetheart,

What a joy to find your perfectly divine letter of 11th on my return here this evening . . . Gud! how my darling girl does spoil me & above all for forgiving me for telling her all those —— lies & for saying they are all forgotten & 'n'en parlons plus'!!

I don't feel I deserve your forgiveness beloved one, but how frightfully happy it has made me; & we won't talk about it all again darling & you have my most solemn of promises, the solemnest I've ever made, that never will I ever tell you another — — lie again & always be straight & frank with you, sweetheart, as I know you've always been, are & will be with me!! (That you've always been an angel is what makes me feel such a — —!) . . .

How grateful I am to my darling little girl for coming into my life as she has & for loving me a little, & what a great incentive it is for me in everything I have to do; I'm beginning to get that 'I just don't care a damn' spirit, & I just don't care a damn for anybody or anything except my 'idol' though this makes me work all the harder at whatever job I have on hand . . . I feel there is something or rather somebody behind it, shoving me on to make a success of things . . .

How sweet of you to want me to stick an E. on to the photo which I return . . . an unsigned photo is such a dud one! . . .

As regards Thompson I'm rather disappointed as although he is nice & helpful yet he is fearfully heavy & seems to be completely devoid of all 'joie de vivre' which is a pity; several people say he's always been like this & they call him the 'mother superior' . . . but, thank God, I've got the Lord Claud & I miss him fearfully now that he's away . . .

What do you think of the Hun reply to Wilson, darling? [*US President Woodrow*]. Surely peace can't be so very far off, though I don't understand much about diplomacy & 'preliminaries' & all that sort of thing are so complex & involved!!

Must stop now as it's after 1.00 & I'm flying early; so bonne nuit . . . all your E's baisers.

Ludendorff had realised for some time that Germany could no longer win the war, and that the only hope was for a negotiated settlement. He wanted to discuss this with President Wilson (who had already put forward his 'Fourteen Points' for peace in January 1918), whom he felt would be a softer touch than the French or English, but he knew that Wilson would not talk with the old German High Command régime. On 1 October, therefore, major constitutional reform took place, and a Parliamentary Government was introduced under Prince Max of Baden.

On 3 October, the new Government sent a note to Wilson asking for his help in bringing about peace. This note, and successive exchanges, were published, but it became clear to Germany that the price of peace was going to be high. Negotiations dragged on as bitter fighting continued through October.

Headquarters Canadian Corps
15th October 1918

My very own darling sweetheart,

Well, here I am with the Canadians . . . my flight was a great success; I left an aerodrome near the C-in-C's train & was flown by a Colonel Carthew over Arras & Cambrai as far as the 'balloon line' West of Le Cateau!! We were up 1 hr & got a good view of the country . . . we landed at a new (old Hun) aerodrome well East of Cambrai where 'our Major Thompson' picked me up in a car!! Carthew then flew over to Hendon & nearly drove me mad by trying to persuade me to cross over to England with him, returning tomorrow; Gud, to think that I had to refuse 48 hrs in England (& no-one need have been any the wiser) which I might have been able to spend unmolested with my darling little girl, & how I was tempted, darling!! . . .

But to return to earth, I then motored to the New Zealand DIV Headquarters where I lunched . . . The N.Z.s are really the nicest & most refined of all the colonials, though I love these old Canadians but I'm coming to them now . . .

This Corps headquarters is a very comfortable hutted camp & I have an absolute palace of a hut with a brick open-hearth fireplace which the Canadian engineers have built for me so that anyhow your E won't be cold at night!!

Old Currie the Corps Commander is a good old fellow in his way . . . he & in fact everybody are very nice & kind to me . . . [*Tall and pot-bellied, Arthur Currie commanded the Canadian Corps from Vimy in April 1917 until the end of the war, and became one of the most successful Allied generals, with his excellent understanding of tactics, and his maxim: 'Thorough preparation must lead to success. Neglect nothing.' He had surrounded himself with a capable staff and was not afraid to listen to their advice. The Canadian Corps' actions in the autumn of 1918 showed his brilliance.*]

How I do miss old Claud, though to my great relief I've just got a wire from him saying he's rejoining me tomorrow!! Poor old Claud, he

On duty with 'the Lord Claud' during a visit to a hospital.

has had bad luck losing his sister like that & how he'll loathe returning au front . . . but I should soon go mad if I only had this fellow Thompson to travel around with as he's getting heavier & more seriously pompous than ever . . . the mere sight of him does depress me . . . he's the most complete wet blanket imaginable . . .

I do get bad fits of depression as you know & which you've warned me against, but that is only surface depression; underneath or inside there is happiness which is the result of knowing that my idol loves me just a little bit!! That keeps me going . . .

I have taken my little pocket frame out & it's standing in front of me as I write & I've been kissing it & feel so much better . . .

Bonne nuit . . . à demain, when I will carry on!!

16th October

. . . Angel you should never have had a 'disc' made specially for me . . . how I'm looking forward to getting it & how I love your idea of having the first letter of each word of those two divine lines engraved on it & I adore them & sweetheart you know they absolutely express my feelings

& it's such fun that no-one else but Toi et Moi knows what that string of letters means!! . . . [*see letter of 20 January 1919*]

Must stop now . . . but I'll carry on later . . . au revoir for the present . . . ton E.

Headquarters Canadian Corps
16th October 1918

My own darling beloved little girl,

It was rotten having to finish my last letter so abruptly . . . but old Currie has a hateful habit of dining at 7.15 which doesn't suit me at all; anyhow I was properly late for dinner tonight . . . the old man can't expect me to be punctual if I have a letter for my 'idol' to finish!! . . .

Sweetheart you are very naughty to feel repentant of that letter 'rubbing it in' as you call it; on the contrary it did me worlds of good . . . The thought that I had told my darling little girl lies when she had always been more than straight with me fairly drove me mad & of course I take it all very seriously & still can't forgive myself & feel the biggest —— on earth . . .

And you are marvellously wise, sweetheart, when you say that 'les petits amusements ne contes pas', of course they don't matter a damn where love is concerned, & now I only call it 'medicine' as you know & I don't feel that I even want that now!! And I can't get it even if I wanted it nowadays, living in this devastated area miles & miles from civilisation, though I only look on England as civilisation nowadays, well let's include Paris as regards 'medicine'!! . . .

But beloved please don't bring up the subject of 'anyone else I cared for more' again, it's so sordid & you know I'll be candid & tell you if there ever was, though pray God there never will be & I never have to tell you this!! . . .

I'm having a pretty heavy & busy time with these Canadians . . . I know your E will return to you with a Canadian accent, it's so catching, though it's the purest King's English compared to the Yanks!! But I do so love their expressions . . .

The news from up North in BELGIUM is marvellous . . . but I've been so busy 'hustling round' & have been out so much this week that I've really hopelessly lost touch with the situation, though how much more important it is for me to 'hustle round', sweetheart!! That's what I'm here for, not to sit in poring over maps . . .

Tous tous mes baisers . . . ton E.

On 5 November, the Prince wrote to his father concerning the epidemic of revolutions and abdications throughout the enemy countries, which were making it hard for the remaining monarchies. He felt that the best way of maintaining the strength of Britain's was to keep in the closest possible touch with 'the people', and that was what he was trying to do – in his case the troops were 'the people'. This also became his guiding principle on his tours through the Empire.

Headquarters Canadian Corps, B.E.F.
19th October 1918

My very own darling sweetheart,

. . . I motored into Douai with Claud & Thompson this morning; our troops only entered it 24 hrs before so that we found it as the Huns had left it & the streets weren't cleaned up at all, but the town is hardly damaged when one compares it to Cambrai or, worse still, to so many villages in this devastated area!! Very few of the houses have been hit (& they mostly by bombs) & except for broken windows & having been thoroughly looted they are mostly intact & will require only a very drastic 'spring-cleaning' to make them d—d good billets!!

But it was a city of the dead today & we didn't stay long; I went into the cathedral & the only decent bit of loot I could find was a rosary in the 'sacristie' which I took for my darling little girl & which I enclose merely to amuse her!! . . .

It's so marvellous to be really advancing East & so quickly on the heels of the retreating & beaten Huns; it's what we've waited 4 years for & it's all so exciting & we all think exactly as you do, darling, that we don't want peace yet, not till the Huns say 'unconditional surrender' & they won't be properly beaten till they do say so!! But I wish they would hurry up & say so, as we know that they must really all wish to, as they know that their number is up or anyhow it will be in the Spring!! . . .

They are fairly legging it now in front of the Canadians & are in Gud's own hurry as they are leaving everything behind except themselves, their mess-tins & water-bottles!! They are even leaving their machine guns behind, which is the best news of all, for it is only these which have been really fighting the past month & causing us casualties!!

We are taking practically no prisoners . . . only a few odd ones who are sick or asleep . . . Tomorrow Claud & I are going up to Lille, where there are 125,000 inhabitants left, though thank Gud we've managed to shake off Thompson . . . he insisted on coming at first & it required some tact to shake him off!!

Tous tous les baisers de ton E.

Headquarters Canadian Corps
21st October 1918

My own very darling little sweetheart,

. . . I'm very fond of these Canadians, but get rather bored with them after dinner & so leave them & go to my room!! Don't think me a snob for saying this, darling, & I know you won't as you understand, I've got absolutely nothing in common with them, & except when we talk 'filth' conversation flags, & I soon get tired of talking filth with people I don't know well; it's so sordid & I always find I have to pretend to have the dirtiest mind of all, to keep them going!! So I soon go to my room to write or read; I've been trying to write my weekly epistle or 'dispatch' to my father . . .

We moved forward today to this château East of Douai . . . & we (I'm a Canadian now!!) should be in Valenciennes tomorrow!! Things are moving & changing some these days . . . I rode here from Queart this morning, just under 20 miles, for the exercise; this place is called Lewarde, if you have a map . . . [*The Prince toured around, sometimes on a bicycle, sometimes on horseback.*]

This afternoon I motored East to the village of Abscon . . . & talked to some of the wretched inhabitants & Gud!! what tales they have to tell, pitiful & tragic, of their treatment & life under Hun rule!!

At 4.30 I had to be at a certain entrance into Douai to meet old

Poincaré [*President of France*], who was bumming round visiting 'les vielles delivrées' [*the liberated*] with a proper horde of French députés etc., a most revolting type of Frenchman as a rule, & this crowd were no exception!! . . .

I'm really quite enjoying being attached to these old Canadians . . . they are d—d good fellows in their own rough way & extraordinarily stouthearted & we owe them a big debt of gratitude, though they are conceited devils & they are always rubbing it in that they are Canadians & not 'Imperial Troops', as they call British troops in a rather disdainful way which annoys me a lot!! . . .

And now I really must stop, though I said this at the top of the page but I've filled it in without knowing it!! So bonne nuit et dors bien . . .

Headquarters Canadian Corps
22nd October 1918 (or rather 1.00 A.M. 23rd Oct!!)

My own darling sweetheart,

We are a very well equipped Corps we Canadians, & we had our electric lights last night but the man who runs the engine gets 'fed up' & sleepy about now & has just shut down & turned in so that I'm writing by the light of two mouldy old candles . . . anyhow I'm not depressed now, having started another letter & I've just lit one of our 'naughty' cigarettes I've just found . . .

I rode from here with old Thompson to visit a DIV & had a 2 hr ride which did me good . . . we ate our lunch in a looted house where I had a long talk with 2 Frenchwomen & a boy who had spent 4 years under Hun rule & it was difficult to believe all the stories they told me!! Still I did as all their hardships & sufferings are writ on their faces; the trouble with these good women is to get away from them; once they collar you & get talking (as only the French can) they won't let you go!

However we escaped & visited a Brigade & Battalion & heard thrilling yarns of the last few days' advance which has been very rapid . . . both these Headquarters were in villages East of the town & there was a certain amount of shelling East beyond them, though trust your E to keep away from shells, angel, & though I longed to go forward & see something, the noise (I never even saw a shell burst!!) put me off!!

After 4 years of war you won't catch me running into barrages for the fun of it & if I haven't got to go forward I won't; I'm afraid your E has become more of a coward than ever & he always was a fearful one. But I don't think old Thompson was any keener to go forward than your E!!

11.00 P.M.   23rd October

. . . Today I spent with 'the Lord Claud' thank Gud . . . we visited a couple of Canadian brigade Headquarters . . . The Huns look as though they are going to hold on to Valenciennes as long as possible . . . they were certainly shelling our positions a lot & fairly strafed poor old Denain, killing about 60 civilians & of course wounded a lot more; I felt yesterday morning that this would happen & they should have evacuated the civilians!!

But 'See here Mrs Ward, enough of this Gawd d—d war shop' as a Canadian would say; I'm afraid my letters are just nothing else nowadays, though the war has become a little more interesting lately (though merely because it looks as if the end is more or less in sight) . . .

I just loved your diary from London & hearing about all the parties. I forgot to tell you that my brother [*Bertie*] said he wasn't going to Mrs Weigall's party (I told him he was a d—d fool not to go) & so his friend Miss Fuller was there, I just long to see her merely out of curiosity!!

But I still maintain what I say about Mrs Castle; she may have a marvellous figure & be very attractive & dance divinely but she is disappointing & doesn't appeal to me at all!! [*Irene Castle, together with her husband Vernon, were a popular ragtime dance team. She turned American fashion upside down with her bobbed hair and trim figure, setting the style for the 1910s. Vernon, an RAF pilot, died in a plane crash in 1918, and twenty-five-year-old Irene retired.*]

The peace talk wave seems to have blown over, though I think it's just as well as the Huns aren't properly beat yet, though they are rapidly becoming so!! But they are putting up a stiff fight South of Valenciennes & are very sticky in front of the Canadians & it looks as if

we shall have to move them forcibly soon . . . however we are putting
that off as long as possible as we don't want to attack & have heavy
casualties if by waiting a few days we can just trek on East again!!

But sweetheart I've started war shop again . . . I hope to manage to
fly south to see my brother who I think joined the Independent Force
R.A.F. yesterday at Nancy & stay there a couple of days!!

Please give my love to 'Poots' if you are still staying with her in
London or anyhow next time you see her; what a divine little house 65
Duke Street is & there is such a wonderful bedroom on the 2nd floor!!
Gud! Beloved one shall I ever forget the night 7th–8th October, the
most marvellously divine night of my life, though pray Gud it may not
be the last.

Au revoir . . . till tomorrow night when I shall write again . . . your
very own E.

In her memoirs, Sheila recounts a tale of when Selfridges ran a promotion involving
the release of balloons with lucky numbers attached to them. Loughie and Poots's husband, Noel, dressed up in tweeds and took their guns and shooting-sticks on to the
roof of the Duke Street house, and proceeded to shoot down the balloons as they
drifted over. They had to lie low when the police called, but the butler managed to
head them off.

Headquarters Canadian Corps, B.E.F.
24th October 1918, 11.00 P.M.

The gods have been kind, sweetheart, & answered my prayer in that I
found a divine new letter on my return . . . So poor Phoebe got cursed
for only putting 1½ d on my last letter, though what did it matter & it
did Buckhouse worlds of good to pay the extra if they had to!! . . .

As regards the Yanks, darling, it is true that they made a hopeless
mess of their staff work during the St Mihiel push, though they've
continued to do so ever since & merely because Pershing is the world's
most obstinate man & insisted from the beginning on forming a huge
American army & keeping it intact to run its own show!!

If only he had agreed to our scheme of sending one US Battalion to
each British brigade what a difference it would have made & it would
have saved the Yanks thousands of useless casualties which they have

suffered in the last 2 months merely on account of ignorance!! But Pershing is an ambitious man & wants to go down in history as the C-in-C of the great U.S. Army!! . . .

The Huns are shelling our forward positions quite a lot . . . though it doesn't seem to worry these old Canadians much; they just don't care a damn for anything or anybody & after the Guards DIV the Huns fear these 4 Canadian DIVS more than any others in the B.E.F.!! We know this from captured documents & it's interesting, though I'm not surprised as these old 'Knucks' ['*Canucks': slang for 'Canadians*'] don't take many prisoners & kill or rather slaughter an astounding number of Huns!

The Prince sent Freda a number of photographs of himself from his childhood and early youth. Several of these (opposite) carry messages expressing the same sentiment: that he had been waiting for her since before he met her.

I have this on good authority & several officers have told me how they think nothing of doing in 200–300 Huns coming over to surrender with their hands up; they turn their Lewis guns on to them though probably ½ are bayonetted; the men see absolutely red & go mad!! But enough of these gruesome details, darling, though they are interesting & absolutely true; you know I wouldn't tell you all this if it wasn't!! . . .

Must stop now & go to bed as I'm so sleepy yet feeling frightfully naughty . . . tous tous les baisers de ton E.

Headquarters Canadian Corps
26th October 1918

You darling darling little sweetheart mine,

As usual I'm totally incapable of being able to thank you properly for the perfectly angelic little disc which arrived inside your divine letter this evening . . . it's easily the most wonderful present I've ever received in my life!! . . . I've strung it on a specially thin & strong piece of string that I found & it's hung round my neck & there it will ever hang . . .

As a result of your divine letter & the disc I'm being very extravagant tonight & smoking one of our cigarettes (that leaves me only 7 now) & it's making me feel so hopelessly naughty, sweetheart . . .

Curse that cigarette & I've lit another; perhaps it's the effects of a long motor trip today which included Lille, though I didn't see any 'bits'!! I think the —— Huns removed most of them though the few that are left don't parade till 5.00 & I had to leave at 3.30.

I left here at 10.00 in an open Rolls which arrived for me last night; this is a car that the War Office have forked out for me as I flatly refused to bring mine across!! And don't you think I was right to get all I could out of a 'grateful country' . . .

I'm very amused to get a letter from my R.A.F. brother [*Bertie*] this evening written from Paris, where he spent a night with old Derby at the Embassy on his way to the 'Independent [*Air*] Force' at Nancy!! But he didn't sleep at the Embassy as, in his own words, 'the deed was done', though he gave me no details & perhaps just as well!! But you see darling, 'C'était le premier fois car il était vierge' [*It was the first time because he was a virgin*] which is why it amuses & interests me so much!! I'm longing to see him & hear all about it . . .

27th October

. . . I see in the communiqué that the old Dagoes have actually attacked in Italy & that with our & French troops have taken nearly 3,000 prisoners!! It is hard to believe, isn't it darling, & how pleased all our people out there must be to at last be able to do something to help end this war! [*The Battle of Vittorio Veneto raged from 24 October until 2 November, by which time the Austrians were defeated. The Allied forces captured 300,000 prisoners and 5,000 guns.*]

So poor Sheila's baby hasn't arrived yet. I've been on the look out for it in the papers; what a life & I'm so sorry for her!!

Must stop now . . . bless you bless you

Thine E.

Headquarters Canadian Corps
29th October 1918

Darling beloved little sweetheart,

This is just the maddest scrawl I've ever written you but I want to catch the bag & I've only got 10 mins!! . . .

Great rumours that Austria & Turkey have 'chucked it' this evening, must have been that Italian push that did it . . . Darling I feel tonight that the war may be over before Xmas as there are so many rumours from Hunland & Ludendorff has gone!! . . . [*Turkey finally surrendered on 31 October, and Austria signed an Armistice on 3 November. Ludendorff had resigned the German command on 27 October; German sailors mutinied at Kiel on 28 October, refusing to put to sea.*]

. . . Tous tous les baisers de ton E sont à toi!!

Headquarters Canadian Corps
31st October 1918

My very own darling beloved one,

. . . I've just opened your letters & see that you think you've got that — — flu; oh!! sweetheart, please take the greatest care of yourself for your E's sake & stay in bed as it's a serious illness nowadays & the number of deaths is fearful, isn't it? . . .

Still more marvellous news this evening, Turkey out of it & 33,000 prisoners in Italy & the Austrians are practically out of it too!! . . .

Ton E.

Headquarters Canadian Corps
1st November 1918 (1.30 A.M.)

My very own darling beloved one,

. . . The 1st Canadian DIV party has been a very good one & great fun; 6 Canadian V.A.D.s were brought up by car from Boulogne & 3 of them were 'divine women' in their way, though of course it was a case of 'single girls are much too tame', not that your E tried to find out if this was so!! But they could dance & the DIV. orchestra is a good one; there were also ½ dozen nursing sisters from a Canadian C.C.S., though they were as ugly as sin . . .

6.00 P.M.

. . . The right Brigade of the 4th Canadian DIV attacked at dawn & was successful pushing forward up to the Southern outskirts of Valenciennes & taking over 1,000 prisoners. I wanted to walk on forward to a hill from where we should have had a marvellous view of the battlefield & there was no shelling, but Claud refused to take me up during a battle & I suppose he was right, darling, as it would be silly to get 'pipped' so near the end of the war & not really 'on duty'!! . . .

Isn't it marvellous news about Austria having concluded an armistice from noon yesterday; we got the news during last night's party; I wonder how long these —— Huns are going to stick it out all alone though I've really got a feeling they may chuck it any day now!! Perhaps not quite that, but anyhow the war is bound to be over by Xmas; I can't see how their men will be induced to fight on when they must see they are beaten!!

Tous tous les baisers de ton petit E.

Headquarters Canadian Corps
4th November 1918

My darling beloved one,

. . . I've just spent 3 hrs in Valenciennes; parts of the town are badly smashed though it's full of civilians & there are whole streets of undamaged houses & so some very comfortable billets . . .

Claud & I had a good day together yesterday & though we didn't go very far forward we walked over Friday's battlefield & saw lots of Hun corpses as well as getting a very good view of our new positions as the Huns started walking East again yesterday morning & saved us the trouble of pushing them as we meant to do!!

And we've gained more ground today . . . it looks as if they are going back to Mons, though then I think they will chuck it as they are retreating in front of the Yanks too now & our 3rd & 4th Armies attacked today & though we have no details we hear that it's gone well. Oh!! sweetheart I think we can count on peace before Xmas if not this month . . .

Sweetheart, it worries me so fearfully when I know you are ill with that beastly flu . . . it is the devil in England though it isn't bad out here, in fact there is hardly any, strange to say . . .

Today has been fine & bright & it should have cheered me up if I hadn't had to spend the day with Thompson who, poor man, has the gift of depressing me more than anyone ever has before; I just can't tell you what a terrible effect he has on me, darling, I feel like death on my return from trips with him!! . . .

Tous tous mes baisers . . . ton E.

By 6 November, Germany was isolated, and not only facing internal revolution but also an Allied invasion as its troops fell back. A German delegation met with General Foch in a railway carriage at Compiègne, and began negotiating an armistice.

Headquarters Canadian Corps
6th November 1918

My very own darling beloved one,

. . . I'm more or less waiting for just the tiniest little note from my darling little girl . . . to say she is better!! Of course I more than understand your not having written for over a week as you've evidently been very ill with that —— flu!! But Gud! how worried your E is not to have any news of you . . . you just can't think what a fearfully depressing effect your long silence (necessitated by the flu) has on your E or how much he longs to get back (& hurries to do so without shirking his daily task) each evening in the hope of finding just a note from you!! . . .

I just can't tell you what a selfish brute I feel writing all this but I'm in such a wretched state tonight darling that I just had to & pray & grovel at your feet for forgiveness!!

7th November

. . . Of course the most marvellous news of all came in this morning when the Hun wireless said 'German delegation to conclude armistice left Berlin for West afternoon 6th November' & G.H.Q. issued the following order: 'Should an officer bearing a white flag of truce present himself at any point of the British Front he will be conducted to the nearest DIV H.Q. & detained there pending instructions from G.H.Q.'

It all sounds too good to be true, doesn't it darling, but this really must be the end now & fighting will stop at the end of the week!! Besides, the Huns offed it in front of the Canadians again during the night & we've been trekking it up the Valenciennes–Mons road all day trying to keep in touch with them & are now several miles across the frontier into Belgium along that road!!

Oh! these are great days just now & everybody is so cheery & how I do envy them, sweetheart, for how can I be without news of you for so long? But will you shut up you ——!! (It's all right, darling, I'm only talking to my rotten self!!) . . .

A friend of mine has just come in to tell me that the Yanks have taken Sedan & the French Mezières; all this good news & big daily advances must mean that the end is very near now . . .

I've got to dine out tonight so I must begin to finish this epistle . . . I meant to tell you some days ago that I saw that Sheila's baby had arrived & that it was a [*the Prince leaves a gap: in fact the baby was a boy, Peter*] . . .

Tous tous mes baisers . . . ton E.

Headquarters Canadian Corps
8th November 1918

My very own darling darling beloved one,

I've just come in very late to find 2 marvellous letters . . . I can see how ill you've been & then that —— toothache on top of it all!! What a —— brute I feel for having written all that yesterday . . .

Tous tous mes baisers . . . ton E.

Headquarters Canadian Corps
9th November 1918

My very own darling beloved sweetheart,

. . . Heavens only knows what will happen to me if there is an armistice, which I feel is almost bound to come next week, though I've still got the Australians to visit & of course it will be months before the troops leave France & I don't suppose any will leave until peace is actually declared.

But as you know Foch [*the overall Allied Commander since March 1918*] has given the Huns till Monday to accept or refuse his terms & then all this sort of revolution in Germany & G.H.Q. tell us this evening that the Kaiser really has abdicated!! . . . [*The German peace delegation had been given the terms for an armistice on 7 November. The Kaiser fled to Holland on 9 November, where he abdicated, and a republic was declared in Berlin.*]

Poor old Reggie, he seems to be pretty 'thick skinned', though I can understand him in a way, sweetheart; you are so absolutely & completely irresistible, though he's a fool not to take a hint!! [*Reggie's letter to Freda of 24 October suggests that he has taken the hint, and realises that their relationship is over.*]

So Sheila's baby is a boy & I forgot to say that when I alluded to the event 2 or 3 letters ago; I'm so glad & as you are his godmother (what a lucky baby!!) one of his names should be 'Fred'!! You can tell Sheila that, darling, though not who said so!! . . .

I must give you my newest limerick, darling:

> 'There was a young lady called Hilda
> Who went for a walk with a builder.
> He said that he could & he should & he would,
> And he did & he d—d nearly killed her!!'

It's a very naughty one sweetheart, though I know you don't mind & your E is as naughty as ever though 'il reste sage'.

Please don't be too angry with your E (who is more than ever only thine) for having been so silly!! Tous tous mes baisers & bless you oh!! bless you darling darling girl.

Armistice

⚜

1918–19

At 5 A.M. on 11 November, the German delegation signed the armistice, to come into force at 11 a.m. Fierce fighting continued in some sectors right up to the ceasefire. In the BEF, among the troops, there was little rejoicing – certainly nothing like the scenes witnessed across England, especially in London.

Haig, and many of his senior staff, were surprised at the suddenness of Germany's capitulation: in mid-October, he had gloomily forecast that the war could continue for at least another year, if not longer, so controlled was the German withdrawal. Although the enemy was in retreat, the Allies had not won any major victories, and there was every indication that the Germans could have fought on. Certainly in the months after the armistice there was a strong feeling within Germany that their Army had never been defeated, and that they had been betrayed by those back home – a feeling which would sow the seeds of the discontent which allowed the rise of Adolf Hitler.

Headquarters, Canadian Corps
11th November 1918

My very own darling darling sweetheart,

What a marvellous day it has been with 'cessation of hostilities' at 11.00 A.M., in other words the end of the war, anyhow the fighting, though we are going to have a rough winter marching on East into

Germany & occupying the Rhineland, which is apparently the terms of
the armistice!! . . .

We got into Mons early this morning though the Huns fought their
machine guns to the last & fought us like hell; a fine spirit though they
were all killed but they caused us casualties, which is a loathsome
thought. What rotten luck to get killed a few hours before the end of it
all, though I fear there must be lots of cases of it throughout the B.E.F.
& one does feel so sorry for them & the badly wounded!!

But sweetheart it all seems like a dream & I've been in a sort of
trance all day; I just can't believe that it's all true & that we shan't want
any more munitions, no more bullets & no more — — shells . . .

2nd & 4th Armies are going to occupy the Rhineland, each 4 Corps
strong & each Corps will have 4 DIVS so that it will be a case of 32 DIVS,
which ought to fix the Huns all right & prevent them 'playing dirty'!! . . .

We aren't to advance for at least a week so as to give the Huns a start in
their evacuation of invaded territories, which will be a hard proposition
for them as apparently they are too hopelessly disorganised for words, &
have been for some weeks now. [*This generalisation is inaccurate: although the
German troops facing the Canadian onslaught were retreating in some disarray,
overall their withdrawal in other areas was well organised.*]

It's quite extraordinary how they have stuck it for so long . . . of
course it was the — — Kaiser, for as soon as he abdicated they accepted
our terms & it only goes to show us more than ever how solely
responsible for the war that man was & how he was the 'kernel of
Prussian Militarism' which is what has kept the war going 4 years.

12th November

After that last rhetoric effort I had to go to bed . . . I was just mad not
to get into Mons yesterday but I was ordered back to Advanced G.H.Q.
to see a Japanese Prince on board the C-in-C's train where he had been
lunching, though I only saw him for a few minutes so it was really a
waste of time!! But I had an interesting talk with Haig, who showed
me the terms of the armistice & the plans & maps of our march to the
Rhine, though I won't discuss these now as it's really 4.00 A.M. 13th as
we've had a dance here tonight. Some of those Canadian V.A.D.s came
East from Boulogne . . .

Claud & I are transporting the V.A.D.s back to Boulogne where we shall stay the night & then motor down to Paris for 24 hrs to meet my R.A.F. brother!! . . .

What about this general election? Will you have to go & live in Southampton, sweetheart; please let me know your future plans . . . [*Lloyd George wanted an early general election, although the King was opposed to it. The Prime Minister argued that emergency legislation had already extended the statutory life of the Parliament by three years, and this concern for the return of democracy was enough to convince the King. Lloyd George, acclaimed as the architect of victory, appealed to the country to return the Coalition Government which had won the war, in order to safeguard the peace.*]

Must go to bed now . . . Tous tous mes baisers les plus tendres & bless you bless you!!

Your own E.

At this point the Prince was obviously unexpectedly called back to London; the next letter is not until 27 November, at the end of his visit. He is en route to France, accompanying his father to the armistice celebrations there, before returning to his programme of visiting Commonwealth troops.

Buckhouse!!
27th November 1918 (2.00 A.M.)

Darling darling beloved little sweetheart,

I am sitting sordidly & pathetically awaiting the dawn; can't sleep & feel 'all dressed up & no place to go' & thoroughly miserable . . .

I'm just dreading the next 6 weeks, though thank Gud it's the last trip & the time ought to go fast . . . I shall be glad when the Paris stunt is over & we've got clear of the place, it will be a very trying 48 hrs . . . But Gud how I loathe all this official work though I've got to be 'British' & not grouse!! . . .

. . . Ton E.

Palais des Affaires Etrangères, PARIS
28th November 1918 (11.00 P.M.)

Darling darling beloved one,

Well, here I am in Paris, though it's pretty mouldy having to live &
be shut up in a —— palace; it's not so much that I want to go out,
sweetheart, but it's the fact of not being able to & being hopelessly
imprisoned that drives me mad! . . . However, thank Gud we leave
early Saturday so that we've only got another 24 hrs 'state' work,
though it is state & no mistake!! . . .

It's rotten having to trot around with the King really, such a waste of
time . . . he seems to like me to hang around!! . . .

We had a smooth crossing to Boulogne where Haig etc. met the
King & we lunched there before motoring to G.H.Q. Montreuil . . . it's
so sordid to find oneself back with all these old men, darling . . .

We reached Paris at 2.30 'descendant' at the Gare du Bois, where
Poincaré met us & we drove down the Avenue du Bois & the Avenue
des Champs Elysées to this old Palais; it was a long procession of open
carriages with an escort of cuirassiers & the streets were lined with
troops to keep back the vast enthusiastic crowd who gave the King a
marvellous reception & cheered themselves hoarse!! . . . It was a very
impressive sight & I got quite a lump in my throat, darling!!

We all called on the President & Madame Poincaré about 4.00 at the
Elysée [*Palace*] & then I had to visit a British leave club where I spent a
hectic hour & had to say a few words!! Finally there was an enormous
male dinner party . . . though Madame Poincaré was there & the King
& the President made speeches; it was a stupendous meal . . . the party
was a very mixed crowd of 150 men, 100 of whom were too revolting
for words . . . ambassadors, ministers, politicians etc., & Foch & Jōffre
were there, though they all said nice things about England (not that
they could well say anything else) . . .

King's Château [Sebourg], *near Valenciennes   30th November*

. . . I went to tea with Diana Capel at her flat before a large dinner (60)
at the Embassy . . . I'm so sorry to have afflicted you with this sordid
sort of a diary . . . however, a little of it may amuse you . . . I'm so

grateful to the Almighty that he gave me a sense of the ridiculous, which is an enormous help on these stunts . . .

Did you go to the Victory Ball on Wednesday? I saw lots of photos in the papers, though they were revolting sights I thought, & I hear that Portia & the whole Cadogan family were 'défendues d'y aller' {*forbidden from going*}!!

And how is that Mike? [*The first mention of Michael Herbert, who was to become the Prince's rival for Freda's affections.*] Gud! that man makes me angry, sweetheart, & I long to tell him off properly, though I'm not big enough!! But he really is the limit & a —— to carry on as he does . . .

Bonne nuit et à bientôt . . . ton petit E.

The Victory Ball was set up on the pretext of being in aid of charity. It was criticised by many as being ill advised and inopportune, and showing the upper classes at their worst, and some families, like the Cadogans, decided to boycott it. It had a dreadful effect in Paris, and there were newspaper headlines proclaiming: 'Dancing on the Dead'.

King's Château, Sebourg, near Valenciennes
3rd December 1918

My own darling sweetheart,

. . . Of course Duddie's fate in the general election must be an anxiety to you for it means everything to him whether he is returned or not!! And incidentally to 'nous' too in many ways!!!!

So my little girl went to the Victory Ball after all, it must have been a marvellous sight & amusing as I'm sure you went with a good party; was it to Eileen's box, or anyhow with her? . . .

I haven't heard another word from 'IT' in Paris so that I hope it's all blown over & that I shan't hear any more; but si ça continue I have expert assistance to hand so I'm less worried than I was, though Gud what a fool your E. has made of himself, darling, & he deserves anything except that he was very young at the time & I don't think he's exactly the first to be had like this!! [*In July 1917 the Prince had spent three days in Paris in the company of Maggy, in his own words a 'pol'. He wrote letters to her which she kept, and she began to blackmail him with them.*]

Gud!! this is a sordid life, beloved one, & I'm getting more 'gaga' each day; I was out with H.M. on Sunday & today . . . brigades are collected in villages or at points on roads & H.M. gets out of his car & walks through & amongst them talking to officers & men while they cheer him!! . . . I arrive back pretty dead each evening, though I can't grouse as this is a joyride as compared to when I have to do it all myself!! . . .

As regards my plans for the next 2 months . . . I shall spend at least 3 weeks with the Australians then go to the Yanks' G.H.Q. to visit Pershing . . . & also call on Pétain [*the French C-in-C who had made his name at Verdun; he lost it in the Second World War as head of the Vichy administration*] to see something of the French army!!

Anyhow I shan't return to England before 20th January . . . if I returned earlier I should have to sit at Sandringham, Norfolk with my family where je deviendrais complètement fou [*I should become completely mad*]!! . . .

I've cut the gloomworthy Thompson right out of my life . . . I think he gets on my nerves more now & he still treats me like a baby; I probably am one but he might conceal this impression he has of me better. But I'm a sort of joke here & an eternal 'butt' for H.M. though I just don't care a d— & I feel I'm doing good & helping the cause as having someone to rag does him worlds of good & relieves many sticky meals!! The fact that I never eat breakfast & prefer lying in bed till 9.00 (wish I could make it noon) is a daily source of amusement & criticism . . .

No more news & must stop to go to bed; it's 3.00 sweetheart & your E is sleepy though so so happy with your letter in the pocket of his pyjamas!!

Bonne nuit et dors bien, darling beloved

À bientôt!! E.

Britain had changed dramatically during the four years of the war, both economically and socially, as had the world with which she had traded.

Lloyd George promised 'a land fit for heroes' for the returning servicemen, while others wanted to 'hang the Kaiser' and 'squeeze Germany till the pips squeak' and make her pay for the war and help restore the economy.

The working classes, who had pulled together and helped Britain in her hour of need, would not tolerate a return to pre-war conditions. The role of women, too, throughout society, had changed dramatically, and for the first time, after the 1918 Representation of the People Act, women over thirty were able to vote.

Red agitators, and the Bolshevism which had swept through Russia, were suspected as the reason behind any working-class disturbance, and the spectre of a Labour Government in Britain was feared by the upper classes as akin to revolution: certainly the end of any hope of a return to their cosy pre-war existence.

King George V could not appreciate the radical changes which had occurred; the Prince, however, was much more aware of the problems facing King, country and Empire.

King's Château, Sebourg, near Valenciennes
5th December 1918

My very own darling beloved one,

Thank you sweetheart for your divine letter from Southampton . . . your present abode must be as sordid as mine & I'm so so fearfully bored & fed up with trotting round like a 'wee doggie'!! But I won't talk about myself till later, darling; I'm so sorry to hear you are pessimistic about D's re-election, though I just can't make head or tail of the details of this general election, of the parties, the questions on which it's being fought etc etc . . .

Still I'm beginning to understand & realise the general conditions & spirit in England & besides hearing a lot I'm sent the fortnightly 'Scotland Yard' reports to read & the last lot are pretty bad reading too . . . the usual revolutionary gas, though alas it's getting more than gas now & it's nothing now to what it will be in a year's time or less!!

I really take a very gloomy view of the future, sweetheart, though as you know I'm not going to own to myself that I've got the wind up properly about everything (which I have) & am fairly going to slave for the cause, far more for the good of the Country & the Empire than for my family!! What a sordid end to the war, beloved one . . . you know that your E hasn't got his eyes shut & is as alive to the imminent troubles & dangers as anybody . . .

Adieu petite amour adorée . . . ton E.

Headquarters 5th Army, LILLE
8th December 1918 (3.00 A.M.)

My own darling sweetheart,

. . . We are staying with Birdwood (G.O.C. 5th Army) & it's a marvellous billet. H.M. went to see a concert party stunt in the huge theatre after dinner which was a popular move & the very best propaganda & it was quite a good show, too, the leading man being Leslie Henson of the Gaiety who is as pricelessly funny as ever! [*William Birdwood had commanded the Anzac Corps until the summer of 1918. Although popular, his military ability was limited, and he was one of many senior officers who had been promoted beyond his capabilities (see also letter of 3 January 1919). Comedian Henson's name was linked to the Gaiety from his first appearance in 1915, until it was demolished in 1957, when he failed in a last-ditch attempt to save it. 'Propaganda' was another word from the Prince's personal vocabulary, meaning 'putting on a show' or 'self-promotion'. George V was very angry when he heard the Prince use the expression, saying that he did things from a sense of duty, not as propaganda.*]

My brother took me on to supper with some R.A.F. friends where we sang & danced & told dirty stories in their mess till 2.30 . . . this last week has been a sort of course for 'how to get old quickly' & my brother & I needed a cheery evening badly!!

I must go to bed soon as I've heard fearful rumours of 'prayers' or some form of worship for 9.00 A.M. which appals me & I know I shan't be able to get up; how anyone can feel religious at that hour is quite beyond me but I suppose I shall have to be British & do my best . . .

9th December   King's Château, Lophem, near BRUGES

What a joy your divine long letter is, beloved one . . . it's so so sweet of you to write & at such length when I know what a hectic & tiring time you must be having in Southampton!! How sordid it must all be for you, darling one, particularly when you feel that D's chances of getting in are somewhat remote & that all your visits to the slums are to no purpose . . . Beloved one, you know how madly interested in all these 'social problems' I am & must be . . .

We left Lille this morning & motored North to Zeebrugge where the old King of the Belgians met us as well as Keyes, the Admiral who ran the April stunt, & the latter took us out to the Mole, where we landed & saw where the 'Vindictive' came alongside etc. Too thrilling for words & now I think more than ever that it was one of the finest stunts of the war!!

Alge Athlone, an uncle of mine [*Queen Mary's brother, who married Princess Alice, daughter of Queen Victoria's son, Leopold*] was also with us & he is coming out here to dinner as well as Keyes, who is a topper!! . . .

Apres le diner!!

We had quite a cheery party for the last night & H.M. was in wonderful form & this trip has done him worlds of good & he is quite human; it's getting away from Buckhouse & the real court life that does it! Oh!! that court life, beloved one, that's what's going to hasten the end of it if it isn't vastly modified; people can't & won't stand it nowadays & how well do I understand it & abhor all that sort of rot!! . . .

I met an interesting Trades Union 'Secretary' yesterday evening who has come out to lecture to the troops & he has been pretty hot & would get up & talk Bolshevism for two pence now, though I think he's playing the game & doing a lot of good amongst the men telling them the truth!! Of course I had to almost cringe before him much though I hated him as he was a thoroughly revolting sight & rude & coarse don't describe him!! But one must look on this type as the ruling spirit nowadays . . . All this Bolshevism & revolutionary stuff makes me do a lot of straight thinking & puts the wind up me . . .

Touching wood I think the Paris trouble is over, though I just must get all those letters back somehow [*Maggy did eventually let the matter drop*]; as regards Diana Capel I can promise you that there are absolutely no grounds for a 'scandale' my sweetheart, & you can tell Sheila!! I did go to tea with her the last evening I was in Paris, though I told you that, darling, surely I did? . . . but I'm sure you didn't believe Sheila, sweetheart, in fact I know you didn't & that you don't now either!! . . .

To return to the Paris scandale, darling, you know it isn't true & that there are no grounds for one, but let the world think so & it's the very finest form of camouflage for us . . . let them think that I have lots of 'affaires' as long as it isn't with my own darling little girl, though of course it's very bad to get that sort of reputation, particularly for me . . .

The cutting you sent is amusing & I could do a lot worse than take on an American, though I just can't bear to even think about marriage let alone talk about it!! . . .

Bonne nuit et dors bien . . . tous tous les baisers de ton petit E.

British Mission with the Belgian Army, BRUSSELS
12th Dec 1918, 2.30 A.M.

My own very darling sweetheart,

. . . We went to look at some marvellous Hun submarine shelters at Bruges which are protected by feet of concrete from bombs; no-one but Huns would ever have thought of that & done it as it must have cost millions!! We also looked at a Hun 15″ naval gun near Ostend which has shelled Dunkirk etc. & the amount of construction for that is amazing!! . .

On Tuesday night we dined at the Palace Hotel full of whizzbangs [*fast young women: 'whizzbang' was trench slang for a mortar or small artillery round*] with whom we all danced & then I went on to a nightclub with Claud & some Canadian friends where we stayed till 4.00 . . .

You must forgive your E as it's nearly 3.00 & he's been dancing more at the Palace Hotel after dining with the King [*Albert*] & Queen [*Elisabeth*] of the Belgians at their palace; my uncle [*Alge Athlone*] went with me & it wasn't fearfully stiff though we were there nearly 3 hrs instead of 2 hrs as we had calculated & I got so so bored!!

Of course this dancing at the Palace Hotel isn't much fun though it's quite amusing . . . the 'whizzbangs' are rather revolting anyhow, very common, but a few of them can dance in a sort of way & there are 2 good string bands . . . of course all these women are 'bochesses' & you can guess what that means, darling, & really life in Brussels is practically the same as when the Huns were here, we 'officiers alliés' have merely replaced the Hun officers & we use Hun paper money!! . . . These Belges aren't any happier with us than they were with the Huns;

Gud! how I hate them though not as much as the Dagoes!!

There are lots of good restaurants & shops here though the prices of everything are ruinous if not prohibitive . . . you would be amazed at some of the 'additions' such as 1 whisky & soda 10 francs & eggs [*gap*] francs each!!

I'm off tomorrow to join Australian Corps at Ham . . . My brother [*Bertie*] returned to England with H.M. on Tuesday to get some more 'clothes' or some such feeble excuse; a curious boy in some ways so that I'm glad to have had this chance of talking to him like a father, which I've been able to do several times this last fortnight!!

Headquarters, Australian Corps, Ham sur Eure, near CHARLEROI
13th December 1918

. . . All you tell me of your further visits to the working people's houses in Southampton is very interesting & encouraging & I'm so grateful to you, beloved one, for telling me all your impressions of the general spirit & conditions. Of course everything depends on L-G [*Lloyd George*] as he is certainly out for a peaceful settlement of everything, wages etc., as he was out to win the war; but will he be able to keep his promises to the people? I'm rather doubtful!! . . .

This is a sordid château, a huge barrack of a place though comfortable; the Corps Commander, Hobbs, is a quaint little man in spectacles who if put into plain clothes would look the completest shop worker or any such type & he has a glorious Cockney accent, though of course that is the Australian accent!! And the rest of the C.C.'s mess are such a dull crowd & rather stiff though they may improve on acquaintance . . . I've got a major (with the unfortunate name Hunn) attached to me & he seems all right though I think he's a Jew; anyhow he looks it!! . . .

Gud! how madly in love with you I am sweetheart & 3 days in Brussels has made me all the more so; it's seeing other women again which has made your own E. far more yours than ever . . .

Headquarters Australian Corps
15th December 1918

My own beloved sweetheart,

. . . Hobbs is the world's completest dud; however I've cut him right
out . . . it cramps my style so hopelessly having any general with me &
Hobbs is one of those prudish & conscientious people who take life
fearfully seriously . . . though I can't help admiring him as he's a self-
made man!! . . .

Most people don't seem to be taking such a huge interest in the
general election as one would have thought; they say it's 'dead snip' on
L-G this time & that unless he makes good there'll have to be another
election next year after peace, whenever that will be signed, & I wish
they would hurry up about it too as the army is bored enough already
& Gud! knows what the troops will feel like in a few months' time!! Of
course demobilisation has more or less started already, though it's going
to be fearfully slow!!

Tous tous les baisers from your very very own loving & adoring E.

Headquarters Australian Corps
22nd December 1918

My own darling beloved one,

. . . Gud!! how utterly sick of soldiering one is, & anything to do
with the army; but one can't help liking all the men & taking a huge
interest in them . . . And how one does sympathise with them &
understand how hopelessly bored & fed up they are getting waiting to
be demobilised; I feel like that myself darling so how much more do
they?

My R.A.F. brother never arrived in Brussels yesterday as he wasn't
able to fly over as he meant to; he only turned up at 11.00 this
morning . . . he was rather stone cold after his 10 days in London where
he seems to have been dancing a good deal besides 'et ça c'est fatiguant'
[*that which is tiring*] . . .

Claud & I stopped at the battlefield of Waterloo on our way to
Brussels to improve our history though it was really quite interesting &

in a way thrilling if one has a certain amount of imagination which thank Gud! I have sweetheart!! . . .

I hear that Diana M. is engaged as well as several other 'girls' in London, though to MOI each one is more unattractive than the other. [*Diana Manners, daughter of the Duke of Rutland, finally married Duff Cooper in June 1919, after her parents initially viewed the match with much disfavour. He had approached the Duchess at the Victory Ball to ask her permission to marry her daughter.*]

Must go to bed now as I've got a heavy day tomorrow; 3 parades & your E has got to 'pin on' about 100 medals!!

So bonne nuit et dors bien . . . ton E.

Headquarters Australian Corps
30th December 1918

Darling beloved sweetheart,

. . . The results of the general election are a pleasant surprise sweetheart, I've just seen a Paris 'Daily Mail' & a long list of successful candidates though alas no Southampton results, which were needless to say the only ones that interested MOI . . . [*Lloyd George's Coalition won an emphatic victory in the 'coupon' election – so-called because of the personal letter of endorsement sent to approved candidates by the Prime Minister – with 526 seats out of 707 in the Commons. The Labour Party won only 57 seats, but polled over two and a half million votes, and was clearly on the verge of a political breakthrough, which finally came in January 1924.*]

I see that old Patsy Connaught (aged 35 or so) has at last 'got off' with a sailor though I think he's rather mad; I know that she is, too, so I wish them both joy!! [*Born in 1886, Victoria Patricia was the younger daughter of the Duke of Connaught. Her mother treated her unkindly, making her wear her sister's cast-offs, resulting in painfully deformed feet from ill-fitting shoes. She married Captain the Hon. Alex Ramsay, son of the Earl of Dalhousie, who had been on her father's staff when he was Governor-General in Canada. He was knighted in 1937, and achieved the rank of Admiral in 1939. She became an accomplished painter, and died in 1974.*]

You know of course that Cynthia Hamilton (Claud's niece) is engaged to Althorp . . . he's such a dud though alas the world's biggest snob & not half good enough for her, who can almost be described as a divine woman, not that she attracts MOI . . . [*Althorp was heir to the 6th Earl Spencer, and grandfather of Diana, Princess of Wales.*]

Too sleepy to write more tonight . . . I wish TOI everything that I possibly can for the New Year 1919 & (selfishly) that we may see far more of each other than in 1918, which has been easily the most marvellous & divine year of my life because in 1918 I met my own darling beloved little girl . . .

Tous tous ses baisers . . . Ton E.

Headquarters Australian Corps B.E.F.
1st January 1919

Darling beloved sweetheart,

. . . I've just seen the official list of successful candidates & am delighted to see D's name on it as the 2nd member for Southampton . . . what an amazing triumph for L.G. if only he can carry on & keep the confidence of the nation . . .

I shall be staying the night of 7th at Spa with my brother at Advanced Headquarters R.A.F. though I hear the little devil was in Cologne for New Year's Eve dancing hard!! . . .

Bless TOI who is never out of my thoughts . . . ton E.

Headquarters Australian Corps
3rd January 1919

My very own darling beloved one,

. . . Birdwood (G.O.C. 5th Army) arrived this afternoon, an interesting man & popular but such a fearful buckstick & advertiser & the world's greatest 'prude' so that guess a very little of him goes a long way with MOI!! How I'm longing to get away from generals!! . . .

4th January

. . . I'm in a rotten mood this evening & depressed, there's a little mutiny going on in one of these Australian DIV Artilleries which doesn't exactly tend to cheer one up!! Although not a big one still this trouble is serious as you know what a terribly infectious disease it is & it spreads like wildfire!!

The men won't parade & demand the removal of their Battalion Commander & the release of 5 men who have been put under arrest for agitating & being the ringleaders, probably Huns or paid Hun agents!! . . . I only hope to Gud the trouble will soon be settled somehow & not spread, though you can understand that it makes one anxious, sweetheart!! . . .

Tous mes baisers till Monday when I'll send tons more

E.

Headquarters Australian Corps
6th January 1919

My own very darling beloved one,

. . . I enclose a teeny calendar for 1919; I've stuck 2 bits of sticking plaster on the cover, the first to cut out a nasty 'vous' & the second to be able to write E. though there's one inside & something else as well!! I just must confess to TOI that it was sent to me, though I think it's rather a sweet calendar & of course all I have to give TOI for Xmas & the New Year . . .

That little mutiny I told you about est tout à fait réglé & the men will parade now that they've got a good C.O. who was sent to them yesterday; it just wanted a gentleman & a strong man to fix it up, that combination in a man never fails; the former C.O. was a ranker!! . . .

I met a very 'boxed' [*drunk*] American '2nd Lootennant' in Brussels last night & have caught the marvellous expression 'jazzing around' from him . . .

Tous mes baisers les plus tendres E.

Headquarters Canadian Corps, Palais Schaumburg, Bonn {headed paper}
9th January 1919

My own darling sweetheart,

I just have to write to you on Hun paper for the sheer joy of being able to write my proper address above the —— palace . . .

Cunningham-Reid [*see letter of 24 January 1919*] flew me over to Cologne yesterday morning & we stunted over the Cathedral & again over the Rhine so that we could spit into it . . .

I lunched with an R.A.F. Wing in Cologne & Claud & I had a stroll in the centre of the town afterwards & had great fun making the Hun men civilians get off the pavement for us; it wasn't difficult as they've all got their tails properly between their legs . . . Gud! how I loathe them all the more now that I'm actually in Germany & it does one worlds of good to know how humiliating it must be for the Huns to see us!! . . .

This palace is a very comfortable house & is the residence of the Princess [*Victoria*] of Schaumburg Lippe, a sister of the ex-Kaiser's & consequently a 2nd cousin of mine I'm sorry & ashamed to say, though it's not my fault & she's still living here!!

I've just met her on the stairs coming up to my room & had a 10 minute talk with her; she did it very cleverly though didn't get much change out of your E despite all her pro-English camouflage; of course she is ⅓ English!! She says the Kaiser was always against U-Boats, bombing, gas etc. & said she knew nothing of the ill-treatment of our prisoners, though a touch of the Prussian came out when she said that but for the revolution the Huns could have fought on for years. That made me mad, her trying to make out that the Huns weren't beaten, & still more mad when she called me 'dear'!! Of course I just took no notice, it was difficult to be rude to her & would have been ignominious, though I just longed to be . . .

Tous tous mes baisers les plus tendres my sweetheart. Ton E.

How the Princess Victoria was one-third English is not explained – her mother was Queen Victoria's eldest daughter, who married the German Emperor, Frederick III, and whose son – the Princess's brother – became Kaiser Wilhelm II. Her first marriage in 1890 was to Prince Adolph of Schaumburg-Lippe; later, in 1928, to the dismay of her family, she married a Russian waiter half her age, Alexander Zoubkoff; within eighteen months he had deserted her and she was financially ruined. Her family refused to help her, and the Schaumburg Palace was the setting for an auction of all her possessions, which, however, failed to clear her debts, estimated at £50,000.

Headquarters 3rd American Army, Koblenz
10th January 1919

My very own beloved one,

. . . I'm very glad I've come up here as it's a real good chance of some propaganda & these Yanks are generally such d—d good fellows & too fearfully kind & hospitable for words; they've got a sort of fascination for me & Gud how they make me laugh . . .

Headquarters Guards Div, COLOGNE
12th January, 11.00 P.M.

. . . Of course I think we are being far too lenient here in Germany & I should like to be an army commander for 24 hrs. No one is more dead against bullying these —— Huns than I am, darling, but I should like to make them feel that they are defeated more than they are & not see all of us live on the Rhine in an atmosphere of 'wash out the last 4 years' which I'm sorry to say we have to do a certain extent due to orders issued by our 'high powers' who have never been near the line & who haven't learnt to hate the Hun!!

Gud! I could just murder some of our staff generals tonight & their orders just make me mad!; I just loathe these Huns a million times more than ever . . . & we aren't half strict enough with them!! The French are giving them hell as compared to us & the Americans & I'm vur-ry sorry to say that there is a good deal of the 'forgive & forget' spirit in the American army; I've advertised the British hatred of the Huns like mad the last 2 days, though of course the Yanks don't look on it all as we & the French do; 1 year isn't as much as 4 years! . . .

Everybody is getting very fed up in the army of occupation &

nobody knows how long they'll have to sit in Germany or what the future of the regular soldier is going to be . . . the Government seem to be making a pretty good mess of demobilisation & I'm afraid there's going to be worse trouble than there was last week & that was bad enough . . . [*The process of demobilisation was causing problems because of the Ministry of Labour's decision that key men, those most required by industry, should be released first. Generally, of course, these were the last men to have been called up, so this stirred up considerable ill feeling among the longest-serving troops. There were mutinies at camps at Calais and Folkestone, and marches in London. Eventually, the problem was solved by Churchill, who implemented a 'first in: first out' principle.*]

I expect Belvoir [*seat of the Duke of Rutland*] was quite pleasant & interesting in a way; I suppose Diana [*Manners*] really is engaged!! . . .

Ton E. is thine & only thine & he only thinks of TOI my sweetheart . . .

Headquarters Guards DIV, COLOGNE
14th January 1919

My own very darling sweetheart,

Thy last divine letter from Belvoir arrived last night . . . I don't disapprove of TOI going to Belvoir at all, beloved one, as I know that TOI wouldn't ever become 'one of them' & I'm sure they are very kind; I wouldn't mind going there myself if I was asked, it would be interesting . . . So 'their graces' don't approve of Diana's 'secret' engagement; what snobs they are . . . [*The Rutlands were part of a very different social set to the Prince's; their children were part of an informal society, known sometimes as the 'corrupt coterie', described by Diana Manners as 'unafraid of words, unshocked by drink, unashamed of decadence and gambling'.*]

The news that TOI is taking another house is too marvellous sweetheart, though this won't be till March; I'm really thinking very seriously of taking a flat as soon as I return in February, though TOI knows it isn't very easy for me; still there's nothing like trying & your E has made up his mind to!! . . .

I do more than agree with TOI about the demobilisation though who is really responsible for all the chaos Gud only knows; but the result is trouble & discontent & grousing . . . Weakness is at the root of all the trouble . . . these concessions & exceptions granted 2 or 3 weeks ago to men on leave who refused to embark for this side should never have been!!

The rest of the men (Navy, Army & R.A.F.) now feel that they are being unfairly treated & so they are really, & there's going to be trouble throughout the months of demobilisation & far more serious trouble than we've had yet, though it's been bad enough already!! It's such a pity as I had high hopes that the demobilisation scheme was going to work so well & so smoothly!! . . .

15th January

This evening I spent ½ hr at the opera, which seems to be the only form of amusement here & TOI can imagine what that's like, all in German with Hun artists & a Hun chorus, though the orchestra is good; I can't remember what the opera was though the music didn't sound too bad, though guess I prefer ragtime or revue music . . . I really went there to look at the revolting Hun women who walk round the promenade during the 'entr'actes', though there weren't many this evening so your E's appetite for dinner wasn't ruined!! . . .

From this very unthrilling account of life in Cologne TOI can see what a deadly existence it is for the army of occupation & everybody is too fearfully bored for words. This Berlin fighting is spreading southwards & there were rumours of a strike somewhere near here this morning & 1st Grenadier Guards were suddenly put on one hour's notice to move while I was lunching with them . . . [*The so-called 'Spartacist' uprising against the German Government was swiftly overturned by the military, which supported Friedrich Ebert, later first President of the German Republic. The Spartacist leaders, Karl Liebknecht and 'Red' Rosa Luxemburg, were murdered by the military police.*]

This is a great secret, sweetheart, but I've just been asking Grigg if he feels like taking on the job of Private Secretary to MOI later; I wonder if TOI has ever heard of him. Probably Duddie has. Anyhow he's supposed to be frightfully clever & to be in touch with a lot of the ministers & leading politicians . . . he won't give me an answer yet &

wants to think it over for 2 or 3 weeks as I think he has several other offers of jobs already!! . . . [*Grigg, later Lord Altrincham, turned the job down, though he later joined the Prince's staff for the tours of Canada and Australia – see letter of 5 August 1919. The post went to Godfrey Thomas.*]

Je t'embrasse très tendrement . . . Ton petit E.

Headquarters New Zealand DIV, *Leverkosen, The Rhine, near* COLOGNE
17th January 1919

My very own darling sweetheart,

. . . Of course I will tell TOI who sent me the teeny calendar which is now thine though it will make TOI laugh a lot; it was that little ——— Lady Coke!! Please forgive your E. for not telling TOI when he sent it; I thought it would spoil it all a little though of course that was all I had to send; my mama sent me a duplicate of it & of course I carry that one in my pocket whereas I couldn't carry Lady Coke's . . . try to forget who the calendar originated from; it's only from thine E & guess Lady Coke only got a very frigid & sordid Xmas card (merely signed) in return!! . . .

How too priceless that I should be engaged to Lady Cynthia Curzon [*daughter of Lord Curzon of Kedleston, later 1st Marquess. She was to marry Sir Oswald Mosley in 1920*] & then that I should still be very 'thick' with Julie Thompson; there's nothing to beat good camouflage, though I fear these rumours are such glorious lies that they would spoil any attempt at camouflage!!

What can TOI mean by saying one never knows what will happen later as regards MOI? TOI knows that TOI would know long before anyone else if anything ever did happen & how could it happen in the near future, beloved one, except 'by order' & then it wouldn't be real, so it wouldn't matter to TOI et MOI!! . . .

This place is all a huge chemical factory where tons & tons of explosives were made in the Great War, but we've requisitioned the Company offices & their best houses & fly the 'union jack' over the former, which annoys the old Hun manager & chairman of the Company a lot . . . it's a relief to find an annoyed & angry & ashamed Hun as they are so thick-skinned!!

18th January

... Guess I'm pretty dead tonight ... I'm nearly through now, only a church parade tomorrow morning & then goodbye-ee to this filthy Rhineland & all these ——— Huns!! [*'Goodbye-ee' is a reference to the popular song, written by R.P. Weston and Bert Lee, with the refrain 'Goodbye-ee, goodbye-ee, wipe the tear, baby dear, from your eye-ee . . .'*]

20th January, Headquarters R.A.F., Spa

I'm in a fever, beloved one, as I arrived here about 4.00 P.M. to find a wire from H.M. to say that my youngest brother [*John*] had died & that I wasn't to go to Paris; I wired back to say that I was returning to England at once for a few days which I thought was a good move & should have arrived in London tomorrow, Tuesday evening ... So of course I didn't finish this letter last night as I had great & wonderful hopes of seeing TOI tomorrow evening if the goddess of fortune had been kind to us ...

I'm so miserable darling as I've just got another wire from H.M. telling me not to return to England, though not to go to Paris & just to carry on visiting DIVS!! Isn't it all too heartbreaking & of course my little brother's death plunges me into mourning; don't think me very cold-hearted, sweetheart, but I've told you all about that little brother, darling, & how he was an epileptic & might have gone West any day!!

He's been practically shut up for the last 2 years anyhow, so no-one has ever seen him except the family & then only once or twice a year & his death is the greatest relief imaginable & what we've always silently prayed for; but to be plunged into mourning for this is the limit just as the war is over which cuts parties etc. right out!! ...

Now I've got to resume trekking from DIV to DIV without Paris or any form of respite & I'm so stale that I've become a completer dud than ever ...

My family should return to London first week in February which will be all right for MOI & what does all the mourning in the world matter to TOI et MOI? I'm terribly sorry for my sister, who was going to a lot of parties in February, though somehow I don't think this mourning will last very long, as I think the funeral was today; it looks to me as if as little as possible was being made of it all & I only hope so. No-one would be more cut up if any of my other 3 brothers were to die than I should be, but this poor boy had become more of an animal than anything else & was only a brother in the flesh & nothing else!! . . .

H.M.'s wire this morning was just about the biggest disappointment of your E's life except when he (or somebody at Windsor Castle) asked TOI to dinner there the last night of my August leave!! . .

I.S.Y.C.T.N.N.O.M.A.E.A.A.O.Y. & Bless TOI for ever & ever [*these letters are those engraved on the Prince's disc and are the initial letters of two lines from a poem*]

E.

The Prince wrote his mother a letter about John's death which upset her deeply. She did not reply, but he heard how much he had hurt her and wrote again, a much more sympathetic letter. His father thought John's death a great mercy, ending his suffering.

Headquarters 32nd DIV, BIOULX (near Namur)
22nd January 1919

My own darling beloved one,

. . . I was very sorry to leave them at Spa this afternoon, I've got to look on Advanced Headquarters R.A.F. as a sort of home on this side now & I'm very fond of my brother now that we've seen something of each other; we used to be great friends before the war but we had drifted apart & become almost strangers! We've had some great talks the last 3 days & got to know each other well again & that's a good feeling, sweetheart; he's a d— d good boy really & TOI would love him & TOI must meet him later!! . . .

I'm thoroughly depressed all round; it must be a combination of the arctic weather & the thought of a whole month of camouflage mourning, though I've got to camouflage myself with crepe bands & keep away from all parties & any form of gaité!! It does seem such a shame . . . not that there's much real 'gaité' in the 'zones des armées' . .

Goodnight my very own darling beloved little one, don't quite forget your very own E.

Headquarters 32nd DIV
24th January 1919

My very own darling sweetheart,

... As regards what Ali told TOI, of course not a word ... I'm sure he's an admirable man for the job of A.D.C. or equerry, which is the same thing, & I won't forget him as I like him very much ... [*Leo and Ali had returned from India, much to the irritation of Leo's mother, Princess Beatrice. She had instructed Reggie to write to Leo and tell him not to come home, though apparently their hosts were not keen on him staying.*]

As TOI knows I'm already fixed up as I have the 'Lord Claud' & then Piers Legh has taken on the job of equerry; but my R.A.F. brother is in search of one & I'll talk to him about Ali in Brussels before we both enter the royal palace where we are to stay the weekend with the King & Queen of the Belgians!!

I should say that Ali would be the very man for him, though of course TOI won't tell Ali I say this or anything else; but I'll tell TOI what my brother says in my next letter; he thought of Bobbie Cunningham-Reid once but not now!! Yes, he is distinctly a bounder, darling ... Of course I hardly know him, I met him my first night at Spa & he gave me a good flip over to Cologne; he seems a stout-hearted lad & is a good pilot though I could see he's a bounder, but not an incurable one!! He's a curious boy & anyhow not at all suitable as equerry to Bertie ... [*Cunningham-Reid was one of the youngest officers in the Royal Flying Corps and had shot down ten enemy planes, winning the DFC. He became Conservative MP for Warrington, and Parliamentary Private Secretary to Wilfrid Ashley, whose daughter Mary he later married. Her sister, Edwina, married Dickie Mountbatten.*]

I'm glad to hear that Michael [*Herbert*] was more 'reasonable' the other night at the party, in other words less of a —— as he was in November; but he's a dangerous man, sweetheart, I'm sure of it; attractive, yes, very, though not to be trusted a yard as TOI knows!! ...

Dors bien petite amour à MOI ... ton petit amoureux E.

The Royal Palace!!, Brussels
25th January 1919

My very own darling beloved little one,

. . . it's just too sweet for words of TOI to write as TOI has about my
little brother's death . . . I've written what I feel about it all & how
mad I was that H.M. wouldn't let MOI return to England for a few days
to my poor Mama, who though really relieved must feel it all, & to TOI
darling; but he's a hard man particularly to MOI & so inhuman
sometimes!! . . .

Thine E 'flipped' over from an aerodrome at Morville . . . though it
was rather a dud day with very low clouds & we couldn't rise above
1,000 ft!! My brother's pilot lost his way & they had to land at a French
aerodrome to locate themselves & they didn't turn up till ½ hr after we
had landed!! . . .

I strolled in the town with my brother till we met Claud . . . we
solemnly drove to this Belge form of 'Buckhouse' where we were met
by old King Albert & we've just got away from a deadly dull & very
trying dinner party with him . . . King Albert is a nice man though
fearfully shy & consequently the completest dud till you get to know
him . . .

Gud how thine E does loathe palace & court life . . . guess he was
never intended for that sort of existence; must have been a mistake, not
that he will ever treat it as anything but a huge joke, & artificial
camouflage & loathing it all more & more intensely!! . . .

26th January

. . . My brother & I had to attend a march past of 4 whole British
brigades . . . & we sat on mouldy old Belge horses for 1¼ hrs & Gud I
was cold just frozen stiff & my feet & hands gave me absolute 'gipp'!!
Of course we couldn't wear 'British Warms' [*officers' thick overcoats*] as
the troops weren't in greatcoats . . .

All the units who marched through Brussels this morning are
billeted in the town for 48 hours so as to give them a 'blow through' &
a change of surroundings which will do them worlds of good & keep
their minds off demobilisation, though it seems to be going better now

that all the unfairness & 'wrangling' has been stopped & the men understand the system & know where they are, poor devils!! . . .

All my love & baisers . . . thine own E.

Headquarters 51st (Highland) DIV, *La Louvière (between Mons & Charleroi),*
(Left Brussels Monday afternoon)
29th January 1919

My very own beloved sweetheart,

It's 3 whole days since I've written . . . I've had to write to my mama & then 1 or 2 business letters. I find letter writing (except to TOI) more of an effort every day & I'm a very slow writer . . .

Of course this Highland DIV. all kilted battalions is one of the first 10 best DIVS in the B.E.F. & has fought marvellously well . . . so I do feel I've been seeing & talking to d—d good men & a lot come from Glasgow & it's very important to get at them before they are demobilised!! [*Britain was in the grip of widespread strikes in January 1919, and much of the unrest was centred in Glasgow.*]

They are loyal enough & play the game as long as they are disciplined soldiers but Gud knows what they won't do as soon as they are demobilised & can get at all the whisky & hear these red Bolshevists talk who incite them to wave red flags!! . . . But though depressing it's everything for MOI to have the chance of getting down to bedrock as regards the social problem & I get it all first hand . . .

I might fly back to England; of course I'm mad keen to learn to fly now & am getting bored sitting behind in the observer's seat!! . . .

How I'm longing for your next letter, beloved one, & perhaps some news & gossip, I haven't heard any for ages & feel terribly out-of-date & cut out of everything!! . . . I suppose 'pa & ma Rutland' really cut Diana's engagement out [*having initially refused Duff Cooper permission to marry his daughter without a year's delay, the Duke relented in April*] . . . I hear that Mrs Wilson [*US President Wilson's second wife, a widow, Edith, whom he married in 1915*] is of doubtful origin & has a strange past & that there are some priceless stories of her stay at Buckhouse . . .

Bless TOI always my sweetheart . . . ton petit E.

Headquarters 36th (Ulster) DIV
31st January 1919

My very own beloved little sweetheart,

. . . As regards thy housie beloved one, I must confess to not knowing the exact location of the Queen's Rd. Bayswater Tube Station, still, guess I shan't have any difficulty whatever in finding it, & I do so agree with TOI about keeping one's money for more amusing things than sordid rents etc.!! And if it can be made 'rather sweet' & is so handy to a tube station guess the 'far away' part of it is rather an advantage & I'm all for it sweetheart . . .

So Duddie is going to America (& I suppose Canada) in April, though I'm horrified by the thought that TOI has even been asked to go to India in March, though I know the Willingdons are charming!! [*Lord Willingdon was, firstly, a provincial governor in India, and subsequently Viceroy.*] Oh!! please please don't dream of going, my beloved one, not this year anyhow, as somebody must stay to help ton petit E. when he returns to England & be kind to him & there's only TOI who takes the least real interest in MOI . . .

My family don't seem to be in the least keen for me to return & are suggesting all sorts of things to keep MOI over on this side; but guess I shall be in London by 13th February unless I get a direct order from H.M. not to . . . I say 13th now as I want to miss Opening of Parliament which is on 11th but hush!! . . .

I'm in mourning for 3 whole —— months according to my Mama, from whom I had a letter last night, & this cuts me out of real parties till 20th April about; I call it rot & most unnecessary . . . Guess thy E. isn't worrying about anything now, mourning or Bolshevism or strikes etc. etc. except thy answer about 'le voyage aux Indes', oh!! please please say NO . . .

Bless TOI my angel for being so so marvellously sweet & delicious to MOI & for making MOI so hopelessly happy.

Ton E. qui t'adore si follement.

My love to Poots when you see her again.

Headquarters 16th DIV, *Avelin (4 miles South of Lille)*
2nd February 1919

My own beloved little one,

. . . All these labour troubles & riots are very depressing, aren't they, sweetheart; of course Glasgow is worse than anywhere else though Belfast & the London docks are pretty serious too; as TOI says the poor old P.M. can't be in 2 places at once [*Lloyd George was at Versailles for the peace conference*] though I do wish he was in England just now . . . I feel he is the only man who will prevent a revolution if anyone can & I'm beginning to get a bit sceptical of that now!! Things seem to be moving so fast, though I suppose these riots are only to be expected after 4 years of war & all these revolutionary & bolshevist agitators on the loose . . . [*In Glasgow, following stoppages around the country, a general strike had been called to try to secure a forty-hour working week, and the red flag was hoisted on the town hall. On 31 January, the Riot Act had been read, and troops were sent to help quell the disturbance. The trouble died down on its own, however, and the strike ended on 11 February.*]

3rd February

. . . there's a wire for me 'in code' from H.M. somewhere so Gud only knows what is in store for thine E., my beloved one, & code sounds important!! . . .

All all my love & tous tous mes baisers . . . ton E.

Headquarters 12th DIV, *Masny (near Lawarde Hd Qrs*
Canadian Corps Oct 1918), East of Douai
4th February 1919

My own darling beloved little one,

Well, guess I've done my job here, which was to present the King's colours to 9 battalions . . . a very easy day for MOI although it meant 3 speeches, though I read them & am getting hardened to 'speechies' nowadays!!

What worries MOI far more is that wire from H.M. . . . I received it

last night though it was in an indecipherable code & when I asked
H.M. to repeat it 'en clair' he wired back to say he had written me an
'important' letter!! Needless to say I haven't received it yet . . . though
of course the thought of it worries MOI a lot though I know it's silly . . .
I always live in a fever & am always waiting for the unexpected to
happen!! So long as it's not going to stop my returning to England next
week I just don't care a —— what it is . . .

5th February   Headquarters 38th DIV near Amiens

The worst possible has happened, my sweetheart!! H.M.'s famous letter
arrived this morning & he says he doesn't want MOI to return to
England till the end of the month & that I'm to push off to the French
armies next week & then go to Paris to do all that Derby has down on
his programme for me!!

Guess this is the final knock-out blow for thy poor little E. & he's
just as miserable & despondent tonight as he's ever been in his life!! On
top of the shock & disappointment of the contents of H.M.'s letter he's
had a 4 hr motor trip across the devastated areas through driving snow
& then he found that the 2 K.M. mails which awaited him contained
no letter from his darling beloved little girl!

Gud! what a thoroughly sordid & mouldy life mine is my
sweetheart, though I suppose this is what I've been kept alive for,
though H.M. didn't fail to rub in the fact that I'm —— mourning &
so mustn't go to parties in Paris . . .

Now I feel like death as I've got 5 more hellish days of visiting
troops to face & then no TOI at the end of it all . . .

TOI knows that he's all & only thine sweetheart & that TOI has all all
his love & baisers.

Ton E.

Headquarters 19th DIV
9th February

. . . I must thank TOI for thy sweet little letter & for the article by
Horatio Bottomley which I'm going to read in bed; yes, there's no
doubt that he has a great influence with the working men & the

soldiers before they are 'demobbed' . . . [*Bottomley, a maverick independent MP with a chequered financial past, had acted as mediator, or 'soldiers' friend', during the demobilisation crisis.*]

I'm afraid that I'm losing faith in L.G. as he has tried to fly too high!! I'm sure he is doing his best at an impossible task, though I'm afraid he's never going to prevent all the strikes & troubles that are coming & they'll be far worse than the present ones! . . .

The Prince's personal note of his Paris itinerary.

What a marvellous thought, Dan & Harvey [*two black musicians who would play at private parties*] at No 65 [*Duke St*], & I of course should enjoy teeny parties 'en cachette' [*in secret*] when I do return as I shan't be able to go to big parties . . .

I think the idea of a little house of thine own in London is too divine & marvellous for words & I know TOI would be happier like that than having to stay with people, or live in hotels in London!! . . .

I'll write again from Paris before I push off to Pershing; it will be interesting meeting the President though still more so Mrs Wilson of universal fame!!

Thine own little E. is loving & worshipping you more than ever tonight . . .

THE PEACE CONFERENCE AT VERSAILLES

The post-war Paris peace conference had been convened on 18 January 1919, with four key aims: to force Germany to accept responsibility for the war; to exact reparations to pay for the material damage of the war; to set up a 'League of Nations' and establish recognised boundaries in both eastern and western Europe; and, finally, to stem the tide of Bolshevism.

While Wilson and the Americans saw themselves as mediators, and Britain's worries had largely already vanished (with the internment of the German Navy in Scapa Flow, and the decision to keep Germany's captured colonies), the French, who had suffered invasion and occupation, were far more intransigent. In their eyes, Germany, though defeated, was still dangerous, and France fought on for a punitive peace.

The peace was eventually signed at Versailles on 28 June; it left unresolved the problems which had led to war in 1914, and sowed the seeds of discontent which would lead to the next, twenty years later.

Hotel Meurice, Paris
12th February 1919

My own darling beloved little one

Well, guess here endeth 48 hrs in Paris . . . Claud & I dined together at Henri's, my favourite restaurant, & we finished up sordidly at a cinema. I daren't go to a theatre on account of this —— court mourning!! . . .

Yesterday I lunched with Lord Derby at the embassy to discuss the programme . . . I paid President Wilson my 'semi-official' call at 2.15 & spent ½ hr talking to him or rather making conversation; I pumped him all I could re the signing of the peace etc. but he wasn't saying much!!

He did say that peace would be signed at the end of May at the latest but that the French were obstructing a lot, though I knew that; I didn't see the famous Mrs Wilson & was disappointed in the President himself & can't see why he's being made such a fuss of!!

He's sailing for the States to meet Congress but guess he's returning to Europe & Paris early next month, not that he's wanted at all; Paris & the French are thoroughly fed up with him, & the Yanks in general, & are longing to be quit of them!! . . .

Hotel Meurice, Paris
14th February 1919

My own darling beloved little one,

. . . So Duddie was here last week; he must have returned with the P.M. on Saturday. Eileen & Geordie arrived on Wednesday night . . . they dined with me at the Ritz last night & I thought her looking divine & in very good form . . . Geordie took us up to their room afterwards & showed us filthy French toys. I'm going to bring back a selection, sweetheart!!

Today I lunched with the old Marquise de Breteuil with whom I stayed for 4 months in 1912 (when I was a little boy!!) to learn French, a somewhat heavy & sordid meal & all rather trying . . .

General Pershing called on MOI this afternoon about 5.00 & I'm travelling back to Chaumont with him in his special train tomorrow night!! Guess I'm moving in high circles . . .

I've been dining at the Embassy . . . Mrs Bate is giving a party in her flat tonight & of course I'm cut right out of it though as they all went on they insisted on dragging MOI with them & making MOI dance 2 dances before the people arrived!! But then I had to fly, sweetheart, as I oughtn't to have gone at all . . . It was a bore having to leave once I had got there though I'm glad I did now . . . I'm really far happier sitting here writing to my darling beloved little girl . . .

I pray that when I return to England I shall be able to spend a lot of

time with the only little girl that I ever want to see!! Of course we
must continue to be as 'discrets' as we've always been though I feel that
it'll all be much easier now that the war is over & when I shall be in
England permanently anyhow for 4 or 5 months till I'm pushed off to
Canada & the States, which I think will be my fate in July or
August!! . . .

There's a fearful amount of work waiting for MOI in England; all
these —— officials & 'big men' are just 'straining at the leash' to
pounce on thy poor little E & he's going to have absolute hell!! . . .

It was Lloyd George's idea that the Prince should make a series of Empire tours to
cement relations with the peoples of the Commonwealth. The throne was looked upon
as the pivot of the Empire, and the regard in which its occupants, both present and
future, were viewed, was deemed critical, especially in the aftermath of war.

Although ostensibly the visits were to thank the governments and peoples for their
contributions to the final victory, Lloyd George was well aware that demands for
reform, which had been merely simmering during the conflict, would now be proposed much more strongly. His view was that a successful visit from the charismatic
Prince of Wales would do more good than any number of solemn Imperial conferences.

Before the first tour to Canada, however, the Prince's life had already been mapped
out for him: the presidencies of the King Edward VII's Hospital Fund and the Royal
College of Music; the chancellorship of the University of Wales; a trusteeship of the
British Museum . . . It was little wonder that the Prince looked forward to his return
to England with some trepidation.

15th February

. . . Claud & I lunched at the Ritz though it was very dull & so we
went off to Geordie's shop & bought some naughty toys & found some
much more filthy ones than Geordie did & I think they'll amuse TOI,
sweetheart . . .

Tous tous mes baisers . . . ton E.

P.S. What does TOI think of Rosemary's engagement? It was a great
surprise to MOI!! [*She was engaged to Eric, Lord Ednam, eldest son of the Earl
of Dudley.*]

Hotel Meurice, Paris
18th February 1919

My own darling beloved little one,

. . . As regards my visit to American G.H.Q. . . . I like Pershing &
he's easy to talk to, & his staff are nice; this 2nd visit to the A.E.F. has
done MOI worlds of good & I'm liking the Americans more than ever
though no-one knows their faults more than I do!! They are quite
different to us & one has to realise this before one can like them; I'm
just longing to go to the States . . . but we just must be closely allied
with the U.S.A., closer than we are now & it must be lasting & they are
all very keen about it & like us as much as they hate & despise the poor
old French; the Americans are hopeless the way they talk about the
'Frogs' & they aren't tactful either!! . . .

The Queen of Italy seems to be staying in this hotel; she arrived on
Sunday & I suppose thy poor little E will have to go & see her some
time today . . .

I've got to motor N. to Chantilly tomorrow to lunch with Maréchal
Pétain . . .

Thine own little E sends all his love & tous ses baisers . . .

Hotel Meurice, Paris
19th February 1919

My own beloved sweetheart,

. . . I had to hurry back to call on the Queen of Italy & managed to
see her about 7.00 & her 2 eldest girls who are with her, though I was
dismissed after 10 minutes . . . I'm in a fever & mad, darling, as
these —— French papers are full of my engagement to the Queen's
eldest girl being as good as official today!! . . . I've asked the Embassy
to get at the French press & insist upon an immediate contradiction . . .
it naturally infuriates me, particularly as the girl has a face like a
bottom!! . . .

As regards Rosemary's engagement it's a relief to MOI, darling,
though I can't help feeling a little sad; TOI knows how I used to feel
about her, that she was the only girl I felt I ever could marry & I knew

it was 'défendu' [*forbidden*] by my family!! I really only know Eric by sight though I'm sure he's nice & that they'll be very happy; I only hope so for her sake as she's such a darling & I guess he's a very lucky man!! Still I just can't bear the thought of having to marry, beloved, though TOI knows that & the reason!! . . .

20th February   *2.00 A.M.*

Some man tried to shoot old Clemenceau [*the French Premier, nicknamed 'the tiger'*] this morning; 6 shots were fired though le vieux tigre was only hit once, in the shoulder, & isn't bad; he's 78 & of course he'll be more of a political hero than ever!! . . .

How madly thy petit amoureux E is looking forward to seeing his own darling beloved little girl again . . .

Hotel Meurice, Paris
21st February 1919

My own darling beloved one,

I started in on Lord Derby's programme this morning . . . I paid an official call on the President & Madame Poincaré, after which I returned here & saw the Queen of Italy & told her how sorry I was that the French papers had written all that rot about my engagement to her girl & she was very nice about it though furious at first . . .

. . . Ton E.

England

1919

The Prince's correspondence during the spring of 1919 is spasmodic, reflecting the fact that he saw or spoke to Freda most days.

Buckhouse SW
10th March 1919 {wrongly dated 10th February}

My own darling beloved little girl,

. . . I just can't tell TOI how utterly ashamed of my —— self I am for that mouldy & disgraceful worm-like effect during last night's crisis & for losing my head so hopelessly. What must TOI think of her —— E after that & he's so miserable, darling, as he knows that TOI must despise him for it. Still that was all typical of me my beloved one, & I just dare not ask your forgiveness now!! . . . [*There is no indication of the cause of the 'crisis'.*]

I'll propose myself to Poots for tea again later on in the week; she is such a darling & is so kind & sweet to me & perhaps I shall get a glimpse of my idol at whose feet lies her petit amoureux fou mais devoué

her E.

Buckhouse SW
2nd May 1919 (11.00 P.M.)

My very own darling beloved Fredie-Wedie,

. . . It's such ages since we've been separated darling that I've quite got out of practice in writing letters . . .

I just loathed seeing you drive away this evening, though how that last divine 'petit regard et sourire' out of the taxi window cheered me up!! . . .

I hope your mama isn't terribly ill & that by the time you get this she will have pulled through her operation all right. But what sickening bad luck that it should all have had to happen this weekend when we had planned out everything so marvellously well.

Still, it was the right thing for you to do, to go up to your poor Mama, one must think of one's family sometimes as I have to, particularly one's Mama!!

I've had a terribly sordid evening & am not thrilled one atom at having been made a freemason; Christ, what I think of it all, particularly heavy men's dinners when I have to get up & make a speech . . . [*Traditionally, replies to toasts were limited to five words: 'Worshipful Master, I thank you', but, unfortunately for the Prince, the rule was relaxed to allow him to speak. He was never, however, an enthusiastic Mason, unlike his brother Bertie.*]

I came in ½ hr ago & have been reading over my speech for tomorrow night's Academy dinner . . . I haven't seen Bertie as he hasn't come in & don't expect him to either till Christ knows when in the morning!! [*The Prince's speech on 'The War in Art' was to be given at the Royal Academy banquet, revived for the first time since 1914.*]

Tonight's stunt was all very weird & mysterious though there are really no secrets to give away . . .

What a divine fortnight this last one has been & I've never been so happy . . . I'm just longing to hear your sweet little voice on the telephone when you'll be able to tell your David [*the first time the Prince calls himself David*] when he's going to see you again . . .

I must finish this letter tonight . . . & I'm so afraid of missing the post, which would make me cry & you 'thulky', & I just couldn't bear to think my little Fredie was 'thulking' when I wasn't there to 'unthulk' her!!!! What babies we both are sweetheart, but I do love it so & it does us both so much good, doesn't it? [*The Prince writes in 'baby talk' throughout the rest of the correspondence. 'Thulky' generally means 'jealous', though here it does mean 'sulky'.*]

I just love your babies darling & think them divine & I'm so longing to see them again next week . . .

'Pleath' oh! 'pleath' come back to your devoted & adoring petit amoureux your little David soon & make him really happy all over again . . .

Buckhouse SW
10th May 1919

My very own darling beloved little Fredie,

. . . I was so miserable to have to leave you so early yesterday though I think it was politic to go & see the Duchess of D [*Devonshire: wife of the Governor-General of Canada*] & I had a useful talk with her about Canada, though what I think of that trip now!!

Of course I was too late to go to the station to meet the Dowager Empress of Russia & lost 'my name badly' over that; I've become too hopelessly vague for words lately as you know, darling, & I really must take a pull.

I dined here last night & signed several hundred more O.B.E.s before going to bed. This morning I've been to a sordid meeting of the Trustees of the British Museum & tonight the 2 'Do's' [*the Prince and Bertie*] are dining with Poots & we are going to see old 'Buzz buzz' again!! We both felt that we just couldn't go to 'Oh! Joy' without the 2 female 'Do's'! [*Freda and Sheila. This is the first reference to the 'Do's' which the Prince uses to refer to the foursome of himself and Freda, Bertie and Sheila. Oh! Joy was an English version of the American Oh! Boy, written by Jerome Kern, Guy Bolton and P.G. Wodehouse. Buzz Buzz was a musical revue playing at the Vaudeville Theatre.*]

Pleath don't be thulky, Fredie darling, but we are going down to lunch with Rosemary tomorrow & then I'm going to play a pompous game of golf with Geordie at Sunningdale . . .

Your devoted & adoring little amoureux David . . .

Buckhouse SW
12th May 1919

My darling beloved little Fredie,

Bless you for your two sweet letters, particularly the last one saying that you are arriving back this evening & suggesting that I should look in after the opera. Oh! no I couldn't possibly do such a common thing as that ——!!!

Sweetheart, how can you say 'or shall we wait till Tuesday?' Of course I must come . . . I ought to be able to get round about 12.00 & I'll let myself in as I've still got the key!! . . .

I only wish I could come earlier but I'm told the —— opera can't be over before 11.30 so it can't be helped though I do say f—!!!!

We lunched & dined with Rosemary & Eric [*Ednam*] at Fleet yesterday & brought Loughie back to 65 in my car afterwards . . . I've been 'slumming' all the afternoon & have just had a game of squash with Do No 2 [*Bertie*], who is writing to Sheila, which won't surprise you . . .

So till midnight Fredie darling . . . how I'm looking forward to 'after the opera' where I shall sleep & probably snore!!

All all my great love . . . your devoted & adoring David.

Buckhouse SW
14th May 1919 (7.00 P.M.)

Darling darling beloved Fredie Wedie à moi,

Just off to this 'me-ha' boxing stunt but I must scribble this teeny weeny little note to send you all my great love . . . [*This was one of the first boxing functions attended by the Prince; he became quite a fan of Welshman Jimmy Wilde, a flyweight boxer of great skill and disproportionate power to his fist roll frame, known as 'The Little Atom' and 'The Ghost with the Hammer in his Hand', who lost only four out of over 300 fights in his fifteen years in the ring. One of these losses had been against Pal Moore in 1918, but he was to have his revenge in July 1919 – see letter of 18 July. Another was in 1921, against the American Pete Herman, who was pounds above weight; Wilde, quite rightly, refused to fight him, until he was told that the Prince had arrived, and would like to see him fight. Despite the odds stacked against him, he fought with incredible bravery for seventeen rounds, until, with sections of the crowd in tears at his display of raw courage, the referee stopped the fight.*]

'Do No 2' left for Winchester [*Lankhills: the Loughboroughs' house*] about 3.00 in my car as he crashed his this morning; he's having marvellous weather for it & I don't expect to see him tonight!!!! . .

Must stop now & dash off to Clerkenwell or wherever this 'me-ha' boxing stunt is, muttering f— the while!! . . .

Your devoted & adoring little David . . .

Bless you sweetheart for making my life such a happy one deep down. [*This is the first time the Prince talks of 'deep-down' feelings, which becomes a recurring theme: his 'deep-down' love for Freda is often overwhelmed by the loneliness and depression he feels 'on top'.*]

Buckhouse SW
23rd May 1919

My very own darling precious little Fredie,

. . . It was such a joy to see you for those few minutes this afternoon . . . it was vewy sad that I couldn't find a 'Mr Thpider' this morning as I tried so hard but I will or anyhow get one made as we must have one!! [*The first reference to spiders, which became the mascot of the Prince and Freda; with a later mistress, Thelma, Lady Furness, it was miniature teddy bears.*]

What big babies we 2 Do's are & I think the other 2 Do's (2nd Grade) are even bigger babies than we are!! What marvellous fun we 4 do have, don't we angel & f— the rest of the world, though guess TOI et MOI are the 'bear leaders' (perhaps too much so sometimes!!) & anyway we look on life more seriously & are so different to the other 2 Do's!!

I hope you've found your family better & your father not too peevish; mine is very trying these days, though the poor old man does have to lead a dog's life, not that he couldn't have more fun if he wanted to, & he is so sour!! . . .

Dors bien as I know your very own little David will!!
Love to Mrs Thpider.

Bertie D sends his love!

*A sketch of the Prince
bearing a message of apology.
In later letters he frequently
lamented his 'foul behaviour'
towards Freda.*

Buckhouse SW
31st May 1919

My darling beloved precious little Fredie,

It was marvellous hearing your sweet voice on the telephone this morning & to know that you weren't too fearfully 'ang-wy' with your poor little David for everything . . . I was feeling so 'down & out' all yesterday . . . you did make your little boy so hopelessly happy (deep down) although I even left you in a depressed mood & am no better today!! I just can't cheer up somehow darling, everything & still more the future does look so hopelessly black & I'm so so hopelessly despondent about it all . . .

Bertie has gone to 42 [*Great Cumberland Place: the house where Freda was living temporarily*] to see Sheila. I hope it's all right, though I expect you know they fixed it up on the telephone this morning . . .

Gud I was sick with my father this morning when he cursed me about last night's speech, though he was quite pleasant after lunch & has as good as taken the ban off me flying!! But I am fed up with him generally & still feel what I said about him to you last night, that he really isn't worth working for, though it's a foul thing to say & you know I'd never say it to anyone else!! . . . [*The Prince's speech was to the Printers' Pension Corporation, thanking them for inviting him to be their next President, and appears to contain nothing which would obviously have upset his father. The dinner was attended by Harry Hawker and Lt-Commander Grieve, who had just been rescued after failing in their attempt to fly the Atlantic nonstop.*]

Your very own little David.

The 'other two Do's', the Prince's brother Bertie, later King George VI, and Sheila, Lady Loughborough.

My very own precious darling beloved little Fredie,

I'm afraid I've got very little news for you today . . . I'm terribly
busy & working so so hard fixing up this —— trip to Canada etc.,
which I've been very idle about, though I just can't raise any
enthusiasm over it or anything else except you . . .

Trenchard [*Chief of the Air Staff*] came to see the King this morning
& I've got leave to fly again which is satisfactory, though even that
doesn't thrill me much now; how hopeless I am but 'that's me all over',
Fredie darling, as you know!! [*The Prince's life was thought too precious to
risk in the air; the ban on him flying was soon reimposed.*]

Bertie rang Sheilie up this morning & fixed up for us both to go on
to 'Rankhills' [*nickname for Lankhills*] tomorrow after we have played
golf . . . I suppose I shall have to try & amuse Loughie so that they can
have a talk though I'll do anything for their sakes, poor darlings,
particularly as they've only got another month to see each other.

What a tragic life poor little Sheilie's is & I'm afraid that a trip
round the world isn't going to make it any better; Loughie's trustees
must be mad giving him £3,000 a year [*at a time when £200 a year was
considered a reasonable living*] & to say that he isn't to work, it's just
asking for trouble!! But enough about Loughie as I'm very fed up with
him, as you are darling; he's cramped our style somewhat lately, hasn't
he, curse him, & I hate him though I'm so fond of poor little
Sheilie . . . [*Lord Loughborough's father and his trustees had decided to try
and cure him of his drinking and gambling by sending him abroad with his
family.*]

All all my love my beloved , , , Ton David

My darling darling beloved little Fredie,

Just back from Winchester & loving you & missing you so so
fearfully . . . I've been too pathetic for words & should never have

thought myself capable of getting in such a state; I do feel so terribly lonely & depressed tonight darling & do want my little baby Fredie Wedie so badly to talk to & comfort me!!

I simply couldn't hit a ball at golf & Bertie beat my head off, f— him . . . we motored on to Winchester reaching Lankhills at 5.30. After tea I managed to lure Loughie away on the pretext of wanting to play a few more holes of golf on the local course, so as to give Sheilie a chance of being alone with Bertie; they said they were tired & we left them, but imagine my horror, darling, when on arriving at the links we found they were closed on Sundays!!

However I kept my head & took Loughie for a walk instead! I really was a little 'Master Clever' & I think the 2 Do's No II were grateful to me & I took Loughie out of the room for a few minutes after dinner before we left, & talked to him like hell all about his family etc., & of course he was discussing his world's trip the whole time.

How poor little Sheilie is dreading it, it's too pathetic, though I think Loughie realises all right; it's all so sordid though I think today has been good propaganda & I'm sure Loughie doesn't suspect Bertie at all! He was really quite nice today & I couldn't help feeling sorry for him, though I hate him!! . . .

4.00 P.M.

I'm having a desperately busy day, sweetheart . . . I'm off to Cornwall at midnight though so dreading the next 4 days & I'm more depressed than ever. I do miss my beloved little Fredie so so desperately . . . It's ghastly but what will it be like when I go to Canada? It's all such a huge nightmare!! We've only been parted for 3 days & I feel like death; Canada will be 3 months, I'm sure I shall never survive, sweetie!! [*Freda was at Dunrobin staying with the Sutherlands; the Prince was about to embark on a tour of the Duchy of Cornwall properties*] . . .

Millions & millions of baisers from your ever devoted & adoring little David.

Sweetheart pleath take care of yourself.

Duchy Hotel, Princetown
10th June 1919

Fredie darling darling my precious beloved one,

Just got back more dead than alive from a 6 hr tour of visits on the Duchy property which included tenants, farms, tin mine & God knows what!!

But I started my sordid day at 6.00 A.M. when I had to step out of the train at Newton Abbot & look happy & pleased with a loyal 'reception'!! Gud! but it was some strain sweetheart & the same thing happened at another little town called Ashburton . . .

2 hrs later I had to attend a fearful service in the church, the installing of the new vicar or whatever it's called by the Bishop of Exeter, & I had to present the man as patron of the living by leading him up to the altar!! Gud! you would have laughed to see your little boy, darling, who was naturally in the biggest 'stupe' at 10.00 A.M. & who walked about like a dazed man quite oblivious of being in church & what he had to do . . .

However the new vicar seems quite a nice little man & has 4 years' service as an army chaplain & has got an M.C. . . . The Bishop of Exeter looks quite mad & is anyway revolting with a scraggy beard; so that besides slapping my sides I was almost sick . . .

Christ! what I think of my life, beloved, & my prospects for the future are so much worse, though it's a shame my going on like this which will only make you loathe my letters . . .

Duchy Hotel, Princetown
13th June 1919   1.00 A.M.

My very own darling beloved little Fredie,

I've only time for a short scrawl as I'm in the throes of writing out 3 f— speeches which I've got to let off in Plymouth later in the day . . .

I spent 2 hrs at Dartmoor prison which was very sordid though interesting. There are only 250 convicts there now instead of 1,000 as before the war, though they are all the worst cases & there are 30 life

sentences. I'll tell you all about it some day, I'm not going to depress
myself any more by talking about it now . . .

Your very own devoted & adoring little David.

Buckhouse SW
14th June 1919   11.00 P.M.

My beloved little Fredie darling,

. . . I'll ring you up from Buckhouse about 10.00 A.M. & ask if I can
'come to tea' which will mean 'can I come & see you about 10.30 A.M.?'
I ask such an early hour as I'm by way of having a 'flip' at Croydon later
during the morning . . . as I'm allowed to fly again I feel it's up to me
to put in an appearance at the aerodrome!! But I just couldn't go there
or anywhere else till I had set eyes on my beloved little Fredie again . . .

I've had a very full day seeing masses of people & then at noon I had
to attend the christening of Georgie and Nada Medina's baby [*Georgie
was Prince Louis of Battenberg's son, who had been given the courtesy title Earl
of Medina, later 2nd Marquess of Milford Haven; he was the elder brother of
Lord Louis 'Dickie' Mountbatten*] as godfather; the boy is called David &
Beatty [*the First Sea Lord*] was the other godfather . . .

I can't get over Fate for having been so vewy unkind as to separate
YOU from me just this weekend!! F— is what I say & I'm saying it a lot
& other things as well tonight.

I do so wonder if Eileen showed you her ragging letter to me which I
got last night . . . it made me laugh & I long to be able to rag her
somehow!! But I'm far too stupid, sweetheart, & unoriginal!! . . .

Je t'embrasse longuement et tendrement bébée chérie à moi

Ton David.

Windsor Castle
22nd June 1919

My very own precious darling beloved little Fredie

It's such a sad depressed & miserable little boy that's writing to you
tonight after such a dreary & pompous dinner party; I've never loathed

any of our partings as much as I did this evening's . . .

Sweetheart, I'm so happy & excited at the thought of your being able to get one room at 1, Cumberland Terrace [*Freda's new house in Regent's Park, which she was renovating*] finished & furnished so that you could live there; it will be so much easier for me than if you lived in the country as I shall be terribly busy in London all July, & feel I should hardly ever be able to get away to see you . . .

Darling your 2 sweet babies [*Angie and Penelope*] were so divine to me tonight & it makes me so happy when they play with me; I do love them so because they are yours angel & they are the 2 most attractive children I've ever seen . . .

I'll write from Cardiff tomorrow night . . . her very own little David sends her all his great great love & millions of baisers.

The Prince was about to go to Cardiff to receive the Freedom of the City.

Cardiff Castle, Cardiff
24th June 1919, 1.30 A.M.

My very own blessed little Fredie darling,

Well here I am in the throes of writing speeches; I had a luxurious 3 hr journey to Cardiff & there were crowds of people in the streets who were vewy kind & cheered me a lot . . .

I'm staying with the Butes [*the 4th Marquess and Marchioness; one of the family's titles was Baron Cardiff, and they had long connections with South Wales*], a vewy weird couple, both rather mad & religious, & she breeds like a rabbit . . . He's got the reputation of being pompous though I've had an interesting talk with him already re coal labour etc. But I'm not going to let him make my visit pompous . . .

There's a huge boring house party here, about 10 'buds' [*young women*] the only one I know being Moira Osborne, who sat next to me at dinner (Lady Bute the other side), & you know what I think of her & she isn't really a 'bud'!! I haven't even tried to talk to the rest of them yet . . .

The guest list for the 'huge, boring' house party in Cardiff.

Cardiff Castle, Cardiff
25th June 1919, 9.00 A.M.

Fredie darling my own precious beloved one,

. . . I had a very successful trip up the 2 Rhondda valleys & got a
marvellous reception from the miners & ex-servicemen who were very

nice to me. I went down a pit & got through a rather trying speech at a colliery lunch all right though my best effort was an impromptu to several thousand ex-servicemen which did me worlds of good . . .

Millions & millions of baisers . . . from your very own little David . . . my love to Penelope & Angie & kiss them from me!!

Cardiff Castle, Cardiff
26th June 1919, 2.30 A.M.

My darling beloved little Fredie

It was such a boring day yesterday at the Royal Show looking at fat cattle & farm implements . . . I rather like a little excitement on these stunts now . . . though I've got plenty today, 2 long & important speeches in answer to the Lord Mayor of Cardiff when I'm given the Freedom at noon & at a vast dinner or banquet in the evening.

Your poor little boy has got the wind up properly & does so long for your sweet comfort while he is working hard at speeches. Not a soul sympathises with me or understands me but YOU, angel; they seem to think that I'm quite used to public speaking & that I don't worry about it, curse them . . .

Only 2 more days hell & then I hope a peaceful weekend & YOU . . . How your own little David does love you . . .

Buckhouse
28th June 1919, 1.00 A.M.

Darling darling precious little Fredie

. . . I shall be terribly busy all this morning & my Mama insists on my showing her over York House at 11.00. [*The Prince was in the process of moving out of Buckingham Palace and setting up an independent household in York House, part of St James's Palace.*]

I'll bring Bertie on Sunday as I know he won't leave me if he can't go to Sheilie & he'll be useful for golf & to talk to your family!! . . .

Till tomorrow, your very own devoted little D.

Buckhouse SW
1st July 1919, 1.30 A.M.

Darling darling precious little Fredie

. . . I must must send you this teeny note just to tell you how much happier than ever you've made me tonight . . . but I'm just a mass of nerves nowadays just as my beloved little girl is & am more distracted than ever tonight by my great great love for you, sweetheart mine!!

I'm so so miserable about that little contretemps when I was ½ hr late in fetching you, & making you wait for me in such a conspicuous place . . .

Gud! if it wasn't for my precious lovely little madonna & the fact that she knew I belong entirely to HER & to her only I swear I should shoot or drown myself, to escape from this —— life which has become so so foul & sad & depressing & miserable for me!! I do get so terribly despondent about everything nowadays & if I hadn't got YOU to live for, sweetheart, I swear I couldn't face it a day longer!!

Unusually, this letter ends abruptly, halfway down a page, and without any sign-off. The Prince usually filled every available inch of the paper.

St James Palace SW [The first letter written from York House]
4th July 1919 (4.30 A.M.)

Darling darling precious little Fredie,

I just can't go to bed without writing you a teeny scrawl to try to thank you for your divine sweetness in coming out tonight feeling as you did!!

Sweetheart, naturally all you said at first was a terrible shock, I mean about 'cutting it all', darling, & of course it has depressed me fearfully & I feel like death!! But angel I do so understand what you must feel . . .

I'm in a far too miserable & despondent mood to be able to say anything now, sweetheart, though what I think of Bertie for having helped to so nearly wreck all that there is left for me in life, our happiness!! . . . [*There is no further indication of what Prince Albert did to*

*precipitate Freda's threat, but from later problems, when the Prince was in
Australia, it would appear that Bertie was prone to overreaction to parental
pressure. From comments in the next few letters, it is clear that there was
considerable gossip within London society about the Prince's relationship with
Freda.*]

Au revoir my very own precious beloved darling . . . your very own
devoted & adoring little David . . . pleath try to forget a few things
though I fear you never will really, sweetheart.

*St James Palace SW
7th July 1919 (2.00 P.M.)*

Darling darling precious beloved little Fredie mine

Bless you for your long sweet divine letter which arrived this
morning; you do say such marvellous things to your poor little boy that
he's been crying!! . . .

I had very high fever last night when I got back over 104 degrees F,
& it was 103 degrees F this morning early though it's only
101 degrees F now. Gud I was feeling ill darling & don't feel good for
much today as I'm so terribly weak I can hardly write so please forgive
this scribble . . . [*The writing of this letter is like a child's scrawl.*]

Hewett came last night & has been twice today; I don't think he's
such a bad doctor really & I hope he'll make me well soon!! . . .

All all my great great love which is so terribly vast . . . your very
own devoted & adoring little David.

*St James Palace SW
8th July 1919*

Darling darling precious beloved little Fredie Wedie mine

Bless you bless you for your letter, sweetheart, & for ringing up
again . . . How could I be angry with you for ringing up, sweetheart,
quelle idée when it thrilled me so.

Fredie darling one, how terribly badly your little boy is wanting you
& he's still feeling rather ill & is as weak as a newborn babe as you can

see from the writing. I had rather high fever again last night & hardly slept a wink & I had such a fearful head!!

But I'm certainly feeling better this afternoon though so lonely & depressed & miserable & Hewett won't even let Bertie come & see me!! Gud if only my darling little girl could come to me I should soon be well; what I think of these conventions, though of course we've loved each other so long now, darling, that we don't realise sometimes that we aren't really married!!!! . . .

Bertie & I will come & see you on Friday if I'm allowed out though I rather doubt it as I've had such high fever & am so terribly weak that it will take me some time to get my strength back!! . . .

If only you knew how much your very own devoted & adoring little David does love you love you more than ever . . .

St James Palace SW
10th July 1919

My darling darling beloved little Fredie

. . . I just can't tell how you entirely dominate the whole of my life which is all wrapped up around your precious beloved little self . . .

Fancy yesterday being 6th anniversary of your wedding day; but you needn't feel old, darling, as you were such a baby at the time & are now my precious beloved little baby!! . . .

Oh! Gud I've got tons & tons to tell you, no gossip or rot like that, only nice things, & then I want to discuss plans!! You see Hewett wants me to go away to the seaside for a few days next week & I'm afraid he'll insist . . . I think Bertie is coming too as he's rather tired & we can play golf down there!!

Of course now I shan't have as much free time as I had hoped for as I've had to fix new dates for ½ dozen engagements postponed on account of this flu . . . I'm now dining with the speaker [*of the House of Commons*] on 25th, & at American Embassy on 21st & there is dancing afterwards but all the better if you are going to be there too . . .

Bertie has just been sitting with me; he's gone off to tea with Poots & needless to say Sheila will be there. My mama came this morning but otherwise I've seen no-one & don't want to except my baby darling & I won't have a woman in this house (unless it's one of my family & they don't worry me much) till you've been into it!! . . .

I love love you so desperately & entirely belong to you except officially & it's only this last tragic thought that makes your very very own devoted & adoring little David sad, darling.

The Manor House, Hove
14th July 1919, 11.00 P.M.

My vewy vewy own precious beloved darling darling little Freda,

. . . Gud, how I loathed having to leave you at 5.00 darling angel . . . I was as usual so hopelessly overcome by your divine marvellous sweetness to your devoted & adoring little boy, darling!!

To think that you've cut out your trip to Canada to a certain extent to help me; baby darling darling what I feel like when I think I should be the cause of all this gossip & scandal which envelops us & of all these —— betas [*a derogatory term meaning 'bitches'*] saying those foul things about you & indirectly upsetting all your plans . . . [*Geordie and Eileen Sutherland planned to visit their properties in Canada at the same time as the Prince's planned visit. Freda and Duddie were planning to go, too, but Freda decided that it could arouse further gossip and cause problems for the Prince if she was there, and decided to stay in England.*]

God how I love you love you love you . . . it's all been more of a heavenly dream than ever since Friday & you've made your little boy so blissfully happy, angel, & he's just not caring a f— for the rest of the world tonight (I'm not a teeny bit toxy darling, vewy sober indeed).

It's such a relief to have thrashed it all out with old Stamfordham [*George V's Private Secretary*] this morning & to have let myself go with Sidney Greville [*Treasurer of the Duchy of Cornwall and the Prince's Comptroller*] during the run down from London this evening, far more vigorously even than at Stamfordham!! And it all went down so marvellous & I feel I've secured two really staunch friends for us both!!

Sidney was as charming as old S. was, & said marvellous things about you, darling, when I told him how you had suggested cutting out Canada; but Gud I rubbed it in how furious & fed up I was with the so-called London 'society', & he's promised to try & spread it about . . . Christ why didn't I do all this weeks ago, sweetheart? I am so so sorry & feel vewy guilty of extreme weakness in not fighting for you, angel . . .

This is a charming little house in its way & Sidney has spent a lot of money on it & has very good taste so that it's quite a work of art if one appreciates all that sort of thing; I do sometimes, sweetheart, but not just now.

Your very very own devoted & adoring little David.

The Manor House, Hove
15th July 1919, 6.00 P.M.

Fredie darling darling precious one,

Bless you for your divine long letter . . . How how right you are, darling, in defining the difference between official capacity & private life; it's that difference which none of these —— old courtiers realise, it's so so vast that their pompous minds can never grasp it . . . [*The Prince did not like to be told by anyone that his private life was not his own: he already felt – as he was to make clear in 1936 – that as long as he performed his official duties, his private life was his own affair.*]

Your vewy vewy devoted & adoring little David.

St James Palace SW
18th July 1919 (11.30 P.M.)

Fredie darling darling little baby mine,

. . . What I think of your having had to go abroad to Brussels, I can't tell you, angel . . . how I bless you for all your divine sweetness to me yesterday despite the foul thing I said or rather asked you.

Sweetheart I do feel so ashamed of my rotten self, & how I loathe myself . . . I'm the happiest man in the world deep down except when I think of 5th August [*the date of his departure for Canada*] & that gets worse & worse each day, the thought of parting for over 3 months!! . . . It's the one great black cloud which is approaching & it gets bigger each day f— it & makes me such a sad, miserable & despondent little boy!!

I lasted 2 hrs cricket yesterday darling & then the big fight at Olympia (Wilde & Moore) was very exciting & I almost enjoyed it!! . . .

19th July   *7.30 P.M.*

. . . This morning's march past was a fine show [*peace parades took place throughout the country; the Versailles treaty had finally been signed on 28 June*] . . .

There was a huge lunch at Buckhouse for all the Allied generals, Foch, Pershing, etc., & we didn't get away till after 4.00!! My family, Mary & George drove in the Park afterwards; Bertie, Harry, Godfrey Thomas & MOI, being off-duty & not wanted, played squash at the Bath Club!!!!

11.30

Just back from dinner beloved one & watching the fireworks from the roof of Buckhouse . . . I have a vewy important speech to work up for this bl—d dinner to the allied commanders & officers at the Carlton tomorrow night!! It's worrying your poor little boy a lot, though he & Bertie hope to get in a round of golf in the afternoon & I think we shall propose ourselves to tea at Fern Hill Cottage [*Freda's new country abode at Winkfield, not far from Kilbees Farm*] afterwards & you know why, darling!! So that I may see your divine little babies, darling, who I love & who are so sweet to me!!

How I'm thinking & dreaming of you in Belgium, sweetheart . . . I hope Duddie took you to Ypres & the battlefields as you wanted him to & that he hasn't been sitting gambling at Ostend, which would be such a silly waste of time & money!!

If only I could have been over there with you, darling, how thrilled I should have been showing you all that devastated country that I pompously say I know fairly well!! But alas anything like that is denied me in this life . . .

I'm quite looking forward to Monday night at the U.S. Embassy & I feel it may be quite a good party, as much as any party can be good, & of course we will be able to dance a lot, sweetheart. I saw Eileen this morning at the march past & she was also at the luncheon . . . she has got Pershing & some of his staff going to Sutton tomorrow for lunch which is very nice of her . . .

20th July (4.00 P.M.)

I have been kept in London all day on account of tonight's dinner &
speech . . . what I think of the Office of Works who have let me in for
tonight's stunt & I can't get a single one of H.M.'s Government to
attend & hold my hand; it really is a shame, though I'm doing my best
to rope in the P.M. & one or two other ministers who certainly ought to
be present as it's a Government stunt!!

They really have carted me properly & I'm vewy angwy & fed up
with them all. It's not cricket or the way to entertain our allies, who are
made such a huge fuss of in all other countries; no wonder foreigners
say we are rude; we are d——d rude & never take any trouble, though of
course it's our nature . . .

Au revoir till tomorrow evening, darling . . . your very own little
David who loves & adores you so madly.

St James Palace SW
5th August 1919 {The early hours}

Darling darling beloved little Fredie mine

Just a teeny line from your broken-hearted little boy to say au revoir
before he leaves London, though he'll write from 'Renown' before she
sails . . . I'm just too hopelessly 'gaga' with love & grief to write any
sense today, sweetheart, so you must forgive such a miserable effort. I'm
keeping my promise & not opening your letter till I get on board
though I'm longing to!!

Oh!! for hier soir all over again, Fredie darling darling, as there's so
much more I want to say; somehow I revel in my despair & misery,
beloved one, as it means that my love for you passeth all man's
understanding.

God! how I'm dreading Canada now & hate my family for coming to
Portsmouth today!!

Bless you bless you for ever & ever, my very own beloved little Fredie
Wedie, your own little David is cwying so hard inside & so is Mrs
Thpider. [*The Prince had a 'Mrs Thpider' mascot; Freda had 'Mr Thpider'.*]

How I long to see you again at 1.00, sweetheart, but I understand,
bless you. [*The Prince had asked Freda if he could call in for a last visit
before he left for Portsmouth, but she had asked him not .*]

France & Paris have already celebrated peace
& our overwhelming victory; the other other allied
nations & their capitals will doubtless do the
same. But just now we are celebrating
it all in the British & London way & I
feel that yesterdays triumphal pageant
was a brilliant success. We feel that it
represented the great war, that it represented
victory in every sense of the word & that no
one who was present could fail to carry away
but the proudest & most inspiring memories
which will last a life time, even far longer
memories which will be handed, passed down to
future generations.

To me as one of the younger generation these
memories will be special particularly vivid as
during my periods of active service in several
theatres of war I often had the priviledge
& good fortune of being closely associated
with many of our allied armies army corps
divisions & even regiments.

I can assure our allied guests that it has
given enormous pleasure to the British people
to have them & their magnificent representative
contingents, here in London at such a time of
rejoicing & to have seen them march thro. our streets

A page from the Prince's notes for the speech he delivered at the dinner for the Allied commanders and officers.

The Canadian Tour

1919

Canada had grown and prospered under Sir Wilfrid Laurier, Prime Minister from 1896 until 1911. The great Canadian Pacific Railway had been completed in 1887, linking the east and west coasts, and offers of free land had attracted homesteaders from Britain and Europe to the developing provinces of Alberta and Saskatchewan.

Considering its size, Canada had made a major contribution to the war: from its population of eight million, an armed force of 600,000 was raised, under first British and later Canadian command.

As well as the enormous economic costs of the war, there were political costs, too. The French Canadians resented being asked to fight what they saw as Britain's war, and conscription became a major election issue in 1917, splitting the country.

Generally speaking, however, Canada's participation in the war brought the country together and increased the feeling of national identity, although this led to many thinking that the British monarchy was an outdated anachronism. The Prince's role, therefore, was to emphasise the Crown's position as the vital hub at the centre of the Empire.

The Prince approached this first tour with an enthusiasm which would be lacking in those which followed. He little knew the physical and mental efforts which would be expected of him, but at least the tour was only for three months, and he had a good team to support him.

The Prince's entourage for Canada included his equerries, Claud Hamilton and Piers Legh; his Private Secretary, Godfrey Thomas; and, on Stamfordham's recommendation, as Chief of Staff, Rear-Admiral Sir Lionel Halsey, who had been Jellicoe's Captain of the Fleet at the Battle of Jutland. Halsey brought with him Captain Dudley North.

Lieutenant-Colonel Edward Grigg, later Lord Altrincham, was also appointed, as Political Adviser. Although exceptionally able, Grigg and Halsey did not get on; Grigg had also been rude about Freda in the past, for which the Prince bore a grudge.

The ship chosen to carry the royal party was HMS *Renown*, an extremely fast battle-cruiser which had been launched in 1916.

Not far behind the *Renown* was the White Star liner SS *Baltic*, which had been due to sail on 1 August but had been twice delayed by strike action. Two of the passengers on board were war widows, Sarah Shaughnessy and Joan Mulholland, friends of Joey Legh and Claud Hamilton.

Sarah Shaughnessy, née Polk Bradford, was the daughter of an American judge from Nashville, Tennessee, and had married Alfred, the son of Sir (later Lord) Thomas Shaughnessy, a Milwaukee Irishman who had achieved great prominence in Canada as one of the builders of the Canadian Pacific Railway, of which he became President.

Her husband had been killed in action in France in April 1916, leaving his widow and three small children in London, where, to the dismay of her parents-in-law, she decided to make her home. In time, Sarah became very friendly with Joan Mulholland, née Byng, a daughter of the Earl of Strafford, whose husband, the Hon. Andrew Mulholland, had also been killed in France. She was lady-in-waiting to Princess Mary, and introduced Sarah to her circle in London society, which included the Prince's equerries.

Sarah first met Joey Legh on 2 March 1919, and he fell in love with her almost immediately, proposing to her on 10 May. She did not accept, surrounded as she was by countless admirers, many of whom wanted to marry her.

The Prince first met her in April 1919, at a dance given by Joey Legh, where, in her diary, she recorded that she danced with the Prince most of the evening. She saw him at several other social functions during the course of the summer, and also met Freda. On 27 July, she and Joey were invited to tea by Freda and the Prince; she noted how happy they appeared to be together, and felt sorry for him. On 29 July, the Prince and Freda dined with them at Sarah's house. She thought the Prince (whom she and Joey called 'The Boy') had great charm and personality, though he seemed very young.

She had decided to take her children to Canada to see their grandparents, and to holiday at St Andrews, New Brunswick, with Joan Mulholland accompanying her. Before they left, Freda had come for tea with Sarah, and opened her heart about still being unsure whether or not to go to Canada with Duddie and the Sutherlands.

Sarah had dissuaded her, especially in view of the growing London gossip about the relationship, which was upsetting Freda.

Sarah's diaries and, later, letters to her from Joey Legh give a fascinating alternative picture to the events described in – or sometimes omitted from – the Prince's letters to Freda.

H.M.S. RENOWN, Portsmouth
5th August 1919 (4.30 P.M.)

Darling darling sweetheart

My family have just left & I'm scribbling this note before we sail!! Bless you for your sweet little letter . . . God! I'm miserable, beloved one, waiting till we sail at 6.00 but it will be better once we shove off & get out to sea.

I wanted to give Bertie a tiny note for you angel but never got a chance to write a word . . .

My very own darling precious beloved little Fredie I did feel such a brute coming round this morning after all you said & when I knew you didn't want me to, but sweetheart I just couldn't keep away; pleath try to forgive me & not be too angwy & I feel happier having seen your darling sacred little self since last night when I was in such rotten form & so foul to you angel!!

God!! how I love you love you, darling darling sweetheart, madly, & I'm merely living for my return to YOU; this trip will only be an existence though I'm going to work so hard to try to make it a success & I shall be so busy that I think the time will go quickly!!

I'll write a little bit every day, & post letters whenever I can to 1, Cumberland Terrace, & you'll always write to St James Palace, won't you, baby mine?

No time for more as last orderly leaves ship at 5.00 & I do so want you to get this tomorrow morning!!

Au revoir petite chérie . . . your v. v. own devoted petit amoureux, your David who will be thinking of you every second Fredie darling darling till we meet again. How I love you love you for having cried so much sweetheart, it was divine of you to feel like that & God I feel like howling just now.

H.M.S. RENOWN, *at sea*
5th August 1919 (11.00 P.M.)

My very own darling darling beloved little Fredie

Here I am, sweetheart, fairly started on this Canadian trip though it's hell for me tonight . . . you just can't think what a huge hole in my life our parting & your absence makes, sweetheart, & I now have to face 'the great blank' & feel so so terribly lost & lonely . . . it all seems so unnatural after the last 5 months when we hardly missed a day when we didn't meet at least once . . .

How I loathe myself now darling for seeming so cold about it all as I know I did the last 24 hrs in London; I can't think what came over me as I was so crammed full of love for my Fredie . . .

My last sight of you . . . lying there hiding your sweet little face will keep me going till I come back to you . . .

Now I must turn in as I am dead beat & no wonder, though it's such a joy to think that the last bed I got into in England was yours; I couldn't get into mine yesterday at 6.00 & I'm so so glad that I didn't now!! Goodnight darling one.

6th August (11.00 P.M.)

Today has been the very worst hell imaginable as I'm missing you & wanting you & loving you so so terribly . . . I feel quite pathetic & Mrs Thpider is worrying me to death from my watch chain trying to get back to Mr Thpider . . .

Sweetheart I'm so so happy with all my precious sacred little souvenirs of YOU; first all my photos, then all my 3 rings, my disc, my cigarette case & last but not least that lovely matchbox which I love so . . .

This is a marvellous ship & I have a vewy comfortable & luxurious cabin . . . the officers seem a nice lot, though I haven't seen much of them as I've been keeping away from everybody as much as possible today, not feeling much like making conversation, as you may imagine darling; I visited a 15″ turret this morning & got some exercise after tea playing 'medicine ball' on the quarterdeck & running up & down. I must keep fit for Canada . . .

Killing time aboard HMS Renown. *Keeping fit with the medicine ball on the quarterdeck* (top), *and getting in some revolver practice* (below left). *The nautical theme — and the Prince's 'waiting' message to Freda — are echoed in another early portrait.*

7th August (or rather 1.00 A.M. 8th August)

I've only just got away from the wardroom, where I dined this evening; they are a cheery crowd & we've been bear fighting and playing vewy wough games . . .

8th August (11.00 P.M.)

As you may imagine from our locality or position (Mid Atlantic) I have absolutely no news for you . . .

Although this is a pleasant enough voyage in the finest ship in the Navy, I'm more bored & restless & lonely than I've ever been in my life!! I'm just longing to get across & land on the other side & to start work; speeches etc. will keep me busy & I shall welcome them as they will prevent my brooding a little . . . but then when I'm in Canada I shall miss my very own darling beloved little mummie so terribly & all her comfort & advice . . [*It has often been said that the Prince wanted a mother figure to dominate him; this is the first of many times he refers to Freda as 'mummie'.*]

I spent this morning in the engine & boiler-rooms . . . we shall get into the iceberg area tomorrow so we may have some excitement, particularly if we run into fog too . . . [*It had been an iceberg that sank the Titanic in 1912.*]

9th August (11.00 P.M.)

It's blowing tonight & there is a bit of a sea & your little boy isn't feeling quite as comfortable as usual, though by no means ill, though I should be laid low if I was in the light cruiser 'Dragon', our escort ahead!! . . .

This afternoon we had some revolver practice & there was the cinema-going after dinner as usual; it's a case of anything to kill time, darling, & I find it impossible to take an interest in anything, though of course I'm pretending to the whole time & my life has now become more camouflaged than ever!!

10th August (usual hour 11.00 P.M.)

The wind fell at dawn & we've had a lovely bright day . . . we've been

among icebergs & have seen about 20 . . . we had fun with one about
6.00 when we fired 60 rounds of 4″ at it & knocked it about a lot!!
We were vewy wough wiv it & at 10.00 we passed a big berg quite
close & turned the searchlights on to it & it was a marvellous
sight!! . . .

We should anchor at Conception Bay tomorrow morning . . .

Fredie darling darling how are you & I do so wonder if you did go
to Scarborough after all; & I hope Burghie isn't being a d—d nuisance
& that his & other barrages [*Freda's male admirers*] aren't too
intense . . .

I wonder if you've seen Bertie since I left; I begged him to ring you
up & try to see you on Tuesday evening & he said he would; queer
boy, that, & I don't miss him a scrap, though I'm very fond of
him!!!! . . .

How are the babies, darling? Pleath give them my love & tell them
I hope they won't forget all about me . . . I do love your 2 sweet little
babies & I nearly cried when I had to say goodbye to them last Sunday
evening as they are so divine to me always!!

11th August (nearly midnight), Conception Bay, Newfoundland

We anchored here & we all went ashore for a walk this afternoon . . . I
leave this ship before 9.00 A.M. & transfer to 'Dragon' to go into St
Johns!!

I enclose all the photos & the diary written up to yesterday though
the latter is too ridiculously pompous for words . . . I know you won't
even read it . . . it's more or less official & is sent to H.M., though I call
it balls!! . . .

But think of having to wait for another whole week for even the
chance of a letter from my beloved little Fredie; oh! the irony of it all &
to think that but for a hard fight on my part (knowing that it was the
right thing for me to do) I should never have set out on this trip at all!!
But I suppose we all have a job in the world, though mine is a bl—d—
one & no mistake & how I loathe it all & all these camouflaged stunts
& having to do the dud hero!! . . .

How I'm loving loving YOU tonight sweetheart & bless you bless YOU
always for everything, which includes all that I could want in this

world except one thing & you know what that is, beloved one!! Perhaps next year, as I'm bound to be away at least 6 months, though we'll do a lot of hard thinking first, not that I want to, though you must, sweetie!! [*What this cryptic paragraph means is never clearly explained: is the Prince talking of wanting a child with Freda? It is more than likely, considering his evident attachment to her two daughters, and especially as when he leaves for Australia in 1920, it is clear that he is waiting for news as to whether Freda is pregnant: see letters of 28 March and 23 April 1920.*]

Your loving & devoted, adoring & upwardly heartbroken & miserable little David, though deep down he's the happiest man in the whole wide world knowing that his Fredie Wedie loves him!! But if only SHE could read HIS heart!!

Government House, St John's, Newfoundland
13th August 1919 (2.00 A.M.)

Fredie darling darling beloved little sweetheart mine,

My first night ashore since leaving England & the only one till Quebec next week . . . I transferred to 'Dragon' in Conception Bay to steam round to this little hole where I landed officially at Noon & it is a little pip-squeak place & no mistake!!

Christ we have laughed as the governor of Newfoundland is the completest old dud & his wife is beyond description!! . . . This seems to be an exceptionally loyal colony & they certainly gave me a good welcome though it's a cold audience & public as compared to Great Britain; it's all very primitive . . . & of course democracy rules but that is very refreshing!!

Sweetheart I'm so glad that I'm not pompous & royal by nature as if I was I might just as well return to England at once!! As I guessed, it isn't wanted & won't go down on this side; all this etiquette & balls & I'm cutting most of it out by degrees, though of course there must be some official stunts where I do my best to be as pompous as possible, though it's hard work!!

This 3 months' trip is going to do me worlds of good, darling one, in your eyes, though perhaps H.M. & the court will have something to say as I shall return more democratic than ever!! And a d——d good thing too!! It's inevitable & I shan't be able to help it as my motto is democracy within bounds . . .

16th August, H.M.S. DRAGON, St John Harbour, N.B. (1.00 A.M.)

Sweetheart I'm really rather bucked & satisfied tonight as today or rather yesterday at St John went off extraordinarily well; I lay a good deal of store by it as it was my first day on Canadian soil & I really received a marvellous welcome despite the fact that it rained on & off all day!!

You know that I don't often derive satisfaction from official stunts darling but from this one I do & I managed to hold forth quite effectively at a club lunch!! . . . there was a garden party at 5.00 where they danced after I had shaken hands with the 500 guests . . .

The Governor General (Devonshire) & Prime Minister (Borden) met me when I landed this morning . . . they all dined on board this evening & I was able to have a good talk to Devonshire & his 2 Ottawa officials & put them right over several matters concerning the policy & programme on which they had hopelessly wrong out-of-date & pompous ideas!! . . . One of the officials is an obstructing old dud of 60 who I cut out right away when it was proposed he should join my staff!! . . . [*The two officials were Major-General Sir Henry Burstall, whom the Prince had met during the war, and Sir Joseph Pope, who had helped to arrange the 1901 tour made by the Prince's father, and who had planned this one along the same lines. The Prince correctly surmised that state drives in horse-drawn landaus, endless civic lunches and official dinners and military parades had had their day, and he decided to put his own stamp on the tour at an early stage, replacing Pope with Martin Burrell, MP for British Columbia, a down-to-earth man of the people who had been badly burned when the Parliament Buildings in Ottawa burned down in 1916. The Prince also decided that he would hold an open, public reception wherever possible – in cities, towns, or at country railway stations – to 'meet the people' and to shake them by the hand. This became so popular that his right hand was damaged, and he had to use the left; finally, when the crowds were too large, they simply filed past him in ranks.*]

17th August (1.00 A.M.) H.M.S. DRAGON (at sea)

. . . This has been an ideal passage to Halifax . . . we had rather fun
yesterday morning as we dropped a 'depth charge' (a new war weapon)
about 10.00 A.M. & then stopped for 1 hr's fishing, or rather collecting
all the fish killed & stunned by the explosion which floated up
afterwards. We lowered boats & I went away in one, 'gaffing' huge cod
& catching hundreds of sardines in a landing net . . .

Fredie, my own darling little precious angel, this is the day when if
fate is at all kind I shall receive my first letter from YOU . . . I'm so
excited & impatient that I just can't contain myself & shall find it hard
to sleep!! . . . I hardly dare think about it for fear that there may be no
mail after all as then my disappointment will be too terrible for words,
darling one!! . . .

It's really a queer coincidence that the letter I'm so so anxiously
awaiting should have been brought across by S.S. 'Baltic' in which Mrs
Shaughnessy & Joan Mulholland booked their passages & of course
Legh & Claud Hamilton (particularly the former) are mad to know
whether she has arrived!! But they aren't as mad as I am, darling, even
a letter from you is far far more precious than either of those 2 women
could be to them!! . . .

I've been reading some of Ella Wilcox's poems in bed the last 2 or 3
nights darling & Mrs Thpider & I have almost been cwying over some
of them . . . [*Ella Wilcox was an American poet whose many volumes of
romantic, sentimental and mildly erotic verse brought her a huge readership.*]

H.M.S. RENOWN, at sea
18th August 1919 (10.00 P.M.)

Fredie darling little beloved sweetheart mine,

. . . We are at sea & on our way to Quebec though I've got to land &
spend the day at Charlottetown, Prince Edward Island tomorrow . . .

19th August (at sea) 11.00 P.M.

. . . Charlottetown is a harmless little spot, very primitive & there was
the completest lack of organisation in the proceedings that I've ever

Photographs taken in the last few days before the Prince's departure were kept as mementos during the long months he and Freda spent apart.

seen, not that it prevented the visit being a success . . . Besides the usual official 'balls' I was shown a silver fox ranch & some trotting races when a fire started in the grandstand to cheer things up . . . I hoped they would give me a silver fox skin, darling, as it's marvellous fur & I said so several times though without effect; I'm vewy disappointed, sweetheart . . .

I'm looking forward to going West & feel that I shall meet & get in touch with live men!! If only WE could settle West (British Columbia or Alberta) darling what heaven & we could be the very happiest couple in the whole world . . .

20th August   Gulf of St Lawrence   11.00 P.M.

. . . I can't remember if I told you that we have Borden on board, he's a crock with a torn leg muscle due to falling down the steps of the club at Halifax . . . he's such a stick & deadly dull except re politics & I can't tackle him on that subject; I leave that to Grigg who I always make sit next to him . . .

Your devoted & adoring little David.

The Citadel, Quebec
22nd August 1919 (3.00 A.M.)

My very own darling beloved precious little Fredie Wedie

Such a terrible blow sweetheart, no mail; it's a real heartbreaker &
I'm fearfully disappointed . . .

The ship must have looked marvellous steaming up this great river
this evening & she certainly looks it from this citadel, which is right up
above the city overlooking the river hundreds of feet below . . .

I landed pompously at 6.00 & Devonshire met me on the wharf &
motored me up here to his wife & family, who have made me vewy
comfortable!! I got several alterations made in the programme & cut
out all dud & boring satellites from my staff for the trip West by
talking to the Duke like a father before dinner; I was very firm but very
polite & he took it all lying down!!

Our little 'ragtime jazz party' as we (my staff & self) call ourselves
are showing these officials a thing or two & giving them lots of new
ideas . . . I think they are surprised that we take so much on ourselves
& won't be run by anybody!!

I like Halsey more & more each day; he's priceless & so sound &
human & so easy to work with . . . Grigg is a very valuable asset & the
rest of the team work marvellously together!! . . .

I've got a heavy day ahead & I'm giving a huge lunch party on board
'Renown' to the Devonshires & all the notables & bores of Quebec . . .

23rd August (2.00 A.M.)

. . . Tonight there's been a reception here followed by dancing from
which I've only just escaped, too pompous to be amusing though I
struck a little bud who could dance & who you would have said was
quite attractive, beloved one, though you needn't be thulky!!!! . . .

I had to read a couple of addresses in French this morning which was
a strain, though these French Canadians like it, though they are a
rotten narrow-minded touchy crowd who haven't played the game at
all during the war & never do!! . . .

Bonne nuit et dors bien petite amour chérie à moi . . . ton petit
David.

The Citadel, Quebec
23rd August 1919 (11.30 P.M.)

My darling darling precious beloved Fredie Wedie

Again no mail & consequently a greater & more bitter
disappointment to your poor little boy who is waiting so anxiously for
the next mail which means almost life or death to him, sweetheart!! . . .

I visited a couple of R.C. convents this morning . . . & a R.C. village
church . . . of course one has to be 'all over' these bl—d— French
Canadians & their priests the whole thing is a vewy intricate & delicate
imperial & political question which I don't pretend to understand,
though I do know they are mostly a rotten priest-ridden community
who are the completest passengers & who won't do their bit in
anything & of course not during the war!! . . .

On my way back I got in a round of golf . . . though I was far too
worried to be able to hit the ball at all & then there were movie men &
hundreds of amateur 'snappers'! It was really a stunt though a good way
of meeting people as of course I had another proper dose of 'pump
handling' (my name for shaking hands, darling!) . . .

I'm sure that taking part in games & sport goes down well & is good
propaganda as it shows I can do more than merely driving pompously
through streets of cities & that I enjoy taking part in Canadian
pastimes & prefer meeting people informally as friends as much as
possible!! Not that I ever want to see many of them again; still it
makes a good impression, which is what I'm always out for! . . .

I don't think there's the least chance of my returning to you with
both my hands, darling; these Canadians will shake my right hand
right off . . . I get so fed up after 1,000 at a stretch though it's always
over the 1,000 for the day!! . . .

I leave Quebec tomorrow afternoon & train to Toronto in the famous
C.P.R. [*Canadian Pacific Railway*] train that the Government is lending
me for my trip West . . . I rejoin their excellencies (Devonshires) on
Thursday though I shall be glad & relieved to quit them & get clear of
this government house party as they cramp my style . . .

They are such a back number & don't keep pace with the times &
the Duchess is really a 'beta', sweetheart, & so pompous & interfering;

no wonder she's unpopular on this side . . . but the Duke is popular & I like him, though he's got almost as little brains as your little boy angel, he is a B.F. & so slow!!

Halsey would of course make a marvellous & ideal governor general but his not being a peer excludes him from any chance of ever being appointed; how terribly narrow-mindedly conservative we are in England & it makes me mad . . . I'm going to talk pretty straight to the Colonial Office when I get back . . .

What I think of having to go to church pompously at the Cathedral tomorrow morning!! I'll continue in the train in the evening . . .

25th Aug (2.00 A.M.), C.P.R. Train to Toronto

. . . This is a very luxurious train & Lord Shaughnessy has kindly lent me his private C.P.R. car, which is comfortable though cramped & there's no bath, only a shower . . . [*Thomas Shaughnessy had been one of the key figures in the building of the Canadian Pacific Railway. He had worked his way up to become President, and later Chairman, and was known as the 'King of Railway Presidents', diversifying into shipping, mining and smelting. Staunchly imperialist in outlook, he had been awarded a barony in 1916.*]

26th August (2.00 A.M. as usual!!), Government House, Toronto

They've done their very best to kill your poor little boy today . . . I've never received such a welcome!! It's been too marvellous for words . . . knocks Cardiff or any place in Great Britain right out & of course this province Ontario supplied ½ of Canadian Corps!!

The diary will show what I had to do & I had to speak at least ½ dozen times . . my big speech was at lunch . . . then another outside city hall after I had held what is called a popular reception when anyone can come in from the streets & shake hands with me!! I did over 2,000 in 1 hr sweetheart, & then there was a huge pompous man's dinner when I had to make a completely impromptu speech after it had been settled there weren't to be any!! . . .

I've got another very trying day before me starting with 4 hospitals in the morning, a university degree & garden party, before a yacht club dinner . . .

I'm staying here with the Lieutenant Governor Hendrie & it's a marvellously comfortable & up-to-date house & a nice change after the train!! . . .

27th August (1.30 A.M.), Government House, Toronto

At last at last a mail & your divine long letter of 9th (2½ weeks old) has revived your poor worn out little boy . . .

I've just got back from the most completely dud party at the Yacht Club . . . though the dinner with 100 returned officers was a good stunt, except of course it was a dry dinner [*there was Prohibition in Canada, though liquor was always available to those prepared to pay the high prices*], which made my speech a worse strain than ever!! What I think of this 'dryness' . . . & it's not going to last, either, there'll be trouble if they don't go wet again!!

4 hospitals this morning with hundreds of limbless & disabled men to talk to which kills me more than anything else as you know, darling, & it took over 3 hours . . .

28th August (12.30 A.M.), C.P.R. Train to Ottawa

Never been so completely 'through' as I am tonight . . . I did get 13 holes of golf this morning before 'being called to the Bar' at a silly pompous ceremony . . . then at 3.00 I was on the exhibition grounds to see 10,000 ex-servicemen whom I had to address & then decorate 200 officers & men!!

It was called a parade but the men naturally broke ranks & did their best to mob me & I had quite a job to get away at the end; it was an amazingly loyal demonstration & they went quite mad!! But ex-servicemen are always an unknown quantity so it was a great strain & I went away a wreck, though I had a 3 hr motor drive round the city to follow which has left me in a state of collapse despite a wet dinner at Government House!!

I've never had 3 such strenuous days in my life though I shall never get such a welcome again . . .

Your last sweet letter made me bless you for it angel & all the divine things you say to me

David.

GOVERNMENT HOUSE, OTTAWA
28th August 1919

My own precious darling beloved Fredie Wedie

I got here about noon after a pompous arrival & presentation of addresses to find oh! the joy of it . . . my blessed little baby's letter of 12th . . . which has thrilled me so, darling, & made me happier than ever . . .

So Duddie sails for Canada next week or rather is due to sail, as I'm sure sailings must be hopelessly uncertain owing to the strikes . . . the coal situation worries me a whole lot & the outlook for the winter isn't rosy!! [*On 18 August, Lloyd George had rejected nationalisation of the mines, one of the recommendations made by the Sankey Commission in June and, later, on 10 September, voted for by the Trades Union Congress. There were problems ahead, too, with the railwaymen and the transport workers.*] . . .

. . . Ton petit David t'aime et t'adore . . . this long separation is absolute cruelty to a child!!

GOVERNMENT HOUSE, OTTAWA
30th August 1919 (2.00 A.M.)

Fredie darling darling little sweetheart mine

What must you think of your little boy always writing at the hour of 2.00 A.M., though the fact is & I have to confess it that I've been dancing again, though only here & so you can imagine it was pompous enough!! There was a fearful 'men's dinner' (what I think of all these 'buck' meals!!) followed by a sort of reception & then we danced: the 2 Cavendish girls [*daughters of the Duke and Duchess of Devonshire*] are very plain, darling, though of course I have to dance with them, staying in the house!! The Duchess is a pompous & terrifying woman . . . she's so officious & interfering & she has no right to be that!!

My 2 letters & some more copies of that fearful diary (which I'm almost too ashamed to send) left at noon yesterday; that was all my mail 3 envelopes all addressed Mrs W. D-W etc. etc. which thrilled me so much, sweetheart!! Godfrey looks after the mails so no-one else knows how much I write to you, my precious beloved darling little baby; as I told you Legh writes the diary & the poor old boy is terribly adrift with it so that I couldn't send anything later than Quebec. It's the presence of Mrs S. in Canada that's upsetting him, & no wonder!!

But yesterday was a great strain as I spent the morning sweating up that terrible speech which I had to make at the Government lunch & which took years off my life & it was a dry lunch too!! But I struggled through it somehow without a crash & it seemed to go down all right with Devonshire, Borden & the other ministers!! Of course Grigg really wrote the speech as it was about the most important I've got to make this trip & it's some relief to have it behind me!!

I held another popular reception in the City Hall at 3.30. I did 2,400 people in 1 hr though my poor right hand stuck it all right. I was able to dash out to the Golf Club about 5.00 & play 16 holes with Legh before dinner . . . your poor little boy's golf is getting worse & worse . . . though of course it's impossible to hit the ball when one's nerves are in the state that mine are nowadays!! . . .

31st August (2.00 A.M.)

I'm afraid I've been dancing again . . . we had to stop at 12.00 on account of the P. of W., not your little boy darling [*the Prince had to stop dancing at midnight on Saturdays; his leisure activities on Sunday were strictly limited*], as there are often occasions when he & his name are 2 different things . . . but Christ it does infuriate me, not because I want to carry on dancing but because of the childishness of all this religious camouflage; they are taking me to church in the morning & they won't let me play golf in the afternoon!! Still I made up my mind to leave England officially & to remain so till I returned . . .

11.00. P.M.

No dancing tonight sweetheart, it being Sunday . . . I had to go to church this morning & then call on old Lady Borden & Lady Laurier (widow of famous Laurier) [*Sir Wilfrid Laurier, 1841–1919, was the first French Canadian and Catholic to be premier of Canada*] before a mixed lunch at the Country Club which was quite amusing . . . but I couldn't really enjoy it, Fredie darling one (how can I enjoy anything without YOU? it just isn't in me!!) . . . No other woman in this world can produce a grain of attraction, interest, excitement or anything else for your vewy own little boy sweetheart, & the only slightest use I have for only just a vewy vewy few that I meet is to dance with them . . .

I can't be bothered to talk to them, though sometimes they say the most pricelessly funny things to me which merely make me laugh in their faces instead of making love to them, which they are often just asking me to do!!!!

Legh feels the same, darling, & we have such fun comparing notes after parties as we generally strike the same women so we can study their various tactics!! And God how they do bore me, though the only thing to do is just to let them carry on; they not only ask me for autographs but shove my cigarette ends down (well, you can guess where, angel!!) & are altogether too silly for words & produce an acute feeling of revulsion!! I'm afraid all this must sound very pompous & conceited, sweetheart, but I know it amuses you . . . being P. of W. is occasionally amusing . . .

1st September (11.30 P.M.), C.P.R. Train to Montreal

. . . It's quite a relief to have got away from the Government House party . . . we are clear of them for 2 months, which is marvellous . . . Tomorrow is to be more or less informal in Montreal . . .

Bless you bless you for ever, D.

C.P.R. Train (going West)
3rd September 1919 (1.00 A.M.)

Fredie darling darling precious beloved one

Again I'm sitting up vewy late sweetheart . . . we've had a successful day in Montreal . . . though it was a case of another extraordinary & overwhelming welcome . . . the great thing was that it was entirely unpompous & more or less unofficial; grey suit & squash hat was the rig & that goes down so much better than uniform on these occasions . . .

I'm quite looking forward to returning to Toronto, Montreal & Ottawa in October . . . of course the 2 or 3 wild trips for shooting & fishing may be good value when we shall be able to lose ourselves more or less, though I don't know how to fish & never can hit anything with a gun!! . . .

I wish you had been with me yesterday morning, angel, to give hell to a small flapper (12–14) who had the cheek to throw her arms round my neck & give me a foul wet kiss as I was going to lunch; imagine my fury, sweetheart, particularly as there was an extra heavy movie barrage, though I've made them cut that revolting incident out & I'm sure the little beta was put up to it, probably by a movie man!! . . .

4th September, C.P.R. Train (1.00 A.M.)

It's been a weary day in the train, sweetheart . . . only two ½ hr. stunts in small towns, though I've always got to be on the watch for small stations & people to wave to!! It's quite amazing how they congregate at stations from miles merely to see this old train roll by & it's so nice that I feel I just have to show myself on the stern walk, though it means doing so every 10 mins!! . .

5th September, C.P.R. Train (12.30 A.M.)

We had an interesting morning at Saulte St Marie & I walked through a paper mill & a big steel works as well as watching the big lock on the canal filled!! These Canadians can teach us a lot as regards inventions & constructions, sweetheart, & I was genuinely interested in all I saw!! . . .

We left at 1.30 & are travelling on a badly laid track (hence the writing) though fine scenery as it runs through absolutely undeveloped forest country!! But it's dull as there's no bird life despite endless small lakes; I've spent hours sitting on the stern walk of this car with my gun hoping for a shot at a duck or something, though I never got one!!

6th September, 10.00 P.M., Camp at Pine Portage, Nippigon River (Ontario)

. . . Well here we are at our first camp on the Nippigon river after a long though mouldy day's fishing . . . we each have a canoe propelled by 2 Red Indians & work down the river independently, fishing or not as we wish; your little boy is no fisherman, sweetheart, & I got vewy bored & fed up flogging this bl—d— old river with never even a nibble & though I had my gun in the canoe I only got a long shot at a seagull & there are vewy few duck & they are hopelessly wild!!

One of my old Indians hooked a 1lb trout late this evening which I played & landed & that's been all my sport; all the others have caught fish themselves 2 over 3lbs. so that I'm the only mug of the party!!

This camp life is vewy wough but vewy good for me & it's only uncomfortable when compared to one's usual ultra-luxury, though I'd far sooner be playing golf or shooting or getting some exercise. But it's a rest from Lt. Governors, prime ministers, mayors etc & yelling crowds . . . [*The Prince never appears to have told the programme organisers how he would like to spend his leisure time, with the result that much of it was spent shooting and fishing, which the rest of his entourage were all keen on, but in which he had little skill and little interest. His periods of relaxation were, therefore, often very tedious for him, having the opposite effect to that intended.*]

Must go to bed as they are turning me out at 6.00 A.M. to fish . . .

7th September (10.00 P.M.)

It's been a bl—d— wet day & I haven't fished at all . . . we are all feeling cold & miserable tonight & not sorry to be breaking camp in the morning . . .

It was divine till 11.00 A.M., bright & hot, then came a series of terrific thunderstorms & squalls & torrential rain . . . my tent was nearly badly worried by a huge tree which was blown down but it was kind enough to fall between mine & the next tent, though it only missed it by a foot!! . . .

I'm sure I shall love Lake Louise . . though I shan't really enjoy it, darling one, as I've told you already; why the hell is this world so conventional, preventing 2 people who love each other from travelling around together!! Why, if my precious darling beloved little Fredie could get herself over this side I'd never want to return to England; I've got thoroughly bitten with Canada & its possibilities, it's the place for a man, particularly after the great war, & if I wasn't P. of W. well, guess I'd stay here quite a while!! But alas I am P. of W.!! . . .

8th September (11.00 P.M.) C.P.R. Train to Winnipeg

. . . We had to leave camp about 7.30 A.M. & it was a bl—d— 3 hr
canoe trip down the river to Cameron Falls where the train awaited us;
& guess it was cold & drizzling & misty & I was such a miserable little
boy, though I shot a species of duck & worked up a speech for
Winnipeg!! . . .

From my detailed accounts of all my stunts the last 3 weeks darling
I think you can see that I've shaken hands with well over 12,000
people; well guess they've bruised the bone of the centre knuckle & it
gives me such hell to be gripped that I've been pump handling with
my left hand for the last week, though luckily it doesn't hurt to use my
right hand any other way!! This was in the papers & I've been making a
joke of it; I'd forgotten to tell you!! . . .

You know what I said about not wanting to return to England if YOU
could get out to Canada, beloved one; well I've been thinking hard
since I wrote that in camp & feel that I'd like to stay on this side more
than ever, though of course only if you could get over & stay too!!

More silly ideas, though you can't think what a joy it is to be clear
of my family & the atmosphere of court, which I shall never get
completely out of in England . . . I don't feel I shall be able to tolerate a
scrap of all that balls when I return in November. I've become the
completest democrat, angel . . . though that doesn't prevent me from
being the loyalist & keenest servant of the King & Empire!! But I've only
got 2 things in life YOU & my job; nobody else & nothing else matters . . .

10th September (2.00 A.M.), GOVERNMENT HOUSE, WINNIPEG

. . . I've had a very strenuous day darling one & have been dancing here
on top of pompous lt. governor's dinner & reception!! . . .

But here's a real joke against myself, sweetheart: Miss McBride
turned up this evening & I had 3 dances with her!!!! She's been back
since March & now I remember she told me she came from Winnipeg;
she's not at all pretty but quite a good dancer & nice to talk to!! It was
the completest surprise to see her again, though guess she was merely
the best of a vewy ugly dull crowd!! . . . [*Miss McBride was mentioned
once previously, in the context of girls in London with whom the Prince was
rumoured to be attached.*]

Two keepsakes for Freda: a childhood portrait, and a contemporary snapshot of the Prince 'relaxing' at Pine Portage Fishing Camp. He had little interest in fishing, but his leisure time had been arranged for him.

Tous tous les baisers of your vewy vewy own devoted & adoring little David who loves his precious darling little Fredie + que hier, – que demain & who never never stops thinking & dreaming of HER!! ['+ *que hier, – que demain', 'more than yesterday, less than tomorrow', was a favourite expression of the Prince's, and Freda gave him a cigarette case inscribed with it. The Prince later had a heart-shaped medallion engraved with it, which he gave to Wallis Simpson.*]

C.P.R. Train (Going West)
11th September 1919 (1.00 A.M.)

Fredie darling precious beloved one,

. . . I went to a terrible lunch given by the Canadian Club where I had to fire off the Winnipeg Speech, & that was some strain, addressing 700 men on a glass of iced water!! Still even the staff were pleased . . . it's about the best I've ever made & I'm so pleased with it that I'm enclosing a copy for your critical opinion!! . . .

I stood from 3.15 to 4.45 on a platform in front of Government House while 6,000 people filed past, a new form of popular reception, as opposed to shaking hands with only 2,000, & I have doctor's orders not to shake with my right hand!!

Winnipeg has been fairly strenuous, though it was amazing to get such wonderful welcomes in a city where only 3 months ago, there had been shooting in the streets, in fact a real battle to prevent a Bolsheviki soviet being formed. I was threatened with petitions though nothing happened, thank God!! [*Canada's best-known general strike had taken place between 15 May and 25 June, leaving a legacy of bitterness and resentment. The police had charged a demonstration, causing thirty casualties, on 'Bloody Saturday', 21 June.*] . . .

Guess I'm terribly tired & worn out so must turn in, Fredie darling, though guess if I dream I'll dream of YOU, bless you, my precious little goddess!! Perhaps you won't approve of this last title, sweetheart, but a man must have some religion & goddess to worship & you know my religion is worship of the goddess Fredie . . . I suppose I'm writing balls as usual . . .

12th September, C.P.R. Train to Edmonton (1.00 A.M.)

Such a trying day at Saskatoon . . . & such a long drawn out afternoon
at a 'pip-squeak' place; usual addresses & inspection of veterans & the
2½ hrs at a 'stampede' on the racecourse, though that was new &
interesting for 1 hr though not for longer. I wonder if you've ever seen
a 'stampede', sweetheart, which is a series of exhibition cowboy stunts,
riding, bucking horses, lassooing cattle etc., & they had fine performers
there, fine tough men as hard as nails who almost put one to shame &
make one feel soft!!

The train left about 6.30 though stopped ¼ hr later & I was able to
get a 3 mile tramp on the prairie parallel to the track. I took my gun &
shot 2 prairie chicken, a cross between partridge & hen pheasant, which
cheered me up as I was feeling peevish after being bored to death at
Saskatoon . . .

13th September, Government House, Edmonton (1.30 A.M.)

I've been dancing tonight at a huge pompous party given by the
Government of Alberta at the Parliament Buildings . . . Edmonton is
of course capital of Alberta & quite a city (over 70,000) though guess
I'm not crazy over it!! . . .

14th September, C.P.R. Train to Calgary (1.00 A.M.)

I'm a vewy depwessed & despondent little boy tonight . . . all this
official work & speeches are beginning to break my heart angel &
though the staff are nice & kind & sympathetic yet they don't really
understand what a strain it all is for me . . .

But as a matter of fact the president of the local G.W.V.A. [*Great
War Veterans' Association*] branch said some very nice things to me
privately as coming from his 6,000 'comrades', though of course that
word is emphasised more on this side than in England & that is saying
a lot, as you know!! . . .

your David.

C.P.R. Hotel, CALGARY
15th September 1919 (12.30 A.M.)

Fredie darling darling one,

I really am down & out tonight sweetheart & feeling like death as I've never taken such a hopelessly miserable & despondent view of life as I do now!! It's hell, beloved one, & all on account of having had to do the P. of W. stunt & play to the gallery until I can do it no more!!

This trip has been a huge success up to the present, I'll take a little credit for that as I have worked hard & no mistake; but it's partly fear of not being able to keep it up & letting down the staff & spoiling the whole trip which has put me into this hopeless state of mind!!

I feel I'm through, & realise as I have so often told you sweetheart that I'm not ½ big enough man to take on what I consider is about the biggest job in the world!! Can't you picture your poor little boy in one of his worst down & out moods that you know so well, struggling with a long & important speech for tomorrow which he knows he's going to crash & so spoil his reputation!! . . . I'm just dreading today as I've never dreaded any stunts before!!

Pleath forgive this long tale of woe sweetheart . . . Halsey has been in my room talking to me & I've given him a slight idea of my state of mind & he's been charming & sympathetic as usual, yet it's not a scrap of real comfort, darling, & that's the trouble!! . . . Your little boy is quite silly to have cracked just now when the worst stunts are over . . .

I like Calgary . . . I've just got away from a vewy wet & noisy dinner at the Ranchman's Club, though I think the title implies tight men, doesn't it darling? They are a fine crowd of Westerners, but God they drink & they don't let dryness worry them much; it was stiff cocktails & Scotch tonight followed by dirty songs & guess I was lucky to be able to escape before midnight having been only roughly handled by one drunkino, though it was kind roughness . . .

I'm not only feeling desperately lonely & miserable & despondent tonight, beloved one, but thoroughly ill as well; over-eating is one of the causes I'm afraid, though I think I've also been poisoned!!

So I'll turn in & cwy myself to sleep Fredie my precious darling . . . Goodnight & bless YOU your vewy vewy own little D.

15th September (10.00 P.M.) Bar U Ranch

This is a real haven of rest, sweetheart . . . I'm feeling better than last night, darling one, though I want YOU just as badly tonight if not more!! . . .

The train left at 4.00 & we had a 1 hr journey to High River where there was the usual mayor & his address to reply to, 20 veterans to inspect, schoolchildren to hear sing & crowds to wave to!!

Otherwise there was nothing but to get in a car & drive out to this ranch about 20 miles East of High River across the prairies with a dear old man called Lane who owns the 'Bar U Ranch', which has its name from the branding stamp on their cattle ($\overline{U}$)!!

This is marvellous country sweetheart & how I wish you were here; we are staying the night with old Lane in his comfortable wooden house & I've got such a huge bed in my room angel that I shall feel quite lost when I turn in!! . . .

Guess this is the country & life for me, sweetheart, if we could live together, though I don't think otherwise; I could never settle anywhere away from you, darling one, though the atmosphere of the West does appeal to me & attract me frightfully!! . . .

17th September, C.P.R. Train Calgary to Banff (4.00 A.M.)

I've done such a lot since I stopped writing last night Fredie darling that I can hardly remember it all & needless to say the reason for the hour of writing is dancing!!

But I must tell you about yesterday on the 'Bar U Ranch' angel as I enjoyed it all & got a huge amount of exercise . . . I started with an 8 mile run at 8.00 4 miles out to a dried-up river & back & at 10.00 we rode off to the 'round-up' of cattle which was an amazing stunt: I rode a nice locally bred horse in a 'stock' saddle . . . we were in time to help the cowboys & Indians round up the last odd hundreds of cattle & they collected close on 2,000 head I guess; it was quite good fun & I got lots of hard riding doing my best imitation of a cowboy chasing refractory calves which wouldn't be driven into the kraal to be branded etc. etc. . . . it gave one a small insight into ranch life on the prairies!!

But of course I should have stayed at least a week on the ranch to get a proper idea of it all; I was walking fields for prairie chicken for 2 hrs after lunch though neither Legh (who was with me) or self shot anything!! Still it was all fine exercise & we were sorry to have to motor to High River at 6.00 to catch our train back to Calgary; it's a real good life that ranching, darling, though a vewy hard one & one's got to be real tough to take it on as a living though it pays if one can make good!! . . . {*The Prince was so taken with ranch life that when he heard that the property next to the Bar U was for sale, he began negotiations to buy it.*}

We dined on the train & have been dancing since 10.00 P.M., a huge party given by returned officers & the best we've struck during this trip . . . we kept going till the train left at 3.00 & I've been listening to the queer & funny experiences of the whole staff, who all had an adventure or experience with one or more women tonight.

18th September (1.00 A.M.), C.P.R. Hotel, Banff (Alberta)

. . . What a happy happy little boy it is writing tonight after a mail yesterday afternoon which brought 2 sweet divine letters from his precious beloved little Madonna . . . & I'm feeling such a spoilt pompous little boy, so proud to think that nobody could ever get such a sweet divine comforting letter which gives & breathes new life to me & I feel quite revived & happy again & no longer depressed or despondent!! . . .

I owe my Mama 2 letters & my father 3 though they do write such balls that they are hardly worth answering though I suppose I shall have to make an effort soon!! . . .

I must tell you my impressions of Banff . . . what a marvellous place & scenery, why, it's just dandy & such comfort & luxury at this hotel & we've been dancing tonight; some of the Calgary girls of last night have followed us up here & we've been bathing in the swimming pools which are heated up & are fine after dancing!!

Gud I do feel fit after these last 2 days with tons of exercise & no worries or speeches or anything; we arrived at 11.00 & I had to attend an Indian stunt before I was allowed to come to the hotel for lunch!! What I thought of Indians or anything else at 11.00 A.M. after such a late night I can't tell you, sweetheart, & I only got out of bed 10 minutes before the train arrived!!

There are ½ dozen nice Canadian girls here, darling, all of them hideous but good dancers & cheery & great fun & good for anything I should say, though that doesn't interest this little boy; I mean more from the point of view of any rag & it was they who made some of us bathe at midnight, though guess if you asked in the right way, why, you'd just get anything you wanted!!

They are amazing people though I may tell you darling that I've been naturally far more interested in Mrs Shaughnessy & Lady Joan Mulholland, who are staying here & remind me far too painfully of England for words!! They arrived on Tuesday & of course Legh & Claud have deserted me entirely, though I'd have made them if they hadn't!!

Mrs S. (or shall we call her Sarah) came up to my room to see me before dinner & we had a perfect though far too short little talk when she told me about your tea party & she referred to you as 'such a darling' sweetheart & I was so so thrilled, angel, & longed to say so much more, though of course I didn't!! [*The Prince still deluded himself that nobody suspected that he and Freda were more than just friends. Sarah recorded that they had a long talk about Freda.*]

I danced once with each of them tonight though no more as I knew they've only got a few hours with the men they really want to see!! . . .

19th September (2.00 A.M.), C.P.R. Hotel, Lake Louise!!

Fredie darling guess I must have fallen asleep last night as I took your 2 divine letters to bed & read them over & over . . . I was on the verge of tears reading all the divine things you say to me sweetheart & I did want you want you beloved one & just held out my arms (I did really!!) though alas nothing happened & I felt more hopelessly lonely than ever!!

Of course I guessed what you were driving at in your last sheet of paper darling one & was so so thrilled though I more than realise that we must look at the whole thing sanely & from every point of view & there are many, though you need never have any doubts as to my being sure, bless you, & I've never felt so sure & certain as I do tonight!! [*One can only guess whether this paragraph refers to the possibility of marriage, of children, or of divorce, though Freda could well be responding to the Prince's letter of 11 August. The Prince later mentions their 'dream', and he is constantly referring to the hope that some day they will be together 'officially'. The purchase of the ranch in Alberta could have been a way for the Prince to pretend to himself that this was really going to happen.*]

But of course I also can't say all that I want to in a letter & there is only one way of discussing it & that is 'de vive voix'!! . . . I adore the way you ended up 'God keep you for me'!! . . .

Oh!! it's useless my trying to tell you what your last letter & everything in it means to your vewy vewy own devoted adoring little David & now I must tell you what I think of Lake Louise or 'Lake Fredie' as I call it & how I'm thinking of you!!

I had 2 rounds on the 9 hole course at Banff yesterday morning though I was hopeless on account of a gale of wind & being worried by people coming up to shake hands or snap me; & the limit came when a hideous Yank girl in huge spectacles came up to me & called me 'dear sweet child' to my face just after I had missed a long iron shot & was using the foulest language!!

This is a marvellous spot as you say, sweetheart, & I adore it because you do & you've been here & I figured out your divine lovely little face in the glacier at the end of the lake. [*Freda and Duddie had spent part of their honeymoon in Canada.*]

We've been dancing in the main building of the hotel tonight with those Canadian girls whom I'm ashamed to say we brought up in our train from Banff & we had them to dinner again, as we did at Banff which I forgot to mention last night!! No, don't be thulky Fredie darling . . . if only you could see them you couldn't possibly be thulky!!

Sarah & Joan are staying here too & Legh & Claud brought them up on another train quite independent of us!! This is an amazing existence though we've really been able to forget that this is an official trip & we feel all the better for it!!

Halsey is a topper & I like him more & more each day; he's so human besides being so sound & is as ideal as chief of staff here as he is during stunts or pompous visits to big cities & he's a very keen dancer & everybody (particularly the women) loves him.

Grigg is apt to be rather a 'damper' sometimes & a little pompous, though he doesn't mean to be, & the Admiral knows how to deal with him when he gets like that . . . The more I think of it, sweetheart, the more I realise what a wonderful staff I've got, though guess I haven't seen much of my 2 equerries the last 48 hrs!!!!

Too thleepy to write any more so good night & bless you Fredie darling darling one. D.

19th September (11.00), C.P.R. Train Field (British Columbia)

. . . I enclose a few more photos angel which may amuse you; that
Indian rig (complete with feathered head dress) was given me by the
Stony Indians yesterday when they made me a 'chief' & called me
'Morning Star'. But guess did anyone ever feel less like a star in the
morning than your little boy, darling; such an inappropriate name to
give me!!

20th September (Noon), C.P.R. Train to Vancouver

. . . How unkind of you to wag me about Miss McBride, darling . . .
but these women out here are as hot as hell most of them & one has to
be on more than one's best behaviour & never relax oneself a scrap when
dancing or talking to them as they are merely waiting for the least hint
for a flirtation & they squeeze one's hand & say the most amazing
things, though all that merely revolts me . . .

It's wonderful to think that we are nearly at the end of our outward
Westward journey & that I shall soon be returning East & nearer to my
darling precious beloved little Fredie Wedie . . . but I can't possibly
reach England before 20th November & my visit to the States is still
very vague; Washington is fixed & I am due there 11th November,
though I think New York is going to be cut out as the Canadians want
me to embark & sail from a Canadian port, though that is only natural
& right . . .

It's lunchtime but I'll write again tonight!!

21st September (1.00 A.M.), C.P.R. Train, Sicamous (B.C.)

. . . We spent a terrible 4 hrs at Revelstoke yesterday afternoon as after
all the balls we were solemnly driven up to the top of a bl—d—
mountain (1½ hrs) in cars to unveil some mouldy tablet to
commemorate my visit!! Christ your little boy was peeved & fierce over
the whole stunt . . .

But I'm about to go 'over the top' again as I have an important
speech at Vancouver tomorrow & as usual I haven't started working it
up yet . . .

21st September (7.00 P.M.), C.P.R. Train to Vancouver

A vewy vewy thleepy little boy was woken up by another divine darling letter from his precious beloved little Fredie this morning & is now ashamed to think he owes her 3 letters so that he must speed up finishing off this one the result of a whole week's writing . . . Although I've never yet gone to bed without writing you at least a page it's no use if I don't post more often . . .

I heard from Eileen last night & I hope to see them at Victoria, though what an amazing stunt of hers carrying you off in her Rolls under false pretences!! What a shame sweetheart & you must have had a bl—d— afternoon with those betas & though you thought Edith Hillingdon [*Portia's sister*] nice, guess she isn't really & of course I can't even think of Portia Stanley without going mad!! Don't you trust that gang an inch, sweetie, it's not worth it & there's nothing to them; I think I know them better than you do & I was once in their clutches & now that I'm quit of them guess I've forgotten them!! [*There is no indication of how Portia Stanley, with whom he had previously been on good terms, had upset the Prince. It is one of the many examples of the Prince turning bitterly against those with whom he had been friendly in the past.*]

And pleath don't feel a hypocrite Fredie darling for as you say it's all our vewy own affair à nous deux & nothing whatever to do with Eileen, however good a friend she may be!!

I feel more & more strongly that it's absolutely legitimate to lie & that we are more than within our rights to do so when it concerns our own private affairs, angel. There can't possibly be a 3rd party, if there is we are done, so that we just mustn't think twice about lying all we can!

11.00 P.M.

I stopped to go to dinner & have had to spend the last 2 hrs waving my hat as we pass through small stations . . . We stopped for ½ hr at Kamloops, a railway city with a population of 4,000, which was a proper ragtime stunt; Halsey & Grigg turned out in knickerbockers & I was chewing gum all the time & nearly crashed when reading my reply to their address!! We are all rather ashamed of ourselves though the people of Kamloops seemed quite pleased & I'm sure they never noticed anything!! . . .

Bless you again & again & for ever & ever for your marvellous letters
& the divine seal which is on my watchchain & which has made Mrs
Thpider so so happy too!! . . . [*Freda had sent the Prince a spider seal,
which, thereafter, he applied to the wax he always used to seal his envelopes.*]

23rd September (4.00 A.M.), C.P.R. Steamer to Victoria (Vancouver Island)

We are having a marvellous trip over to the Island sweetheart & it's a
divine calm day . . . Sarah & Joan are crossing over today too so Legh &
Claud are going to be happy again, though I have great hopes of seeing
Eileen & Duddie on Saturday & Sunday . . .

We land at Victoria about 6.30 where I'm going to stay with the
Barnards (Lt. Governor of B.C.) who I hear are nice people, though I'm
sorry in a way that I shan't be at the hotel where most of the staff will
be & where Eileen is sure to stay!! Still I don't get much peace at
hotels . . .

*An envelope containing one of the Prince's letters to Freda, sealed with the spider seal she gave
him, which he kept on his watchchain.*

24th September, Government House, Victoria

Bless you bless you & thank you thank you Fredie darling for that most
divine & marvellously sweet letter of 4th September which was handed
to me just as I was going down to dinner . . . all you say thrills me to
death angel & I just don't know what to do with myself tonight. I'm
almost going mad with love & joy & guess in a way it's lucky you aren't
here tonight sweetheart as I would just kiss you to death!! . . .

And what has really finished me off, darling one, is what you say
about the little gun you saw in Purdey's shop [*Purdey was, and still is,
one of the premier London gunmakers*]; of course I can guess what you were
driving at & I do love it so when you refer to our precious sacred little
dream, angel, which makes me happier than anything else; sweetheart
when you ask me 'do you really love me like that?' my answer is 'do'
because nothing I ever wrote could possibly or adequately express how
madly & desperately I love you love you Fredie mine & worship you &
want you & miss you!!

I really am quite silly & gaga & dazed after reading this last sweetest
& most divine of letters & I can't think of anyone but YOU & have
almost forgotten about my arrival here about 7.00 P.M.

There was the usual kind welcome cheering crowds etc., though I
always loathe the 1st drive through a city before they get to know one
& that the cheering is merely for the P. of W. & not for me; I get my
look in the 2nd day sometimes!!

Sarah & Joan came in after dinner & I had 2 dances with S . . . she's a
divine little woman & so sympathetic . . . I like her awfully as she's
now a link wiv you, angel . . .

So Michael wanted you to ask him not to go to America, curse him,
though I bet you gave it him good & true & I only hope it was his last
appeal as he said; but I have my doubts as to this, darling, & that his
barrage will come down again as soon as he returns to England, though
guess it doesn't worry you, sweetheart!! Has Burghie's been as intense
as ever lately & has he been following you around any more?!! . . .

You know that Legh has become my really great friend now,
sweetheart; I think because of Sarah, Claud doesn't mean ½ so much to
me as he used to. He's a curious reticent boy [*Claud was aged twenty-nine
at this time*] & has very little feeling or sympathy in his nature!! He's

always been like this but this trip has brought out more than ever & he says & does pompous little things sometimes which either annoy me or hurt me . . . we've drifted apart, or shall I say we aren't as intime as we used to be, though of course we are still great friends.

Bonne nuit & bless you for ever Fredie mine. D.

26th September 1919 (3.00 A.M.), Train on Esquimalt & Nanaimo Rly (Vancouver Island)

. . . I've been dining & dancing at the Dunsmuirs' house about 10 miles out from Victoria & I was too thrilled for words to hear that you had stayed there angel . . . It has been quite an amusing party as again it was far from dry & one of the Dunsmuir daughters was a bit toxy & of course several of the men; Sarah & Joan were there of course & I danced 2 or 3 times with S & sat out with her for quite a time & she was so sweet & sympathetic about everything. [*The Dunsmuirs were a wealthy and influential British Columbia family whose fortune was based on coal and, later, railways. James Dunmuir became Premier of the province in 1901, and from 1906 to 1909 was Lieutenant-Governor. His wife, Laura, was renowned as a great hostess, but after her husband's sudden death in 1920 she lived quietly on their estate, Hatley.*]

There is one little bit here who is quite attractive & dances well, a Miss McPhillips . . .

I had a heavy morning visiting Esquimalt dockyard & naval college as well as 2 hospitals & other odd stunts . . . I'm sleeping the night in the train . . .

Bonne nuit & all your little David's love & blessings.

27th September (2.00 A.M.), Government House, Victoria

. . . I'm disappointed on opening a letter from Eileen that she only reaches Vancouver Monday 29th, the morning I shove off East again, so that I don't see any chance of seeing her which is tragic!! . . .

Sarah wants me to go out with her & Legh on Sunday afternoon though I don't think I will as it's their last day together & I shall feel 'de trop'!! [*Sarah recorded that the Prince had requested the lunch, and a drive afterwards, but that she was worried that this might offend Claud and Joan. In the event, she went out for a drive with the Prince, but without Joey.*]

Christ what I think of life sweetie & being caged as I am; the fact
that every second of my life since we left London has been public is
getting rather on my nerves at last & I feel like a caged animal!! . . . it
maddens me never to be out of the public eye & to have to lead this
eternal official existence without the break of a second.

Still I told you I left London on duty & should be on duty till I
landed in England again . . .

28th September (2.00 A.M.), Government House, Victoria B.C.

There's been a kind of farewell party here tonight sweetheart & it being
Sunday morning & a question of stopping at midnight, old Barnard the
Lt. Governor put the clocks back 1 hr & we danced ¾ hr after
that!! . . .

I'm getting to know Sarah quite well now darling & like her more &
more & we danced 2 or 3 times tonight & my little bit Miss McPhillips
was here so that it hasn't been so bad!! . . .

Yesterday afternoon we looked in at Hatley, where the Dunsmuirs
showed us the marvellous Japanese garden, the daughters I mean, as
the old man is gaga & dying really; the only son that mattered was
drowned in the 'Lusitania' on his way to the war; the other is a rotter
who lives in S. America!! [*The Cunard liner* Lusitania *was torpedoed by the
German submarine U-20 without warning on 7 May 1915, and sank off the
Irish coast within twenty minutes of being hit. Twelve hundred of the 2,000
passengers drowned, 128 of them Americans, among them Alfred Vanderbilt,
the millionaire yachtsman, together with close friends of President Wilson.
Although the Germans had given clear warnings of the dangers of travelling in
the war zone, and although the ship was carrying a substantial quantity of
war material and was, therefore, a legitimate target, the sinking caused a
great outcry, especially in America, and was instrumental in causing a
reconsideration of her policy of neutrality.*]

29th September (1.00 A.M.), C.P.R. Steamer to Vancouver

We shoved off at midnight & I was really quite sorry to leave Victoria
where we've had a really pleasant 5 days . . .

I lunched at the Empress Hotel with 'The Quartette', guess you
know what I mean, which was cheery & then I motored with Sarah &

Joey [*not according to Sarah!*] afterwards along the shore & had a walk & a good yarn & laugh; it was the first time I had really seen her except at parties & she was quite divine, angel, & I was sorry to say goodbye when she left Government House after tea, though I shall see her again at Montreal; of course she is quite attractive, but so sweet in the way she's a link with YOU my beloved one. She said she longed for YOU to have been at Victoria this week & what a shame that you couldn't come out, till your poor little boy nearly cried . . . [*Sarah simply recorded that it had been a wonderful week.*]

Only a small dinner tonight though we danced to a gramophone afterwards waiting till it was time to go & my little bit was there & came down to the pier with Lady Bernard to see us off!! You know I'm only ragging, don't YOU sweetheart, about this little Miss McPhillips & that there's absolutely nothing to her except that she isn't quite as ugly as the rest & that she dances quite nicely . . .

I'm just living for your next letter though I daren't hope too much for fear of being disappointed & that would upset me for my work . . . your love is such a great incentive to it all bless you, I should just die or shoot myself if YOU didn't love me darling darling one!!!! . .

And now I'm going to say goodnight to my vewy vewy own blessed little Fredie Wedie whose vewy vewy own devoted & adoring little boy HER little David sends her all & everything that he can on paper to his divine little goddess whom he worships & worships.

29th September (4.00 P.M.), C.P.R. Train to Penticton (B.C.)

Well guess I saw Eileen & Duddie & Geordie at Vancouver this morning though only for about 5 mins alas & that was entirely my fault sweetheart & what they must think of me I don't know!!

But it was like this; the steamer got in about 8.00 A.M. & Johnnie Fordham [*with whom Freda and Duddie had stayed on their honeymoon*] fetched me at 8.30 to play squash at his house as arranged, though I meant to get back to the hotel to see Eileen as soon after 10.00 as I could as I only had till 10.30. But we played squash so hard that I forgot all about the time & it was 10.00 before we left the court!!

Gud! I was furious with myself darling & when I did reach the hotel I only had 8 mins before I had to shove off for several stunts!! I went straight up to their rooms & found all 3 waiting for me though I only just had time to realise it really was them when I had to go!!

It just maddened me to have to go without having had a decent talk with Eileen & D. I casually asked how you were & D. said he hadn't heard from you yet & that you weren't too well when he left & you were fussing about your new house!!

Fredie darling darling precious one, what could he have meant that you weren't too well? & then he said he was worried about YOU on account of the strike . . . Guess all he said about you has fairly upset me angel & I just can't bear to think of YOU in any danger in England!!

Of course Duddie may be recalled at once on account of the terribly serious railway & mining situation which seems to me as near a revolution as nothing!! . . . What I think of the bolshevik agitators getting at the railwaymen as they do at the ex-servicemen, or any big community, however loyal; & I'm confident that it's all the result of agitators who can talk, though such a strike was inevitable & far better get it over before the Winter!! [*There was widespread industrial unrest in Britain during September, culminating in a national rail strike – which Lloyd George declared to be an anarchist conspiracy – which began on 27 September and lasted until 5 October. The Prince overreacted to the strikes, however, thinking that they presaged the start of the revolution he feared.*]

30th September (11.00 P.M.), C.P.R. Train to Nelson (B.C.)

. . . It's only the strike in the U.K. that I'm thinking about now & your safety, sweetheart, & I long & want to be near you at this most critical & dangerous moment in our history & I just loathe being 6 thousand miles from YOU as I am though otherwise I'm d—d glad to be missing it all!! . . . I've got the wind up me properly . . . & I'm terribly anxious about your safety & can only pray!! . . .

The strike has upset me completely & instead of inspiring me to make good I sort of feel what is the use of all this official balls, it can't last . . .

1st October 1919 (9.00 P.M.), C.P.R. Lake Steamer on Kootenay Lake (B.C.)

We reached Nelson about 1.00 P.M. & embarked on this steamer landing at Balfour 2 hrs later where there is a T.B. or consumptive sanatorium for ex-servicemen where I had to talk to over 100 men, which was a strain, & see all around the establishment, which was a C.P.R. Hotel, though of course I'm keener on that sort of work than anything else. The welfare of war veterans & that far from being balls is just about the most important stunt for me!! . . .

There was slightly better strike news this morning from Reuter [*the news agency*]; everybody seems to be volunteering in the most marvellous way to save the U.K. from revolution & disaster which thrills one & is encouraging, though it doesn't make the general situation any less serious, though I feel that it's the nation & not the government that is fighting the railway & other unions now & showing that it's not going to be ruled by any single community!!

2nd October (1.00 A.M.), C.P.R. Train to Macleod (Alberta)

Although I got back to the train 2 hrs ago I've been kept at a sort of conference with the Admiral, Grigg & others discussing future plans, particularly our visit to the States as we've been getting silly wires from Lord Grey, the Ambassador, & others at the Embassy at Washington who don't know me or my methods & who will spoil the whole show if we don't watch it & make it all far too pompous!! [*Lord Grey had been Secretary for Foreign Affairs from 1905 until 1916, and is remembered for his oft-quoted remark on the eve of war in August 1914: 'The lamps are going out all over Europe; we shall not see them lit again in our lifetime.'*]

So I've asked Grigg to go to Washington next Saturday & talk to them all like a father & tell them what I want to do & insist that they should fall into my way of thinking . . . your little boy is not going to let the Foreign Office make a b.f. of him in the States, particularly at New York .   That F.O. is a corrupt department & no mistake!!

7.00 P.M., Lethbridge (Alberta) C.P.R. Train

What a marvellous change in me today Fredie sweetheart mine having got your divine sweetest of letters of 10th & 13th . . . your letter is a real inspiration & incentive & I'll do any thing for anybody & bless you for it . . .

But the London Reuter news is better & far more hopeful this evening & I'm vewy vewy relieved indeed. I have confidence in Thomas of the railway union & know him to be a white man. [*J.H. Thomas was leader of the NUR 1917–31, and became Colonial Secretary in Ramsay MacDonald's 1924 Cabinet. A great favourite of George V, who admired his down-to-earth nature, he held several senior Cabinet posts, including Dominions Secretary 1930–5. He came to an ignominious end, being found guilty of revealing Budget details in 1936, and retired from public life.*]

We arrived at Macleod & after the usual balls had a conference about the ranch with George Lane of the Bar U who came down from Calgary to meet me. I think he's going to clinch with his next door rancher who is selling out, only 2,000 acres & it won't mean an actual expenditure of more than £12,000 & it's going to be a very good investment & old Lane will be able to keep an eye on it as it's next door to his!! [*George V was dismayed at the Prince's purchase, foreseeing, wrongly, that the Prince would now be under pressure to make similar purchases elsewhere in the Commonwealth. As it turned out, the ranch was a poor investment, and the Prince lost a great deal of money in later years in an abortive attempt to extract oil.*]

I'm afraid all this about the ranch will bore you sweetheart, only I feel that the idea will appeal to YOU & I know it's a good move & will create a good impression in the West, which is my part of Canada . . .

5th October (1.00 A.M.), Government House, Regina (Sask)

I'm happier than ever tonight Fredie sweetheart with another divine letter of 13th September . . . so you're actually living in 1, Cumberland Terrace at last angel . . .

The news of the strike was mouldy yesterday & put the wind up me as Thomas seems to have broken off negotiating with the Government, no settlement being possible, though I pray the Government won't give in to the railways & this for the sake of the nation . . . I wish Duddie was in London as he is just the sort of man who is wanted during such an unprecedented crisis, who has so much influence & experience as an MP!!

Pleath give my love to Poots & Sheilie, angel, I haven't written to either since 'Renown' on the voyage out . . . Poots is such a real friend of yours & always so sweet to you as she has been to me & I've never shown her how grateful I am for all her great kindness to me & what she must think of me I dread to imagine!!

Fredie sweetie I was so thrilled to hear that Lavery [*Sir John Lavery, a portrait painter of the Glasgow school; his work, especially portraits of women, enjoyed great popularity*] is going to paint you, though I can't see what Lady Cunard has got to do with it; I insist on giving it to YOU, no-one else must have it. I couldn't possibly tolerate anybody else having a picture of my darling lovely little Madonna, though of course you must buy it yourself so that nobody should know & we'll fix things when I get back!! Of course you'll be furious with me for insisting but pleath pleath say Yes & don't be obstinate over it . . .

And darling don't be angwy wiv me if I implore you to steer as clear as possible of Lady Cunard, though I know she's always worrying you as she does me & that she's vewy kind & all that sort of thing; but I know she's a proper 'beta' & there's always some dark motive behind anything she does camouflaged by kindness!! She's a vewy dangerous woman & not to be trusted & she terrifies me; do you remember how she used to try & ask us to the opera together last Summer? [*'Emerald' Cunard was born Maud Burke and married Sir Bache Cunard, grandson of the founder of the Cunard line of steamships. She became one of London society's premier hostesses, and changed her name to Emerald in 1926.*]

As regards my father's letters I enclose 3 or 4 for you to read & keep for me, sweetheart; not vewy thrilling do you think? though what do I care what he writes as he doesn't understand!! . . .

The Prince enclosed six of George V's letters written from Buckingham Palace and Balmoral between 10 August and 14 September 1919. The King talks generally of the situation in Britain with the strikes, of the worse labour troubles in the USA and of the White Russians' success at Archangel, with the Russian forces being smashed up and 2,500 prisoners taken.

The fourth letter suggests to the Prince that the shaking of hands is overdone and undignified if carried too far. He is, however, complimentary about the Prince's speeches. He laments the death of General Botha in South Africa, saying that his great personality and guiding hand will be greatly missed. The fifth congratulates the Prince on the extraordinarily enthusiastic reception he has received in Canada, but the final letter, dated 14 September, mildly criticises the Prince for continuing to say that he is a Canadian, suggesting that it may cause him problems when he visits other Commonwealth countries and has to repeat it wherever he is: will he say he is a Hindu or a 'Mohamadan' when he visits India? The King also laments that the Prince never wears gloves, which fails to protect his hand while it is being shaken, and is concerned over the dirt from thousands of hands.

5th October (11.00 P.M.)

I've never been so relieved in my life as when I got the marvellous news this afternoon that the strike was over!! What a triumph over Bolshevism, sweetheart, & it's the nation that has won, not the government, as it had become too big a thing for the government to settle!! . . . Being a pessimist I feared the worst angel & that it was the start of a revolution & I pictured starving mobs from the East End breaking into your house darling or wherever you might be living; I was sure they would make straight for YOU, sweetie . . .

Yes, I've had the wind up me properly . . . I am particularly pleased & comforted at the way the ex-servicemen have behaved & how they've been breaking up railway meetings & taking the place of strikers; of course they are the ideal force to break strikes; in fact it just isn't safe to use armed troops nowadays!! Now that the strike is over & that it's been peaceable I look on it as the very best safety valve!!!! . . .

So Sheilie & Bertie are planning great things & you are being divine to them as usual, angel, though you must watch it with Loughie on the warpath & I'm always nervous about the other 2 'Do's' & their assignations!! . . .

I guess my letters to YOU are easily the best account or diary of this tour particularly as I've written every night since I left England . . .

I don't suppose your poor hard-worked little boy will get more than 4 months in England before he sails for Australia & so time will be vewy precious for us both when I do get back at the end of November.

Au revoir Fredie darling God keep YOU safe for ME . . . Oh! for just one baiser tonight . . .

6th October (10.00 P.M.), Shooting Camp, Qu'Appelle Valley (Sask)

We arrived here about 5.00 P.M. & are living in tents though it's a very luxurious camp run by that marvellous force the R.N.W.M.P. [*Royal*

North West Mounted Police – the 'Mounties'} who are absolutely spoiling us . . . they are such a magnificent smart body of men & over half of them fought in the war & I love their uniform!!

We left Regina at 2.00 P.M. & had 1½ hrs in the train to Edenwald, an old Hun settlement, & though the children sang the 'God bless' at the station they are all very Hun in spirit & had to be closely watched during the war!!

The police loathe them & say there's nothing to them as they do about the Indians, though I've told you what a foul decadent lazy crowd they are & what I think of them!! But this camp is pitched right inside an Indian reserve about 20 miles from the railway & we have hundreds of the mouldy local tribe camped around us at the West end of a long lake which is absolutely teeming with every species of duck & teal. We were out 'flighting' till 7.30 when it was quite dark!!

Wonderful sport & great fun for anybody who can shoot, darling one, though your poor little boy can't hit anything & his score was 0, while the next worse bag was 10!! . . . and I'm supposed to be enjoying myself . . .

We have the 2 Lakes with us (the Lt. Governor & his brother) who are the absolute limit in the line of pious duds & dinner was too sordid for words tonight!! I had one each side of me & Dudley North described me as being in the 'Lake district' which I thought rather clever though thank Gud they haven't brought their terrible old wives with them!!!! . . .

Sweetheart I must tell you how I've dreamt of you so vividly the last 4 nights running & I woke up at 4.00 A.M. this morning after the last dream with both my pillows on the floor & feeling very cold as I had kicked all the clothes off me!! Pleath forgive all these sordid details but they illustrate better than anything else the state of mind I've got into . . .

7th October (10.30 P.M.) 8th October (9.30 P.M.)

Our last night in this shooting camp thank Gud as it's blowing a whole gale & trying to snow . . . I don't think I've ever felt so miserable or cold or down & out as I do tonight & I've quit the others to sit down & gloom to YOU . . . I was out at 6.30 A.M. & my first shot was a 'recud' fluke as it brought down 3 duck & one was minus its head, though needless to say I never even touched another during the 2 hrs I was shooting!! . . .

But what I think of camps & shooting in Canada in October I can't tell you angel; I'm absolutely fed up with this scheduled tour & our long separation & merely want to get on with the rest of the work in the bloody East & the States & sail for England to my precious darling beloved little baby as soon as possible!! . . .

Of course the staff are enjoying the shooting & having the greatest fun bringing down the duck & the bag is over 300 in 48 hrs to which your poor little boy has contributed 7 & those were flukes!! And this is supposed to be rest & recreation for him, the only one of the party who not only hasn't enjoyed it but loathes it all!! . . . [*The* Sketch *of 12 November shows a picture of the duck bag from the Qu'Appelle Lake shoot, with the caption: 'The bag for the 2 days was 480, and the Prince accounted for more birds than any other member of the party.'*]

What a marvellous speech the PM made at the Mansion House 3 days ago, striking absolutely the right note, he is a marvel!! [*Lloyd George had spoken at a lunch in honour of General Allenby, who was being given the Freedom of the City. As well as honouring the General, he had spoken of the ending of the strike being proof that Britain was a democratic country where public opinion ruled, and where the people would not be held to ransom.*]

Too frozen to write on sweetheart so bonne nuit & bless you & may I dream of YOU!! D.

11th October (4.00 A.M.), Royal Alexandra Hotel, Winnipeg

This terribly late or early hour will give you the impression of a regular debauch, my beloved one . . . the huge party of over 1,000 people preceded by a dinner for 400 returned officers were dry & so fell flat . . .

I've been too bored for words, Fredie darling, with it all, particularly the women, even Miss McBride who was there revolted me, though I danced quite hard for the exercise & to camouflage my intense boredom . . .

I've got to go to this foul lake to shoot duck . . . it's on the 'schedule', that haunting word, & so has got to be gone through with!!

But I write again from whatever miserable housing or tent accommodation there will be . . .

So 'au revoir' & all all my vast intense love . . . ton

David.

12th October (1.00 A.M.), Shooting Club Hut, Lake Francis (Manitoba)

. . . It's freezing hard tonight & though the centre of the hut is warm on account of a good stove, guess the wee rooms off it & otherwise unheated are arctic & I've only a hopeless oil lamp & can hardly see to write . . . I'm not looking forward to tomorrow or rather today as it's Sunday & of course I'm not allowed to shoot & there's absolutely nothing else to do in these prairies . . .

There came a very mysterious wire from H.M. last night giving us to understand that he & the embassy at Washington have cancelled my visit to the States, though no reason was given & I'm not going to concur till Grigg rejoins us at lunchtime & I know the reason!! . . .

Of course I'm delighted deep down, Fredie sweetheart, as it would mean my return to YOU about a fortnight sooner, but on the other hand, duty & my conscience tells me that my not going to the States now wouldn't be understood by the American public at all & would create a werry bad impression!!

6.00 P.M.

Oh!! it's been such a deadly dull day sitting here, though restful I suppose . . .

But here I am grousing again . . . & now the Chink servant is clearing me off the table wanting to lay the dinner though I'm not a bit hungry & feel rather ill!! Still a cocktail may revive me which old Patton [*one of the party's hosts*] is just shaking for me & he's an expert bartender, though I'm glad I'm not staying here long as I'm drinking too much darling, & I know it!! . . .

Now I'll try to tell you briefly all about the States! Apparently Wilson has been & is far more desperately ill than the bulletins have said (haemorrhage of the brain) & so he won't be in a fit state to receive me or entertain me officially next month; for this reason the U.S. State

Department don't seem over-anxious for me to go to Washington &
Lord Grey & the Embassy naturally concur!! [*President Wilson, his doctors
said, had suffered a complete nervous breakdown.*]

But as Grigg says the American public don't care a d—n for the
President or the Government & won't take his illness as sufficient
excuse for my abandoning my visit which might produce a bad
impression & undo all the hard work & trouble that I've taken to make
good with the Yanks!!

So I've wired to Grey (repeating to H.M.) to this effect & have
insisted that if my visit is postponed to next year that this is
announced by the U.S. Government who must take all the
responsibility!! . . .

As it's a case of 5.30 breakfast I really am going to bed . . . What I
think of having spent 1 hr this evening drafting wires with the
Admiral & Grigg re the States when I'm just longing to cut my visit
out so as to get back to YOU sooner . . . Of course it really is everything
to have a man like Grigg to keep one up to the mark as but for him I
should have jumped at the chance of cutting out the States since it has
been practically ordered by the higher authorities & here I am fighting
them!!

Christ I am fed up with the job of P. of W. It's such a hopelessly
thankless one, though I've never been rewarded for all the misery of it
as I have in this marvellous Dominion, & don't feel I ever shall again,
not that I appreciate it all as I should do!!

13th October (7.00 P.M.), C.P.R. Hotel, Winnipeg (Man)

. . . We (the Admiral, Grigg, Godfrey & Joey) are going to a private
party tonight given by a certain Lady Nanton (I'm vewy vague as to
who she is, darling) [*Augustus Meredith Nanton was a prominent westerner
who ran a highly successful broking firm and financial agency in Winnipeg*]
though I'm far too tired a little boy to be looking forward to it as we
were all out shooting at 6.00 A.M. & guess I spent 3 hrs in a canoe on
Lake Francis though no more as I just couldn't stick the pain of my
frozen feet any longer!! . . .

We had a hearty & somewhat toxy farewell lunch . . . & I walked 5
of the 6 miles to the station so guess I've had some exercise today,

though the weekend has been rather a drunken orgy really & I feel it!! . . .

14th October (3.00 A.M.)

You see that despite my saying that I wasn't looking forward to the party I'm not camouflaging the hour of writing, though we left the Nantons before 2.00 & have been sitting up talking as usual; the Admiral & Grigg are devils for starting an argument about 2.00 A.M. into which I'm always called as arbitrator!

We've been discussing the States again & we all feel sure that my visit will be cancelled despite all our wires . . . I'm only praying now that Washington & New York may be off so that I may return to YOU earlier in November which is such a marvellous marvellous thought as I just don't feel I can even exist let alone try to live much longer without you, my precious darling beloved little Mummie!!

And they played 'Hindustan' tonight darling & I just loathed & resented having to try to dance to it with one of the 'bum faced' women at the party . . .

God bless you & keep you for ever . . . your vewy vewy own little David.

15th October (1.00 A.M.), C.P.R. Train to North Bay (Ontario)

. . . I've heard that the fact & the news that I've bought a ranch in Alberta has gone down vewy well & has been the success I hoped it would!! . . . I've got it far cheaper than I ever expected to & I'm going to send stock over from my home farm in Cornwall!!

Gud it must make you laugh darling to hear your little boy doing the heavy rancher & agricultural stunt knowing how gloriously ignorant about it all he is . . .

16th October (1.00 A.M.)

. . . We are a vewy cheery little party nowadays . . . General Burstall makes the 6th member of the party who I haven't mentioned for ages [*one of the Canadian officials responsible for setting the itinerary, whom the Prince had, in fact, never previously mentioned*] & he's very good

value, a huge fat man who makes a great butt for jokes, & we rag
him the whole time . . . he was drinking too much at Victoria but a
hint from the Admiral soon put him right; Halsey really is one in a
million . . .

I'm really getting to know Godfrey at last who is the most dear &
charming fellow & then I like Joey more & more, though Claud seems
to get further & further away the whole time . . . we are the best of
friends but I know we irritate each other!! . . .

7.00 P.M., Train bound for Hamilton (Ontario)

Thank Gud today is over as I don't like this mining area [*Cobalt*] at all;
it's vewy bolshie with a huge alien population . . .

But let me give you the news re the States, sweetheart, that I've been
so anxiously awaiting!! I got a wire from H.M. this morning to say that
on account of the President's illness he couldn't let me visit the States
this year; of course it's rot & H.M. is wrong in not letting me go, bad
narrow-minded policy; still I'm naturally mad with joy as I ought to
reach England by 20th November.

17th October (1.00 A.M.)

Visit to States not definitely cancelled yet as we've just got a cable from
Grey who quite understands my wires & has asked H.M. to defer
decision till U.S. Government makes one, though they cordially agree
they must take entire responsibility of abandonment of visit & make
announcement if this is decision . . . but we must hear definitely by
tomorrow Saturday . . .

We've been playing 'poker' again hard tonight darling finishing up
with 1 hr of 'vingt et un' & I'm about $60 down getting for $100 since
I started this card craze, though I couldn't expect anything else playing
with a lot of old sharks . . .

18th October (3.00 A.M.), Royal Connaught Hotel, Hamilton (Ontario)

What I think of myself staying on at a mouldy pompous dance till this
mad hour sweetheart . . . but as it was a programme dance I had to stay
till the end as the people had gone to enormous trouble & expense to

give this dance & took most of the hotel for the purpose, though no bedrooms!!

But I'm a happy little boy tonight as my visit to the States is now definitely cancelled . . . we got another wire from Grey saying that U.S. Government had decided against the visit on account of President's illness; guess they are wrong angel & what I resent most of all from the P. of W. point of view is that my father gets his own way in a matter of which he is completely ignorant & takes the craziest narrow-minded view possible, though he's always thwarting me & spoiling my chances of making good . . . he maddens me, beloved one, & I often feel like turning Bolshy as it's so hopeless trying to work for him!! . . .

Au revoir & bless you for ever & ever . . . your vewy vewy own devoted adoring little David.

19th October (2.00 A.M.), C.P.R. Train, Niagara (Ontario)

Just returned to the train after motoring out to see the Falls illuminated, sweetheart, rather a marvellous sight in its way though nothing to go crazy over & it's kept me up late again & I had a terribly strenuous & irksome day at Hamilton which we left at 10.00 P.M.!! . . . After the usual balls at city hall I motored miles & miles merely opening a school & visiting a hospital, so little to show for the time & distance!! We lunched at the 'Tomahawk' club (the Hamilton Country Club) . . . I held a veterans parade at 4.30 which I had to address & present over 150 decorations & then go to tea with an old woman because she had entertained King Edward VII!!!!

I only had 1 hr at the hotel before the civic dinner at which I had to reply to the 'dippy' mayor who I had with me in the car all day & who talked such high balls that everyone was convulsed!! . . . Oh! these bl—d— mayors & this one was quite toxy after lunch at the club which, though dry, produced gallons of Scotch both before & after & he became vewy twying & Joey & I all but hurled him out of the car!! . . .

20th October (1.00 A.M.), Clifton Hotel, Niagara Falls

Oh! Fredie darling darling mine mine forever how can I possibly try to start to thank you for 2 most marvellously sweet divine letters . . . I feel such a vewy vewy pompous superior little boy knowing that I belong to my precious beloved little Fredie & am as much a 'married man' as I ever shall be, far more so, & consider myself as such & am the happiest man in the whole world to have such a lovely precious darling darling little 'wife'!! That's my life in a nutshell baby mine . . .

I'm so interested in all you tell me & feel about the strike though simply shudder when you suggest being murdered in your bed, which was the sneaking sinking fear I suffered under during that ghastly week when I was so desperately anxious for my precious beloved one's safety & that of HER sweet little babies had there really been a revolution!! It just makes me sick to think of it . . .

I must send you the enclosed libellous cuttings from a Hamilton paper re the dance there on Friday night, which I hope will merely make you laugh, angel, though they disgust me!!

The girl in question was the least plain of a vewy plain crowd & danced well & being fed up I must own to having danced with her 4 or 5 times but merely because I had to see the dance through & I just couldn't face lugging mouldy faced women who couldn't dance round the room after 2.00 A.M!!

They are the limit these Canadian papers, though the Yank press is worse & are always on the look out for any personal touch which is the dope the public likes & seems to want!! Even the staff, who are all out to rag me, agree that I didn't make myself the least bit conspicuous with the girl or that I danced too much with her!! . . .

So Reggie has been worrying you again darling one; how hopelessly thick-skinned he must be. It's a great pity as I know you like him & so do I & as you say there's nothing worse than scenes!! . . .

21st Oct (1.00 A.M.), C.P.R. Train stopped for the night near Guelph (Ontario)

. . . You'll think me dippy sweetie mine when I tell you that on the strength of a press wire stating that the King & Queen of the Belgians are being entertained at Washington by Marshall the Vice President, we've wired to suggest the same should be done for me, so strongly do I feel that I ought to go down to the States somehow from my official viewpoint before I sail for England!!

The local newspaper cuttings offering 'the dope the public likes & seems to want'.

Overheard At the Ball

A Number of Them Were Evidently Made by Young Ladies

"There's that smile!"—Everyone.

"I think he's just too sweet."—One of the "fortunates."

"Well, I don't mind if he has taken my partner."—Magnanimous gentleman.

"The best dancer in the room."—Many.

"Look at his pink cheeks and his golden hair."—Just a Girl.

He's dancing with her again."—Everyone.

"Look, he's encoring the dance."—Someone.

"Well, she takes her honors well."—An Observer.

"Please, where is Miss Wilkinson?"—His royal highness.

DANCED SIX TIMES WITH PRINCE.

But the "sensation" of the evening was undoubtedly given by a charming young debutante, Miss Blanche Wilkinson, daughter of Mr. and Mrs. H. L. Wilkinson, with whom the prince danced the second dance, ofr this lucky young lady was singled out for more attention from his royal highness than any other girl in the room, having no less than six dances with him. Miss Wilkinson, by common accord was a fit partner for the prince with her blonde beauty and her exquisite dancing. She was gowned in an extremely fetching creation in black satin, which was embroidered in silver, and she carried a peacock blue fan. This debutante was quite the "talk" of the evening, and her quiet, composed manner of taking the honor added greatly to her charm, which was lost to none—not even to those girls who were dying to have one of these dances with the prince themselves!

We've only wired to Grey . . . though I don't think we shall get any change out of Washington as my father's wire was as good as an order to cut it all out!! . . .

22nd October (1.00 A.M.), C.P.R. Train stopped for night near Woodstock (Ontario)

. . . Besides those revolting Hamilton cuttings I enclose a few amateur snaps of that famous veterans parade at Toronto in September which aren't too bad . . . I'm vewy sad & disappointed that I've not received any new ones of my vewy vewy own precious Madonna, though am so so happy to think no foul man has taken HER since HER little David did in August!!

23rd October (1.00 A.M.), C.P.R. Train stopped for night in London (Ontario)

Oh! how I wish this was really London England . . .

Grigg & I are both amused darling to see that Nancy Astor has become a baroness. How she'll hate it, & we sent her a joint wire of congratulations & she'll hate that still more won't she? I see Plymouth want her to stand as woman candidate . . . [*Waldorf Astor was MP for Plymouth until his elevation to the House of Lords; his wife, Nancy, was then invited to stand in his old constituency and in November 1919 became the first woman MP to sit in the House of Commons. (In 1918 a Sinn Fein woman MP had made herself ineligible by refusing to take the oath of allegiance to the monarch.)*]

Goodnight & au revoir Fredie darling darling of my heart . . . Bless you & God keep you for me

Ton D.

24th October (2.00 A.M.), C.P.R. Train stopped for night at Windsor (Ontario)

. . . As usual it's the early hours though there's been no dancing. I'm afraid we just sit up & yarn every night, at least some of us, & the Admiral's the worst offender, & I can't write till they've all gone to bed!! . . .

Windsor is the largest of these border cities with the huge U.S. City of Detroit (over 1,000,000) on the opposite bank of the river & guess ¼ of the crowd this evening were Yanks so it was good propaganda!! . . .

This evening's stunts have bucked me up as I was the completest wreck in the train all the afternoon between London & here & lay on my bed in a state of collapse feeling I just couldn't ever face a crowd or shake hands or speak again!! . . .

Of course Detroit is the world's auto centre & I met Henry Ford at dinner whose plant is right there, rather a striking looking man though I couldn't forget his peace campaign in 1915!! . . . [*A fervent pacifist, Ford had tried to negotiate a European peace.*]

If only you could realise just a scrap what YOU mean to your poor lonely fagged out & stale little boy . . . it's only you who keeps him alive & going . . . if only you knew how you were helping the Empire's cause, angel!!

What an unnatural life for a poor little boy of 25 . . . I do get so terribly fed up with it & despondent about it sometimes & begin to feel like 'resigning'!! And then I should be free to live or die according to how hard I worked though I should have you all to myself sweetheart & should only then be really happy & contented.

25th October (2.00 A.M.), Train stopped for night near Kingston (Ontario)

The reason for the usual 2.00 A.M. touch is that we received the long expected wire from Grey at Toronto . . . the U.S. Government now want the visit & it is 'to proceed' . . .

I have still got a terrible month ahead of me before we can possibly meet again . . . & I only hope I shall be returned to you sane though guess the betting is against it & I'm in a completely dazed state right now in a proper bewildered stupor!! . . .

26th October (1.30 A.M.), In train at Kingston (Ontario)

So endeth a bl—d— week, sweetheart . . . finally it was a case of one of the worst civic 'banquets' which we've ever been through presided over by a completely 'dippy' major who recited poetry instead of making a speech to which I had to reply!! . . .

I heard from my father before dinner, a letter full of advice & more or less orders, though all such balls & more or less showing how hopelessly out of touch & ignorant he is of everything on this side & his studied hostility to the States, which is a national disaster to my mind. [*George V disliked 'abroad' generally, and in particular the United States, which he saw as epitomising everything he hated, being brash, boastful and mercenary. After 1923, he never made an official visit overseas, thinking state visits a waste of time and money.*]

27th October (1.00 A.M.), In train at Kingston (Ontario)

My last free peaceful night before Montreal, sweetheart, though yesterday was hardly a rest . . .

There were 200 people waiting when I returned to the train at 7.00!! I shook hands with them all & was signing my name on queer bits of paper for ½ hr; it's such a curse this autograph hunting . . . but these Canadians really are too amazing for words & tickle me to death the way they'll wait for hours around this train & some of these girls are quite touching the way they give me flowers & quite a pretty little girl waited 4 hrs to give me a box of chocolates!!!!

It's all very marvellous sweetie this amazing loyalty & they don't do it for ME but for the P. of W. & that is for the King, which is all that matters, though he ought to come over to Canada next year; he must & my Mama & my sister Mary too & I'm going to work hell for that when I return to England . . . it's up to my father to show he belongs to Canada or any other dominion just as much as to the U.K. & that he must circulate more!! . . . [*The Prince was unsuccessful in his efforts to make his father revisit Canada, which had been on the itinerary of his Empire tour of 1901.*]

. . . YOUR vewy vewy own devoted adoring little

David.

> *Ritz-Carlton Hotel, Montreal*
> *28th October 1919 (2.00 A.M.)*

My vewy vewy own darling precious beloved little Fredie Wedie,

. . . My first pompous drive here yesterday afternoon was amazing & the public seem to be quite 'dippy', must be the French temperament, as they fairly mob me & it's really a great strain trying to circulate even privately in the city!! . . .

Of course Mrs S. (Sarah) & Joan are here & Joey & Claud are happy what I think of their having seen so much of their 'bits' on this trip . . .

29th October (4.00 A.M.)

. . . I regret to say a proper little beta of a flapper (aged 14–16) jumped up on the car this evening & clung to me with an iron grip imploring me to kiss her, curse her!! Needless to say one of my 4 trusty marine orderlies pulled her off gently but firmly & she was never near gaining her objective, thank God!! . . .

30th October (4.00 A.M.)

You just can't think the huge joy & relief that your sweet divine long letter of 12th has been to me, sweetheart mine . . . I'm so so proud to feel that I'm YOURS & yours only & as such & as long as I'm privileged to be yours I'll never look at any other woman in this world!! And it's not only that I won't look at but I just couldn't look at anyone else!! . . .

We've just returned from a private party given by Lady Davis (Mortimer Dav   wife) [*the Prince was obviously not sure where to put the apostrophe and the 's'*] in their marvellous house where we've all been dancing hard!! . . . quite fun & not too crowded, though I was too tired to talk to all the women & merely danced, which was the choice of 2 evils . . .

I had another long talk with Sarah & danced 2 or 3 times with her though she's different, isn't she darling, & she is so divine & sympathetic & feel she is a link with YOU bless you. Lady Davis told me she met you at a party of Wimborne's about 3 weeks ago just before she sailed; I don't think there's much to her though she's clever but I can't tell you what I think of her revolting fat opulent husband who is a tobacco king & 'nouveau riches' personified!! But they have a marvellous house & I'm using his Rolls here which he's lent me though I rather resent being under an obligation to the bounder as of course I didn't ask for it!! . . . [*Mortimer Davis had built up his father's cigar business into a hugely successful concern, and was often known as 'The Tobacco King of Canada'. The Wimbornes – Ivor Guest, 1st Viscount, and his wife, Alice – were celebrated London party-givers: the Prince was later to write of a striking occasion at their house in Arlington Street, when several hundred guests danced to the light of thousands of candles.*]

31st October (4.00 A.M.)

You'll be thinking me such a nasty dissipated little boy sweetheart being up every night at 4.00 A.M.

You'll be amused to hear that I've struck a good dancer here in the shape of a girl called Marion Coke or Cook (don't know which, anyway it sounds the same). What a queer coincidence & how ironical!!

2nd November (4.00 A.M.)

It's a vewy vewy sad & ashamed & repentant little boy that writes at this silly hour to finish this belated letter as he hasn't written for 48 hrs!

Fredie darling you would just have loathed & hated me last night as I got rather toxy at a club dinner & worst of all went on to a private party in that state too though I pulled through all right & I don't think it was really noticed!!

But I was absolutely incapable of even trying to sit down & write before I went to bed, the first night I've missed writing to you since we parted beloved one & I'm so furious & disappointed with my loathsome self as I wasn't living up to my ideal YOU or doing what you expect of me!!

Today has been more or less free; I staggered out of bed about noon & played squash before lunching with some returned officer friends who did their best to oil me up again but guess I wasn't for it & have been feeling so ill all day . . .

And now I've just returned from a party at the Shaughnessys' house (old Lord & Lady S.) though I've been such a good little boy tonight angel & danced with all the right people . . . I only enjoyed dancing with Sarah as she is such a divine sympathetic little woman & such a link with YOU . . .

But it's marvellously satisfactory to feel that the official schedule is over; it was over Friday & that's my only slight excuse for getting toxy, beloved one, though I was vewy vewy vewy naughty to do it in the presence of women, though they do put away a lot at these Montreal clubs!!

But now it's my turn to scold YOU Fredie darling; it's vewy vewy naughty of you to have started this hypnotising stunt which Sheilie tells me about. I heard from her yesterday & it's somehow connected with Dimitri [*Prince Dimitri Obolensky, one of Sheila's circle*] & she asked me to write & tell you not to go in for it as it's bad for YOU though I do this on my own!!

No, but ragging apart sweetie, please cut that out as it must be vewy bad for you & Dimitri has no right to mesmerise my precious darling beloved little Madonna, though of course I don't know what it entails or anything except what Sheilie tells me . . .

Grigg returned from New York this morning prophesying success for the visit though says there's quite a lot of anti-British feeling in the States just now which we've got to try to live down & propagand against!!

So goodnight & bless YOU bless YOU Fredie darling darling angel à MOI & please twy to forgive last night & I think it's all right though you would have disowned me . . . All all my love & baisers from YOUR vewy vewy own devoted adoring grateful though repentant little David.

9.00 A.M.

Just woken up sweetie & scribble a few more lines before I seal this up . . .

After reading your delightful letter over again . . . What a priceless card from that beta Irene [*Carisbrooke*] & of course it's true that Princess Victoria has made mischief about her though I'm so glad as Gud! I hate & loathe that foul woman!! [*Princess Victoria was George V's favourite sister, who had her brother's ear, and liked to whisper mischief and gossip into it. A spinster and hypochondriac, who had – she claimed – sacrificed her own happiness to care for her ageing mother, Queen Alexandra, she particularly despised the Prince's mother, poking fun and disparaging her remorselessly.*]

Then Duddie amuses me when he says 'you'll have to watch it' about me & how splendid that he thinks that way . . .

Love to the babies & kiss them from 'P. of W.' mummie darling . .

C.P.R. Train, Montreal to Toronto
2nd November (11.00 P.M.)

It's ages since I've written to you in the train sweetheart & this is actually the last night we shall spend in this '780,000$' train as it's often described in the press, though how much better than calling it the 'Royal train' as it sometimes is & which I resent!! . . .

I've had a vewy strenuous day . . . starting off with a mouldy service at the Cathedral & then I had to call on the old R.C. Bishop of Montreal who is laid up with a skin disease . . . before lunching with the Allans at their marvellous house!! Sir Hugh & Lady Allan, one of the richest families in Canada, & they had quite a little party which included Sarah & of course Joey . . .

I wonder if you've met Lady Allan in England sweetie as she was running a hospital at Sidmouth the last 2 years of the war, though she's had a bad time as she was in the 'Lusitania' with her 2 youngest girls who were drowned & then the only son who was in the R.A.F. got shot up & crashed & was killed!!

But her eldest daughter is a proper beta & vewy weird & mysterious & I don't think she has much use for men, darling, though I may be wrong . . . [*Sir Hugh Allan was a wealthy industrialist, with a wide business portfolio based around Montreal, as well as being keenly interested in hunting and racing. His wife had both legs broken when the* Lusitania *was torpedoed, but survived to set up a hospital for Canadian war-wounded.*]

We eventually left Montreal about 3.00 though we really had a vewy touching send-off & there were lots of people lining the streets to wave us goodbye . . . even the track was lined for several miles out & we all felt quite sloppy about it & in a way it is the most wonderful thing that has happened to me since I've been in Canada & is more than reward for my labours of last week!! . . .

I'll leave telling you all about the States till Ottawa beloved one as I shall be in the throes of this fearful Toronto speech as I have to address the joint meeting of 4,000 members of the Canadian & Empire Clubs . . . I'm crazy to make a success of it & that it should go down well & Grigg has produced some marvellous dope; if only I can come up to scratch, angel . . .

5th November (3.00 A.M.), C.P.R. Train at Toronto

Well, the speech is all over & I'm so relieved . . . though Christ it was a strain & I really don't know why I didn't crash & how I'm still alive . . . it was the largest audience I've ever addressed as well as the longest speech I've ever made!! I held your darling little 'thpider' seal in my hand all the time beloved one & that kind of gave me marvellous comfort & inspiration . . .

I'm such a wreck tonight that I really must flop off to bed Fredie sweetheart so 'bonne nuit'.

6th November (3.00 A.M.), Government House, Ottawa

. . . I've been talking to Joey in his room as he had to say goodbye to his Sarah on Tuesday for a few months!! . . . I do feel so full of sympathy for the poor old boy as he loves her desperately, hc's almost as

much in love as I am Fredie darling, though that's quite impossible . . .
*[Joan Mulholland recorded in her diary that she and Claud Hamilton were
convinced that the Prince had fallen in love with Sarah Shaughnessy, and they
hoped he would propose to her. Certainly, around this time, Sarah records a
certain amount of friction between herself and Joey, which appears to have been
caused by his jealousy of the Prince, though, naturally, there is nothing in the
Prince's letters to Freda to suggest that he saw Sarah as any more than a friend
and the love of Joey Legh, whom she was to marry in 1920.]*

I don't like Ottawa much & hate the atmosphere of this Government
House & all its pomp & etiquette & balls . . . though one has to be
tactful here, particularly as this beta of a duchess is a great friend of my
mama's & writes her everything I say let alone what I do!! . . .

12.00 Noon

At last a mail & another divine sweet letter from my precious darling
beloved little mummie . . . Godfrey brought me your letter as I was
dressing for the Investiture from which I've just escaped . . . I knighted
one old general with my own sword, the 1st I've done . . .

Fredie darling how can you accuse yourself of being a fig as regards
Irene. I told you what I think of the beta in my last letter & how I loathe
her with a loathing that passeth all understanding & please don't let her
worry you the way she does sweetie as she's just a mass of snags & vewy
dangerous & I'm never going near her again, curse her!! It's just too bad
that she rings you up as she does darling & I wish you would throw her
& her 'baby to be' out of the window. Can't you get Leo to tell her not to
make such a B.F. of herself, though I know he hates her & I wonder what
that ass Dreno thinks of it all, or doesn't he know she's dippy? He must
be a mug, though she's never written to me, thank Gud . . .

I'm getting quite excited about my new Rolls cabriolet, angel,
which ought to be finished a week or 2 before I get back & guess YOU will
be the first real passenger, baby, & you'll have to christen it. I've
ordered a large Thpider mascot for the radiator, I'm just dippy about
thpiders & Mrs Thpider is more of a companion or camarade than
ever!! . . .

Bless you for your last sweet letter Fredie Wedie mine & for loving
your vewy vewy own devoted adoring petit amoureux ton David.

7th November 1919 (2.00 A.M.)
Government House, Ottawa

Fredie my darling darling precious beloved one,

I've been to another party tonight though I escaped from it at 1.00 as it was at the hotel here & vewy large & public & I hated it . . I've been sitting up talking to North & one of the A.D.C.s [*aides-de-camp*] for the last hour which is such a silly habit I've developed!! Still we've had a good laugh about the women of Ottawa & they are a scream . . .

I wonder if you danced with the King of Spain sweetie or perhaps kings don't dance; & I wonder why the Queen is ill? Is she going to have another baby?!! . . . [*From later references it is clear that King Alfonso XIII had joined the 'barrage' around Freda. The Queen was Victoria Eugenie, sister of Dreno and Leo.*]

I was working on speeches for 3 hrs till dinner here & guess I've got to put in another hour before I go to bed as I've got 3 vewy important speeches to give in Washington next week . . . I don't think I'll ever get over my nervousness or you might really call it terror at the thought of getting up on my hind legs; I did think I would once, but now I know I never will & to think that I'm going to spend my life talking hot air!! [*Despite the Prince's continuing fear of public speaking, it is apparent from contemporary reports that he delivered his speeches very well, rarely using his notes, which reflected the hours he spent copying out the speeches and then making précis of them. The* Times *correspondent in Canada reported: 'You hear without effort every word he says. He has a happy knack of saying the right thing in the right way, and his clear boyish voice has a quality of sympathy and sincerity which makes the speaker one with his audience.'*]

I'm like YOU angel, want to die young & how marvellously divine if only WE could die together; there's absolutely nothing I could wish for more though perhaps you don't quite feel like that darling one & why should you? But I'm just dippy to die with YOU even if we can't live together though I'll explain what I mean when we meet & about dying young, though I've developed a mad craze for that lately, sweetheart mine . . . [*Perhaps the Prince had heard the romantic tale of Crown Prince Rudolph of Austria and his adoring mistress Marie Vetsera, whose doomed affair led to their suicide together in 1889, immortalised in the film* Mayerling.]

9th November (11.00 P.M.)

Well, so endeth our last day in Canada proper, sweetheart, & I feel quite sad about it in some ways as I know I shall never have such a marvellous time from the public viewpoint again & Canadians have absolutely spoilt your little boy darling!! . . .

We leave for Washington tomorrow afternoon . . . though the U.S. programme won't really be strenuous as compared to Montreal etc. . . .

I went for a walk this afternoon & we've been playing some jazz both before & after dinner though there was no big party!! That Miss Marion Cook I was telling you about as being a good dancer is staying here sweetie as well as Miss Marguerite Shaughnessy (Sarah's sister-in-law), though the latter is a proper beta & we all loathe her & she's only a duty guest!!

Miss Cook on the contrary is a nice little bit & a friend of Dorothy Cavendish's & I've been dancing quite a lot with her as she can dance, though for no other reason, as you know, angel! As a matter of fact I think she's the nicest bud we've struck in Canada & we are in 'Her Ex's' 'good books' for liking her!! Still this Government House life is rather a strain. I shan't be sorry to leave Ottawa, though Ottawa isn't Canada; it's all so unnecessarily pompous here . . .

This is my very last letter from Canada, darling one . . . as though I do return to the Dominion when I go up to Halifax after the States it will only be for the last 24 hrs before I sail for England . . .

Now I'm going to be pompous for a moment sweetheart mine; I think you'll find your little boy slightly changed when he returns!! Of course in no way that concerns ourselves TOI et MOI Fredie darling & only as regards my general view of life & other people . . . I'm a little more self-confident than I was & less frightened of other people, particularly of my father!! . . .

You just can't think how absolutely divine & marvellous it is to feel there's someone waiting for me in England & guess I'm just the luckiest man in the world to have TOI waiting for me bless you!! . . .

So au revoir till Washington . . . More than ever ton devoted little amoureux ton David.

Any letters written from Washington are missing. The Prince arrived in Washington on 11 November, where he was met by Vice-President Marshall (as President Wilson was still too ill to receive him formally), together with General Pershing and Lord Grey, and he attended an Armistice Day dinner that night.

He travelled to New York on 18 November, where he received the Freedom of the City, and a 'ticker-tape' parade.

H.M.S. RENOWN, *New York Harbour*
18th November 1919

My vewy vewy own precious beloved little Fredie darling

. . . I had a marvellous welcome here this morning & got through the freedom ceremony & speech all right!! But I've got at least 2 speeches a day here & I really don't know how I'm going to pull through it all alive. It's a hellish schedule programme & enough to break any man's heart let alone your poor little boy of 25!! . . .

I haven't written since Sunday as they told me it was no good but Godfrey tells me there is a mail at 6.00 so I'm just scribbling this last little letter to you before landing for a huge pompous war workers' dinner at the Waldorf followed by a gala performance at the Opera, of all terrible stunts!!

Christ it all makes me so tired & sick of life all this useless official balls & it's such a cruel misinterpretation of me, isn't it, Fredie darling?! . . .

Bless YOU oh!! bless you Fredie Wedie mine & God keep you safe till your vewy vewy own devoted adoring & crazy little amoureux YOUR David can return to you . . . It's nice to get back to this little old ship in a foreign country.

After the Prince's visit to New York, Lord Grey wrote: 'It has done more good than any number of political speeches. The same can be said of his whole Canadian tour, where, by the sheer force of his personality, and his apparently genuine interest in everyone whom he met, he inspired a real devotion.'

In these letters, the Prince seems to take little credit for his accomplishments, and only rarely admits to Freda that he was moved by the welcomes he had received. He omits any mention of the mass hysteria which had erupted during the early stages of the tour in Quebec and Toronto.

He does appear to be two different people – the smiling, extrovert Prince on the surface, and the totally different, depressed young boy, expressing his 'deep-down' feelings to Freda.

It would be easy to suppose that, in order to elicit sympathy from Freda, he kept from her that he was really having a marvellous time. However, it should be remembered that whole pages expressing his love for her and bemoaning his lot in life have been removed from the correspondence. It would appear that the deep-down feelings were the true ones, but that the Prince was a brilliant actor, at this stage of his life, who managed to play the role expected of him.

As he grew older, however, he became less able to hide his impatience and boredom with this public role.

England

❧

1919–20

CHRISTMAS AT SANDRINGHAM

As Edward VII's widow, Queen Alexandra, lived in the main house at Sandringham until her death in 1925, George V and his family stayed in York Cottage, on the estate, when in Norfolk. 'Cottage' is, however, rather a misnomer, as the building now provides the Sandringham Estate Office, as well as five flats.

It had been built by Edward VII, when Prince of Wales, to put up the overflow guests on some of his larger shooting parties, but was no thing of beauty. Despite its description by Harold Nicolson as 'a glum little villa . . . the rooms inside . . . are indistinguishable from any Surbiton or Upper Norwood home', York Cottage was a favourite residence of George V, who had personally arranged the furnishings from Maples in Tottenham Court Road, much to Queen Mary's discomfiture.

Its claustrophobic atmosphere, however, was anathema not only to his grown-up sons, but also to many of the courtiers whose duty it was to stay there. The poky rooms and the persistent smell of cooking added to their discomfort.

The King loved playing the country squire, and was very keen on shooting, being one of the finest shots in the country. Although the bags at Sandringham were no longer the huge ones of his father's day, much of the Christmas break would be spent out shooting. The Prince, as has already been seen during his Canadian tour, was not in the same league as his father or, indeed Bertie, when it came to shooting, and was easily disheartened after a series of misses.

Christmas itself was a programme of rituals followed year after year, and the Prince looked forward to the festive season with trepidation, especially as it would separate him from Freda – who was at Lamcote with her parents – for two precious weeks of the time left to him before his next tour, to Australia and New Zealand, scheduled for March 1920.

York Cottage (F–ck it!!!!), Sandringham
23rd December 1919

My vewy vewy own precious darling beloved little Fredie

I can never never tell you how I loathed our parting this morning angel, although only for a fortnight; 2 weeks out of the short 10 weeks that remain before my next f–cking world trip!! . . .

I feel so so lost sweetie & as if I'm a guest in a strange house instead of staying with my family; I only feel at home in your house, darling one, & how I'm longing & longing for us both to return to London!!

Bertie & I arrived safely about 6.00. We took 4 hrs to come via Newmarket as the roads were greasy & we tore an outer cover which meant changing the wheel; but the car ran fine & we overran 60 mph twice though how I wanted you to be sitting beside me instead of Bertie, darling one!! It really would have been a marvellous joke to have brought you here sweetie & we could be so happy!!

My father received me rather coldly though my mamma was divine & can't do too much for me so I hope for the best & that they won't be too foul to your poor little boy . . .

But how I'm going to sit through dinner without dozing off in my chair I don't know as I really am dead to the world tonight & going to bed vewy early, midnight at latest . . .

. . . Ever your vewy vewy own devoted adoring little David. Dless you.

York Cottage, Sandringham
23rd December 1919 (11.00 P.M.)

Fredie, my vewy vewy own darling beloved little sweetheart,

I'm just going to bed so as to be asleep by midnight (according to your orders) but I just can't till I've written you a few lines to say how

An excerpt from the Prince's disconsolate letter of 23 December. Freda later took him to task about his increasing use of bad language.

I'm missing you & wanting you tonight & how hopelessly lonely & lost I feel!! Sweetie I've already said this in my letter this evening but I can't help saying it again & it's hell!!

It's been such a bloody sordid dinner party you just can't imagine what it's like though all is peaceful & my father wasn't as criticising as usual though he got in a few digs at me!! He is a most extraordinary man, in fact as I've so often said he isn't a man at all & he is so queer in many ways!!

Thank Gud my 3 brothers are here though they are nearly as bored as I am . . . & to think I've got a whole fortnight to face!!

I'll finish this tomorrow as I'm so so thleepy & you must be too; baby mine pleath do take the greatest care of your precious little self; now it's my turn to preach!!

Be vewy vewy careful of the 'hunt horses' they might give you to ride if you do hunt as one can't trust them & then you haven't ridden for such ages!! I'm vewy vewy worried at the idea of your riding rotten horses, you just mustn't!! If only —— but then it's the usual reason why I shouldn't lend you horses, merely because I'm the bloody f–cking P. of W.!!!!

24th December (7.00 P.M.)

Sweetheart the crash came this morning, I mean the cross-questioning re YOU & ME that we've been awaiting, though it was a double-barrel one angel as not only did my mama talk to me but the King did too!!

But don't worry my beloved one as I didn't crash at all, that's only my way of describing such an interview; on the contrary all is well sweetie & we could neither of us have come out of it all better & I'm quite happy about it, though of course it was a difficult subject to handle & be questioned on!!

They know absolutely nothing, darling one, except odd rumours that we danced together a good deal last summer & of course it was the bad luck of that bloody silly wire of mine going to the King that made him a little suspicious!! . . .

The situation hasn't altered at all so pleath don't worry or think about it again till we meet sweetie mine!! They couldn't have been nicer about it all & not in the least sour or accusing, they merely asked a few questions which were easily answered to satisfy them that I didn't know you better than I did anyone else!! . . .

What I think of the foul bitches who first talked about us; I rubbed that in as well & the King agreed that it was entirely idle female gossip that he had heard.

Fuck the bloody post going in a few mins & forcing me to stop . . .

Bless you bless you Fredie . . . I'll write tonight before I go to sleep. All all your v v own little David's love & baisers. Love to your sweet babies.

The Prince must have taken his parents for complete fools if he imagined that their intelligence of his actions and friends was so poor. His 'friendship' with Freda had been well known in London society, and within the Court, since soon after they met, and it is inconceivable that, by now, the King and Queen had not been fully informed of it.

25th December (Xmas Day) 7.00 P.M.

I'm going quite mad sweetheart as besides hundreds of important things my staff are asking me to settle I'm being overwhelmed with Xmas letters & cards & have become quite incapable of even trying to think!! I'm getting absolutely no rest here beloved one & am worried to death with every sort & kind of complex brain-racking problems!!

I'm sure I'll end in a madhouse soon as my brain really is going & I feel so hopelessly & utterly lost; my brain hasn't really recovered from Canada yet & I don't think it ever will!! But here I am grousing again angel though of course I can't tell anyone else all this; but I'm really getting quite frightened about myself!! [*Despite the Prince's assertion that he could not tell anyone else, he wrote to Godfrey Thomas the same day, in much the same vein. Thomas was sufficiently concerned by the letter to reply to the Prince, telling him quite clearly that he would have to change his lifestyle, for both his own sake and his staff's, if he was to avoid disaster. The heavy smoking, drinking and late nights would have to be curtailed: the Prince thought his letter marvellous, but took no real notice of it.*]

I went to church this morning with my family & took the Communion & I prayed & prayed for YOU till I worked myself up into a sort of religious frenzy, though that's all passed away now though it's done me good!! . . . I went to church at 11.00 A.M. Perhaps we were both in church & praying for each other at the same moment . . .

After eating far too much lunch I played 14 holes of golf on the little course here & beat Bertie which made him rather sour, as you may imagine, angel; you remember what he used to be like . . .

A demain & I'll phone one evening soon!! More love than ever from your little D.

York Cottage, Sandringham
26th December 1919 (1.00 A.M.)

Fredie my darling precious beloved one,

We all dined up at Sandringham House with Queen Alexandra this evening . . . it was an improvement on the usual sordidly dull & boring evenings here & Bertie, Harry, George & I gave them a few of our old 'Buzz Buzz' choruses which went down quite well!! . . .

The King looked rather sour all the time though we didn't care. I know he doesn't approve of me though nor does he approve of my 3 brothers either so we're all in the same boat & after all, what does H.M. matter, as you would say . . .

But this deadly slow life is telling on me, beloved one, as it gives me so much time to brood & gloom & think all by myself . . . it's hell when I'm all alone & depresses me more than I can say; there's only one remedy & that is bed, though I can't turn in till I've written you just a few lines.

We are shooting tomorrow so I'll be able to tell you how badly or otherwise I perform with my gun; of course my brothers will put one over me in that respect which I'll resent & which will irritate me . . .

Ever your v v own little D.

York Cottage, Sandringham
26th December 1919 (11.00 P.M.)

Fredie darling precious beloved one,

. . . Not quite such a sordid dinner tonight as my family are in fairly good shape, though of course it's too dull & boring for words!! Christ how any human beings can ever have got into this pompous secluded & monotonous groove I just can't imagine . . . It's really quite interesting for 2 or 3 days when one hasn't seen it for so long though it's become maddening by now & I want to shriek & yell or do something.

And that poor little sister of mine is the greatest tragedy of all, darling, though it's not her fault as it's the way she's been brought up & she's quite happy & not to be pitied as far as she is concerned!!

But I do resent (as you know I do) the foul way my father treats her in imprisoning her at court & not letting her lead a normal life & ruining her chances of getting married or even existing as a girl of 23 should do!!

Christ it makes me mad sweetie, though I can't do anything more; you know how hard I tried last spring when I first came back when I chose her clothes etc. Of course I've no time now as I've far more work to do than I can ever expect to do properly however much I slaved!! Still it is a bloody shame & my father is as unwittingly foul to her as he is to me!! . . .

27th December 7.00 P.M.

I rang you up about an hour ago beloved one . . . though what a disappointment to find you are away from Lamcote till tomorrow afternoon!! At Belvoir I suppose; Christ what wouldn't I give to be at Belvoir tonight & I'm going mad to think that that bloody fucker (excuse these adjectives please sweetie!!) Michael may be there !!!! Oo-oo-oo-oo what I think of life & how I envy Godfrey who is there for the weekend . . .

Your vewy vewy own devoted & adoring little David.

York Cottage, Sandringham
28th December 1919 (1.00 A.M.)

Fredie darling darling one à moi,

Here beginneth another of my daily sordid little letters; we've got a bishop down here for the weekend to preach tomorrow, Bishop of [*gap*] though he's quite a boy & he made us laugh quite a lot at dinner!! You see I'm getting my own back a little sweetheart with my Americanisms when I'm away from you & you can't scold me!!

But Christ how I wish you were here to scold me angel & how I do miss being kept in order & everything that you do to & for me!! I hope I haven't said anything naughty!!

We've been making the bishop play the piano & we yelled choruses & I longed to make him play some of our 'Buzz Buzz' songs, though perhaps some of the words might have been inappropriate for him in my mamma's presence!! But fancy the only weekend guest being a bishop; how typical of my family & of the court & of life down here, though I often wonder if my family is in the least religious or if it's only mere marvellous camouflage.

Bertie & Harry & I are motoring over to Brancaster today to play golf, though of course we shall have to do church first; but I believe it's a marvellous course & I'm longing to beat Bertie on it!! . . .

By the way 'the Turk' [*Philip Sassoon*] has sent me a most lovely Xmas present, a vurry vurry ancient snuff box; that will make you 'laff' angel though do pleath send me any letters he or any other members of the 'barrage' write you . . .

Can't think why I'm so late tonight except that my brothers always foregather in my room before they turn in & we get spinning yarns mostly 'latrine stuff' & quite unfit for publication!! . . .

7.30 P.M.

. . . I'm a vewy sad depressed little boy as I've just got through to Lamcote to find that you are what they call out!! . . . The queer part was that they told me they would fetch you when I asked for you & said my usual that you were expecting a call & when a very faint woman's voice started speaking I thought it was you, angel!!

I'm afraid whoever it was, your mamma or Vera [*Freda's sister*] I hope, must have thought me very mysterious when I only answered 'ME' when asked for my name & when I was finally told that 'Freda is out' I rang off!! Vewy rude only I didn't feel up to facing a long conversation on an indistinct line when I didn't know who the woman was the other end!! . . . I'm afraid I lost my head as usual . . .

We played golf this afternoon & I'm ashamed to say Bertie beat me '4 & 3' which I resented as I know you'll be disappointed darling . . .

The Bishop preached a rotten sermon when I expected a good one from what I saw of him last night, so nothing has gone right for your poor little boy today & another crash on the phone is the climax & I long to do something desperate this evening & shrink at the thought of dinner!!

I enclose 2 of last week's gamecards, darling, which may amuse you; we are shooting the next 3 days though I dread them really as I hate displaying my bad shooting!

All all your little D's love & baisers.

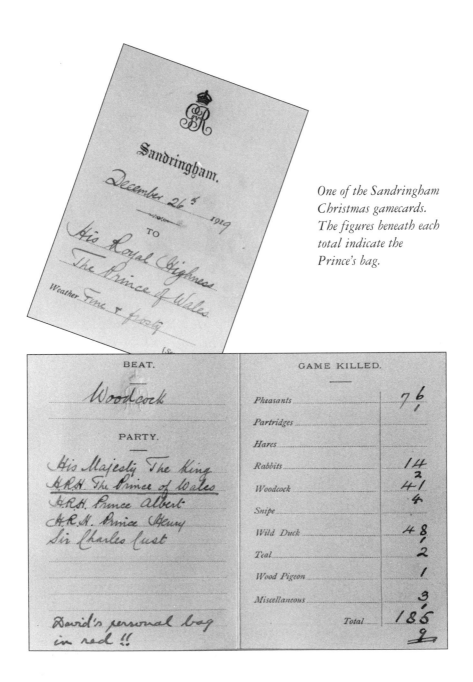

One of the Sandringham Christmas gamecards. The figures beneath each total indicate the Prince's bag.

York Cottage, Sandringham
28th December 1919 (11.30 P.M.)

Fredie my precious darling beloved one,

I'm late again tonight because we've still got that old Bishop staying here & at my suggestion we've been singing hymns ever since dinner; why, wasn't that notable & I think my Mamma & my sister were duly impressed!!

Vurry fine camouflage I guess darling one, though of course those 3 foul brothers of mine were slapping their sides the whole time watching me singing hymns!!! Christ only knows how I raised the energy to do such a thing feeling as miserable & down & out as I was . . .

Christ it was a blow not being able to talk to you this evening . . . I wonder who it really was speaking; I feel strongly that it was your mamma (anyway it wasn't that fucking Violet) [*Freda's mother-in-law, sister of the 2nd Viscount Esher*] & it may have been Vera!! I wonder if you'll be told you were rung up by a madman!

Rather queer we met Tom Coke [*Marion Coke's husband*] & a party from Holkham at Brancaster today darling where they had been playing golf; I never realised the 2 places were so close together & I had never answered Lady Coke's letter!! So I sent her a polite little Xmas card this evening saying how glad I was 'to see Tom again'!! Rather a good one I feel, don't you? . . .

That old fucker Horace Farquhar who lives near here is celebrating his silver wedding with a huge dinner & dance party in Grosvenor Square on 5th January & he's urging me to attend, though guess nothing in the world will make me go, sweetie, as I happen to be dining out already that evening, at least I think & hope I am !! . . .

29th December, 7.30 p.m.

Just dashed back to my room after talking to you beloved one & Christ I do feel so much better & happier after hearing your divine voice again sweetheart . . .

So Godfrey talked to you about me; I heard from him this morning & he said my letter to him had worried him, though no wonder!! I did let myself go something like what I do to you sometimes sweetie or vewy often in fact nowadays, though he's my greatest man friend & I felt better after I had written the crazy letter that I did though I really thought I was going mad on Xmas Day & wouldn't have thought twice about shooting myself if it hadn't been for YOU Fredie darling darling who I've promised to warn before doing anything so drastic.

Christ to think I've got another week to face here, though I was beginning to kill a few birds out shooting this afternoon which improves my morale a little!!

But you know what a bloody difficult life mine is sweetie & how I live on my nerves & when I'm away from you & can't talk to you & get terribly easily upset & worried to death!! If I can't talk & unburden my soul . . . then I get thinking & brooding & that is fatal & something in my tired little brain seems to snap & I feel I'm going mad!!

I'll carry on after dinner as the post is just off & I just can't miss it!!

All all my love & baisers . . . & bless you for writing daily & for talking to your v v own devoted & adoring little D.

York Cottage, Sandringham
29th December   11.30 P.M.

Fredie, my precious beloved little darling,

. . . Our talk on the phone tonight has worked wonders with me & I feel a new & changed man & was able to be quite hearty at dinner for the first time since I've been here!! And the old Man (H.M.) was in good shape too & told what he considered a few risqué stories though they were really only harmless 'balls'!!

Since dinner we've been playing mad games on the billiard table which hasn't gone towards improving it but we don't care & H.M. never uses it!! . . .

Christ how I'm looking forward to Monday & it's so so kind of you to ask me to dine, angel; I do hope that M.P. dies darling & that Duddie will be kept busy & out of London with another by-election; what a marvellous thought!! I feel like going & poisoning that M.P. if only I could find him . . .

30th December (7.00 p.m.)

I just returned from a Xmas tree stunt for the servants, keepers & other employees & their families which takes place annually at Sandringham House; not such a bad way of spending an hour, darling, in fact it was about the best stunt there's been since my arrival & I saw a lot of old friends!! . . .

I can't help worrying & thinking over all the foul things I've got to do in the near future & worst of all that bloody New Year, that fucking 1920 which I dread so!! . . .

I heard from that beta Irene [*Carisbrooke*] this morning & I enclose her letter which will amuse you sweetie; Christ I just couldn't loathe her more bitterly & she is not to be trusted an inch!! [*The letter contains innuendo, offering the Prince 'comfort'; the Prince has written 'Oo-oo-oo-oo-oo-oo!!' beside it.*]

There was slight sourness when I told my Mamma I had to leave on Monday though she quite understands now that I've explained that I must see the Admiral & Godfrey & that there are masses of things to fix up for the next fucking trip!! All that is true sweetheart though of course I couldn't tell her the real reason why I have to be in London on Monday evening!!

As a matter of fact I'm quite the 'blue-eyed' boy here now as she is divine to me in her way & H.M. is quite affable or as much so as he ever could be & he hasn't ticked me off for 2 or 3 days!! Wondurrful!

Must stop now as I've 2 or 3 bits of business to get off to Godfrey. How I'm longing for my thrill on the phone tomorrow evening!! Bless you Fredie darling all your little E's love & baisers!!

York Cottage, Sandringham
30th December 1919 (11.00 P.M.)

Fredie my precious darling beloved one,

Your sweet divine letter of 29th arrived this evening . . . still not another word from Godfrey though I'm so thrilled inwardly to think he really talked to YOU about ME sweetie & how nice of him to say marvellous things about me!!

But he really is my greatest man friend & the only one to be trusted absolutely. Joey Legh is my other real friend though in a different way & I don't trust him in the same way either, not that I'm referring to our sacred friendship, beloved one . . . I put Joey & Bertie on about the same level of trusting only Bertie is such a d——d simple little boy . . . but Godfrey is a uniquely charming man, isn't he, darling? . . . But I've got to fix up my permanent private secretary next week & it's the choice of Godfrey or Grigg as I can't hope to get both & I want Godfrey of course, though H.M. & Stamfordham are urging for Grigg!! You'll say forget him angel I know & so do I, & I expect that's what will happen; in fact I don't feel I could carry on my official work or leave for Australia without Godfrey !! [*Godfrey Thomas remained in the post he had been carrying out for most of the year.*]

But here I am discussing my own affairs & grousing to you as usual beloved one as if I was writing an article in the Times instead of writing to you darling darling.

Of course it was me that Violet talked to last night on the phone though I never recognised her voice; & how priceless that she thought it was Reggie [*Seymour*], though you know angel that I would never ask him to help me over anything that concerns us now . . . Still it was good camouflage, though I hope it will be YOU & not that fucking Violet tomorrow evening!! . . .

6 more days to wait, oh!! hell!! I've never never missed you or wanted as much as I do now sweeheart mine & what is a week compared to 7 or 8 months!!!!

Your little David loves you loves you.

31st December (7.30 p.m.)

I'm such a happy little boy again this evening after talking on the phone though I'm vewy vewy ashamed & penitent for having signed myself E instead of D in my letter of last evening beloved one; but it's always such a rush to catch the post that I quite lose my head when I'm finishing my letters to you angel & get quite 'gaga'!! Still I'm miserable about it sweetie & curse myself; can't think how it could have happened!! . . .

My precious darling little Fredie would have been quite pleathed with her little David's shooting today, particularly as he shot better than Bertie & he's quite pleathed with himself for a change & Mrs Thpider got vewy excited!!

But it poured all the afternoon so we came home early & I went up to see that old bitch of an aunt of mine, Princess Victoria, who pumped me hard about Irene, though she was divine; she's laid up with flu or something though I was on my guard as she's vewy dangerous & the divineness is mostly camouflage!!

We've got the Queen of Norway [*Maud, George V's youngest sister, married to Prince Christian of Denmark, who had been invited to take the throne of Norway as King Haakon VII. She regularly spent the winter months at Appleton House near Sandringham*] coming to dinner this evening so guess I mustn't be late & that means I must stop to have my bath & dress, sweetie; but what a way of spending New Year's eve my beloved one . . . I'm not going to wish you a happy New Year sweetheart as that's impossible but may God bless you & give you all good luck in 1920 & keep you safe for your v v own devoted adoring little D.

York Cottage, Sandringham
1st January 1920 (12.30 A.M.)

My vewy vewy own precious darling beloved little Fredie,

I've waited till after midnight to start writing sweetie as I want my first letter of 1920 to be to YOU, not that we've been sitting up to see the bloody New Year in or anything silly like that!! Still the thought of beginning a New Year always makes me rather sentimental angel & always makes me do a lot of hard thinking & particularly so when I know I'm not going to spend much more than a ¼ of 1920 in 'the old country'!! . . .

The Queen of Norway, her son Olav & her lady in waiting (a young Norwegian bit) cheered us up at dinner & we tried to dance a little bit in the billiard room afterwards & the Norwegian girl (I'll say thulky for you) wasn't too bad on her feet though of course she can't jazz . . . How I resent dancing with anyone else but you baby mine & I just can't screw myself up to put any 'pep' into it whatsoever!! The greatest strain is when my Mamma makes me valse [*waltz*] with her & you've seen me do that at Windsor Castle! . . .

Well guess I'm going to bed sweetie. Reggie arrives tomorrow & I'll try & draw him out in a vague & abstract way about YOU & just to see how much he'll say, though guess I'm 'the village idiot' as usual should he ask me any questions & I'll be vewy much on my guard & so so tactful!! I think I might have rather fun with him & my breaking the ice re you will be good camouflage!! . . .

Must stop now as they've come for the letters . . . Au revoir & bless you Fredie darling darling Ever your v v own devoted adoring little D.

York Cottage, Sandringham
2nd January 1920 (12.30 A.M.)

Fredie, my precious darling little Mummie,

Reggie is responsible for this vewy late hour; Bertie Harry & I have been bucking to him in that famous billiard room . . . Christ the poor devil is fed up with the prospect of 31 days here!! I just long to remind him of what he wrote to you on the subject sweetie, how he longed for this bloody York Cottage to be burnt down, though of course I can't!! . . .

It snowed a little about 9.00 . . . it will be bad luck on Mary if we can't hunt as she is so looking forward to it & Reggie is coming too as 'chaperone' as of course I am not considered old enough or sufficient; makes one laugh, doesn't it, beloved one?!!

I'm terribly thleepy again as we were walking most of the day out shooting, at least I was as I always asked to so to keep warm, which one can't do standing around!! . . .

I heard this evening from my mamma (though I think it happened a week ago) that Boy Capel (Diana's 2nd husband) has been killed motoring with Rosslyn on the Riviera I think!! I'm not surprised if R. was driving as he was probably thoroughly well 'oiled' on port, though I think she is d——d well out of it as he was a proper '4 letter man' & she wasn't happy! But it's sad for her to become a widow a 2nd time!! Still there are advantages in being a widow!! . . . [*Harry, 5th Earl of Rosslyn, Loughie's father, was an inveterate and unlucky gambler who reckoned he had lost £250,000 by 1926 – at least £5 million at 1998 prices – when he nearly went bankrupt*

for the third time. He claimed that he could hold a daily quart of
champagne, and another of port, like a gentleman. On 25 January 1920,
Geordie, Duke of Sutherland, his nephew, reported he was gambling heavily
at Monte Carlo, and had lost £6,000.]

7.00 *p.m.*

Oh!! what happiness & bliss your sweet long letter of New Year's Day
brought me this morning my precious one; I got it just as Mary,
Reggie & I were leaving for hunting!! We got as far as the meet over
20 miles away though as it froze 10 degrees F it was too hopelessly
hard & slippery for hounds to attempt to hunt!! So we stood around for
½ hr trying to look 'horsey' . . . & then motored back gloomily to a
sordid lunch here!! . . .

How I long to be at Tamcote tonight for the party . . . I'll want to
hear all about that party on the phone at 7.00 tomorrow evening when
I'll ring up; 7.00 London time!! [*The clocks at Sandringham had been set*
half an hour fast since Edward VII's day to allow more time for shooting on
short winter days. During the night after his father's death in January 1936,
Edward VIII ordered the clocks returned to London time (GMT), an insensitive
action which upset many of the old retainers and courtiers.]

Yes, Vera is divine & I'm so glad she's a real companion to you
darling. I long to know her better (thulky you'll say bless you!!) . . . [*In*
1922, the Prince and Freda discussed Vera as a possible wife for him. The
Prince dismissed the possibility, although he admitted to loving Vera a little bit,
mainly because she was Freda's sister.]

No time for more so au revoir till after dinner, angel . . . only 3 more
days for your v v own little David to wait for the only thing he wants
in life, to see YOU darling.

> *York Cottage, Sandringham*
> *3rd January 1920 (1.00 A.M.)*

Fredie darling beloved one

It's my 3 brothers who have kept me up so late tonight sweetheart
though I'm always using other people as excuses for not going to bed
early!! . . . I've been giving them some of my early experiences in Paris

etc. which you've heard so often! But I think it's rather a good thing to talk to Harry & George about all that, don't you, darling, as of course they are both going to get far more chances of getting themselves into trouble than I ever did & they are both very hot by nature!! . . .
[Prophetic words about Prince George, who kept bad company and had a drug problem in the late 1920s, which the Prince helped to cure.]

Such a deadly dinner tonight though it's nice having Reggie here as he is such a young & live man & I like him vewy much except for one thing & that is such ancient history, isn't it? . . .

I don't feel a bit thleepy tonight & have that 'caged' feeling strongly & long to take the car & buzz right over to you darling darling.

How I do pray that Duddie may be out on Monday evening & better still away from London . . . I shall have to get H.M. to get a hustle on & open Parliament; the old man has his uses sometimes! . . .

Just heard that Grigg's mother died yesterday which will be a blow to him as he was devoted to her; died at Cliveden as they were both staying with the Astors for Xmas!! Can't think why I mention this sweetie only I just always write as I think of things.

I haven't promised anything or tied myself down at all angel & we'll talk it over; but I'm half thinking of returning here on Wednesday afternoon till Saturday next week!! The hounds are meeting here on Thursday & they are shooting on Friday so that it might be a good thing to do & Mary is imploring me to! . . . I won't fix it till I've seen you; it's merely a question of 'phoning here as I think my family just eat out of my hand now, I'm training them well . . . *[This is an extraordinary turnaround by the Prince, after his earlier lamentations about his wasted two weeks at Sandringham: however, a day's hunting was one of the few things which would take him away from Freda.]*

I really must go to bed now sweeheart . . . I loathe thinking of you dancing with all those foul men at Lamcote!! If only I was going up to London tomorrow too sweetie I am a B.F. not to have fixed that up!!

7.00 p.m.

Bertie, Harry & I went over to Brancaster again this afternoon & had a good game & I put a real one over Bertie, beating him '5 & 3' & winning the 'bye' as well!! So that I feel quite your proud little boy this evening though it was a real case of oo-oo-oo-oo when we found that little bitch Lady Coke there . . . I suddenly saw her standing outside the clubhouse as we got out of the car though I didn't lose my head angel & went up & shook hands with her & was coldly polite!!

And Christ what she looks like, beloved one, I must have been mad to run after her, which I own I did until I met YOU Fredie darling, though you know there was never any love about it & I was merely a silly ignorant & green little boy!! But the mere sight of her upset me terribly for the first few holes, though thank God she had gone when we returned to the Club.

Well I'll go & ring you up now sweetie & finish this afterwards . . .

They've put your letter in my room while I was away talking to you . . . Christ I'm so restless & fed up now I'll find it vewy hard to be polite to all the Queens at dinner & as for that little Norwegian I'll kill her!! . . .

I loved our talk on the phone . . . I'll give Reggie your message darling though it will only be your love & not your best love & also to Bertie & your George as you call him; vewy thulky!! Now I really must go & doll myself up for this fucking party . . .

All all my great love & mes baisers. Your v v own little David does love & adore you so sweetie mine.

> *York Cottage, Sandringham*
> *4th January 1920 (12.30 A.M.)*

Fredie darling darling precious beloved one,

. . . The Queen of Norway's party was naturally a frost though she's a nice kind little woman & I'm fond of her as an aunt as she's always been vewy nice to me & I stayed with her in Norway for 3 weeks in April 1914.

We turned the gramophone on afterwards & tried to dance on a carpet but I got tired & couldn't face it so I sat down with my little jazz box & had quite a succès accompanying the tunes!! And mind you darling that was supposed to be a hell of a night out & treat for us; the best part was getting back to our old billiard room where we've all been talking to old Reggie for an hour!!

I like him awfully as man to man, sweetie, he's a very nice fellow & a sportsman & I'm awfully sorry for him as he never really feels fit with that bullet in his lung & can't stand much exercise. I gave him your message angel & it seemed to cheer him up as of course he's nearly as hopelessly bored and depressed here as I am, though I don't know if he appreciated getting it through me.

Only one more bloody day to get through, though Sundays are the worst of all here as there's no shooting & instead church parade & then a terrible kind of stroll round the gardens . . .

I want to give my car a rest so as to be in good shape to take me back to YOU tomorrow in good time!! I'm going to have a cut at a record trip darling now that I know the road, though how I wish you were going to be sitting in wiv me behind the Thpider [*mascot on the Rolls*] which by the way has been intriguing my mamma & Mary & others a lot though they admire it vewy much!! It thrills me so when our intime little things are admired by other people who can never know their origin!! . . .

7.00 p.m.

Oh! it's been such a dry & tedious day & has seemed so long & drawn-out as all days are when one is impatient & longing vewy vewy much for something to happen & that thing is going to happen the next day! I'm so terribly restless & excited sweetie as you couldn't possibly ever know how I'm looking forward to seeing my sweet divine marvellous precious lovely little mummie again!! I feel far more elated than a child on its last night at school before the holidays. I can't tell you what a marvellous thrilling feeling it is!!

We all trudged off to church at 11.00 muttering foul oaths & talking filth with Reggie in the wake of H.M.'s firm stride!! . . . I had tea with my grandmother & I'm spending a hectic evening packing up (thank God for it) as even if I do return here it will only be for 2 or 3 days sweetie; & it's such a relief!! . . .

. . . Love & baisers from your ever v v devoted & adoring little boy your D.

York Cottage, Sandringham
14th January 1920 (1.30 A.M.)

My vewy vewy own precious darling beloved little Fredie,

. . . Sweetheart you just can't think how miserable I am & how furious I am with myself for having blurted out the idiotic & mad remark that I did last night!! How false I was to myself & my ideals & how I must have hurt you, my beloved little Fredie, though you were such a complete darling little angel (that you always are to your foul silly little boy) as to forget what I said & to forgive me!!

I just can't realise that your faith in me hasn't been shaken sweetie & how could I blame you if it was; I more than deserve anything that you might think of me now darling & that's what makes me so so terribly unhappy as I've been merely living to be true to YOU both in deed & speech; YOU the only person & thing I live for!! . . .

How I do bless you & love you for being so so marvellously lenient & realising & understanding that the foul & painful though entirely volunteered thing I said last night (re that little Belgian bitch) was a hopeless & silly lapse of memory; I clean forgot about the episode in the car when I was toxy & I'm oh!! so so repentant sweetie . . .

I just can't bear living away from you like this Fredie darling darling particularly when it's entirely my own — — fault (words omitted) [*Freda had chided the Prince on the bad language which was creeping into his letters*] I am a hopelessly weak little fool & how I curse myself for everything as I've really been foul to you lately (or anyway what I consider foul) by coming to you day after day in such a hopelessly depressed & sloppy mood; I feel that it just isn't fair on you, sweetheart . . .

You know you ought to be really foul to me sometimes sweetie & curse & be cruel; it would do me worlds of good & bring me to my right senses!! I think I'm the kind of man who needs a certain amount of cruelty without which he gets abominably spoilt & soft!! I feel that's what's the matter with me . . .

6.30 p.m.

We've had a very nice day's shooting, sweetie . . . It's been cold though fine & bright, divine really, & I didn't shoot too badly & got 8 woodcock so I'm quite pleased with myself this evening & I think H.M. is favourably impressed as he's rather inclined to judge people by their powers of shooting, though of course that is silly!! . . .

Cromer has arrived to take over from Wigram [*Assistant Private Secretary to George V since 1910: he eventually succeeded Stamfordham in 1935*]; I quite like him though he's rather too pompous & affected!! How I do crab everybody darling; Reggie hasn't gone mad yet!! . . . [*'Cromer' was Rowland Thomas Baring, the 2nd Earl, who since 1915 had been aide-de-camp to successive Viceroys of India, Lord Hardinge and Lord Chelmsford.*]

Post just off darling so au revoir till after dinner . . . Love & baisers David.

York Cottage, Sandringham
15th January 1920 (1.30 A.M. *again*)

My precious darling beloved little Fredie,

It's the Admiral's [*Halsey's*] fault tonight & I've been trying to get to bed since midnight; Harry & George stayed talking for 1 hr & of course the Admiral & I have masses to discuss & then we started yarning!! . . .

George is off at 11.00 A.M. for which I'm sorry as he's such a good boy, though I'm glad he's going to get at least one night in London before he returns to Dartmouth. Harry returned from his Birmingham & Manchester trip about 10.00 having got through his first 'stunt' very well; old Sir Brian G-F [*Sir Bryan Godfrey-Faussett, George V's equerry*] went with him just to cheer him up & help him through!! . . .

7.00 p.m.

The Admiral & I are having a desperate evening with the Colonial Office who are being foul to me in fact vewy vewy wuf wiv us re the date of my sailing in March & we've been on the phone with them for an hour!! Christ what I think of Government departments & officials as they are so hopelessly inhuman & forget that it's your little boy who has got to undertake this bloody trip & not them . . .

I talked to old Bertie this morning & he told me he was probably going to see you at tea chez Poots so I told him to give you my love, I couldn't well ask him to say more.

I'm so worried about this mix-up re dates darling one, it really is bad luck & just as I was trying to take a pull & get keen on it all!! I hate putting people's backs up as I seem to have & I hate to think of the Admiral being blamed for it all as of course he is!! Christ what I think of it all & how I loathe public life!! . . . [*The Prince was trying, without success, to get his date for sailing deferred by three weeks.*]

Bless you bless you my precious beloved darling little Fredie all all my love & baisers Your vewy vewy own devoted adoring little David.

York Cottage, Sandringham
16th January 1920 (1.00 A.M.)

Fredie darling, my precious beloved one

It was divine having such a marvellous talk on the phone tonight & it's raised my morale a lot which was badly needed after this evening's 'flap' with the Colonial office which H.M. became far too interested in & wanted to know all about!!

Of course I'm furious that they worry him with all this balls as they do, as it only complicates matters & doesn't give the Admiral or myself a chance. And H.M. invariably gets hold of the wrong end of the story for which I get cursed!! Christ it's a thankless job sweetheart & no mistake, though thank Gud I've got the Admiral, who just doesn't care a f—, well you know what angel, & he's such a huge help & standby though I'm able to help him too!! . . .

Bertie rang me up at midnight & told me he had met YOU chez Poots & of her invitation for dinner on Saturday!! I told him I couldn't give an answer yet sweetie . my view is say NO if we can be 'seuls' but otherwise say YES as we needn't stay late & can always dance a little together . . .

How I'm longing to leave this bloody house, angel, first & foremost because life away from you is mere hell & then because my mamma was too foul for words to me at dinner tonight & flared up at some harmless remark of mine re Australia without any warning!! She is an amazing woman & has vewy distorted ideas & both the Admiral & Reggie, who were as taken aback at her outburst as I was, unhesitatingly take my part!!

Of course my reply was to maintain a stony silence the rest of the meal & I shan't refer to the matter unless she does . . . It only shows that it doesn't pay to see too much of one's family, doesn't it, angel, though I've only got myself to blame this time!! . . .

. . . Your ever vewy vewy devoted & adoring little David.

St James Palace, SW
23rd January 1920   6.30 P.M.

Fredie darling darling sweetheart,

I'm so utterly miserable for having said I couldn't look in this evening after dinner that I'm sending this little note to implore you to wait up till 11.00 for me in case my f——g dinner is over before then!! I'm feeling so sad & lonely beloved one that I'm going mad at the thought of not seeing you again tonight & to have to write this note which is the only thing that can give me the tiniest atom of comfort!! . . .

I can't think what made me say I was too busy darling except that I didn't want the Admiral, who has been so foully treated the last 3 days, to think me idle & not keen about everything. But as he won't be here there's no use my staying in & as Duddie is going out after dinner I implore you to let me come round & say 'goodnight' . . .

In great haste ever your v v own devoted & adoring little D.

The problems that the Prince and Admiral Halsey were having were the result of arguments with the Government on the composition of the Prince's entourage for Australia. Halsey was criticised by Leo Amery, Under Secretary at the Colonial Office, for incompetence, his indifference to political considerations and his poor relationship with the press on the Canadian tour. Amery wanted Grigg put in charge, but the Prince had serious reservations about him, and much preferred Halsey. Eventually, the Prince met with Lloyd George and was forced to give way.

St James Palace, SW
14th February 1920 (3.30 P.M.)

Fredie darling darling sweetheart,

Joey is coming in for a moment to see me before he takes Sarah to Trent [*Philip Sassoon's house*] so I'm writing this little note for him to take to you my beloved one just to send you all all my great great love & to apologise for having been so foul to you this morning, darling.

I said such unkind things & I'm so so unhappy & miserable about everything. I just loathed seeing you drive off with Philip & this evening without you is a ghastly ordeal to face, not that I could cheer up vewy much even if we were going to see each other, sweetheart, as I've really become a broken man!!

I'm really rather dreading going to Trent tomorrow & facing the others, angel, & I don't suppose we shall be able to be alone at all, anyway not for long. I've become such a hopeless wet blanket for any party & just sit & gloom silently with a face as long as a mile!!

Left: *'I hope you've had a good game of golf and played well with my clubs darling!'*

Although unpopular with the Government, Admiral Halsey was a firm favourite of the Prince's, with whom he is seen here at the races (above).

Still I should just die if I couldn't see you my beloved one so of course I'll come as early as I can & stay as late as possible, though how I wish you were here tonight & just going there with me tomorrow!!

I hope you've had a good game of golf & played well with my clubs darling!! I promise to be in bed by midnight & you must do the same please.

I'll ring you up between 7.00 & 7.30 on the chance of a talk. Bless you bless you Fredie mummie darling precious beloved one a demain Tous tous les baisers from your v v own devoted & adoring but sad little D.

I love you love you

Other letters from this period show the Prince constantly apologising for his foul behaviour, and emphasising his love for Freda, which he says he never shows to her. The departure for Australia was weighing heavily on his mind, and not only that, as a further tour, to India, had been scheduled to start in November 1920, less than a month after his return, which would keep him out of England until July 1921.

The Prince tried to enlist Lloyd George's help to get him out of the India trip, suggesting that Bertie should go in his place, which Lloyd George said he would think about. The Prince then went and related the conversation to his parents, who were furious that the Prime Minister had not discussed it with them first.

St James Palace, SW
26th March 1920 {misdated: probably 26th February} (6.00 p.m.)

Fredie darling darling sweetheart,

Christ how miserable I am about tonight, my beloved one, but you'll see from the enclosed letter from my mamma that I've got to go to their bloody party to prevent a bad row with my family!! But it's all my fault for having no guts angel & being weak & allowing myself to be ordered about as I am!!

So that I thoroughly deserve the fearful punishment of not seeing you at all today my beloved; in fact I couldn't blame you if you refused to speak to me or to see me ever again, darling, the foul way I've behaved to you the last week or so!!

Christ how miserable & unhappy I am, sweetie, though there is still just a faint ray of light when I think of just the teeniest chance of talking to you on the phone soon after 11.00. I daren't hope to see you as I feel you don't want to tonight & I'm not surprised, either, though it would be so so marvellous angel.

And what I think of you going out with Burghie while I've got to attend this bloody official party to which you've not been invited. What you must think of me this evening I daren't imagine . . .

I feel I'm going quite mad & only 10 days more before I leave you!! I'm not at all normal just now though you must know that . . .

Bless you & please forgive this mad letter, though it's from a madman mad with love which is your v v devoted but miserable little baby

David.

In his later letter of 16 April, the Prince enclosed a press cutting from the *Toronto Globe* of 23 March, which he had been sent, which tells of his refusing to attend a party at Buckingham Palace in his honour because he had had no hand in putting together the guest list – in other words, Freda had not been invited. Apparently, he also persuaded his brothers to boycott the party too. From the letter above, it would appear that this was not what happened, as the Prince's initial opposition died in the face of strong maternal pressure.

In the train
{16 March 1920}

My sweetheart my blessed darling beloved little Fredie angel,

How can I start this devastatingly sad little letter which I'll give to little Bertie to take back to YOU?

There's only one way & that is to tell you that I love you love you far more than ever before my vewy vewy own beloved one & our parting is almost more than I can endure!!

What I'm going to do for 7 —— months without my Fredie God only knows, darling, but as you said I feel that God is on our side &

will watch over us both & bring us safely together again!! . . .

I'm glad you didn't come in the car wiv me sweetie & that we were able to have a good cwy in your darling little room that I love so much. As it was I was whimpering the whole way back to my house though I managed to pull myself together for the pompous drive to the station & the ⸺ family & official farewells, but Christ how I hated them all though there was quite a large crowd in the street & the P.M. & other notables were there.

I long to open your letter beloved one but I'm being firm & won't till I get to bed (vewy early) when we get to sea as I must have something to comfort me my first night away from you sweetie!!

But I gather you've written something about ties & that I mustn't feel I'm bound to you, darling. Well, let me tell you again, Fredie darling mine, that it's the feeling that I am so so fastly tied to you that's going to keep me going the next 7 months & keep me going straight.

I'll never do anything that I know you wouldn't like me to do sweetheart; you can't think what a high standard you've set me to live up to beloved & to live up to it & not disappoint you, will be my constant aim!!

Christ I'll cwy when I get alone in my cabin Fredie darling how can I ever forget my last sight of you on the sofa with poor little Peggy [*the Prince's puppy, which Freda was looking after*] standing by not understanding. Today is the saddest & yet in another way the happiest day of my life beloved, for I think we both showed each other that our love was so so sacred & so tender!! . . .

This is getting such a hopeless scrawl sweetie & I've had to borrow odd bits of paper!! . . . What heaven if only you were coming wiv me & how how happy we would be. I can't even start to thank you for everything sweetie, all your divine sweetness to me & I've done so little in return & feel so ashamed.

Bless you bless you for it all & for saying that you'll cut out that ⸺ Michael Herbert, who is no fit friend for you beloved one!!

This last week has been a marvellous dream & I'm really only dreaming now as I'm such a 'thleepy head' & you know why, sweetie! I'm so happy to think that I had my last meal in your house & my last sleep too!!

We are nearing Portsmouth angel so must stop now as I shan't have time to write on board before we sail. But I'll give Bertie lots of messages for you & make him promise to ring you up as soon as he gets back to London this evening to find out the earliest moment he can go & see you.

And Fredie darling one, twy & cheer up a little bit, though I'm not the one to say that as I can't be happy till we meet again sweetheart!!

Au revoir till I can post from Barbados in a fortnight's time, though what an age that does sound & that's only ¹/₁₄th part of 7 months . . .

All all & more my great great love & more amour amour God keep you & bless you for ever & ever your your your your David.

My love to the babies & Peggy.

The Tour to New Zealand
and Australia

❧

March–April 1920

In his memoir, *A King's Story*, the Duke of Windsor reflected back to his Australian tour, writing: 'The message I carried went something like this: "I come to you as the King's eldest son, as heir to a throne that stands for a heritage of common aims and ideals – that provides the connecting link of a Commonwealth whose members are free to develop, each on its own lines, but all to work together as one . . ."'

He saw his job as '. . . to make myself pleasant, mingle with the war veterans, show myself to schoolchildren, cater to official social demands and to remind my father's subjects of the kindly benefits attaching to the ties of Empire'.

It is clear from the following letters that he did exactly that, with the same success as in Canada the previous year. What was less apparent, except to his immediate staff, was the Prince's state of mind as he embarked on the trip, even before the hard work had started. His depression of the previous months increased with his departure to the other side of the world for seven long months, with only Freda's letters to look forward to and keep him going. It is likely, too, from the comments in his letters of 28 March and 23 April, that he hoped that Freda was pregnant, and he longed for news of this.

His tears when he finally left Freda were witnessed by his young cousin, nineteen-year-old Lord Louis 'Dickie' Mountbatten, whom he had invited to join his staff for the tour. Nominally Flag Lieutenant to Halsey, his actual role was more as companion to the Prince, and Mountbatten immediately saw the extent of the challenge facing him.

A letter from Mountbatten, signed 'Dickie', enclosed with the Prince's of 16

March, thanks Freda for her kindness to him and promises to look after the Prince and to try to keep him cheerful.

Mountbatten's secondary role was as writer of the 'unofficial' diary of the tour. Besides the official diary, again written by Piers Legh, the Mountbatten diary was intended for distribution to a select few courtiers and officials, and only twenty copies were produced on HMS *Renown*'s own printing press.

One of these copies was sent to Freda with the Prince's letters. It is indiscreet and lighthearted, but very frank about certain people and events, and its contents could have caused political waves had they been known at the time. Indeed there was a scare when one of the copies was stolen and offered to the press for £5,000, but it was recovered in time. The diary has been published, edited by Philip Ziegler, and is interesting to read alongside the Prince's own letters.

H.M.S. RENOWN
16th March 1920 (11.00 P.M.)

My darling beloved precious little Fredie,

I've just read your most marvellous sweet & divine letter sweetheart & what a huge comfort it is to me this first sad lonely night on the ocean far away from YOU my beloved one!! . . .

I find it vewy difficult to write tonight as I'm such a thleepy head so that I think I shall go to bed vewy soon & lay my sad tired head on your darling little pillow which is the joy of my life . . .

I found going out of harbour a great strain on my self-control & all but cried like a baby again; luckily I was able to keep my feelings down to mere misty eyes. I never knew I could cry like I did those last precious 5 minutes together beloved one though it did me worlds of good & as you say it's so marvellous to know we both feel the same about parting 'hard for you but hard for me too'.

I dined with the staff, same as before plus Dickie & the Admiral's secretary paymaster Lieut. Commander Janion R.N., a sad little party & conversation didn't flow!! We tried a few new records on the gramophone but when Dickie put on 'The land of might have been' I had to beat a hasty retreat to my cabin saying I was turning in; & now I'm sobbing!!

Oh!! if only you knew how ill from grief I feel tonight . . . it's such a complete and devastating hell to have left you for 7 months. I'm sort of waiting for you angel & feel you'll be coming into my cabin in a few minutes to comfort me & make me feel happy on top again . . .

17th March (11.00 P.M.)

. . . We are getting settled down by degrees though it always takes a few days anyhow for ME & I can never get really settled down!! My only happiness is derived from all your darling sweet presents & souvenirs, particularly your divine photos, darling, which I've stuck up all round my cabin! It's a proper 'Fredie's picture gallery' . . . & I'm so proud that other people should see you in a dozen different poses . . .

My 2 real friends who are a link with you are Joey & Dickie; poor old Joey is nearly as sad as I am & so down & out while Dickie is keen & cheery about everything, though of course he is such a baby!! But he's a vewy clever boy & goes out of his way to be nice & kind & sympathetic & attentive to me as I think he guesses a little how I'm feeling.

I'm so glad I've got him with me & I think we are going to be great friends, or as much so as our different ages will allow as of course he is terribly young. But he's been such a help to me today angel & I'm grateful to him.

As for the rest of the staff they are all as nice as ever but I haven't got the same bond with them & they don't know you except Godfrey, & then he is so vewy reserved. Only Grigg I hate, though not openly of course as one must play up, though I know you understand why I hate him & you hate him too!!

Good night bless you bless you Fredie darling.

18th March (11.30 P.M.)

We've had a movie show after dinner so I'm later than I meant to be. What a rotten form of amusement but it breaks the monotony of life at sea a little bit.

But I hate movies now sweetheart when I think there's a chance of you going into them if only for a short time. Christ!! how I hope you won't though I suppose it would be silly for you to refuse a good offer!! But you are far too marvellous & divine to go on the movies Fredie darling, how I long & wish that you should never be troubled by money matters as you never ought to be!! [*Film producers were on the lookout in London society for potential film stars. Diana Manners, by now Diana Cooper, was one who had a successful and lucrative career.*]

Dickie has been sitting in my cabin for ½ hr while I undressed & has told me all his 'love affairs' as he calls them!! He makes me laugh sweetie, particularly when he mentions the word love!! . . .

19th March (11.00 P.M.)

Such a divine bright warm afternoon sweetheart; that means day to me as I didn't turn out till noon . . . I had 1 hr's squash with Godfrey at 4.00 p.m. & have been reading the rest of the time; just started that amazing book 'Susan Lenox'; terribly sordid it's going to be I think but instructive as a study of human nature!! [Susan Lenox: Her Fall and Rise *was a long story, written by D.G. Phillips, and published in 1917, of 'a girl who learnt to live, but paid the price'.*]

You know angel, I think a book of that sort is good for me in my present state; you know me as no one else does & you know what a baby & what a backward baby I am & such a book gives one an insight into the lower world which is hard for me to get in any other way!! But it's essentially a man's book, you would loathe it sweetheart, & I should hate to think of you reading it!!

But it does bring out a man's love if he is in love as desperately as I am; I do feel that our love is so so sacred & holy my beloved one & I still can't get over that last most marvellous & heavenly of divine letters that you gave me to read after we had sailed on Tuesday.

That last glorious sentence when you said you loved me as people loved once long ago, as they love no more & as they will never love again!! Oh!! mon amour if only I could make you realise that those words just express my own feelings though of course I could never write like that . . .

How I admire you & look up to YOU angel, most lovely & marvellous & beautiful of women; I feel more strongly than ever that fate & time will bring us together forever some day my blessed darling. I'm obsessed with that thought & idea more & more each hour since we parted & feel confident that something will happen some day that will make me belong to you legitimately, not that I could ever feel I belonged to you more than I do now!!

Again bonne nuit & bless you

20th March (11.30 P.M.)

Of course I've been desperately 'Fredie sick' (my form of homesickness) ever since we sailed sweetheart, but I've never felt it as I have today or tonight; particularly as it being 'Saturday night at sea' we drank the usual toast to 'sweethearts & wives' & I vewy nearly broke down!! . . .

I feel so utterly lost & hopeless without you . . . I knew I should feel like this before we parted but I never guessed I would feel it as much as I do!! It's the most fearful hell imaginable . . . How I'm just living for your first letter which might just catch me at San Diego . . .

I had my game of squash this afternoon [*the Prince had the court booked for an hour every afternoon*] & other exercise & I'm shortening up on my food to get thinner, sweetie, which you'll be pleased to hear!! I'm no good on these official trips if I don't keep myself terribly fit & I can only do that by eating little, working hard & taking lots of exercise . . . [*Coupled with staying up late, and a consequent lack of sleep, this was the regime which had caused exhaustion in Canada, and was to take its toll in Australia.*]

I nearly go crazy when I think of where we were this time last week; at Trent, my beloved one, though if I remember rightly we were sad that night as I was such a thleepy head & we both cwied!!

Still those marvellous weekends are so so divine to remember & to think about; I suppose you are down at Lympne this weekend to look at the cottage Philip is going to lend you for the summer & which alas I've never seen, which I resent!! Then as you know I hate Philip doing all these things for you sweetheart while I can do nothing of material use. [*Port Lympne was Philip Sassoon's estate near Folkestone in Kent.*]

But Fredie darling darling I can & I do love you love you madly . . . I've done that ever since I first set eyes on you only I suppose it was a baby's love till you educated me & brought me to my right senses!! . . .

I can never even start to thank you for that or for everything else sweetie; how you've spoiled me these last 4 months till I've become such a blasé little David & it's not till I've left you that I realise how much you've changed me & improved me since my return from Canada!!

It's amazing darling one & I've become more of a man & less of a boy . . . if only we could live together I would become of some use perhaps & have a will of my own & be strong!!

But alas I'm not strong by nature & so have to rely on other people for help in my work & have to be bolstered up though I know it's silly & unnecessary; if only I had some guts . . . However my beloved I promise for your sake to try & mend myself & to develop a will of my own & be more independent in both my thoughts & actions. I can never hope to make good if I don't make an effort & above all be true to myself as you've so often told me to be, mon amour!! . . .

I'm going to finish this letter now as it's getting so bulky & start another tomorrow; & I know you like lots of short letters sooner than a few long ones & so do I darling!! . . . Then you shall have our diary by instalments which Dickie is writing up each day; not a pompous one (as of course Joey is still on that job) but a private diary for the staff which is supposed to be more or less funny though I doubt if it will be!! . . .

Now I really must turn in angel . . . Ever your vewy vewy own devoted adoring petit amoureux. Your David.

Letter No 2
(At sea)
22nd March (11.30 P.M.)

I've had 2 games of squash today & a good run, all this to get rid of what I call 'cold weather fat' & get in shape for the tropics; the rest of the day I've been reading 'Susan Lenox' which gets more & more sordid & depressing & I haven't finished the 1st volume yet as I read so slowly!! I really wish I was reading something else just now but I must finish it now that I've started!! . . .

I had my hair cut this evening (quite an event & worth writing down on this long monotonous trip) & then dined in the wardroom, where I tried to be cheery & beat the jazz drum for a rag orchestra they've organised!!

But I'm no longer the little boy that sailed for Canada, angel; Surgeon Commander Newport who was our doctor in Canada sat next to me at dinner tonight & said to me: 'You haven't got the same pep as you had the last trip' & those are the truest words any one could say about me.

No, I haven't a scrap of pep left in me sweetheart & know I shan't ever have again when I'm separated from my precious darling little Fredie; of course I'll do my utmost & go 'full out' to come up to the scratch darling one, but I'm afraid it won't & can't be natural as it used to be!! . . .

24th March (11.00 P.M.)

We are all depressed tonight (which means that I'm extra depressed) as we lost a man overboard about 3.00 P.M. He was apparently leaning up against the rails on the port side of the ship when the top one parted & he fell overboard; he was a private of marines & though we dropped both lifebuoys & turned the ship about & lowered a lifeboat & searched for the man for 1 hr we never saw him again. So we hoisted in the boat & held an impressive but very sordid funeral service on the forecastle & then steamed on!!

Of course one man's death means nothing, sweetheart, only it's a depressing event in a ship on the 9th day at sea & has a depressing effect on everybody!!

Otherwise it's been the same usual sort of deadly dull day at sea; you can't think how monotonous a long sea trip in a man of war is & how everyone gets almost to loathe the sight of everyone else!! . . .

We are due to anchor at Barbados at 5.00 P.M. tomorrow & we've got the old governor & a few local officials coming to dinner on board followed by a reception & a dance afterwards which I'm dreading more than I can say!! Never have I felt less like all that or setting eyes on any woman but you darling angel; the idea absolutely revolts me & I guess the realisation of it all will be worse!! . . .

BARBADOS   26th March (1.00 A.M.)

. . . I haven't landed yet sweetheart but it looks a proper bum island this Barbados . . .

At 8.00 we gave an official dinner . . . & there was dancing though I stopped it at midnight!! I only danced 3 dances towards the end &

never loathed anything so much, beloved one; but I just had to though I've appointed Dickie my 'procureur' of partners & only take on a 'young woman' that he has vetted as being possible!! But Christ! they were the absolute limit tonight . . .

Christ! how I'm loathing this trip; there isn't a single thing to it as far as I'm concerned as what's the use of it all!! I'm afraid I'm becoming a bit of a bolshie, sweetheart, rather a bad confession to make & I wouldn't make it to anyone else, but it's the truth though it's a trait or feeling I have to keep down . . .

I hope you've given that bloody Michael the push sweetie which is no more than he deserves as he's absolutely bum!!

Good night my beloved . . .

27th March (2.00 P.M.)

It really is hot now darling; my cabin was 90 degrees F when I woke up at 10.30 & I was just dripping . . . But as to yesterday at Barbados . . . it's a unique sort of scenery, very ugly, & I didn't take much to the coloured population, who are revolting. There are over 170,000 of them; the white population is very small & they aren't much of a crop to look at, too deadly dull & of course depressingly primitive . . .

We finished up with a ball at the House of Assembly where we stayed about 2 hrs & I danced quite a lot sweetheart: Dickie found me a little American bit who wasn't a bad mover but the rest of the women were impossible . . .

The young marine who I'm going to play squash with has just turned up so I must stop now angel . . .

11.00 P.M.

It's desperately hot . . . so I'm going to sleep out on deck tonight . . . I feel much better after my squash & they've rigged a canvas salt-water bath in which Dickie & I spent 1 hr after tea before the rush of ship's officers . . .

28th March (10.00 P.M.)

Usual Sunday routine this morning; I inspected the whole ship's company before church & bathed in the sea bath before lunch . . . some squash this afternoon & I've been listening to a lecture on the Panama canal . . . not a vewy thrilling day sweetheart . . .

How are the babies . . . and then how is Peggy? I'm so happy that she's with you sweetie & has therefore got such a good home as I'm so fond of that little animal & she does love you . . .

And finally but overwhelmingly important, how are you my precious beloved little Fredie? Not too many painies I hope & pray & then —— well —— it's too soon to know, isn't it!! It's such hell not being able to write all I want to & I'm so so worried . . .

I've got the feeling that some day we shall belong to each other officially beloved sweetheart so so strongly again tonight & it's such a marvellous divine feeling too . . .

29th March (10.00 P.M.)

. . . I spent 1½ hrs visiting engine & boiler rooms this morning, all of them over 100 degrees F & one up to 120 degrees F so it was some sweat though a good stunt for me to do & I think the men appreciated it. I'm going to make the habit of doing it at least once a week & the other forenoons at sea I'll visit other parts of the ship so as to see

With Dudley North and the engine commander aboard HMS Renown.
The Prince captioned this photograph: 'After a forenoon in engine & boiler rooms (Average temp 110 degrees F)'.

something of the men, who are, after all, far the most important thing in the ship . . .

Au revoir till tomorrow night when I'll start my 3rd letter . . . all all my great great love & paper 'baisers' but oh! for a real one which would do me more good than anything else in the world. Your D.

Panama

31st March 1920 (1.30 A.M.)

Fredie darling darling precious beloved,

The mail doesn't close till 3.00 P.M. so I'm just writing you a final little letter after our 12 hr trip through the canal.

We've been dining at the local Ritz, the Tivoli Hotel, with Bennett (British Minister) & his wife . . . and there was a ball afterwards & we've all been sweating away for nearly 3 hrs & dancing with impossible women!!

You just can't think what they were like sweetheart & the only one that Dickie found for me who could dance at all was an American girl who works behind the counter at a store!! However she was preferable to the so called 'monde' though I also danced with Miss Bennett.

But the canal was interesting angel; we entered it at Colon about 8.00 A.M. yesterday (30th March) & the President of the Republic of Panama [*Belisario Porras*] came on board at the Gatun Locks 1 hr later. That raised the ship the 80 ft into Gatun Lake through which we steamed & on into the Culebra cut where we were delayed 1 hr by a landslide which are frequent occurrences & it wasn't an easy job getting this huge ship round the corner there with only half the width of the canal in use.

Then came the Pedro Miguel lock where we shed the President & other officials & finally the 2 Miraflores locks which brought us down to Pacific level & we tied up at Balbao, the suburb of Panama city in the U.S.A. canal zone at 8.30 P.M. We had a Yank pilot & other Yank officers both naval & military on board & as it was really hot they became rather trying at the end of 12 hrs.

Panama is a deadly spot the end of the world almost & I was the first to want to leave the party, beloved!! Must turn in now . . . they tell me these letters will take 3 weeks to get home sweetheart & as I've been gone a fortnight you will hear from me in 5 weeks!! . . .

I'll try & land about 10.00 in plain clothes & see something of Panama privately & have a walk to stretch my legs . . . This continuous life on board ship . . . gets very trying though it's rather early for me to say this, isn't it, sweetie?

I hope you like the 3 photos of Dickie & I bathing; we posed in the canvas bath specially for you darling; I'm rather pleased with my thin legs!! [*George V hated these bathing pictures, which were widely published around the world.*]

Au revoir again . . . your vewy vewy own devoted adoring little amoureux

ton David.

Panama
1st April 1920 (2.00 A.M.)

Fredie darling darling beloved one,

I've only just got back from the official dinner & dance . . . I've been jazzing around some; sorry for breaking into real Yank, sweetie, but it's being in the canal zone & amongst Yanks ashore which is always bad for my accent . . .

At sea (2.00 P.M.)

But now as to yesterday at Panama!! I landed informally about 10.00 with Grigg, not being able to get anyone else, & we bought some Panama hats in the filthy little town before motoring out to Naos Island to see the Yank big gun defences which are tunnelled in the rock no doubt to keep the Japs out of the canal some day!! . . .

I landed officially to call on the President, inspecting over 100 returned West Indian soldiers on the way!! There are 20,000 British coloured people working on the canal & they gave me a good welcome; they are mostly from Jamaica & smell too revolting for words, poor brutes!!

It was all a proper old pantomime & we all laughed a lot as the

Panamanians are a very queer people, all dagoes of course, though very pompous & dirty . . .

Then back to the ship at 5.00 for some squash & to work at my speech before the President's official dinner . . . when he spoke in Spanish though guess I didn't sweetheart & they were a sticky audience & the heat terrific.

The dinner was followed by a bloody awful dance, about 200 Panamanians besides the motley crowd of Yanks of the night before so it was a terrible squash & dancing almost impossible . . . My 'store girl' was again the only mover though I was too tired for more than one with her, particularly when she said I could take her home if I wanted to, although she was already booked up with a man for that pleasure, I think the man who kept her!!!!

Christ she was awful though I got first prize when we got back to the ship & were all telling what women had said to us during dances!! It all revolted me angel & it's a relief to be at sea again, now in the Pacific on our way North to San Diego . . .

10.00 P.M.

Christ it is hot tonight sweetheart & my cabin is 90 degrees F & I'm just dripping & have to keep my face away from the paper so as not to drench it . . . I'm feeling more Fredie sick than ever before tonight . . .

2nd April (11.00 P.M.)

Good Friday today so Sunday routine & we had church this morning . . . I've had a long yarn with old Joey this evening who is feeling almost as 'Sarah sick' as I am 'Fredie sick' . . . he's such a dear when you get to know him . . .

An for Claud he drifts further & further away from me as a friend & seems more aloof each day & I've come to look upon him as merely of use officially . . .

3rd April (10.00 P.M.)

I'm so sorry my letters are so dull & boring just now sweetheart but you can understand how uneventful & monotonous official life at sea in a battlecruiser is . . .

I've censored Dickie's letter as you'll see by the alterations angel, though of course it's only a rag letter on his part & he put in those items I made him alter just to annoy me; so I know you'll believe the amendments darling though of course he's such a baby & can't understand my viewpoint, particularly when he says I take life too seriously!!

Of course he can't make me out at all when we go ashore & I take no interest in the bits he picks up for me to dance with except as regards their dancing!! He is naturally out to kiss any woman that attracts him sufficiently if he gets the chance & why not at his age & heart free?!

But how glad I am that I'm not heart free beloved one & that on the contrary my heart is locked up inside YOU . . . All all ME & all & everything that's in me is yours yours Fredie sweetheart, nothing else or anyone else exists for me except YOU though I'm still trying to carry on with this thankless & rotten job of P. of W. which is the only reason why I've left you now!! . . .

Still you are my idol, my goddess my goal my —— everything sweetie . . . I feel as if we were having one of our heart-to-heart talks tonight darling. What a lot we had those last 3½ precious months together & they often made me temporarily sad, in fact miserable down & out & d—d near to shooting ourselves.

Still we didn't shoot, angel, so we've always got that up our sleeves!! I've promised & do again never to shoot away from YOU sweetheart: you've promised & please do again by letter that you won't shoot till we are together once more!! . . .

4th April (10.00 P.M.) Easter Sunday

How I wonder where you spent today sweetheart? How well I remember last Easter Sunday afternoon in the garden at Fern Hill & we bicycled over to Kilbees you standing on the step of the machine . . .

I thought of you so much & felt quite sloppy at Holy Communion this morning though it was a sordid little service on a very hot mess deck taken by our naval parson, quite a good fellow in his way though high church, which I abhor, & how he sweated!! . . .

Otherwise the usual monotony of life at sea; you can't think what a Godsend the squash court is angel & the Admiral & most of the staff &

officers have got very keen & we are organising a handicap competition with a sweep on it !! . . .

We are now off the coast of Mexico & it's cooler . . . How I'm longing for San Diego & just the faintest chance of a mail though I'm not letting myself count on one or even expect one for fear of being disappointed as of course that would be the very worst hell imaginable angel!! . . .

Oh! I've forgotten to tell you that I bought a couple of what they described as ladies' Panama hats which I'm mailing to you with this letter; there are 2 sizes & I do hope one of them will fit you & be of use for tennis or something, though I know you love being out of doors without a hat which suits you so marvellously!! . . .

I'm just going to turn in on deck where I know I'll be really cool tonight as there is quite a fresh breeze. Of course I always take your darling little pillow up with me sweetheart but always take the precaution to pin it to me for fear lest it should be blown overboard when I roll about which would be the end of everything! . . .

5th March {misdated} *(11.00 P.M.)*

. . . I visited a turret this morning & have been dictating letters to my father & Lord Beatty today asking that I get 'Renown' for my next bloody trip (to India, Malay Straits, China, Japan & home via Canada) instead of 'Malaya' which any amount of alterations & expense couldn't ever make one tenth as comfy or as suitable as this ship!! But what I think of having to even think about India just now, sufficient unto the day etc.!! [Malaya *was a Queen Elizabeth class battleship on which Prince Albert had served as an acting lieutenant in 1917.*]

Good night & bless YOU.

6th March {misdated} *(7.00 P.M.)*

. . . I enclose a few more photos, sweetie; one more bathing one which really is the best . . .

I'm also writing to old Bertie; I hope he goes to see you sometimes angel as I love to think that you & he are friends & that you see something of each other when I'm away, though we both think exactly the same about him!! . . .

Although George V was irritated by the 'bathing' photographs, the Prince was evidently pleased with them: he sent Freda an additional shot. 'Dickie' Mountbatten is on the right.

How are Sheilie & Ob [*Prince Serge Obolensky – a married emigré Russian with whom she had fallen in love*] getting on & above all are you much worried by the 'super barrage' Michael & Philip, not that I class them together in any way as I like Philip; but I loathe Michael with a hatred that passeth all understanding!! . . .

I've at last finished that famous book 'Susan Lenox' which Philip lent me; it's too devastatingly sordid for words & you just mustn't even so much as open a page of it as I know you would hate it!! It's a book for men only & I really mean that angel, not in any way from the prude's point of view as I don't know how to be a prude!! But it's an interesting & instructive book for men though merely 2 volumes of unadulterated filth for a woman!!

Our programme for tomorrow at San Diego is very vague though I know we are to lunch on board U.S.S. 'New Mexico' about 1.00 & there's a sort of official landing & a drive through the city is planned for the afternoon with a mayor's dinner & dance in the evening at Coronado Beach which Duddie urged me to visit!! . . . I've had an invitation from a Los Angeles film company to fly over the 20 miles to see a film made; of course I've had to refuse as I've been made to cut out flying . . .

Au revoir & bless you bless you forever & God keep you for me D.

San Diego (California)
8th April 1920 (1.00 A.M.)

Fredie darling darling beloved à moi,

I've never never felt so utterly down & out & miserable as I've done ever since we anchored here at 10.00 A.M. yesterday as there was a fat mail & nearly everybody in the ship got the letters they wanted except me!! Most of them were dated 17th March but there were newspapers as late as 19th; the only letter I did get was from Philip, a charming letter & he gave me news of you sweetheart but I don't count anything but YOUR letters!!

Fredie darling I'm not blaming you or grousing in any way though you can understand how miserably sad & disappointed I am!! I was a fool to count on a mail here though how could I help it when everyone else got letters?

They are still talking vaguely of another mail about noon but I'm more than sceptical now angel & have quite given up hope of getting any news of you for a least another month if not 5 or 6 weeks!! Oh! it's intolerable hell & I feel so so desperate tonight as I do love you love you so madly madly & no news of you after 3 whole weeks is heartbreaking!! . . .

We've just got back from the most bloody awful dinner & dance at the Coronado Hotel; I've never hated a party as much as I did this evening's though of course I couldn't have been in worse form as I've been all day as a result of a blank mail . . .

I'm so so near unto cwying that your little pillow may get wet.

Various writers have suggested that the Coronado Hotel dance was attended by Earl Winfield Spencer and his wife, Wallis (when they divorced, she married Ernest Simpson); however, though they had lived in Coronado and frequently used the hotel during the early part of 1920, in her autobiography *The Heart Has Its Reasons* she states clearly that they were not present. Other writers have suggested that Wallis and her husband were, in fact, presented to the Prince on board USS *New Mexico* earlier in the day, which she conveniently forgot in a fit of pique, as neither the Prince nor Dickie Mountbatten had any recollection of meeting her.

(5.00 P.M.)

There's a mail train due at 6.30 P.M. at San Diego so we are delaying our sailing a whole hour on the chance of their being another mail for the ship sweetheart. I need hardly tell you that I was the first to suggest waiting for this possible mail angel though of course it's for everybody's sake!! . . .

All all my great great love & paper baisers & may God keep YOU for your vewy vewy own devoted adoring petit amoureux

ton David.

> *Letter No 6*
> *At sea, San Diego to Honolulu*
> *8th April 1920 (10.00 P.M.)*

My vewy vewy own precious darling beloved,

The very worst possible has happened this evening as the mail we waited for arrived & was put on board but oh! the bitter pain of it, not a single letter for me!!

I'm completely stunned & shattered though I must be brave & pull myself together & try & be a philosopher though it's d—d hard & so I've shut myself up in my cabin & am just writing you these few lines before I turn in to cwy myself to thleep!! . . .

I'm glad for his sake that whoever is the cause of the delay of your letters isn't within my reach as I wouldn't hesitate to kill him!! Christ it makes me mad with rage as my Fredie letters are all I've got in this ghastly existence . . . people can do any d—d thing they like to me as long as they let me have my sacred Fredie letters; not that I'm accusing anyone of stealing them or tampering with them, only someone's been a d—d fool somewhere & hasn't hustled them on & has held them up somehow!! . . .

Of course the cruel part of it all is that I've now got to wait 4 or 5 or 6 whole weeks till New Zealand before there's the least chance of our mails catching us . . . no words can ever describe to you what I feel like tonight; I feel quite ill from the bitter ghastly disappointment of it all though thank God I've got 5 whole days to get used to it as I just couldn't face official stunts with my morale as low as it is now!! . . .

All I have to console me is Philip's letter & he does give me a few lines of news of you mon amour . . . so he dined with you the evening I left sweetie & it produces fresh sobs sweetie when he says 'She was terribly miserable'!! I'm afraid it makes me 'terribly happy' to hear that beloved & I'm so so thrilled though I long to hear it from YOU instead of Philip!!

I'm afraid there's going to be a bit of trouble about India & that quite unconsciously I'm becoming involved in an ugly row between H.M. & the P.M. or what might become a row between H.M. & Me backed by the P.M.!! I know which side is the strongest really though as you know such a row is the very last thing I want as I'm afraid I wasn't born a fighter though you are training me marvellously, angel!! [*Sir Philip Sassoon was now Secretary to Lloyd George, and so could keep the Prince supplied with inside information from Downing Street. At Victoria Station, where the Prince had taken the train for Portsmouth on 16 March, the King and Queen were 'extremely frigid' with Lloyd George – according to Lady Lloyd George's diary – and Queen Mary would scarcely shake hands with him, resenting the fuss that the Prime Minister had made of her son.*]

So that I'm also longing for Philip's next letter to know what's going on between Buckhouse & Downing Street & of course inwardly I'm delighted as I dread India now more than I did.

But I guess the P.M. won't stick at anything to get his own way which in this case seems to be to stop my going to India this Winter . . . I guess I'll be getting some fairly rude letters from Buckhouse, not that I care a d—!!

It's a vewy pathetic & dejected & miserable little David that is just going to lay his sad tired head on your little pillow sweetheart but he loves you loves you so madly & desperately.

9th April (10.00 P.M.)

. . . But now I must tell you about San Diego, though how I loathed our 36 hrs there . . . we visited the USS 'New Mexico', being shown over the ship and lunching on board. Then came the official landing at San Diego city . . .

From the landing stage I motored through the city to the Stadium in the Exhibition grounds where there were several thousand people (San Diego's population is close on 100,000) & after driving right around I had to say a few words from a platform . . . all this is illustrated by the photos enclosed in my last letter sweetheart & it terrified me having to talk at those magnaphones which are the latest invention!! . . . [*Magnaphones were an early loudspeaker system.*]

Now for a typical example of 'graft', the Yanks' name for bribery, as perpetrated by the mayor, an absolute wrong 'un who may be 'jugged' any time!! Mrs Charlie Chaplin (alias Miss Harris, a movie star) [*Mildred Harris was in the process of divorcing Charlie Chaplin at the time*] was bent on meeting me & came down from Los Angeles for our visit getting in with the mayor & paying him so many thousand dollars to get herself introduced which I regret to say she succeeded in doing before I had the least idea who she was, though the mere sight of her all but made me sick!!

When we discovered her identity we stopped her attending the dinner & getting a ticket for the reception on board the next day (Thurs) though she was at the dance & I was rather sick with Dickie for dancing with her!!

We didn't in the least take exception to her as a movie star but as she's up to the eyes in the white slave traffic & every other of the most revolting trades of that sort & is besides the most revolting looking 'beta' we got rather fed up!!

How I resent even having had to shake hands with her & her press agent bribed our photographer to snap her standing near me & more than made it worth his while; so you can see how one has to watch out in the States sweetheart!! Not a v interesting or edifying little yarn but I thought it would amuse you . . .

10th April (11.00 P.M.)

. . . We are due at Honolulu at dawn on Tuesday . . . we sail again early on Wednesday for Fiji & shall 'cross the line' [*the equator*] before we get there which entails quite a ceremony as you probably know!!

Well goodnight my precious darling beloved little F̂redie, though you'll probably be thinking of getting up by now!!

Love love D.

11th April (11.00 P.M.)

Late again darling but we've been dining in the gunroom tonight which naturally was God's own rag what with jazz traps & yelling to accompany 3 of the band & we finished up by de-bagging Claud (at my instigation, needless to say) on the quarterdeck though it was d——d good for him & he took it very well indeed!!

Yes I'm afraid the young lord's dignity was temporarily badly knocked sweetheart but he's such a boob really & never plays any games or does any of the things a man of 30 ought to do; of course I know nothing of his intime life!! . . .

Otherwise it's been a usual Sunday at sea . . . I played Joey [*at squash*] . . . it is luck & a godsend having this court, though alas I don't have you to watch me play.

I'll never forget that final at the Bath Club & I was so thrilled to have you watching me sweetheart, though how nervous I was, though that wasn't why I lost; on the contrary it gave me such confidence but I was in rotten form that day somehow!! [*Despite playing off a handicap of seven – equivalent to starting each game of tennis thirty–love up – the Prince had still been well beaten by the well-known sportsman Captain Eric Loder. Despite great enthusiasm for squash and golf, the Prince had little natural talent.*]

I'm rather pleased (pompously) with a cutting from the Times of 18th March which I enclose; & to YOU and only YOU Fredie darling I can say that it isn't all balls, only the part where Drummond says I led him. Of course that is, but as you know I did go 'all out' every day I hunted & at every hunt I rode, sweetheart, so that I feel quite proud of the cutting & that it's something of a reward for my labours, though I'm crazy about hunting as YOU are & it's such a d——d shame that you never get a day to hounds nowadays!! [*Sir Charles Frederick, Master of the Pytchley Hunt, was quoted, and was complimentary about the way the Prince rode on the hunting field. After the Prince had fallen, the Master had spoken to Captain Drummond, who had been asked to pilot the inexperienced Prince. Drummond had replied that '. . . before we had gone very far, he was piloting me'.*]

Oh! if only we were married Fredie darling beloved, but then —— well I suppose it's silly to talk of such a thing for the present, anyway, though if only you knew how utterly & completely obsessed with that thought & ideal I am, sweetheart, & as I've said before I feel so so strongly that something radical is going to, must happen to our lives to make us really belong to each other!! By really I mean lawfully darling darling, for I'm sure we couldn't belong to each other much more than we do now, at least I know that I couldn't!! . . .

God bless you again beloved one & may he keep YOU safe for your vewy vewy own Yes! your very very own little David.

Letter No 7
Honolulu
14th April 1920 (3.00 A.M.)

My own darling beloved little Fredie,

I'm just as surprised as you'll be when I wrote the hour 3.00 A.M. but we've just been out to a Hawaiian 'Luau' or festival put on for us at a private house 12 miles out from the city which didn't start till midnight as it followed a ball in the city!! . . .

I'm vewy sad not to have had any reply to my first 3 cables darling & hinted at that in my cable to you from here yesterday!! I've become so desperate with no news of YOU for a whole month sweetie & as I can't get a letter from you for another month a cable is the only thing that can relieve & comfort me!!

How I loathe being separated from YOU & so cut off from you angel; it will be more tolerable when I at last begin to receive your sacred precious letters!! Oh! the joy & happiness they will bring me mon amour & I can't help beginning to get excited about mails again!! . . .

Dickie & I sent you a silly postcard from the hotel out at Waikiki where we 'surfed' for 1 hr before dinner but I mustn't enter into any details now as I'll only write nonsense!! . . .

Goodnight & bless you bless you Fredie darling beloved; à plus tard!!

At sea (10.00 P.M.)

There was to have been a concert or singsong this evening but thank God there's a bit of a blow & seas are coming in over the quarterdeck . . . we none of us feel at all like singing as we still haven't recovered from last night's Hawaiian orgy; I didn't turn out till 11.30 & have done nothing all day except play a game of squash though I'm still terribly thleepy sweetheart!! However I'll anyway start to tell you about yesterday at Honolulu . . .

We anchored about 7.00 A.M. & landed officially at 11.30 for an hour inspecting British & returned men . . . then back to the ship for a lunch party before landing again semi-officially in plain clothes to attend a terrible Hawaiian pageant to celebrate the centenary of the arrival of the first white missionaries. You can imagine how fearfully boring that was darling . . .

We motored to the Moana Hotel at Waikiki Beach where without any ceremony we got into 'tenue de bain' [*bathing costumes*] & spent 1 hr in the marvellously warm sea learning how to surf!! I need hardly tell you there was quite a crowd on the hotel beach to see us off & return & we all felt rather shy though most of the crowd were clad like ourselves . . . it really is lots of fun that 'surfing' as they call it, which is done either in a special sort of long canoe or on a flat board shaped like a tiny boat.

The whole game is to catch a big breaker coming in at the right second & it shoots you inshore for several hundreds of yards so long as you can steer & keep your board on the slope of & just below the crest of the wave & one gets up a good speed.

I only caught one wave & surfed properly once angel though that wasn't so bad for a beginner; of course I got terribly 'ducked' several times & my board came up & hit me on the head once & I cut my toe on some coral on the bottom!!

So I emerged rather sore & bruised after my hour in the water & oh! so tired. Then they've got an amazing aquarium near the hotel where they've got some 'varwy queer' (as Angie would say) fishes . . .

I attended a terrible masonic stunt though it only lasted 10 mins [*Halsey's father, Sir Frederick Halsey, was a high-ranking Mason who encouraged the rise of both the Prince and Bertie through the Craft*] & then went for 1 hr to a huge ball where there was too much of a crowd to dance & 2 of the most completely bum bands that couldn't keep any sort of time!!

And then the women, sweetheart!! I only found one who could dance

& who was in any way tolerable so that we were all glad to quit at
11.00 & motor out to Pearl City where the Hawaiian 'luau' was given
by some Yanks called Atkinson . . . it was worth seeing as a unique
native stunt though the Hawaiian food we were made to eat was too
revolting for words . . .

We (100 people) sat down on the floor at low tables with leaves
instead of table cloths laden with the queerest 'mélange' of foods
anyone has ever seen; roast pig & fish cooked in leaves, seaweed & some
stuff that tasted like sticking paste were among the dishes so you can
imagine how revolting & nauseating that supper was, particularly as I
had an enormous fat Hawaiian 'princess' (though civilised & much
travelled in Europe) next to me who ate enormously of all the
disgusting foods & expected me to as well!!

I picked at 2 or 3 of the messes but struck after the seaweed as I
thought it would be regarded as an insult had I been sick where I sat!!
I'll never forget what I went through angel!!

But of course the best part of the stunt was the Hawaiian singing &
dancing sweetheart though one got rather tired of the native songs &
longed for some of our tunes in the steel guitars & ukuleles!! But I was
glad they didn't as just hearing those instruments made me think more
poignantly than ever of YOU, beloved, as they were of course identical to
YOURS and Sheilie's!!

It was all a weird but quite picturesque show though, as most things
of its kind, very overrated & 2 hrs was far too much of it . . .

The Hawaiian women who danced were too disappointing for
words; I expected natives & I expected them to be hideous, though I
heard they had good figures!! But no, au contraire they were very fat
& such legs & ankles, though they knew how to waggle their fat b——
——s!! . . .

I'm still shy of several hours of sleep as unlike the staff & officers of
the ship I never sleep in the daytime as it doesn't agree with me at all!!
If I do succumb I invariably wake up feeling like nothing on earth
though it's a desperate job keeping awake after lunch sometimes!! . . .

15th April (11.00 P.M.)

. . . We actually cross latitude 0 [*the equator*] in 24 hrs time & then
we'll be busy with all the 'crossing the line' stunts which really bore

me to tears, angel, only one has to try & show some interest as it amuses everybody else . . .

16th April (11.00 P.M.)

The curtain raisers to the 'crossing the line' stunt took place at 9.00 P.M. sweetheart when King Neptune & his court & 'bears' went through the motions of coming on board which were accompanied with the firing off of rockets on the fo'c's'le & he came up onto the bridge & he & the captain exchanged greetings in the most pompous way & Neptune informed him that he would arrive on board officially at 9.00 A.M. tomorrow!!

Of course the whole stunt is the most thorough balls but it's a very old naval custom & worth keeping going & doing properly nowadays!! . . .

Otherwise merely squash, beloved one, 2 more handicap games; I beat poor Dickie 54–6 out of 60 though he took it very well & understands that the game can't be learnt in a few days . . .

I feel sure the enclosed cutting will amuse you darling as much as it does me; it's out of a Toronto paper & was sent to Godfrey by Henderson, military secretary at Ottawa!! Of course it's somewhat incorrect in detail but the gist of it is true enough, except for 'best girl pals' it should read 'pal'!!!! [*See letter of 26 February 1920.*]

I'm delighted darling & only hope it gets to that bloody Buckhouse; how I loathe them all there & how embittered I am against them & look on them with contempt! So I'll turn in now loathing them & loving you more fervently than ever Fredie mine . . .

17th April (10.00 P.M.)

I won't go into a long account of this morning's Neptune stunt angel as Dickie is writing it up well in the diary; sufficient to say that 'His aquatic majesty' started in at 9.00 A.M. with a lot more pompous talk & a rag investiture after which he progressed forward to a huge canvas bath on the fo'c's'le above which there was a platform & 3 'tip-up' chairs & the ceremony of initiation of 600 novices, officers & men began & lasted 2 hrs!!

Your little David was the first to be put through beloved & after having vile concoctions of soap smeared over my face & a revolting pill (dough mixed with quinine) shoved into my mouth the chair was dipped up & I fell backwards into the saltwater bath where the 'bears' were waiting for me & who dragged me the whole length of it, ducking me all the way!!

Of course I swallowed tons of water & felt rather sick when I escaped from the clutches of the 'bears' as I didn't spit the pill out quite quick enough & so had the taste of quinine in my mouth the rest of the forenoon, or rather until I had a couple of cocktails!!

I think Neptune's party & all the warrant officers are being dined in the wardroom tonight angel, anyway it sounds like it though I'm glad I'm out of it all as to enjoy those stunts one always has to drink a good deal & I just loathe that sweetheart; yes, I swear it, & you know it, not that I'm a pussyfoot, though you know that too!! I'm not such a hypocrite as to pretend that I haven't had spells of drinking too much beloved one, & guess I couldn't exactly pretend anything to YOU, though I'm your good little boy this trip after all you said to me before I sailed sweetheart & I feel ever so much better & much fitter too!! . . .

I weighed myself this evening 'starkers' & scaled 9st 4lbs. which pleased me as I was afraid I was more. I suppose I'm about 2 stone heavier than YOU darling, which puts me to shame, though a man always weighs more than a woman, though I am just a teeny bit taller than you angel!! . . .

18th April (11.00 P.M.)

Sunday today so church again but I wasn't bored as I've stuck a lot of odd snapshots of you into my prayerbook sweetheart & I felt oh! so sloppy & I did pray for US beloved though I'm so so terribly depressed just now . . . everything looks so inky black ahead of me; starting real hard work again in N.Z. & Australia, which I'm dreading more than I can say, & then there's that — — Indian etc. trip looming up which means another long & gloomy separation from you, beloved!!

I honestly don't think I can face another like this one without going quite mad; I honestly want to die as soon as we are together again though you know I've promised YOU not to use that little 6 shooter till we meet again, though Christ I long to tonight!!

It's desperately hot in my cabin, 90 degrees tonight & damp heat which is rather trying if one is feeling as hopelessly lost & lonely as I am!! . . .

Now I'm going to write something that I know I ought not to really & you'll say 'bloody impetuous short-sighted fool' when you read it!! But mon amour I swear I'll never never marry any other woman but YOU!!!!

I've been doing a hell of a lot of thinking this last month at sea angel & I'm quite quite decided!! Of course there are terrible obstacles for both of us; we know we are both 'up against it' & as I think it all over soberly it would be a d—d shame to even ask you to take on the job of wife to the P. of W. In fact I don't think I could ever summon up the courage to ask you to & I know you would hate it all as much as I should!!

It just would not be fair on you sweetheart though who knows how much longer this monarchy stunt is going to last or how much longer I'll be P. of W. I dread to think how you'll curse me for writing like this but I just can't help it as I love you so so desperately. It's doing me worlds of good getting this off my chest which I've had bottled up ever since our tragic parting . . .

I feel it stronger than ever the thought (I can almost say knowledge) that one day we really will belong to each other!! It's by far the most marvellous thought that could ever come to me & I'm nearly going mad just writing it down!! Oh! if only I could see YOU & talk to YOU . . . though I know you'll say 'why the hell didn't he say all this before when we were together?'

Well beloved I suppose I am rather a unique & hopeless sort of man & how I loathe myself for some of the terribly unkind things I've said & done to you unconsciously!! I could honestly shoot myself even for that alone, beloved, so ashamed am I!!

But as regards the marriage part I'm absolutely decided now, sweetie; YOU are now the one & only thing that matters to me in my life & it will always always be the same with me in the future!! I don't want to live & I'm not going to live if I can't live with YOU my sweet precious beloved darling little Fredie, my vewy vewy own lovely blessed little angel. I don't care a damn for the rest of the world which means absolutely nothing to me. Oh! how much better I do feel after all that sweetheart . . .

As I've told you Dickie & I have become very close friends & after all we are relations & he knows YOU & so means a great deal to me away from you. The result is that we are more or less inseparable & are in & out of each other's cabins all day (he's generally in mine) & when we sleep on deck our beds are always next to each other!!

Well, would you believe it sweetie, the rest of the staff have for this reason become jealous of him & object to him & have gone to the Admiral with a long list of what they consider his misdeeds!! Of course they don't mention a word about me & our being so intime but I've just had a long yarn with the Admiral who has just had a long talk to Dickie.

All this happened this afternoon & I'm furious about it all, though the Admiral was so human & sympathetic & understanding about it all as usual!! Dickie is so young & inexperienced (not 20 yet) & it's only natural that he should make a slip sometimes & he wants to be ticked off . . . Oh! why is it that anybody who gets involved with me or who I get to know & like suffers & must finally regret it all? I'm talking now of men sweetheart . . . [*Mountbatten alone, out of all the staff, called the Prince 'David', and was envied by the longer-serving members of the entourage because the Prince clearly preferred his company to theirs. Dudley North is reported to have chided Mountbatten for his informality with his cousin, telling him to remember, in company, that he was addressing the future King. Joey Legh, in his letters to Sarah, refers to Mountbatten as 'Dirty Dick' and 'the Hun', and says that 'The Boy' was ignorant of how much the rest of the staff detested Mountbatten.*]

Oh!! I could go on for ages about all this my beloved but I really must turn in now . . .

Bless you bless you forever my precious beloved little Fredie darling & God keep you for your ever devoted adoring little amoureux

ton David.

Suva, FIJI Is
20th April 1920 (11.00 P.M.)

N.B. As we've crossed 180th Meridian we've had to skip a whole 24 hrs. We've skipped Monday 19th so we call today 'Muesday'! . . .

22nd April (1.00 A.M.)

. . . It's been quite an interesting day with an official landing, inspection of returned soldiers both white & Fijian, a municipal stunt & schoolchildren to see . . . this afternoon we watched a 'Meke', a typically Fijian native stunt, in Government House grounds when several hundred natives dolled up in coloured grass danced & chanted weird songs or rather made queer noises & presented me with whales' teeth (ivory), grass mats etc. All very acceptable & I'll keep some of them for you beloved, not that they'll be of the least use as furniture or decoration, though they are quaint & original & it isn't everybody that goes to Fiji!!

Then I made Rodwell take me for a walk in the country above Suva . . . I did get hot all right, sweetie . . . I've never dripped before as I've done today as it's such damp heat . . .

I helped to fish for 1 hr last night off the bottom of the ladder near the light with a landing net & got some species of striped sea snake though North & several others caught some quite big fish on rods with live bait, 'Kabally' up to 12lbs!! But it's difficult to imagine me fishing

'Quite an interesting day.' Inspecting the Fijian guard of honour at the official landing.

at midnight, isn't it, beloved one, though it's a change from the ordinary routine!!

Bonne nuit Fredie darling   D.

At sea (11.00 P.M.)

. . . We've got 2 Digger officers on board as well as Tahu Rhodes (Grenadier Gds.), military secretary to Liverpool, G.G. [*Governor-General*] of New Zealand, who met us in Suva with programmes for the 2 tours & we've been discussing them today; Fredie darling they are going to do your little David in completely in N.Z. if not physically anyway mentally, & it's going to be worse than Canada, while I was so sure before I left you that it was going to be less strenuous. [*After the Prince's exhaustion in Canada, the authorities in both New Zealand and Australia were given guidelines for the preparation of the official programmes, which included no ceremonies before 10 a.m., three half-days a week for relaxation, and at least one public reception in each big city to enable the Prince to meet the people. The New Zealand visit had been planned as a rehearsal for the more important visit to Australia, but the programmes presented, especially in the former, ignored most of what had been requested. Lord Liverpool had passed a schedule which both Halsey and Godfrey Thomas thought impossible for the Prince to carry out and then be in a fit state for the Australian leg of the tour. Although frantic efforts were made to change the Australian programme, little could be done in the time available to improve the New Zealand schedule. Lord Liverpool was to be held responsible for most of the problems that arose in New Zealand and, later in the year, was replaced by Viscount Jellicoe, the former C-in-C of the Grand Fleet.*] The Australian programme is a trifle better though not much; no, I'm in for a real hard 4½ months sweetheart & being with my back against the wall I've got to work as I've never worked before!! If only I had the pep that I had last August, darling one, but I haven't, though I could do twice as well again if only I knew that India was postponed, which I fear it won't be now or I should have heard before!! . . .

It's no use my writing any more tonight as I feel so rotten so I'll turn in Fredie mine . . . Blessings D.

23rd April (1 1.00 P.M.)

. . . I went down to the wardroom after dinner, where we've been ragging & singing latrine songs, a very popular pastime in the senior service!! But I'm still oh! so desperately depressed beloved one which is a bad augury for landing at Auckland about noon tomorrow!! It makes it all seem ever so much worse feeling as sad & mouldy as I do & that old screw will have to be so tight to be of any use!!

I got a cable from Poots this afternoon to announce the birth of her son (my godson) sweetheart, though I'm sure you were the first to be told & aren't you godmother, angel? How I hope you are & I'm sure you are & I'm furious to think I can't attend the christening! But I told Sidney Greville to represent me before I left & send Poots my present for the child!!

Oh! Christ that makes me think & worry more than ever about —— well I needn't say, though how I long for news & wish it could happen!! But then that's selfish of me to say that beloved, & it's hardly fair on you!! Oh! but curse this separation . . .

It really is getting near the arrival of the mail bringing me your first letter so I can't help repeating how madly excited I'm getting about it . . . I know I've never looked forward to anything half as much before, except of course our sacred reunion . . .

A demain soir at Auckland when I'll have reached my —— destination & cabled you!! How I love you love you . . .

Your v v own little David.

New Zealand

❧

April 1920

New Zealand had been given Dominion status in 1907, but had remained firmly attached to Great Britain. A hundred thousand men had answered the call to arms and served overseas during the Great War. Over 16,000 of them had been killed, many in the disastrous Gallipoli campaign, where they had fought, with great courage, alongside the Australian contingent.

The Prime Minister, William Massey (who also held four other ministerial posts), led the Reform party, which had broken from its wartime coalition with the Liberals in 1919.

By 1920, New Zealand had developed into a rich agricultural economy, with vast areas having been turned into pasture land for cattle and sheep. Its economy had been helped by the building of the railway, but this, in turn, led to industrial problems, and the railway union was threatening to strike as the Prince's tour began.

Letter No 9
Government House, Auckland
25th April 1920 (1.00 A.M.)

My v v own precious darling beloved one,

Well, here we are arrived in New Zealand enfin sweetheart & it's really rather a relief to feel that one has at last 'struck bed rock' as regards the object of the whole trip, though the mere thought of the programme they insist on my carrying out is staggering . . . Christ only knows how far gone towards insanity we'll all be at the end of it when we go to Australia!!

However you'll hear more of all this in a day or 2 & perhaps I'll be able to send you a programme to show you how they are absolutely going to kill us all or anyway do their best to . . .

I've had a very good welcome here sweetie though such a trying day . . . I spent a bad 2 hrs driving round the city & receiving & answering the usual hot air addresses at various points!! We didn't get lunch here till about 3.00, where we are staying with the Liverpools who are both very trying indeed & make me tired!!

But you'll hear more of them later as well angel! At 4.00 I inspected a huge parade of returned men which took over 1 hr to do . . . like all those parades it left me rather a wreck as the mental strain is so great & I got back here with a bad head though I got rid of it by taking Aspirin & going to bed before dinner!! . . .

I've got to work hard beloved & I'm afraid I can't stick it in the same way as I could in Canada. Yesterday was a proof of this though the truth is I've never really recovered from Canada and never shall!! . . .

There's been a bit of a jazz party this evening . . . I was glad it was Saturday evening and the Governor General stopped it at midnight . . . the Admiral has been in my room saying exactly what he thinks of Liverpool, who is really the cause of the ghastly N.Z. programme; he is a proper ———— (4 letters darling one, you know what I mean!!) & no mistake & how he's lasted 7 years as G.G. I can't tell you!! . . .

(11.00 P.M.)

Sunday, the day of rest, sweetheart but oh! the irony of it all when I think all that I've had to do today!! Church at 11 oo lasting over 1 hr, then lunch here at 1 oo & I had to attend an Anzac Day returned men's service, a memorial service really, to commemorate the first day N.Z. troops went into action when they landed on Gallipoli on 25th April 1915!!

Quite a thrilling show if one hadn't been to church before though also trying angel as lots of the women were crying & it depressed me which was the last thing I wanted. From there I had to visit a returned soldiers' hospital where I found 100 men, mostly T.B. cases, & they are sordid too!! . . .

Massey, the Prime Minister, dined, otherwise merely the G.G.s & my staff . . . the Liverpools are the absolute limit, beloved one; he is too hopelessly pompous & impossible for words while she is so shy that she hardly ever utters & I've given up even trying to make conversation!! So she is the completest old 'dud' while he infuriates me so much that we just long to do him in somehow anyway to put him out of action till we've left N.Z.!! . . .

He won't let the Admiral see Massey & other N.Z. officials alone who would certainly ease up on the schedule if it wasn't for 'Liver' (as we call him) who rubs them all up the wrong way!! . . . It makes me so angry to have my job bitched by other people, darling, especially by hopeless ——'s like 'Liver'!!

But despite another hard day my morale is just a teeny bit higher as the crowds everywhere today couldn't have been more enthusiastic . . .

Dickie was so nice & sympathetic & encouraging during our walk before dinner . . . what an asset he is to this trip as besides meaning a lot to me as a man friend he takes over more important little items of staff work each day!! I really don't know how we would carry on without him though the rest of the staff don't appreciate & in fact refuse to recognise that he does anything as they are so jealous of his ability & charm!! . . .

Christ! what a terribly long way I am from you now sweetheart, over 10,000 miles . . . but I don't feel so far from England apart from YOU darling as the people here are so intensely English, more than the Canadians in some ways & certainly more than the Australians!!

They are amazingly respectful to the 'P. of W.' as well as delightfully natural & democratic to me & they always call me 'Digger', which is the highest compliment they can give me!! Do you remember how we used to rag Sheilie about the Diggers, though I don't think I'll get much respect in Australia, sweetie, anyway I'll be very surprised if I do!! . . .

26th April (11.00 P.M.)

Just returned from the Town Hall where I've had to shake hands with about 2,000 people though my right hand hasn't given out yet . . .

This afternoon I spent 2 hrs at the local races where I was fairly well mobbed though 'I asked for it' as I was strolling around between each race & there were a lot of returned men with their bits!! . . .

My only free time was from 5.30 to 8.00 when I took 'Liver' down to the ship to give him some squash as he is very keen & not too bad at it at all though I had him pretty cold as he is grossly fat. He has a large court at Government House, Wellington where I hope to give him hell next week!! . . .

New Zealand does seem quite the model dominion that one has always heard it to be & their loyalty is quite amazing . . . of course the Admiral has a great succès here & is very popular as he was captain of H.M.S. 'New Zealand' when she came out in 1913 to show the dominion their 'present' to the Empire; that's fine hot air!!!! . . . he's one in a million & he gets so shy when (as has already happened several times) they give 3 cheers for Halsey!! . . .

He is such a charming & sympathetic man though of course a bit old for me, though he's very young for his 48 years below the surface. He's really the only one of the staff (except Dickie) that I really talk to somehow; I could to Godfrey & Joey & have been talking to Godfrey a bit, though they are both, particularly Joey, rather hard to penetrate sometimes!! Of course Grigg & Claud are complete strangers except for work!! . . .

Christ!! how I long & pine for news of you after 6 —— weeks away from YOU angel; how I wish you could cable me just the one word 'Venus' darling one, & you know what that means in our code books!! . . . [*Mountbatten later used the same codeword on cables to his wife, Edwina, admitting he had copied it from the Prince, and that it stood for 'Missing you terribly'; in the Prince's code it meant 'I love you'.*]

Bless you bless you . . . your David loves you as no man has ever really loved before!! Love to the babies & to 'Peggy' who I hope has been behaving!!!!

Fredie my precious darling beloved

Just back from a desperate little party . . .

Gud! I'm tired again tonight Fredie darling though it's the same every night nowadays; quite a new phase sweetie & I'm worried about it as I so seldom got tired in Canada, where I was really far harder worked particularly as regards speeches!! However I think this new phase started a few weeks before I sailed, didn't it, beloved? I seem to remember being called 'Thleepy Head' . . . *[Joey Legh wrote that the Prince had made a poor impression compared to Canada, and did nothing but grouse, and that this would probably continue till he received a letter from Freda. On 27 April, the Prince had drunk more than he should have at dinner, and Halsey had to have a word with him.]*

'Stunting' in New Zealand. 'Talking to aged veteran', the Prince comments on the back of this picture . . .

. . . and with his entourage at Christchurch races on 15 May.

28th April (7.00 P.M.)

Today's stunts although terribly boring & irritating would anyway have been a little interesting if it hadn't poured in sheets till 3.00 P.M. . . . I had to go through long & tedious Maori ceremonies & had to submit to being made to look the most hopeless B.F. dolled up in mats while inane Maoris danced & made weird noises at me!!

Some of the Maori women sang & danced quite nicely though they spoilt their stunt by revolting me by kissing my hand when I shook hands with them all & 2 of the betas infuriated me by trying to kiss me. That was too much sweetheart & was the last straw & then my boredom changed into bloody-mindedness when they made me stand for a whole hour by a hot geyser to watch it blow off & it never did!! . . .

The railway strike is the main topic of conversation . . . I think they are using me & the upsetting of my tour as a weapon against the Government to try & force the premier's hand though old Massey won't soften!! . . . so we are all somewhat disorganised though we aren't caring or worrying much . . . of course Liverpool is more trying than ever on account of the strike & fusses more than any man I've ever known!! . . .

11.30 P.M.

. . . What a hopeless state the whole world is in just now & each day I long more & more to chuck this job & be out of it & free for YOU sweetie; the more I think of it all the more certain I am that really (though not on the surface yet awhile with Britishers) the day for Kings & Princes is past, monarchies are out-of-date though I know it's a rotten thing for me to say & sounds Bolshevik!!

But this railway strike which might become a general strike which completely upsets a so-called 'Royal Tour' (how I loathe that ——— expression) makes me do a lot of hard thinking angel & I really do feel rather helpless & bolshie tonight!! . . .

1st May (11.00 P.M.), H.M.S. 'Renown', Auckland

Well, here we are still on the ship at Auckland sweetheart, & till a few minutes ago we were sailing at 6.00 A.M. Now we've suddenly had a phone message from old Massey at Wellington to say the whole railway strike is off so that we are to resume our tour of the North Island tomorrow by train!!

What a life beloved one & we have been properly messed about & I'm furious & bloody-minded about everything though I'm glad we are able to carry on with the official tour as of course the places down to be visited spend quite a lot of money on various items such as entertainments, decorations etc. etc. & it's a shame to disappoint them however much I loathe it all!!

Meanwhile we have all these bloody women on board . . . & we've all had to turn out of our cabins for them which has 'fed' us more than anything else angel!!

I just loathe the thought of having to give up my cabin to anyone else but you & old Mrs Massey is sleeping in my bunk tonight & I'm camping out in the Admiral's day cabin!! Lady 'Liver' has Claud's cabin for special reasons (she objects to anyone passing through her cabin!!) . . . 'Their Ex's' & the rest of the 'refugees' came on board for dinner & it's been a painful job fixing them all up for the night . . .

I sign myself Bolshie David tonight!!

Letter No 11
4th May (1.00 A.M.) 'Imperial Hotel', Wanganui

Fredie my precious darling beloved,

. . . Such a pompous address beloved but it's really a miserable hole; no electric light & the hotel boilers elected to burst before dinner so no baths & a vewy nasty dinner!! But we are all pretty peeved tonight as we've really had a desperately twying day . . .

We first spent 1 hr at New Plymouth . . . then we had ½ hr stops at small places at 12.15, at 1.20 & again at 2.15 after a rush lunch . . . I slept for 1½ hrs and only woke up as we arrived so that I was half asleep during the big returned men's parade & was completely 'gaga' particularly when the men insisted on dragging the car off the ground!!

But we've had a bad evening too darling . . . 2 ghastly concerts and a civic supper party in a huge marquee where there were 3,000 people!! Oh! & I forgot a big school I had to visit after the parade!!

Christ! how dead I am beloved & no chance of rest till Saturday & to add to my troubles I have an important speech at Wellington at the official Government lunch on Thursday which Grigg hasn't even started in to write yet as he says he's fagged out & has no ideas!!

Of course that brute is going to let me down before we've finished angel & the Admiral & I have just been discussing it!! He's taken far too much on though we knew that in London in February at the time of the famous row when the P.M. was brought in!!

Oh! how difficult everything is my beloved little sweetheart, though how I loathe writing you all these grouses & moans & never anything cheerful; as a matter of fact today was very successful & the people couldn't have been nicer or more enthusiastic!! But somehow I don't get the same thrill from these crowds as I did in Canada though it always boils down to the same thing, darling, that I'm stale & that this programme is too strenuous for words!!

Luckily it's been fine today though it's much colder down here & I'm frozen as there's no heating in my room & I'm sitting huddled up in an overcoat!! . . .

(11.00 P.M.) Hawkes Bay Club, Napier

. . . We had a few local authorities to dinner & then had to attend a worse concert than either of the 2 terrible ones last night though I got one of the worst fits of giggles I've ever had which made it less sordid as not only were the performers very funny (unconsciously of course) but I found myself seated between the mayoress & deputy mayoress, both over 60, who never uttered!! But the whole staff were similarly convulsed as most of them had queer neighbours though I won!!

Grigg has at last produced some material for my big speech . . . but it's going to be a real hustle to get it up in time as I've got hell ahead of me tomorrow, 7 places to visit before I reach Wellington & so little spare time in the train in between . . .

But I'll be glad to get this —— speech off my chest & I've got the wind up worse than usual sweetie as I've got so little time to prepare it, though that's Grigg's fault, curse him!! . . .

5th May (11.00 P.M.) Government House, Wellington

. . . We had a marvellous welcome here in the capital of the Dominion & it took us 50 minutes to motor from the station to Government

House & the crowds were so dense that I had to stand up in the car the whole way!! It really was marvellous & for once I was gratified & felt quite the cheap little hero!! . . .

It's been a nice bright day & we managed to keep fairly cheery despite never 1 hr free from returned soldiers & schoolchildren!! Christ their cheers & 'God saves' & 'God blesses' get on my nerves . . . [*The 'God bless' was 'God bless the Prince of Wales', originally written in Welsh, and translated into English by George Linley.*]

8th May (1.00 A.M.)

You'll be getting so tired of my everlasting saying 'I've had another cruel day' sweetheart but I must say it as it's merely the truth & the only way of describing another 24 hrs of my present existence unless I added some bad language, which first of all you've forbidden in writing & which isn't effective unless you say it!!

I did get a good game of squash with that old —— 'Liver' & regret to say he beat me 3 out of 4 games though he's a fine player. But at noon the stunting began again . . . I really am feeling quite ill tonight as apart from being thoroughly worn out I've got a fearful cold & that is always very exhausting . . .

It is a real hard life this . . . I know I'll not last long at this P. of W. game, I just can't sweetheart & I'm so so miserably unhappy & despondent about everything just now!! . . . I know I'm a —— hard proposition & as I've so often said before I often wonder how you've managed to tolerate me for so long though that's the only thing that keeps me alive . . . you are probably having lunch now just as I'm going off to bed to try & sleep off this terrible fit of blues though I know I'll be worse instead of better when I wake up . . . I really think I've become a trifle mad.

9th May (1.00 A.M.)

. . . Dickie has been in my room as usual & he's been telling me lots of interesting things about the staff etc. . . .

Even Joey is rather hard but Grigg, Claud, & Dudley North are the worst offenders in this respect & according to Dickie say the foulest things behind my back!! Christ! how I loathe the first 2 named though Dudley is a good fellow really; but he's certainly become rather a courtier after nearly a whole year's contact with the P. of W. . . . but of course one can't collect a staff indiscriminately as I have without having one or two hostile members; of course if only the hostile members had any guts they would chuck their 'ands in on our return but they are far too big snobs to do that sweetie & it's hard for me to give them the sack though I long to drop Grigg & Claud!! . . .

H.M.S. 'Renown' (11.00 p.m.)

. . . I got a free afternoon & so was able to play squash again though I'm ashamed to say that absolutely revolting little man 'Liver' knocked me again though not badly.

We've just had a desperate official dinner party on board for 'Their Ex's' the Mayor & Mayoress & other notables of Wellington which was the absolute limit; I'm writing home to old H.M. by this mail & telling him all about Their Ex's & how unpopular they are out here & how they've done their best to bitch this tour; they really are too intolerable for words & besides being —— (4 letters!!) he's a liar & a cheat at any games, cards, golf & everything. And he's too pricelessly pompous for words. I could never tell you how much I loathe him & she is an old cat that —— Annette & such a deadly bore (no, not Dudley Ward!!) . . .

I shan't get another free day again . . . it is a rotten way of seeing a fine country like N.Z. & I shall have to quit without having seen any of the up-country life or anything that might be the least bit instructive!! Returned soldiers & shrieking people & schoolchildren are all that I shall remember of my visit beloved though I might add drunkinos as half the men are overflowing with Scotch at most of the places I've been to, celebrating my visit I suppose, though they don't worry me . . .

I'm leaving North & Claud behind so that they may get some of the deer stalking I've had to cut out on account of the railway strike, though I'm delighted to be quit of them for 2 or 3 days, though I've let Dickie go too which I regret selfishly as I'll miss him & his sympathy . . .

    ton David.

Letter No 12
Dawson's Hotel, Nelson (South Island)
11th May 1920 (1.00 A.M.)

My precious darling beloved little Fredie,

Well here endeth the first of 4 more terrible days jazzing round doing small places, only I've got down to the South Island now, though we are at the top or North end of it!! . . .

A most irritating day sweetheart . . . this is a terrible little hole though the people are exceptionally enthusiastic . . . there were the usual stunts for 1½ hrs & we've just returned from the most pricelessly funny party that one could imagine.

There wasn't a single woman who had the least idea how to dance, & the 'squeejee band' & the floor & everything . . . We stuck it out like heroes till the supper & tried to lug those wads of ham-faced women around although we were all feeling very weary & thoroughly peeved. But perhaps it's unkind to talk about these poor people's gallant efforts to entertain us in this way though we've been suffering under these ghastly sordid entertainments for over a fortnight now!! . . .

11.00 P.M., Grand Hotel, Reefton

This is a teeny place where we are stopping for the night; only 2,000 inhabitants, a mere village in the foothills of the mountains of the province of Nelson . . . We didn't get here till 7.30. We had the civic stunt & I shook hands with most of the inhabitants at 9.30 after some dinner so it's really been an easy day . . . we are more or less 'roughing' it as these little country hotels are far from comfy & vewy cold & there generally isn't any hot water & so no baths which doesn't exactly cheer us up . . . [*Mountbatten reported – although he was deer-stalking, so another member of the party must have related the episode to him – that the Prince had caused offence in Reefton when he did not attend a returned soldiers' dance, though the Prince makes no mention of it. As he was particularly careful not to cause offence to ex-soldiers, and also appreciated the trouble that people had gone to on his behalf, the diary may have misreported the problem encountered on 14 May.*]

We got a cable from the deer stalking party this evening; Dickie has shot a stag with my rifle which I lent him & Claud & 2 of the ship's officers have also killed one each!! I must say I envy them though of course I'm out here & away from you for work only so I don't really care a d—, though a little recreation occasionally does make a change . . .

12th May (11.30 P.M.), Keller's Hotel, Hokitika (Westland)

. . . I drove back from Westport myself in a Cadillac which is rather a come-down after the Rolls Cabriolet though it relieved the monotony of the return trip & it was quite a dangerous road to take on for the first time . . .

We've just escaped from another fearful one horse party where they had the most pricelessly funny old dances, lancers, quadrilles etc. . . . We did our best though the wretched women were too revolting for words; in fact it was a proper rustic or village crowd, though it's the 'milieu' we've been living in ever since Wellington . . .

14th May (2.00 A.M.), Christchurch Club, Christchurch

. . . We left Hokitaka & trained to Otira up in the mountains the Southern Alps where the railway ends . . . the southern Alps are being tunnelled from Otira to Arthur's Pass though the tunnel won't be completed for another 18 months; so we had to do that lap of the journey in a weird old coach . . . again the most marvellous cloudless day & the mountains looked fine, particularly Mt. Cook (12,500 ft) highest mountain in N.Z. . . .

We've been to quite a good private party tonight, beloved, given by the Rhodes' . . . hideous girls but the ½ dozen I struck all had some idea of dancing, which was a relief . . . but these N.Z. women really are too amazingly plain & unattractive for words sweetie & their powers of conversation nil . .

I may tell you that it hasn't all been so easy this past week on the West Coast as it's very Bolshie, though there were no incidents!! A few of the returned soldiers' leaders were rather truculent (though not the men themselves) & we had to be very tactful as of course the most important item of this trip are the returned men & all would be over if I got wrong with them!!

Then the Mayor of Christchurch [*Dr Thacker*] is an absolute wrong

'Schoolchildren's parade, Dunedin 19.5.20. (There's nothing to be thulky about!!)', the Prince's caption assured Freda.

The Empire's pin-up, May 1920.

'un & anything else bad one could think of calling him; he is being exceptionally truculent too though he's quite tame now that the Admiral has had a row with him, though he was foul this evening trying to pile a lot of extras on to the already overloaded programme for this city!! But then he's a socialist 'of the people, by the people, for the people' & worst of all he started talking politics & was most offensive!!

But of course the Admiral is marvellous at dealing with all these brutes . . . Grigg is too hopeless for words, in fact he is quite useless as soon as he puts his pen down though he does know how to use that . . . he's such a lazy brute as soon as there's any dull spadework to be done; he just clears off as he gets bored anywhere & gets more hopelessly inconsistent every day!! . . . Oh! how lost I shall feel in India without the Admiral if I have to go & he doesn't come too . . .

(11.30 P.M.)

Just back from a terrible 'citizen's ball' sweetheart, which charming entertainment consisted of shaking hands with 3,000 people, dancing in an official set of lancers with the Mayoress & then taking her into supper!! It was all a great strain . . .

But it's been quite a successful day angel despite the bloody mayor Dr Thacker having tried to put us wrong with the returned men (by telling them I would go to a dance which they had organized for the men of the 'Renown' tomorrow night, when we had refused a whole fortnight ago). 6,700 of them turned up & I shook hands with all of them & said a few words afterwards, so I haven't done badly in the shaking hands line today, have I, my beloved?

The Admiral & some of the others are turning out at 4.00 A.M. to shoot duck before the races tomorrow but not your little boy, sweetie!! Dickie & the stalking party rejoined us this morning & I'm glad to get him back again & I think he is quite pleased to see me again as they are all inclined to treat him like dirt except me!! . . .

ton David.

Letter No 13
Fern Hill Club (the name seems familiar somehow!!), Dunedin
18th May 1920 (7.00 P.M.)

Fredie darling darling precious beloved à moi,

. . . Oh! how I've been shrieked & yelled at this afternoon till I could cry, sweetheart, though I know it's ungrateful & rotten to talk like this; I've had a marvellous welcome here as everywhere, though I'm so stale & tired now beloved, though can you be surprised? But I've only got 2 more days' stunting in N.Z. now & there's above all things the mail & then a day's hunting to look forward to on Friday!! . . .

But how I'm counting the minutes & almost seconds till I get the mail, my beloved; I'll hardly be able to believe my eyes when I do see your sweet & marvellous handwriting Fredie darling though I'm so so sad you've never cabled even just once!!

19th May (12.30 A.M.)

It's been a terrible evening my beloved as there were 10,000 people at the citizens' concert & I had to say a few words to the multitude which

was a great strain!! . . . I'm only just scribbling you a few lines as I've
promised to play golf with the Admiral at 8.00 A.M., our only chance of
a round as we start stunting at 11.30!! So I'll never be able to see the
ball unless I turn in right now beloved . . .

20th May (1.00 A.M.)

. . . I'm dead tonight sweetheart as I did play 18 holes of golf with the
Admiral from 8.15 to 10.45 though we had 2 hrs stunting before
lunch . . . I really think that Dunedin is the most enthusiastic city of
all in N.Z. though they have worked me here, angel!! There was the
usual sordid dinner to which I had to invite the usual 4 local boring old
men as I do each night & then another 10,000 people, concert & a few
more words, though it was easier as it was mostly returned men &
their families & then lots of next of kin, which is always sordid &
pathetic! . . .

It will be such a huge relief to get back to the ship at Lyttelton on
Friday evening & feel that the N.Z. tour is over!! And there'll be no
holding me that night, sweetie, if I've had a letter or letters from YOU &
on top of it or them there's a decent hunt . . . But I mustn't build
'castles in the air', Fredie darling, or I'll come a bad crash & get more
hopelessly miserable than ever, though I've got into a state of perpetual
misery & unhappiness now angel so so far away from YOU . . .

21st May (12.30 A.M.), In the train Invercargill to Christchurch

Fredie darling darling beloved,
    My intense great joy knows absolutely no bounds tonight sweetheart
as we've just stopped at a wee station & taken in a mail & it contained
your No 3 letter!! Bless you bless you for it my angel & I'm oh! so so
happy & relieved tonight & feel more my old self again . . .
    How madly thrilled I was when my servant brought me my letters &
yours was on top; besides my family & Mary, Bertie, Philip & Sidney
Greville have written though of course I haven't even opened
them!! . . . Oh!! bless you & thank you my beloved amour for making
your petit amoureux so so happy & saying you love him; please say that
in every letter as I do so often in mine sweetheart & believe that my
intense & devoted & all absorbing love for YOU increases every moment

of my life! You come before everything else & you are always going to, my sweetheart mine.

Am dropping off to sleep so bless you again & bonne nuit sweetie D.

22nd May (1.00 A.M.), H.M.S. 'Renown', Lyttelton, N.Z.

I'm absolutely overwhelmed & quite silly tonight as on top of everything else I found 2 more sweet divine marvellous letters (nos 1 & 2) waiting for me in my cabin . . . I've only just glanced at them my beloved as I'm leaving reading them properly till I turn in!! . . .

As for today (or rather yesterday) we reached Christchurch at 9.00 A.M. & Tahu Rhodes took me to his house to change into riding clothes for hunting & we motored to the meet of the Chch Hounds or rather harriers as there are only hares to hunt!! But we had 3½ hrs of the best fun to be got out of riding & we were 'lepping' the whole time!!

We had a fast 20 minute hunt to start with & killed, & though they didn't kill again hounds were running the whole time!! I was lent a perfect little wire-jumping mare as every fence is wired & we had to take on ½ dozen plain strand wire fences, which is really a very dangerous game & put the wind up me properly at first sweetie, though I never shirked one & rode hard & kept at the top of the hunt all right!!

Please forgive all this about one day's N.Z. hunting though you know how I enjoy it & how it's rather my stunt & I think I did manage to impress some of the hard-bitten crowd with my riding . . . what really made me enjoy it all so much was having your 3rd letter in my pocket; I just don't care a curse for anything or anybody now!! . . .

I was the only one of the whole 'royal outfit' to hunt . . . They are a soft crowd; Dickie was there but in a car with some bits (he's lost a bit of his large heart to a girl in Chch) . . .

Oh!! Oh!! Fredie darling darling I rode hard for your sake & nothing else as I knew you would want me to make a good show which (pompously) I think I did, though I did cut 2 'voluntaries' in the first hunt . . .

(11.00 P.M.), At sea

. . . I was on the bridge with the Admiral when we left Lyttelton
though alas it came on to blow hard after tea & we are now in a gale
with a heavy sea running & your poor little boy feels so ill, too ill to
write much, though he longs to write & write as he's so much to tell
you & discuss with you . . .

So my morale is low tonight sweetie though there wouldn't be any
morale at all if it wasn't for YOU . . . YOU are more my all & everything
in life than ever & there's not a single thing that I wouldn't do for you
my beloved including die for you!! Doing things for YOU is my only
pleasure in life . . .

Christ! how I loathe & despise my bloody family as Bertie has
written me 3 long sad letters in which he tells me he's been getting it
in the neck about his friendship with poor little Sheilie & that TOI et
MOI came in for it too!! But if H.M. thinks he's going to alter me by
insulting you he's making just about the biggest mistake of his silly
useless life; all he has done is to infuriate me & make me despise him &
put me completely against him & I'll never forgive him for insulting
you as he has!!

God! damn him! though in a way he's done me good sweetheart by
his extra display of foulness to Bertie & me as it's cured me of any
weakness that was left in me!! Christ! I'll be firm with him when I get
back & tell him to go to hell & leave me alone as regards my friends;
I'll have whatever friends I wish & what is more I won't have them
insulted or I'll bloody well insult him!!

What a tirade Fredie, but words could never describe my hatred &
contempt for my father tonight & it's going to be lasting, though I
won't tire myself over it as he really is such a negligeable quantity & as
you say he can't do anything to me!!

Poor old Bertie seems to be having rather a warm time just now
though I'll discuss him later; I only hope to God he'll keep his head for
our sakes, yours & mine sweetie!! . . .

All all my on top & deep down love & then all my baisers

YOUR David.

Letter No 14
HMS RENOWN
23rd May 1920 (10.00 P.M.)
At sea Lyttelton (N.Z.) to Melbourne (Australia)

Fredie darling darling precious beloved angel,

I did succumb to sea sickness last night sweetheart & though I did turn out for a short time during the forenoon the mere mention of the word lunch drove me back to bed again where I've been ever since, though 3 hrs sleep this afternoon did me good!! But the ship has been knocking about a lot all day & is still though the gale didn't last long!!

But it's bad luck getting this weather just now when I was so utterly exhausted & wanted 4 days' peace before starting in stunting again at Melbourne on Wednesday 26th. And I've got such a phenomenal amount to do in the writing line, vewy important things to tell H.M., important to YOU too my beloved & then there's Bertie & Philip & 2 or 3 speeches to prepare, & I'm not at all in good shape & my brain won't function; all I'm capable of is writing to you my sweetie as that doesn't tax my brain at all as it's always thinking only of YOU & so I'm able to write down just what my brain dictates without having to ask it to work!! In fact writing to you is so so restful besides being such a joy I just don't know where to start Fredie darling.

First of all I hate to think of you travelling through France & Italy without me, beloved, for all those dirty little Frenchmen & unspeakable & revolting Dagoes to gaze & fall in love with as I know hundreds of them must have, in fact all who saw you!! And what I think of missing seeing you spitting in all their faces bless you. I'm just longing to hear all about Rome though how I loathe that Dago city for the misunderstanding to which you refer!! It's 2 years ago almost to the day that I spent that week there & may I never go there or to Italy again anyway without you, and even if you wanted to go I think I would try to dissuade you sweetie; you see I know Italians fairly well after a whole year in their land!

As regards Paris it's somehow different because it's unique just as London and New York are, & I used to love Paris too when I was 'jeune homme'. I've never been there as a 'married man' which despite all you are sweet enough to say, angel, I feel I am more than any man could feel!! The shops must all be terribly tempting & it must have been a hard fight to keep your head darling knowing you as I do though how I wish that if you did go a bust there you would let it (or any way part of it) be my birthday present for 28th July!! Surely you will allow me just that one pleasure so so far away from YOU sweetheart, when you know the joy it brings me to give you little things you want sometimes!!

I quite understand why you've never cabled & I was a B.F. to send all mine from the beach, though I hope you'll cable to the ship after my last cable from Lyttelton!! I don't care a —— who sees yours to me sweetie; as they would probably be in code they couldn't get anything out of them!! I promise you beloved that all that idiotic self-consciousness & shyness that I used to feel about YOU for some still unknown reason has long disappeared, though you used to feel a little the same about me didn't you angel?

Perhaps in a way it was only natural at first & then you know how I was brought up & the poor miserable weak little baby I was when we first met over 2 years ago!! And I would be just the same still if it hadn't been for you sweetheart to give me strength & bring me out as I know you have!! But now I'm being pompous though I think you like me to try & be a little pompous sometimes. But now I'm wandering!!

That bloody London Mail [*weekly magazine*] & did you see another hit at us which Sarah sent Joey & which I enclose? But what do we care for the London Mail or any other filthy rag? They all write such balls that they aren't worth reading though sometimes they are amusing!!

There's still a big swell though the wind has gone, but here's to hoping it will die down tomorrow if we don't get another blow. We are in the Tasman Sea which is noted for bad weather, as all the Australasian seas seem to be, so that it's a bad omen for the next 3 sea trips which are part of the Australian programme, though what I think & how I shrink from & dread the mere mention of the word programme or schedule as they call it in Canada!!

It's all such a nightmare just now & ever will be sweetheart as I'm too stale to ever really recover again!! But goodnight now & bless YOU bless YOU!! D.

24th May (6.00 P.M.)

The sea has gone down a lot though I stayed in bed for lunch & only got up to play squash at 3.00 P.M. though I feel all the better for it sweetheart & am more or less myself again this evening, though not quite; & then I've been discussing India all day with the Admiral & Godfrey who are both all out to get the Indian trip postponed. The Admiral is writing a marvellous letter to H.M. putting my case very strongly & appealing to him!!

   The gist of his letter is pointing out that a fellow of 26 can't go on leading an abnormal life (such as these official trips entail) for ever & that it isn't fair to ask me to take on 7 more abnormal official months in India & the Far East within 1 month of my return from this abnormal 7 months' trip. And the Admiral does more than agree with all you say against my being mixed up with all these political reforms sweetheart; in fact he volunteered it all & then I had to tell him that it was YOU who had written it to me beloved & he was so impressed!! [*The Prince's trip to India was planned to coincide with the setting-up of a new constitution. Several of the provincial governors in India thought the proposed visit ill-timed, as the situation was tricky enough without the added complication of the Prince's presence. George V, however, had decreed that the tour should go ahead, and did not want to change it.*]

   I'm longing for Philip's next letter to know what the P.M. thinks about it all now & with any luck we'll find another mail awaiting us at Melbourne!! I'm sorry the P.M. wasn't more impressed with Bertie; must have been one of his 'off days' or something as I'm sure he would do well in India, sweetie, where it's all apparently so pompous as he's rather pompous himself!!

   But what the Admiral & I are aiming for (though much against my own personal feelings, darling) is to do South Africa on our way home either direct from Australia or after the West Indies in September as that would prevent anyone saying I returned in October, & so had plenty of time to go to India. By doing South Africa I'll alas delay my return nearly 3 months, though it would make India out of the question until October 1921!!

   Then I'll get 8 months in England which will mean 8 months more or less together; oh! just think of the joy of the mere thought of it baby

darling though 3 extra months added to our 7 months separation is an
equally ghastly sordid & depressing one!!

But this is all 'castles in the air' as we haven't even written all the
letters yet & I don't suppose H.M. will listen to our appeals; however
here's to hoping, sweetie, though I needn't rub in how frightfully secret
all this is, though none of the staff except Godfrey know that the
Admiral & I are writing!!

Now as regards old Bertie & Sheilie; B. talks a lot of hot air about
H.M. making him a duke on condition that his name ceases to be more
or less coupled with Sheilie's though it certainly need not have been
ever since January anyway – if not earlier!!

You & I both happen to know that they neither of them really mean
anything to each other at all, do they sweetheart? & never will (not
[*that?*] they ever have) so that personally I'm all for their really
breaking apart properly & cutting out the camouflage love stunt!!

From what he tells me S. & L. [*Sheila and Loughie*] are living on top
of a hotter volcano than ever & anyone in love with her is sitting on top
with them!! We both of us know she really loves Ob so surely it would
be better for Bertie to drift away from it all & just be one of Sheilie's
friends, like Ali!!

Oh!! I'm so hopeless at expressing all I want to say on paper
Fredie darling & I don't know what you'll think of all I've written
but we've discussed 'the other 2 Do's' so often recently & I think we
came to this conclusion though I've naturally kept Sheilie's secret re
Ob so so faithfully & Bertie knows absolutely nothing & never will
from me!!

It is so hopeless trying to discuss letters 6 weeks old & Bertie may be
a Duke now for all I know as I think that his rather pompous nature
makes him want to be one. Of course if he really loved Sheilie he
wouldn't care a d— about dukes or anything else; but the point is that
he doesn't really love her & she loves him less so that I would strongly
advise him to quit the top of the Loughborough volcano as fast as he
can if it's as hot as he says it is!! [*Prince Albert became Duke of York on 5
June 1920. A much-reproduced letter from George V tells him that he has
behaved well in a difficult situation for a young man, having done what the
King asked of him: what the King had asked was not generally known,
however. In late May or early June – biographers disagree on the exact date –*

Prince Albert attended a dinner party given by Lady Farquhar, at which he met Elizabeth Bowes Lyon, who became his wife in 1923.]

But perhaps it isn't, beloved, as you've never said a word about it yet, though apparently it's all carried on from the last weekend row at Trent!! But you haven't felt comfy having either Ob or Bertie in your house for Sheilie to play with lately & I'm not surprised, so I don't feel I'm on a new line of thought!!

If only YOU could talk to Bertie sweetheart & warn him against being too thick with Sheilie, though it seems a hard thing to ask you to do when we know that they can be so happy together in their own way!! But what I mean is that there's no thrill about it for either of them, without which any sort of trouble with that — Loughie just isn't worth the candle!!

Do talk to B. Fredie darling, as I know he would listen to you. And I feel that it would help TOI et MOI so much beloved as we've long felt the weight of them on our hands & it's been growing heavier anyway for you whose house they invariably use for their — —, well shall we call them 'causeries'!! They've often been a — — nuisance and vewy much in the way, haven't they darling, & yet you are so fond of them both as I am that you've risked it often!!

Do you know that I've a funny feeling that I know Sheilie better than Bertie does really & that she's more fond of me & would do more for me than she would for him?!! That's a good one isn't it, sweetie? but I wonder if you'll agree or just be 'thulky'! (no! of course I'm only wagging). So as there's really nothing entre S. & B. I can't see why they can't agree to just be great friends but as I've said before cut out the love stunt!!

Oh! if only I could talk to you about it all sweetheart though I've really written nothing that we haven't already discussed & agreed upon, in fact you opened my eyes about the other 2 Do's!! But my point is that while my family (who Bertie seems to be up against) regard TOI et MOI & 'the other 2 Do's' in the same light we are really so so utterly & entirely different, aren't we, beloved?

But Fredie darling darling of my heart what I want to rub in (I say rub in because you already know it) is that whatever Bertie does or says about Sheilie has absolutely nothing whatsoever to do with your vewy vewy own little David who loves you loves you as he's never never loved or will ever love again!! No — — Kings or Queens or newspapers or anybody or anything can ever stop him doing that or being with YOU & seeing YOU as much as he possibly can!!

I'm never going to stick any more rot about YOU and least of all insults my precious sweetheart & YOU will continue to be the greatest friend & all & everything to me in this world as long as you are sweet & divine enough to care to carry on with it!!

Christ! what reams I've written bless you & it's all so incoherent that I fear you won't be able to understand much of it; but I had to get all this off the chest in case you should be in any doubt if Bertie should do (or even has done) anything, not that I really imagine you ever would be sweetheart!! But I know you like me to write like this.

25th May (11.00 P.M.)

I'm later than I meant to be tonight sweetheart as the gunroom insisted on my going down below to them after dinner & we've been ragging & making a bloody noise down there; in fact I left them all getting rather tight and breaking up everything doing Maori 'hakas' (native dances)!! . . .

How I'm dreading landing at Melbourne tomorrow, my beloved; I haven't had anything like a long enough stand-easy from 'stunting' & being yelled at & don't feel at all strong & Melbourne is a huge city to take on!! . . .

How I wonder what you'll think of all I wrote about Sheilie & Bertie last night though I'm sure you'll agree with it all . . . You see I'm selfish sweetie & look on it all from our point of view & am so so anxious that they or anybody shouldn't embroil us, not that anybody could, though we want to keep clear of other people's troubles . . . We've both of us got quite enough troubles of our own without that.

The other thing I wanted to tell you about & which I vaguely mentioned in my letter was that if I do have to go to India I insist that the Admiral shall come again as Chief of Staff & he's kind enough to say he is willing to stick to me & see me through another of these official tours (the 3rd)!!

Of course you know I've more or less asked Cromer to come as C. of S. but I can't help it if I·do hurt his feelings & say he can't be C. of S. as

I must have the Admiral!! What I want is to keep Cromer & let him replace Grigg, who I refuse ever to take overseas with me again!! [*In fact, Cromer would be the Prince's Chief of Staff in India, replacing Grigg, although Halsey went too.*]

I'll explain why another time though I told you all about the row in February & what a dirty crooked brute he showed himself to be. Well that ought to be enough & I loathed taking him on this trip, though there was no alternative as he got round the P.M. before I really knew the latter & the —— is very uscful with his pen!!

But he's the limit now & too impossible for words and it's one long fight for the Admiral & me sweetheart though we've made up our minds not to really quarrel with him!! . . .

Australia

∽

May–August 1920

Australia had become a Commonwealth in 1901, when the six former colonies, now called states, joined together in a Federation.

Australia traditionally possessed the most left-wing, militant and republican working class in the Empire, so the Prince's party looked upon the tour with some trepidation.

The Prime Minister, W.M. 'Billy' Hughes, had upset his Labour colleagues in 1916, when he had formed a national government. He was re-elected convincingly in December 1919, but economic problems were causing widespread labour unrest.

The seat of the Parliament was in Melbourne, but plans were already underway to build a new federal capital of Australia, at Canberra.

27th May (2.00 A.M.)
Federal Government House, Melbourne

Well, here we are arrived in Australia sweetheart & oh! Fredie darling beloved the joy of receiving another mail & with it your No 4 letter from Rome!! Oh!! I'm so so happy & in such good shape tonight although worn out & so windy about everything somehow sweetie; there's been a huge party here tonight which wasn't such a bad stunt as these Australian women do seem to be able to dance a bit & I took quite a lot of exercise tonight, particularly after Dickie had handed me

Inspecting the guard with Governor-General Ferguson after the official landing in Melbourne.

a fat envelope from YOU!! There was no holding me then & I cut a dance & dashed into a faraway room to open that divine fat envelope & just peer into it & read the end which comforted me so sweetheart!! . . .

Today or rather yesterday was a proper old hustle as we got befogged in the 'Renown' about 8.00 A.M. off the Heads or entrance to Port Philip (the harbour of Melbourne) & we had to anchor out there. As my official landing had been timed for 2.00 P.M. & the ship couldn't move till 3.00 on account of tide we got a Royal Australian Navy destroyer out about noon when the fog lifted & came in & landed from her!!

Of course I was furious about not being able to land properly in the ship though the destroyer stunt went down quite well!! So we were only 1 hr late & we landed at 3.00 P.M. but oh!! Fredie darling no words of mine could ever describe to you the pompousness & state of my landing or of my first official progress through this city (the capital) to this 'palace'!! Vast carriages drawn by 4 horses were provided for us & after being received by Ferguson (the G.G.) [*Ronald Munro-Ferguson, later 1st Viscount Novar*] & Hughes (the P.M.) & hundreds of other bearded old men we drove solemnly for 2 hrs through the streets in cocked hats till I thought I would die!! I was livid although I had been warned of the carriage stunt, though I just couldn't have been more furious with everybody & everything except the Admiral!!

The people gave me a most marvellous welcome though how could I appreciate it or look as if I did under such conditions, dolled up in a state carriage escorted by cavalry & police & God knows what else!! Of course there were any number of tight returned men who most of them tried to jump into the barouche [*carriage*] in their efforts to do in that unfortunate right hand of mine, which, I'm afraid I've never told you, sweetie, struck again as early on as Auckland!! But it really was a marvellous show & there were over ½ million people in the streets; if only I had been in a car as usual. [*Mountbatten recorded that the official estimate was three-quarters of a million people, more than the entire population of Melbourne, as so many people had come in from outlying areas to see the Prince.*]

I've already told you I've got the wind up tonight my beloved though it's really this —— speech this evening & it's important as it's addressing the Commonwealth Government, but then that's nothing new!! I really must get down to it again & can't turn in till I've copied it out a 2nd time which means I can't read your letter till I've done it!! That is to be the reward for my labours & there couldn't be a more marvellous one . . .

The 'pompous official drive', as the Prince's caption described it, through Melbourne.

This ghastly existence of mine really seems to get more intolerably strenuous & difficult each day Fredie darling . . .

I just don't see how I'm going to avoid a nervous breakdown my beloved one, & what makes me more unhappy than anything else is that I know this eternal strain is ageing me prematurely darling which is the very last I should have said was desirable for ME, when being & keeping young is my only weapon or tool or whatever you like to call it!! . . .

11.00 p.m.

Just back from the Commonwealth dinner sweetheart & it's a relief to have got that speech off the chest which was a reply to Hughes' & I think it went down fairly well!! Great crowds in the streets tonight though it was the first time I had been outside Government House since my arrival yesterday . . .

I slipped out this afternoon with Godfrey for a short game of squash . . . Of course you'll think me mad to try & play squash when the programme is so impossible, sweetie, but I can never tell you what a help it is to be able to hit something like a squash ball & hit it hard, besides the getting hot part which prevents me getting soft . . .

But bless you bless you more than ever for No 4 letter . . . Yes I remember your telling me about that —— Yank Channon who had joined the barrage, though how dare he pester you again, & then how right I was when I wrote 2 or 3 nights ago about the Dagoes falling in love with you beloved one. But how happy it makes me when you say they nauseate you darling . . . [*'Channon' was Henry 'Chips' Channon, an American who fell in love with England, married Honor Guinness, the daughter of the Earl of Iveagh, and whose published diaries of the 1930s are an informative commentary on the times.*]

29th May (3.00 A.M.)

What an hour, but we've all been to a private party tonight mon amour though didn't get there till after midnight & it was miles from here in the 'Clapham' or 'Balham' of Melbourne . . .I'm too dead beat to be able to give you any account of the day though you'll get it in the diary & I'm afraid I'll have to condense my letters more in these big cities angel as I can't compete with life any more!!

I think I've put up quite a good fight against it but I'm afraid I'm beaten!! Enough to tell you darling that I left here at 10.00 A.M. & only returned for ½ hr at 6.15 P.M. & it's past 3.00 A.M. now, though I suppose the 3.00 A.M. touch is really my fault!! . . .

Of course I can never begin to tell you what the word 'driving' through this city means sweetie; it's far more overwhelming than anything in Canada or that I've ever struck before, though I'm not saying that the people are really more enthusiastic!! Only their street demonstrations are so much rougher & the Admiral & I really do get hell in the first car . . . [*Confetti was thrown in great quantities, and the Melbourne crowds developed a 'touching mania', although the touches were more like blows.*]

The people have all gone quite crazy in this city sweetheart & though no-one could possibly not appreciate their marvellously kind enthusiasm yet we are getting rather tired of being held up in the streets every time we drive through & made as much as one whole hour late for everything sometimes!! And these drives are becoming so dangerous, not for me angel but for the crowds, more than ½ of which are women with masses of tight returned men around!!

I feel I'm becoming a bit pompous now sweetie though I only wish I could tell you properly what marvellous welcomes I've had from 'le peuple' here in Melbourne, which is full of Bolshies, as are all Australian cities or anyway very very Labour!! If only I wasn't so hopelessly worn out I would be so much more touched & appreciative darling as it all really is a marvellous demonstration of loyalty . . . [*At the 'popular reception' it was estimated that 20,000 people filed past the Prince in two hours; over 100 people fainted, and three had to be taken to hospital, such was the crush.*]

30th May (1.00 A.M.)

. . . I was so dead last night my beloved that I forgot to tell you I met a Mrs Armitage at the private party who was Pamela Tustin & was engaged to your cousin who was killed in the R.A.F.!! She suddenly asked if I knew you sweetie & I was so thrilled & we talked about you a little though I'm sure she hasn't seen you since we met in February 1918 & from all she says I gather that she broke off the engagement just before your cousin crashed & had a row with your uncle & you probably hate her!! Still that's only my surmise . . . she asked after 'that bloody Violet' too, so she evidently does know your family a bit!! . . . How small the world is!!

Christ! I'm becoming such a wreck & I'm afraid I'm beginning to look it now as I'm always hearing 'Oh! isn't he tired' muttered in the crowds, though I like that, angel, & am glad a few of them do realise what a fearful existence this is with never a moment to oneself till after midnight!! . . .

I'm so stale that I've just ceased to worry now & just drift along from minute to minute & hardly ever look at the programme & often haven't the least idea where I'm going . . . Thank God! there is a squash court without which I know I would become a raving madman!!

11.30 P.M.

As usual my first chance of putting pen to paper sweetheart & yet it's Sunday & the programme says I've had a free afternoon!!

Of course there was —— church followed by facing 50 photographers here planting a tree then a rush lunch before Billy Hughes (the premier) motored me out to some hilly bush country where we rode for 2 hrs . . . then he took me back to his house where I dined with him & Mrs Hughes . . .

I didn't get back here till 9.00 P.M. & I found that Their Ex's had asked a dozen girls in to amuse me which was the very last thing I wanted as I hadn't had a moment to myself all day!! However I did the best I could to be sociable & I tried to dance to a gramophone but it all fell vewy flat though the whole stunt was well meant!!

The women here can dance, though Christ how they bore me & there's only one who could be called pretty & she's the biggest boob of the bunch!! But then Fredie darling you know perfectly well that you've spoilt me for ever as regards women & I just can't look at any of them . . . it's the very best thing that could be as there's no possible chance of my name being really coupled with any other woman's which would just be more than I could bear angel!! . . .

Grigg & Dickie were with me this afternoon & I'm a little cheered as 2 girls (both very plain, angel!!!) who met us where we mounted the horses gave me a baby 'wallaby' (small species of kangaroo) which we brought back & which is such a sweet little animal & is only 2 months old!!

He's asleep on my bed now sweetie though I'm afraid he'll have grown a lot before you see him if we can ever get him back alive!! If only he would remain tiny as he is now so as one can hold him in one's arms . . . Dickie has gone crazy about him & he & I are going to keep him all to ourselves & not let any of the staff have anything to do with him. We've appropriately christened him 'Digger'!!

Tomorrow is 4th anniversary of Jutland & I've got to take the salute at a naval march past here (luckily here) at 9.30 A.M. which will shake me some . . .

1st June (2.00 A.M.)

I'm far more dead than alive tonight sweetheart so can only just scribble a few lines to say I love you love you + qu'hier mais – que demain as you wrote in my cigarette case my beloved!! How I love & hold on to all our precious little sayings sweetie!! . . .

I got through the naval parade all right at 9.30 A.M. . . . it was a fearful strain trying to address over 1,000 men at that hour & I've lost my voice, though not badly . . .

I did have the rest of the forenoon free & played squash though I was stunting again at 1.30; first a huge but marvellous schoolchildren's demonstration followed by a visit to 800 badly wounded men at a hospital, which entailed miles of 'driving' & there were addresses en route!!

Then ½ hr to change & I attended a naval Jutland dinner . . . I was at a vast 'smoke night' for returned men at 8.30 whom I had to address . . . the hospital ball at the Town Hall which followed was a worse bullfight than on Saturday night & I was almost killed in my efforts to dance with the Lady Mayoress!!

On top of it all I was fool enough to go on to a private party about 11.00 which some nice people had well-meaningly & kindly organised for me & of course we had to go though it was silly. But isn't that a staggering day Fredie darling . . . Of course the squash & the private party were both my own fault sweetie. I know from experience & you understand that I can't carry on without some relaxation!! . . . Of course I've been like a man in a trance all tonight angel . . .

2nd June (2.00 A.M.), Glenormiston, Victoria

Aren't I just too hopeless for words sweetie sitting up dancing again till this idiotic hour . . . there was quite a decent band . . . & Dickie & I spent most of the time playing the 'jazz traps' for the band!! It became quite a cheery evening . . .

It was an easy day compared to Melbourne . . . a very luxurious train & only 4 places to visit . . . we are staying with a charming middle-aged couple called Black; I don't know much about them but they seem to be prominent landowners . . . I feel quite homesick tonight sweetie as it is all so English here, though I should say Fredie sick!! . . .

But my most exciting news my beloved is that on account of not only ME but the Admiral & most of the staff having had such a strenuous 6 weeks stunting (N.Z. & Victoria State) we are postponing our departure from Melbourne a whole week which will merely mean postponing the whole programme a week without cutting out any place or item at all!!

But we came to the conclusion last night that we just couldn't carry on at this rate & yet last through the remaining 2 months of the tour, particularly as the Fergusons & many others urged this scheme!! We've left Grigg behind in Melbourne to see Hughes (the P.M.) etc. & we've been phoning him the whole evening & hear that all is well & the G.G. is making an announcement in the press!!

So we'll stay on here all next week angel free of all public engagements; what I would call a holiday if YOU were here & we could spend next week together Fredie darling darling!! But this will give us all the breather we all want so terribly badly . . .

I'm not the least bit ill sweetie, in fact vewy fit physically but mentally I'm utterly worn out; of course I could carry on if I wasn't going on immediately to Sydney, which will be far more strenuous than it's been here!! But as it's a case of tackling the biggest city of all next week I just can't look at it anyway as regards making the visit a success!!

But I'm not going in for a rest cure by any means angel, as you know

I don't want that & I would go mad; all I want to do is lead even a semi-normal life for a week with lots of sleep (midnight to 1.00 A.M. sort of time) lots of exercise & above all comparative freedom, not being tied down to that eternal & wearing schedule which is slowly killing us!! . . . But anyway I hope to feel less gaga than I do now though I really am 'N.B.G.' at present!! . . .

2nd June (11.30 P.M.), Federal Government House, Melbourne

We arrived back about 7.00 P.M. after all day in the train . . . The Fergusons are really charming people & such a contrast to the Liverpools, though he (the G.G.) sent such a silly cable to H.M. last night while I was away & my family now have the wind up about me, though I've now cabled myself to make it all right!! . . .

I love you love you YOUR David.

'Digger' the baby Wallaby sends his love to 'Peggy'. Also love from Dickie!!

Letter No 15
Government House, Melbourne
3rd June 1920 (6.00 P.M.)

Fredie darling darling precious beloved à moi,

The mail has gone sweetheart though I must anyway just begin my next letter . . . I feel more or less at home in Australia now; at least I feel I understand the people & the general spirit though it's taken me longer than it did in Canada; but I must say I like these diggers & their women better than I thought I was going to as I liked the Canadians much the most during the war!! But comparisons are odious.

5th June (1.00 A.M.)

How how happy & comforted I am with your divine little wire my sweetheart & you said such marvellous things in those 4 words & Venus the last one!! . . . Dickie brought me your wire while I was still in bed & half asleep on the train & I've been in such good shape all day as a consequence! . . .

You can never know how it's bucked me up that you should have said you were anxious about me & wanted news angel; I guess there have been headlines in the home papers about me being tired or perhaps Bertie let you know . . . [*The Times of 4 June contained a report which stated that the Prince's doctors did not believe it would be possible for him to continue without a period of recreation, except at the price of serious strain. Halsey, the report continued, appeared to be under even greater strain than the Prince. The report complimented the Prince on his ability as a great artist in the difficult craft of public appearance.*]

The Admiral has been in my room discussing hunting!! There are 2 or 3 good packs round Melbourne & there are 3 meets next week & naturally I'm crazy to go out sweetie though the G.G. & others are opposed to it on the grounds that I must be 'kept in cotton wool' for the Australian people & that should I crash & knock myself out they would be furious & not look upon it from the sporting viewpoint as people would in the Old Country!! . . .

Of course I don't see this at all & just couldn't be more disappointed . . . & also terrified lest the hunting crowd here who know I made urgent enquiries as to the chance of hunting might think I wasn't for it & wasn't what they call out here 'a sport'!!!! . . .

(11.30 P.M.)

Here endeth the last day's stunting in Melbourne, thank God . . . I went to the races at Flemmington . . . but I only got 2 hrs racing as I had to go to a hospital for incurable returned men to visit about 20 spinal cases which was sordid & pathetic!!

I only got back at 6.00 & I've just returned from what they call a 'gala' show at one of the big theatres where they are giving 'The Bing Boys on Broadway' which might have been a lot worse though they added a few terrible extra numbers such as operatic dope to give the local 'Melba & Caruso' a chance, which was more than out of place!!

Do you remember in March 1918 when you & Burghie & Rosemary & I went to 'the Bing Boys', sweetheart? That was the only time I ever saw it & hearing the 'First love best love' song made me feel so so infernally Fredie sick . . . The theatre was marvellously decorated & the house was packed & they gave me a good welcome which I appreciate all the more no longer being a novelty here!! . . .

6th June (6.00 P.M.)

Having been a good boy & gone to church I was allowed to play golf this afternoon at a good course called 'Sandringham' . . .

I see that old Bertie has become 'Duke of York' though I'll never get used to it; personally I think he's an ass to accept the title as he's universally known as P.A., which is what he was in the war & who cares a —— about 'The D. of Y.'? However that's his own look-out, though I personally loathe addressing him D. of Y. as I've just done in a cable!!

8th June (11.30 P.M.)

Another small private party again tonight but as you can see by the hour such a good little David again . . .

My best stunt today was getting a ride out at Caulfield racecourse this morning; I took Dickie though I didn't see much of him as I was riding a very hot animal that has been raced in its young days & it bolted with me completely for a few hundred yards till I got comfy in the saddle (after no riding for a month) though all was well after that & I got him over a few small hurdles!! . . . I'm going out every morning as it's so good for me & goes down well with the jockeys & the toughs who hang around racing stables!! . . .

But nothing can ever thrill me like our rides together last April in Windsor Park & how I pray God will be kind & let us have many many more; as you know my one ambition is to take you out hunting as I know how keen you are & how marvellously you ride & go!! I just live for the day when it might be my happy privilege to pilot you & give you a lead in a marvellous long run at the top of a hunt!! More castles in the air, sweetie . . .

10th June (1.00 A.M.)

Oh!! Fredie darling precious beloved what huge joy your 2 letters Nos 5 & 7 have brought me & I've never been so happy since we parted . . .

though I've only just peered inside the envelopes & am keeping them to read in bed so I won't answer them till later!! . . .

I had an even better ride this morning . . . the jockeys & toughs became quite enthusiastic & one of them said to me 'You don't do so bad' which is very high praise from a digger, angel!! . . . I took Dickie again but the poor boy is so so sore & very sorry for his —— well 'you know what I mean'!!

(5.00 P.M.)

Fredie my beloved each letter of yours is if possible more marvellous than the one before; bless you bless you & fank you fank you fank you for ever for Nos 5 & 6 & 7; I underline 6 as I was woken up with it . . .

I'm so so touched that you should have thought of sending me the only 4 leafed clover you've ever found accompanied by such a divine little wish that it should bring me safely back to you!! Oh! Fredie darling how I love you love you I'm so glad we made that tiny little word VENUS to mean that sweetheart & I've got into the habit of repeating it after FREDIE which means that through my thoughts my brain my mind & my soul are always always running the 2 words 'FREDIE VENUS' . . .

Oh! & you've thrilled me so & made me so so happy by saying that your thoughts fly to me whenever you feel émotionée or happy or unhappy or when in trouble & that your soul consults mine across the thousands of miles that separate them, poor lonely little things!! How sloppy I'm becoming angel . . .

I've got 3 more letters from Phillip by this mail . . . also a nice one from Reggie all about hunting & horses though old Bertie has written me a mad one which I can't fathom at all!! He mentions long yarns with you & Sheilie & arrangements & suggestions & you wanting to make things easier for me!! God knows what the boy is driving at & I'm quite worried as to what he could have said to you my beloved re MOI!!

I wish to God he would leave TOI et MOI alone & settle things with Sheilie; & above all get the absurd notion that WE & our affairs in any way resemble them & their affairs out of his silly head!! Christ! the boy irritates me angel as he doesn't understand though I know you won't take the slightest notice of anything he may have said or says or will say about me!!

What I think of him, though he wrote a nice letter & he means well (that damns him!!) & I'm glad he is at last taking a pull about Sheilie as I'm so keen for him to as I explained at length in my last letter!! But I also told you not to take any notice of his actions, didn't I, sweetie, or anything he may say, though again I'm quite happy & confident that you won't listen to anyone except MOI!!

How I'm longing for your next letter which may report your yarns with him & how I'm longing to know what the B.F. has said to you!! Curse my family & of course the boy has the wind up like I've had it but that's all past history now & I'm going to be so so strong & firm instead of timid & weak . . . Christ where should I be & what should I be like if YOU hadn't come into my life & saved me Fredie mine? I just shudder to think!!

It's you & only you that have made something approaching a man of me & have helped me to be successful sometimes!! I'll ever ever be so so colossally grateful to you for that alone my beloved one & I'm sure everybody must know by now that it's you & your marvellous little soul & ideas & advice that govern one & all my actions!! And it's so unfair that I should get all the praise of what I now call the firm 'Fredie & David'!!

The pressure exerted on Bertie by his father, and the 'yarns' he had with Freda, convinced her that her relationship with the Prince was doomed, that the gossip about them was doing her children no good, and that the best solution was for the two of them to give up their love. This she wrote to the Prince in her 'Letter No 8', which was on its way to him.

(11.45 P.M.)

Just got away from another small & select party here at Government House, the usual crowd though good dancing . . . I must tell you that Dickie has been taking my dancing in hand lately (just as I've been giving him riding lessons) & I really do think I've improved & that dancing with me won't be such a physical strain as it used to be!! . . .

Dickie & I rode again this morning & I took on the biggest steeplechase fence on the course twice; but poor old Dickie finds it so painful to sit down tonight that he absolutely refuses to come out with me tomorrow morning!!

I smashed that — — Grigg at squash this afternoon so that
altogether I'm in some shape now darling & have become so hard &
fitter & thinner . . . I really do feel a new man & oh!! —— well, I do
feel so frightfully fit mon amour & —— well, 'you know what I
mean'!! Curse our separation; it's driving me mad!!

11th June (3.00 P.M.)

. . . I've had 2 more letters from H.M. but no news in them; they are
merely sarcastic & finding fault with 2 or 3 details as one would expect
from him!! Christ! what I think of him & my contempt for him
increases daily . . .

I hope you found your sweet babies well & happy please give them
'Ickle Prince's' love!!

(11.30 P.M.)

. . . We've been to yet another teeny party . . . Dickie & I found some of
our host's clothes & opera hats & tennis boots in his room (he was away)
& we dolled ourselves up & made everybody laugh too which was so
amazing! But as you can guess my beloved my mild hilarity was merely
due to some very good brown sherry His Ex gave us for dinner though I
wasn't in any way toxi-boo . . .

Dickie by the way thinks he's 'crashed' & that he's in love with a girl
here called Gwenda Grimwade; she certainly is quite pretty &
attractive though she's only a baby & it will pass off & he'll soon forget
her at Sydney!! Dickie is such a baby too & he's got such a large heart
too, darling . . .

We sail for Sydney at dawn on Sunday & I'll really be glad to be
getting on with the work again; I've been feeling all this week that
we've been marking time . . .

Of course you can put your letters to me in K.M. bags, you know I
don't worry about those trifles any more. On the contrary I'm so so
proud & thrilled that people should know that YOU write to me though
of course we don't exactly want it published in the press!! . . .

your vewy vewy own devoted adoring petit amoureux

your little David.

Letter No 16
H.M.S. RENOWN*, Port Melbourne*
13th June 1920 (1.00 A.M.)

Fredie my darling precious beloved,

We've had a farewell party on board this evening & it took some time to get all the women away as there were several rather pathetic farewells between officers in the ship & their bits!! How I sympathised with them all, sweetheart, & Dickie was all over his Grimwade girl as he's quite lost his heart to her! . . .

As a matter of fact I danced most of the evening with a certain Miss Nancy Moule who I've danced with quite a lot this week merely because she can jazz & has nice scent & so doesn't stink as most of the women out here do!! I just can't tell you how nauseating it is dancing with them angel & this girl also has a certain amount to say for herself which hardly any of them have.

Pleath don't be thulky sweetheart . . . she's neither pretty nor attractive; merely chic & a good dancer!! I know you like me to tell you & what is more I should say she was 'as cold as an Eskimo' as far as flirting goes, though you know I've forgotten what that word means angel let alone how it's done!! . . .

My route down to the pier at Port Melbourne was published in the papers & it was somewhat of a stunt drive & a rough one too, as there was quite a crowd in the streets & many of them gave me hard farewell slaps on the shoulder which became very painful!! . . .

14th June (11.00 P.M.), Jervis Bay, N.S.W.

We anchored here at 1.30 P.M. & landed at the Royal Australian Navy College where I was shown over the buildings & watched a rugger match between our ship's officers' team & the R.A.N. 'cadet midshipmen' . . . & needless to say our team was smashed as 2½ weeks of Melbourne's hospitality hasn't been exactly conducive to keeping fit for the officers of the ship!! . . .

Must get down to my speech again so bonne nuit & bless you Fredie darling.   D.

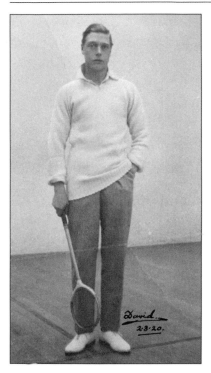

'Looking the completest stable hand!! Talking to 2 of Renown's rugger team at ½ time during the match against R.A.N. College at Jervis Bay. This was on my return from a ride in the "bush". P.S. I'm swinging a cane in my hand & please note how thin my legs look in canvas gaiters!!!!'

The Prince was a keen, though by no means talented, sportsman.

16th June (1.00 A.M.), At sea

I've been up on the bridge while we weighed & steamed out of Jervis Bay & I've been giving the Admiral a final recitation of my speech which all account for the late hour!! I have to 'faire mes excuses sweetheart as you might be angwy wiv me for sitting up!! . . .

I've got to 'break ice' in Sydney today & must be on the bridge at 9.00 A.M. which is when we are due to enter Port Jackson!! . . . Christ! what I think of having to face huge crowds again & I've got to go through with another terrible & pompous carriage drive through the streets when I first land which 'gets my goat' & upsets me . . .

17th June (1.00 A.M.)

Well I hope & think I've broken the ice fairly successfully in Sydney today angel & it's all been far easier than landing & arriving at Melbourne!!

We entered Port Jackson at 9.00 . . . it's a marvellous harbour & it
was a good stunt steaming up being saluted by the Australian fleet &
escorted by masses of small craft & the ship must have looked well too!!
I landed at 11.00 & was received by the Lord Mayor (the completest
Bolshy) . . .

The Government dinner was at the Commonwealth Bank about
150 ——— ——— politicians is the only way to describe them & I got my
speech off all right sweetheart & I think it went down all right though
Billy Hughes the P.M. was in hopeless shape & was quite incoherent &
no-one could hear him though he is a fine speaker!! So that he didn't
give me much of a lead though perhaps that made it easier to avoid
'crashing'!!

Finally we went to a vast ball . . . & there I met Sheilie's great friend
Molly Little & had 2 dances with her & of course we talked about S the
whole time!! S writes to her a lot & so she's heard about you & Bertie &
Poots though I hope to meet her again at other parties & make her tell
me more!! She seems a nice girl & she dances well & she certainly has a
look of Sheilie, particularly about her mouth!! . . .

We are sleeping on board tonight & I only wish we were living on
board the whole 10 days at Sydney instead of having to stay with those
pompous 'boobs' the Davidsons [*the Governor of New South Wales*] . . .

Sydney is easily the largest city in Australia & by far the most
important in every way . . . you must get Sheilie to explain my doings
here to you which she'll be able to do if I name a few places and
buildings . . . Sydney is the London, Paris or New York of the Southern
hemisphere (good phrase that) & is very cosmopolitan, though I can't
think what that's got to do with my saying goodnight Fredie
darling . . .

18th June (*1.00 A.M.*), GOVERNMENT HOUSE, SYDNEY

I landed at 10.00 & had 2 terribly pompous & trying hours official
decorating & receiving 70 addresses & shaking hands at this bloody
house; I could have killed Davidson & so could the Admiral & the staff
as he was too impossible for words . . .

I nominally had the afternoon free but I thought it was a good
propaganda stunt to go voluntarily & unofficially to the races at

Randwick, the course of Sydney, & I got there in time for lunch with the Australian Jockey Club & who should I sit next to but Mr Harry Chisholm, Sheilie's father, & I spent the whole afternoon with him though all his tips were useless & I lost every quid I put on as well as a side bet of £4 to him on the last race!!

He's such a sweet old man . . . & he's just crazy about little Sheilie & was so grateful for all the news of her that I could give him & no-one has given him as much as I have since Mrs C. returned!! Of course he's heard of you sweetie though I didn't like to say much about Loughie, particularly as Sheilie seems to write home & say she's happy with him!!

But then we know she isn't always quite quite truthful, even to you, is she darling, so how can one exactly expect her to be to her family, though I hope she's more sincere with hers than I am with mine, what!! . . .

I've just escaped from a terrible official party . . . the evening started with a ghastly dinner & the only saving clause was that I managed to get Molly Little asked . . . I just couldn't have been more furious with 'Dame Margaret' (as the beta of a wife of Governor Davidson calls herself) when I mentioned Miss Little's name to her & she said she didn't know her & I since find she did really!! The ——— 'Dame' had

'Waving to huge crowds from balcony of Town Hall Sydney', wrote the Prince.

heard that Miss Little & I were mutual friends of Sheilie's & knowing that she was attractive & could dance guessed that I would dance a lot with her if she came & so she wouldn't ask her!! And just to spite the old beta I've spent most of the evening with M.L. & we've had such a marvellous talk about Sheilie . . . there's practically nothing Sheilie doesn't tell her; anyway she knows almost everything & I'm sure all about Bertie, though probably not about Ob!! . . . [*Joey Legh wrote that Mollee Little was not highly regarded within Sydney society – he twice uses the word 'vulgar' about her – and that the Prince's request for her attendance at the dance had caused a real fuss. He also reported that the Prince's selfish, ill-tempered and irresponsible behaviour was daily becoming more difficult for the staff to put up with, and that he could not contemplate accompanying the Prince on the tour to India with him in his current mood.*]

19th June (2.00 A.M.)

Vewy late tonight I'm afraid sweetheart but we've been to a rather good private party . . .

I haven't really seen anything of the city . . . I'm not keen to, really, though anything to escape from this — — Government House & the — — Governor & the — — 'Dame Margaret' Davidson O.B.E. They are the absolute limit & I just can't be polite any more.

20th June (1.00 A.M.)

There's been another party here tonight sweetheart . . . of course the pompous boobs tried to make it all as official & pompous & serious as possible though somehow I was feeling in fairly good shape & ragged a bit & managed to make everybody treat the party as a joke which it was & Molly Little & I laughed till it hurt, my beloved!!

God! she's so like Sheilie, I can't help saying it again & she gets the hysterics just like Sheilie does!! We (or rather I) wrote out a short cable for her to send to S. during one of our sit-outs & it runs like this: 'We wish you & F were here. Love Molly & E.' I had to add the F. Fredie darling or I couldn't have added the E!! . . .

My only stunt today has been the races at Randwick again though as usual I lost everything I put on & I'm sorry to say that I've lost over £100 in quiet 'punting' (as they call betting in Australia) . . . I must be

a regular 'Jonah' darling as the horse I backed in the steeplechase fell at
the first fence & was killed, though the jockey was all right!! . . . I'm
getting vewy tired of never spotting a winner or even backing a horse
that ever gets placed!! However luckily for me I can afford to lose
though it's irritating . . .

(6.00 P.M.)

I'm going up country tonight for 24 hrs & leave by train at 10.00 P.M.
so I'm scribbling a few lines now . . .

Church at the cathedral at 11.00 was more painful than ever & then
I visited Randwick soldiers' hospital, the largest in Australia, & had to
shake hands with over 1,000 wounded men & there were over 200
amputation cases which was vewy twying as one has to have a short
yarn with each & I returned here vewy exhausted & dazed . . .

I've managed to get Molly Little asked to dinner here tonight
sweetie & fixed up that she should sit next to me so that's something &
she'll be able to help me through another desperate evening here as I
can hardly bring myself even to talk to these —— —— Davidsons!!

However they are tamer than when we arrived, not that that is
saying vewy much; they really are the most impossible couple & no
wonder the dominions get fed up with the Old Country & want to
abolish all Imperial Governors if the Colonial Office will insist on
sending out such hopeless boobs!! I'm going to tell L.G. & Milner etc.
what a lot of harm is done throughout the Empire by the rotten
governors they appoint who are nearly always pompous duds who they
don't want in London!! [*Alfred, 1st Viscount Milner, had been a member of
the War Cabinet, and in 1919 had become Colonial Secretary.*]

How pompous I am this evening sweetie but I feel I might be able
to help in this direction & even poor ignorant little David can't travel
around the Empire officially without getting a little experience!!!!

22nd June (2.00 A.M.)

I got back from the up-country trip at 10.30 P.M. beloved but was
enticed to a party by Mollee Little (she spells her name Mollee) though
I wasn't there 2 hrs & didn't get in more than 7 dances . . . however I
got 3 with her . . . I wanted some exercise after a ghastly political sort

of day in the new federal district or area called Canberra which is the site of the new Commonwealth capital!! . . .

We motored to Duntroon military college . . . & then motored on a few miles to 'Capitol Hill' which is to be the central point of the new city, where I had to sit through a fearful lunch in a tent & then lay a foundation stone of one of the proposed federal buildings, though it was the 15th stone that has been laid at Canberra in the last 10 years & they haven't made any effort to even start building as yet, though they seem to have laid out some roads & done some irrigation work as the district & site is the most desolate 'bush' & station country that one could imagine & miles from anywhere!! . . . [*Mountbatten checked this stone on subsequent visits to Canberra, and in 1976 was irritated to find it had been removed.*]

It's sad & pathetic for me to think that this is the end of 'aged 25' & that in 24 hrs time I'll be in the 2nd quarter of life!! [*The Prince's calculations are a year out: he started the second quarter of life on his twenty-fifth birthday, in 1919.*] What a sordid little thought my Fredie & I do feel so terribly old away from TOI; how well I remember my birthday last year angel as it was the end of Ascot & I had to go to Cardiff!! Do you remember? Yes I know you do!!!!

24th June (3.00 A.M.)

I'm an absolute disgrace & so so terribly ashamed to appear so gay sweetie but the fact is that the old Davidsons insisted on organising a mild form of birthday party for me tonight, though we've all been too dead beat to be able to enjoy it!! They asked a few bits to dinner (M.L. being one of them) . . . it's really lucky it's our last night in Sydney Fredie darling as life here is too strenuous for everybody & we are all B.F.'s for having sat up so late so often & for nothing too!! . . .

We've got 2 bad days ahead of us beloved but I'm so excited at the chance of the mail (which I hear has arrived) being sent up to Toronto (where we stay the night) by the afternoon train!! Goodnight my darling little Fredie . . . all all my blessings & baisers.

10.00 P.M.

Yes, the mail has come with a vengeance my little Fredie darling &

though I've only skimmed through parts of your No 8 letter I can see that besides being the most marvellous divine one it is a terribly sad one, my sweetheart, & the little I have read is making me cwy!!

It's the result of your yarn with old Bertie I suppose, though there's also your letter No 9 & such a sweet little birthday note you enclosed to Dickie!! But I just daren't read your letters any more tonight angel for fear of breaking down altogether as we've had almost the worst day of the whole trip, certainly the most jarring to the nerves as we've had to spend 5 hrs in a steam boat on the Hawkebury River with the New South Wales labour premier & 10 of his labour government!!

Their scheme was to get poor little me all to themselves & more or less interview me & as the whole crowd are Bolshies one had to be frightfully careful!! However as they made me the excuse for an oyster & champagne orgy at lunch on board & all of them got toxy except Storey, the premier, there wasn't much serious interviews about them, though some of them struck out some nasty little bolshie ironies at the Admiral & me which hurt & then they began singing!! Oo!oo!oo!oo! what we went through this afternoon & you know what wrecks we were when we left Sydney this morning!!

So that when we reached the train I couldn't have been in a weaker state both mentally & physically to receive the first shock of a mere glance through your No 8 letter, for of course I've got the gist of it, that we must make the greatest sacrifice of our lives & give up our LOVE!!

But oh! oh! my beloved darling little Fredie I just mustn't talk of it all or write any more tonight or I'll never be able to face bolshie Newcastle tomorrow, where anyway I should have had to make an extra effort!! It now seems a superhuman task to me to even live through the night my sweetheart, though perhaps a real good cwy when I get into bed will help me as of course I can't let myself go till I can bury my head in your little pillow.

Oh!Oh!Oh!Oh! I'm cwying already sweetie & you know how I can cwy . . .

Whatever might happen Fredie darling you'll always know that your poor sad worn-out little David so so entirely faithful & devoted to his precious sacred blessed divine little goddess & idol his Fredie whom he loves & adores & worships as no man has ever loved adored or worshipped before or ever will again!! . . .

What you must think of the ultra frivolous tone of this letter up till 3.00 A.M. this morning my beloved but I never camouflage my moods to you as you know sweetie & I was a fairly cheery little boy (not a happy boy, as I'll never never be happy away from my Fredie) at the end of Sydney having gone through with the 2 biggest (& the only 2 really big) Australian cities sans accident!! And the photos I enclose are cheery too; I'm glad none have been taken since your No 8 letter though I received it after dark, thank God!!

Blessings   D.

The Mountbatten diary records the arrival of the English mail, and the fact that 'H.R.H. was the only one who apparently did not find his mail very cheering'.

Letter No 17
H.M.S. RENOWN, *At sea, Sydney to Perth (W.A.)*
25th June 1920 (10.00 P.M.)

I did as I said I would last night sweetie & didn't really read your long tragic No 8 letter till the train left Newcastle at 3.00 P.M. I just funked reading it properly & I'm glad I didn't now as I just couldn't have gone through today, which was an important & wearing one; if I had, anyway I shouldn't have been able to stunt properly & as it was the 'screw' was jammed & couldn't go another turn which is the first time it's happened.

You know what a shock No 8 letter was to me last night Fredie darling & I cried myself to sleep on your sweet little pillow which is all the more sacred to me now than ever because I love you love you far far more than ever though you know that angel!!

But having read it & re-read it till I've almost memorised it sweetie & had a little time to think (though not much & I'm dead beat) I'm knocked right out & life has never looked as black as it does tonight & it's often looked vewy vewy black, hasn't it, darling one!!

But everything everything seems so so terribly & pathetically sad now mon amour; even this old ship has become sordid where I used to feel my best before No 8 letter!! But then No 8 letter marks & means the beginning of the 3rd phase of my life Fredie darling; Christ what a lot of hard thinking I've done in the last 24 hours!!

The first phase of my life was before WE met; the second phase of my life was after WE met; & now the third phase which has alas alas just begun is after No 8 Letter!! I'm as near to mad as nothing tonight sweetie as I'm terribly exhausted both mentally & physically & not at all in shape for receiving such a knock as No 8 letter, let alone even trying to answer it!!

I had made up my mind to get it all off the chest tonight mon amour but now that I've sat down to the job I find I just can't face it properly without some sleep first!! But let me tell you at once Fredie mine that I'm afraid either rightly or wrongly, kindly or unkindly I just can't bring myself to do as you suggest & ask me, or even to help you until we meet & until we can talk!!

You know I can't express myself on paper & I'm not going to let YOU go out of my life 'in writing'; my reasons (& you'll probably think them both selfish & cowardly) I'll give you tomorrow beloved or I'll try to give them though I fear I won't succeed!!

Of course No 8 letter is easily the most marvellously divine & sacred one you've ever written me sweetheart & the most wonderful one as regards soundness & ability as besides being the only only woman I've ever loved or ever will love you are the soundest & most able I've ever ever met & you know how intensely I admire you & look up to you & listen to you besides loving you loving you & adoring & worshipping you!! This must all sound terribly pompous sweetie but perhaps I do get a bit pompous when I'm as serious & earnest as I am now though that's only in writing!!

But first of all bless you bless you bless you my beloved little Fredie for writing all the divine marvellous things you have in No 8 letter & being sweeter to your petit amoureux than you've ever been before; of course it ought to & does make me happier deep down than I've ever been but my deep down feelings are all but drowned tonight by all the utter misery & despair on top!!

But of course they aren't really drowned & never could be my sweetie & you've said just all the little things that alone make it possible for me to try to bear the shock of your so so sensible (though how it breaks my sad Fredie loving & adoring little heart to have to say it) suggestion that we should try & be brave & give up our LOVE!!

I'm quite hysterical & am cwying as I write though when you say you'll never ever love anyone else or console yourself by flirting with other men my sobs abate for an instant & I kiss your photo & little lockets round my neck!! But I'm unreasonable tonight & just can't think as I've said before angel so that the sooner I turn in & cwy myself to sleep the better!! And we've had such a wearing day though I can hardly bring myself to bore you with my usual diary though I want you to have my full account of this —— trip as well as Dickie's diary . . .

We reached Newcastle at 10.00, quite a big city & port & vewy bolshie so I wasn't looking forward to it much. I was there 5 hrs launching a ship & going over the biggest steel plant in Australia . . . there was the usual drive through the city & civic reception & lunch which was nauseating. However the people were fairly enthusiastic, though it was a great relief to get away at 3.00 . . .

'Renown' had left the harbour during the afternoon because of the tide so that we had a ¾ hr trip to get out to her . . . Dinner was a great trial as I was on the verge of cwying the whole time & I was too worn out to even twy to camouflage my misery & depression & I particularly don't want anyone except Dickie to know there's anything wrong with me!!

Thank God! I've got that boy with me angel as although he naturally knows nothing of all my troubles yet he knows me well enough to guess that it's the result of yesterday's mail, though he asks no questions but is just extra sweet & sympathetic. It's his 20th birthday today & I'm afraid I've been so worried that I've forgotten all about it & never even drank his health!!

But I must turn in now so as to have as clear a brain as possible tomorrow.

26th June (5.00 P.M.)

I didn't turn out till noon as I was so dead beat after yesterday & cwying myself to thleep . . . my brain is clearer this evening though I'll have to hurry writing as the glass is going down & it's coming on to blow as it generally does in this foul Australian Bight, though it's been calm the first 24 hrs.

But now to getting all you want me to say about giving up our LOVE off the chest Fredie darling!! –

I told you last night that I'm not going to let YOU go or slip out of my life in writing angel & the reason is that I just can't lose all that remains to me in life in this cold-blooded way & in the middle of this ghastly Empire tour!!

You see we never made any resolutions when we parted did we sweetie (perhaps it's a pity we didn't) & the only thing that's been keeping me going up to now (3½ months) is the thought that at the end of this ghastly 7 months' existence TOI et MOI will meet again, that YOU are as usual my goal!!

I'm afraid you'll be terribly disappointed with me & say I've failed you when you read this & you'll think I'm not going to help you to be brave & strong as you've asked me to!! But my Fredie beloved how on earth am I going through with the rest of Australia & everything else if I write to you & say that we'll never meet again or something like that?

You see mon amour for the moment or till we do meet again the most important thing is that I should be able to 'smile' at crowds & look as if I appreciated their enthusiasm. Well this I could never do if I gave you up in writing by this mail, as you see angel (& as I've so often told you) you'll never never know how much I love you love you though it's all my fault that you don't know & Christ! how I curse myself for it now!!

So that although you are sweet enough to say that you know your suggestion will give me pain, my beloved, you'll never know how much pain or how terribly it's affected me, coming as it does in the middle of this —— ghastly tour when I'm worn out & yet must carry on as usual with camouflaged 'smiles' & so-called cheeriness!! Oh! what I'm going through & what hell mon amour when I can read so easily between the lines in your letter that you are trying so hard to help me to do the bravest deed of my life, to give up my LOVE for YOU!

This is all so disjointed & there's no sequence whatsoever in all that I'm trying so hard to write & explain sweetie . . .

There's another thing you say darling that I don't at all agree with (& there are 2 or 3 more that I'll come to later on) & that is that you can never be any good to me in my life!! Sweetheart you know perfectly well that it's YOU & no-one & nothing else that has made me capable of doing & going through all that I have in the last year so 'what in

thunder' should I do if I suddenly lost your marvellous influence &
advice & if we couldn't have some more talks?

What would become of me, beloved? I just dread to contemplate &
I would never never do any good anywhere again!! Perhaps I would
become something like my bloody father or even worse if I lost you &
surely that is more than undesirable if I've got to carry on as P. of W.
I'm afraid I'm being vewy obstinate angel but I must get all my
contradictions off the chest now that I've started!!

You say that we've so often tried to make resolutions when we've
been together & have always failed; that it will always be useless to
actually discuss changing our lives!! But sweetheart you know perfectly
well that never have we ever really faced the facts before, at least I
know I never have . . .

And of course when you bring in sweet little Penelope & Angie
darling I just can't discuss your suggestion at all for as you say they are
our care (& how I love the way you say our) & you know how devoted I
am to them . . .

TOI et MOI are going to discuss it all so so sensibly & calmly as soon
after I get back as possible & we'll have such a marvellous talk,
probably the most divinely marvellous one we've ever had as it will
bring out our unique mutual understanding as nothing ever has
before . . .

I've got over 3 months to practise getting a hold on myself &
keeping my feelings under control; in fact you'll hardly know it's your
little David who will have returned to you so calm & easy will he be,
though he isn't now by God!! He's just mad & crazy my beloved the
completest caveman & Christ! how cruelly bitter he's become towards
his bloody family & their still more infamous crowd of satellites known
as 'the court' if they really have been surrounding our poor little
molehill & making it vulgar & notorious, as Bertie seems to have told
you they have, God's curses be upon them; bad luck to them all!! . . .

But it's blowing up fast angel & we are going into a gale so that
although I'm going to try & face dinner I don't suppose I'll last
through it & anyway shall be incapable of writing & have to turn in
soon after!!

So à demain Fredie darling to carry on with this pathetic screed . . .

27th June (3.00 P.M.)

. . . It's been blowing a Westerly gale ever since midnight sweetheart &
I'm feeling oh!! oh!! so ill mon amour . . . it is bad luck getting this
bad weather just this trip when I was so in need of rest & peace of mind
& soul so as to be able to write & write to YOU!! I'm at present
scribbling in Dickie's cabin laying back in his big armchair as I've
removed to his wee cosy cabin which is far more comfy than mine &
where there is far less motion & I'm going to sleep here tonight . . .

What was I discussing last night my sweetheart? Oh! yes; my bloody
family & the court!! Well what infuriates me more than anything else
is the fact that apparently it's only they who have cast all this mud &
dirt at poor little TOI et MOI . . . What does old Duddie say about it all,
darling? I do so long to know or perhaps you haven't discussed it at all
with him any more!! . . .

If we do change things when we meet again & can talk calmly, let it
be understood at once & before all else, that we will be changing things
for OUR sakes & for the Babies & not for anyone or anything else!!

Freda with her 'sweet babies', Penelope and Angie.

If Duddie produced that big stick beloved then I suppose it would be different but as he hasn't yet & as far as I know isn't likely to (& you would be the first to warn me) our pride mustn't suffer such a blow or insult that it would if we felt that we had been intimidated by anyone except your husband into changing things!! . . .

If only you knew how this bloody old ship was knocking about as there's a big sea running & I'm feeling so wretched & ill besides utterly miserable & worn out!! No doubt I've got blacker days ahead of me in my ghastly & loathsome career as P. of W. but they'll never be blacker than these last 3, anyway I'll never feel them as much . . .

Trent!! & you & Sarah there together; oh! the irony of it all & Joey & I over 10,000 miles away Philip writing 2 or 3 letters by each mail saying he's building squash courts both there & at Lympne so that I can play when I stay with him for weekends!!

Dickie & I have just been having a little tête-à-tête dinner in his cabin . . . he asked me why I was so sad & I told him our little intime meal made me feel vewy homesick!! . . .

But to return to Philip sweetie he also tells me that India is very much on & the reasons!! How sad this news would have made me before No 8 letter Fredie darling, whereas now I'm really relieved as I think one month under our new conditions will be just about as long as TOI et MOI could stick to start off with, though we must meet & talk as soon as we possibly can so as to be able to readjust & re-set ourselves . . . You know I'll not ask for anything else (I'll get into practice not to) & you know I'll make it all so so easy for you . . .

From now onwards I'll twy to teach myself to look on you only as Fredie Mummie though it's going to be the hardest task of my life sweet one; but I swear I will twy, though a chap can love his mummie & so I'll never stop saying 'Fredie Mummie Venus'!! . . . [*Joey Legh wrote that the Prince had been in an appalling fit of depression since the arrival of the mail, and was sending endless cables in code, and that he had never seen him so upset. The Prince had given himself away by announcing that he now didn't care whether or not he went to India, and Joey realised that the relationship with Freda was the cause. Despite the problems with the Prince, however, he wrote of the extraordinary success of the tour overall, and the effect it had produced of bringing Australia into the Empire, even more so than the war had done.*]

28th June (5.00 P.M.)

Today has been the absolute limit my sweetie as we steamed into a new
& far worse W. gale this morning & have been ploughing through a
mountainous sea all day; only the Admiral & 2 or 3 of the officers can
remember ever having seen bigger waves & we are fair taking it in
green on the 'fo'c's'le'. [*The waves were estimated to be at least thirty feet in
height.*]

It's a fine sight from the fore bridge where Dickie & I spent about 1
hr during the forenoon though it made me feel more squirmish than
ever . . . feeling ill gives me an excuse for cutting all meals in the mess
so that I can dodge the staff!!

Dickie & I have all our meals tête-à-tête in his cabin . . . though they
are vewy teeny meals as far as I am concerned & it revolts me to see him
eat hugely as he always does as of course it takes a destroyer or small
craft to upset him!! . . .

I'm just beginning to be able to think a little more soberly as I
slowly recover (though only vewy vewy slowly) from the shock of your
suggestion in No 8 letter . . . & isn't your suggestion if we even try to
carry it out just the biggest sacrifice we've ever made, my beloved? . . .
Oh!! bless you bless you forever mon amour for writing more divinely
than you've ever written before . . .

I'm afraid I've been repeating myself a lot since I started this long
screed but you know I'm neither mentally or physically normal just
now!!

Poor old Bertie, I've been reading his letter (which arrived by the
same mail as yours) again & it is indeed a tragic little tale of woe
sweetie & as you say my —— —— father has been vewy vewy wuff
wiv him!! But Fredie what 'gets my goat' is when he still persists in
referring to 'Us 4 Do's'!!

I could just murder him for that, though perhaps it's as well the poor
brute doesn't know the truth about Sheilie!! But now I wish he had
known it so that he could have given her up of his own free will instead
of having been intimidated into doing so & having his hand forced!! If
only he knew what a futile farce his & S's so called love was & what a
lot of trouble & worry he has given himself & H.M. for absolutely
nothing!!

And my precious beloved that is why I insist on TOI et MOI
re-adjusting our lives entre nous; I'm not going to have Bertie trying to
do so with you for thank God he knows nothing whatever about our
own affairs & I object to what he calls trying to fix things up with TOI.
I've never heard of such an idea, it's too much, sweetie, though I must
admit that he naturally & obviously has later & fuller information of
H.M.'s attitude towards US & the least he could do was to tell you all he
knew & warn you as he did & he is out to help you from all you & he
say . . .

I was a selfish little David & I didn't think enough about my Fredie's
future or those of her 2 sweet babies. But as I've never really ever worried
seriously about the foul idle gossip that has been circulating for over a
year about US & the only danger 'Duddie's big stick' being negligeable
unless you warned me of it which you never have, it was easy to lose
sight of everything except our sacred LOVE? wasn't it Fredie darling one?

But perhaps I'm getting involved now & I can't write for very long
continuously without getting all muddled up mon amour & as Dickie
& I feel it's time for some dinner (anyway he does) I'll pack up & carry
on tomorrow . . .

29th June (6.00 P.M.)

The gale has abated somewhat my angel but it's shifted from right
ahead to the port bow so that we are now rolling & I feel — — well
less well than I did yesterday!! Guess I'll never forget the 'Bight' as
long as I live though I've been with the Admiral most of the day
concocting a letter to H.M. (& I haven't written to him since
Wellington N.Z.) on the subject of India!!

Before No 8 letter I had made up my mind to fight against going to
India but now I know it will make everything easier for US if I do go
Fredie darling although it breaks my heart to have to say it!! . . .

I've made up my mind that the Admiral shall go with me to India as
C. of S. which I've already asked Cromer to do; & I'm equally
determined that I won't take Grigg!! I'm writing all this to H.M. . . .
I'm insisting that I shall choose my staff for India, pointing out that it's
the least concession I'm entitled to for being shot away again within
one month of this 7 months' trip!!

'"Renown" in Australian Bight 28.6.20. Looking ford. Taking in a 'green sea' on the fo'c'sle!! Dickie says he stood by Brooks the photographer counting "1.2.3.Go!" & so is trying to take the credit for it!!!!'

And I couldn't be more genuinely delighted Fredie darling that 'enfin' I've found a really strong & just cause for a row with H.M. which I feel very confident is bound to follow this letter, the hottest I have ever written to him!! And Christ! I'm going to fight him & everybody will be on my side as you've so often explained to me & assured me!!

I happen to know that the appointment of my staff is one of his cranks & that he looks upon them as one of his own 'pigeons'; well he s guessed wrong about this 'pigeon' & I'm quite looking forward to the battle sweetie in which I know I'll win!!

The poor Admiral is naturally rather worried about it all as first of all he doesn't at all want to come on my next trip, being badly in need of a long leave (he hasn't really had one since 1912), & he can see that a battle King v P. of W. is a certainty. Still he realises that I just couldn't face the next trip without him . . .

Of course if the Admiral comes Grigg won't . . . you will remember the row in February which had to be settled at 10 Downing St. & how the Admiral & I swore we would make a point of not falling out with Grigg!! Well we haven't angel but Grigg hasn't played the game as regards the Admiral as C. of S. & he becomes daily more difficult to work with!!

Apart from his mad uncertain & impetuous nature he's saturated in politics . . . I now look upon him as dangerous as I never know when he won't land me in a political row & we have to watch him like hawks!! A charming situation, isn't it, sweetie? . . .

No doubt Cromer will scratch his head somewhat when I tell him he's to be supplanted by the Admiral though I'm sure he'll understand; if he doesn't —— well he just needn't come!!

Of course Godfrey will come & Joey & Claud, though I'm going to tell the latter that at the end of the next trip he'll have to quit as we never have been kindred spirits & never will be & that he had better look for another job when we return in October if he doesn't want to go back to the regiment.

You'll say that David is becoming a bolshie though I know you'll really be delighted that he has become such a vindictive little boy, though you'll also think that it's a pity he didn't have this spirit a long time ago!! Just one more point about my staff for India; I'm intent on Dickie coming again!! I just couldn't do without that boy on the next trip & the Admiral likes him & wants him too & it won't harm his naval career, in fact he'll benefit by it!! . . .

More food is being produced for us & as I'm going to work at that letter again with the Admiral afterwards it's a case of bonne nuit . . . the 2 enclosed photos taken yesterday will show you what the sea has been like!! D.

30th June (3.00 P.M.)

These are only a few rush lines before we land in Western Australia to tell you how much I love you love you & that a mail was brought on board as soon as we anchored but alas alas no letter from my little Fredie . . . I'm sadder than ever, particularly when I've received 2 letters from the faithful old Philip; still I'm always grateful for his screeds . . .

But I'm puzzled angel as I've just had a cable from him & in our code sweetie (which means that you must have worked it out for him from our little unicode book) to say that he thinks he'll be able to fix

things up to my satisfaction, which means that he thinks he'll be able
to prevent my going to India which is what he's working very hard for,
isn't he darling?

But in his last 3 or 4 letters he says he doesn't see any chances of my
getting out of it now as the P.M. is still keen & if he wasn't won't face
H.M. on the subject again!! So I really give up the unequal contest my
little Fredie & just don't know what to say in reply to his cable or
whether to answer it at all or what!!

I know perfectly well that TOI does not want MOI to go to India this
year & yet I've a feeling that Fredie Mummie wants David to go
because she thinks that it will make her suggestion of readjusting their
lives easier!! Has any man ever been faced with such a problem beloved;
am I to tell Philip to abandon his efforts or encourage him? And yet
why do you let him continue with them or anyway why don't you put
the brake on if you think I ought to go!! Oh! my little Fredie what am
I to know about it all & everything so so far away from YOU . . .

But no time for more now as we leave the ship in a few minutes (&
for a whole fortnight) to land at Albany & then we sleep the night in
the train & reach Perth tomorrow morning . . . What a hopeless
rambling & contradicting yarn this letter has become my sweetie
though what a hopeless rambling & dazed brain mine is now!! Oh!!
bless you   D.

1st July (5.00 P.M.), Government House, Perth S.A.

We arrived here after a terribly cold night in the train . . . Perth seems
terribly sordid & dull & slow & primitive after Sydney . . . Perth isn't
much over 100,000 which seems small after close on a million in
Sydney!! . . .

There's a bloody 'ball' here tonight to 'cap' this 'perfect' day so that I
really am thoroughly fed up this evening . . .

2nd July (6.00 P.M.)

. . . We motored back from Fremantle visiting a home for permanently
disabled men on the way & there were groups of people out the whole
10 miles & as it was pouring it couldn't have been a more devastating
day & I've got such a ghastly fit of the blues this evening my little

Fredie, though these fits are becoming so frequent that I'm getting quite used to them!!

Yes, last night's ball was a strain as the women of Perth are too sordid for words . . . The governor Newdegate & Lady N. [*Sir Francis Newdigate-Newdegate*], with whom we are staying here, aren't at all a bad couple as governors & their wives go, though their looks are against them & he is rather pompous, though who's ever seen a governor who isn't? . . .

Oh! & Fredie darling, Philip also tells me in his last letters that Loughie is willing to let himself be divorced, which is the only way out of it for poor little Sheilie, though I wonder what her plans are? I suppose 'Ob & Alb' etc. etc. are clear of trouble, at least I hope so, & that it will all happen quietly!! . . . poor old Loughie, one can't help feeling just a teeny bit sorry for him as he'll sink & sink now that the only thing that has kept him on the surface, his Sheilie, will be gone, though he is such a miserable rotter & I'm so glad for her sake!! Bertie didn't quit what I call the 'volcano' any too soon, did he, angel? . . . [*In fact the Loughboroughs were not divorced until 1926.*]

4th July (10.00 P.M.), In the train to Pemberton

. . . I've quite chucked even trying to find out where I'm ever going let alone knowing, though I'm always quite safe in expecting to find diggers & schoolchildren everywhere & every day!! . . .

I had a great yarn with the Admiral & Godfrey this evening re India & they are both so adamant about my not going this year beloved that I just don't feel justified in cabling Philip to abandon his efforts on my behalf!! And now I wish to God I had never said to you that I thought one month would be enough for us to be together under the changed conditions, if we do change them, my ickle Fredie . . . I want you to cable me 'VEPRES', the word under 'VENUS' in our private code in the 'unicode', to say that you agree with all I've written.

5th July (10.00 P.M.)

Still in the train but not in the same coach sweetheart as we've had a slight railway accident this afternoon; merely our coach & the next ahead derailed & turned right over on a slight embankment.

We've really had a miraculous escape & have been let off very lightly indeed, my Fredie, as there are no casualties except Newport (our doctor) who has a nasty cut on his right leg from broken glass & we've lost none of our gear!! But it's shaken us all up a little bit . . . [*Luckily, a cow on the line had slowed the train just before the accident occurred. The Prince, on emerging from a corridor window, remarked that finally something had been done which was not on the official programme: it was a rule only to do what was on the schedule. The derailment happened because of the effect of the recent heavy rain on the unballasted railway track, and the combination of a lightweight rail and a heavy train causing one of these rails to bend on a curve.*]

It's worse writing conditions than ever tonight as of course we are all 'doubled up' in this train now that we are 3 coaches shy (as a 3rd derailed though didn't turn over) & the Admiral & I are sharing the teeniest cabin ever built . . .

The train crash. '. . . I was in the rear coach & one can see how far we were dragged "overturned" by the darker colour of the earth on track which was ploughed up by coach sliding down embankment . . . Railway track is a perfectly good imitation of a "strafed" section of track "au front" during the Great war!!!!'

'. . . Salving our gear!! I've had to sign my name against my face {on the back of the picture} as it's hardly recognisable. I mean I hope I don't always look like that.' Behind the Prince is Mountbatten, and in the foreground is Burt, the Prince's private detective 'and anything else you want him to be!! A marvellous man!!'

We left Pemberton about 1.00 P.M. & lunched at once & we were given our great thrill about 2.30. We were all glad we were crashed after lunch instead of before although the lunch was vewy nasty!! . . .

I would honestly sooner go through a cushy accident like today than make a speech any time. Of course as soon as we all realised that no-one was really hurt we all laughed like fools & there were several priceless incidents!!

The best was that the local state minister for forests (a most offensive & revolting old rustic who we loathe) was what he described as 'being in the convenience' & ended up with 'one leg in the pan' & emerged from the wreckage in complete 'déshabille'!! We all had to laugh then, even those who were shaken!! . . .

But my beloved little Fredie I'm so so happy to remember that during all the long long seconds from the moment we derailed, the toppling over, the being dragged along overturned till the moment we stopped, seconds of real mental agony which really put the wind up me I — — well, where do you think my terrified little thoughts were mon amour? Chez TOI as usual . . . I didn't wish you were with me . . . I instinctively thought of just YOU bless you . . . I felt sure I would in a real crisis or moment of danger but now I know!!

Of course I always used to when I got shelled during the war sweetie but then I was always windy when I went up the line whereas I'm not generally in a train & one gets no warning of an accident it all happens so quickly!! Thank God I've lost none of your sacred precious little souvenirs & am so happy that I was able to salve your little pillow from the debris of my bunk . . .

I really feel just a teeny bit religious tonight my little Fredie & have thanked God in a little prayer for saving me today & keeping me safe for YOU & our reunion beloved!! . . .

Oh! the squalor of this nauseating little cabin & I hate the look of the sordid little upper bunk above the Admiral who's asleep but mercifully he doesn't snore; still it will be less depressing asleep than sitting up so bonne nuit my Fredie; all my love & blessings.

My own darling precious beloved,

Enfin the mail left about 4.00 P.M. which takes you 2 long long letters, sweetie, containing nearly a whole month's hard writing, though how bored you'll be not hearing from me for over 3 weeks!! At least I hope you'll be bored & fed up & angwy wiv your little David angel; he would be vewy sad indeed if you weren't . . .

I got up at 8 00 A.M. & finished my long ultimatum to H.M. re India & my staff though I felt far from well . . . that railway crash has affected far more than I at first realised sweetie; I live so much on my nerves that an extra strain like that exhausts them a good deal as I've not got a big reserve of nerves!! . . .

There's yet another big ball here tonight though this is our last in Perth as we leave at noon tomorrow . . . we'll have 4 days in the train before we reach Adelaide though I'll be able to write you a lot during the trans-continental trip!!

So à demain my precious sweetheart.

9th July (10.00 P.M.), Federal Trans Australian Railway

We've spent today on the Western Australian goldfields . . . I was shown over the surface workings of one this afternoon after an hour's racing at the Boulder course where my luck changed & I put a fiver on a winner at 10 to 1!! . . .

There was a fearful civic dinner before we left in this marvellous federal broad gauge railway. You just can't think what a relief it is to be off that bloody narrow gauge at last mon amour as I didn't enjoy last night in the train at all & I couldn't sleep much!!

I'm sure I told you that the Admiral had written to my father strongly deprecating my going to India this year & giving my mental breakdown in the Commonwealth capital as sufficient reason for urging postponement!! Well H.M. cabled a reply to that letter this evening & I enclose what Godfrey has just decyphered from which you will see mon amour that I'm 'for it' all right!! . . . [*George V's reply states that the only possible reason for not going to India is the Prince's health, and asks for the Admiral to cable him again when they leave Australia. He also states that a visit to South Africa is impossible, but that the West Indies trip should be carried out.*]

I'm sure you'll be sad, though not half as sad as your poor little David is!! Apart from TOI he does so want at least 6 months in the Old Country to try & make good there & carry out a scheme or two he has in mind which would help him quite a lot he thinks if they came off!! . . .

My schemes are quite mad I'm sure but as you've probably gathered from my letters I'm more crazy about riding than ever I was & I just long to make somewhat of a name for myself as a horseman & own & ride the winner of a race, a steeplechase or point to point or anything!! I'm lucky enough to have the dollars & light weight & certainly the keenness!! But it's got to be done in the Old Country & it's got to be done young angel & I'm 26 already!! . . . but what's the use of even talking about it when I'm going to be away another whole hunting & racing season?

All my little schemes are shattered by my father's cable for although he does give me a loophole by saying that my health is of first importance yet my health is the only excuse for postponing India &

Racing in Australia. The Prince nursed an ambition to 'make a name for myself as a horseman'.

that would mean having to play the invalid in England all this Winter & invalids can't ride or hunt!!

Of course if H.M. didn't want me to go to India he could so easily prevent my going as we know L.G. doesn't want me to go now & there would be no trouble in his direction!! No it's more & more evident & proof that H.M. couldn't be more delighted at having an excuse to keep me out of the Old Country on account of his bloody bitter but wholly unreasonable & unnecessary jealousy; you see he has got so used to my being away practically for the last 6 years that he just dreads the thought of my returning for any length of time! But it's vewy hard on poor little David, don't you think, beloved?

10th July (10.00 P.M.)

I was in vewy bad shape altogether last night . . . not only sad & miserable but also in a bad temper though I'm afraid my good temper isn't anything like as good as it used to be though it has been tried so phenomenally hard this past month . . . But a day in this comfy train across the Nullarbor plain or Australian desert free of stunts has soothed me somewhat!!

You see yesterday in the goldfields was one of the most trying of the whole trip as besides being very long & strenuous, the people weren't over-enthusiastic, though mining cities never are & there's always a small 'red flag' element though it only affected the show indirectly!!

Then H.M.'s cable came on top of it all & got my goat completely angel so that I was a vewy peeved little boy . . .

This is amazing country through which the Trans-Australian railway passes & the line runs dead straight for 300 miles across the immense flat plain . . . there are tiny little stations every [gap] miles with a population of ½ dozen railway employees & 2 or 3 wives & their children who live in little wooden huts with tin roofs, vewy uncomfy & Christ! how devastatingly monotonous!! Still they seem fairly happy & half the men are returned soldiers!! . . .

11th July (11.00 P.M.)

Still in the train sweetie . . . the mere thought of tackling another capital (Adelaide) tomorrow overwhelms me completely, angel!! The whole thing has become too big & vast for your poor little David so that he's a permanently dazed little boy now.

Oh! I forgot to tell you that they showed us some of the native aborigines at a wayside station in the great plain yesterday afternoon though they were the most revolting form of living creatures I've ever seen!! They are the lowest known form of human beings & are the nearest thing to monkeys I've ever seen; they danced for us & threw spears & boomerangs, though the whole interest of this native stunt (& you know how I just loathe any form of native stunt sweetie) was spoilt by the fact that they had all been transported (vermin & disease & all) over 100 miles by train for the purpose!!

The authorities must think me the biggest fool God ever created if they imagined they were going to hand out to me that these filthy nauseating creatures had just drifted in from a waterless district to see me without my finding out the truth!! . . .

I don't at all like the look of my bunk as I think the mattress etc. etc. will slide off during the night & I'll hate that!! However I must turn in hope for the best so bonne nuit . . .

13th July (2.00 A.M.), Government House, Adelaide S.A.

Yes, the mattress did slide off during the night & I was rudely awakened about 6.00 A.M. by crashing; however we arrived here safely at 11.00 A.M. met by Archie Weigall [*the governor of South Australia*] & after a really ghastly pompous drive through the city we landed here & found 'Grace' [*Lady Weigall*] in very good shape!!

Of course you'll laugh at what I'm going to say beloved when you remember all the foul things I used to say about her before I knew her; but you know, angel, she's a very charming & amusing hostess & I'm going to add a sweet woman in many ways though I know elle est dangereuse & a cat at times & I'm on my guard!! . . .

You can't think what a marvellous atmosphere is at this Government House as compared to any I've ever struck before!! The Weigalls are real live people instead of boobs & we've had quite a cheery evening despite a pompous dinner & reception as they asked a few bits in to dance about 11.00 & we got a jazz band under way & Archie conducted & we had a proper rag. And for the last hour Grace has been cooking

eggs & bacon in my room & we've had a quartette supper with Archie
& the Admiral & we've laughed a lot!!

She's got some priceless yarns & doesn't care a d–mn what she says
which is vewy refreshing & we feel better already!! They've only been
out here about a month but are very popular already & I'm sure they'll
be a great success out here . . .

Grace has very kindly turned out of her boudoir for me & whose
photo should I find on a shelf above the writing table (where I'm
sitting now) but that of a queer but oh! such a lovely little girl called
Freda Birkin!!

Oh! mon amour I was so thrilled when I saw that photo . . . it made
me feel quite at home at once & no longer in such a strange land
though this ménage is easily the nearest approach to home I've struck
out here!! . . .

It hasn't been such a strenuous day really & I played 6 games of
squash at one of the schools here this afternoon . . .

I'm vewy worn out but I must get down to a speech I've got to hand
out at a government dinner in 16 hrs time!! . . . if want to get any sleep
I must get down to the —— —— now!!

You've never seemed so so near to me as you do tonight mon amour
D.

14th July (2.00 A.M. again!!)

Oh!! my little Fredie I'm such a miserable little boy tonight as the mail
arrived about 10.00 A.M. but no letter from Toi!! What can have
happened that you've missed or that your letters have missed 2 mails
sweetie though I've received such a sweet little one from Penelope
evidently dictated by TOI & anyway TOI printed the address. This fresh
blow has knocked me out completely darling . . .

It's had a desperate effect on me tonight as I just couldn't face a
single woman at the party here tonight except Grace (I can't think why
I call Lady Weigall Grace, but it's shorter), with whom I danced only
once round the ballroom & then sat talking to for 1 hr & she really was
very sweet & sympathetic as I told her of some of my trouble & worries
on this trip!! . . .

3 more long yarns from Philip all about India & a few mentions of

TOI & best of all some photos of TOI . . . I couldn't be more thulky than
to see you standing arm in arm with old Burghie curse him though
thank God it's not that bloody Michael & I feel you really have
forgotten all about that brute & as you've never mentioned him in your
letters, I hope he hasn't been worrying you!! . . .

There seems to be just the faintest hope there is still another bag on
its way up from the ship that had its label eaten by rats on its way out
so that I'm not going to give up all hope of a Fredie letter till the
morning, my sweetheart!! . . .

6.00 P.M.

You'll never know how happy I am with your No 10 letter my
sweetheart & a cable saying you've sold the house though of course
both make me vewy vewy sad & sloppy on top as you were so sad when
you wrote & all you say is too too pathetic for words & now I've got to
try & cheer you up . . .

No 10 letter was in that last bag which only turned up this morning
(it would be) & after reading it over hurriedly the first time between
stunts I was too miserable for words!! But my angel all you wrote at the
end of the last day has bucked me up more than you'll ever know & I
feel it's more or less wiped out No 8 letter till we can meet & talk
which is exactly what I want . . .

My precious beloved how more hopelessly & desperately madly you
make me love you by saying how worried you were to hear that my
week in Melbourne had nearly finished me & that I was stone cold &
that you were distressed that you couldn't be with me to comfort me &
do all the little things to revive me that only YOU can do!! . . .

Of course I'm absolutely livid over what you tell me about Bertie &
Harry having cut you at Farquhar's party sweetie & there's absolutely
no excuse for them whatsoever; cutting YOU who has always been so
divine to them both, particularly Bertie, & how often you've hated &
I've hated his coming to your house to meet Sheilie!!

Little — — well, no words can say what I think of them both & I'll
give them absolute hell on the subject when I see them again if I don't
write for first of all letting H.M. influence them into chucking their
friends & secondly for insulting them.

I also heard from Bertie by this last mail darling one & was staggered when he told me he had seen you at old Farquhar's party but had not danced with you because you left so early & that surprised me & made me think vewy hard!! The little liar & I couldn't be more disappointed in him; it's shown him up properly!!

Harry is such a child, such a baby, my angel, that I don't consider anything he does & I'm sure he longed to dance with you only perhaps that — — old Bertie told him not to; quelle difference to last summer indeed my little Fredie when 2 Do's were so so blissfully happy together & 2 others thought they were, though how I curse the other 2 now not for themselves oh! no, but for having been Do's when it meant absolutely nothing to either of them & they've always been a source of worry to us, haven't they, sweetheart?

Must go & dress for dinner now my Fredie though I'll carry on again later . . .

15th July (6.00 P.M.)

I'm afraid I'll sit up desperately late every night I'm here sweetie as the Weigalls insist on the late supper parties in his dressing room & it means such a lot to the Admiral & I to have them to talk to!! The result is that I was far too thleepy to write at 4.00 A.M. which was when the party broke up & I need hardly tell you there hasn't been a chance of writing since then as it was a hospital, demonstration of women war workers (no need to be thulky, angel) & then a statue of my grandfather to unveil & no less than 10 blinded soldiers to talk to & all that before lunch!!

Last night there was a ball at the Town Hall though we escaped before 11.00 but Grace insisted on asking a dozen girls in to Government House who I had failed to tackle the night before when I was feeling so ill (sans lettre de mon amour) & I did my duty like a man & a Britisher though it was a strain as I wasn't for it at all, though I came up to the scratch & helped the jazz band on the drum, which was infinitely better than dancing!! . . .

Mais ça suffit about all my boring doings & stunts & I must get down to bedrock again where I had to leave off 24 hrs ago as I've got to make such vewy vewy vital points . . . First of all my angel please get that amazing notion that you mustn't be in my life or that you aren't doing me any good right out of that divine but in this case silly little head of yours!! Fancy David calling his Fredie silly . . . & what is more he is scolding her for saying such a thing . . . You know it's only YOU that has made sufficient man of me to carry out my work & far more than ½ the succès I've had is yours mon amour à moi & that I'll never never be able to carry on without your future help & comfort!! So don't you ever dare to make such a statement again my angel; I'm the caveman this evening as you see!!

Another thing I won't tolerate is your kind of including me in the 'YOU all' when you referred to Bertie & Harry being up against H.M. re TOI: I just couldn't be more hurt beloved & absolutely refuse to be in any way even associated with them re TOI!! You already know how much I despise old Bertie for having cut you at a party, whatever H.M. may have said to him, & I do so want YOU my Fredie to remember how vewy vewy different Bertie is to MOI & how still more different are our relations with H.M.

Of course you don't know how much I've changed re my family & in my dealings with officials & I may add the outer world in general; the change is quite amazing sweetie it even amazes me but thank God it's happened & it's happened because of YOU & nobody else!! Oh! I know TOI will be pleased with MOI when TOI sees me again!!

But I've got to scold you still further angel & I really am vewy angwy wiv you for imploring me to go on believing in YOU & not to believe any lies I might be told about YOU!! My little Fredie how could you implore me to do anything that you know I will always always do & that you can trust me to always do!! . . .

. . . I know how sad & depressed you must have been . . . my sweetie, & how more than ever do I curse Bertie as I know his cutting you & insulting you at that party must have reflected just a little onto me in the eyes of the public, for I bet they noticed it & he couldn't have done (apart from the insult to YOU) a more silly thing towards helping us if that was his scheme!!

However it's up to me to show the public that I don't cut my friends whatever they may all say . . .

I hope your house sold well & I wonder who has bought it; I do hope nice people as I'll always be fond of that house & just don't feel I could ever drive past it again & will always go the other way round Regents Park if I ever go through it again . . .

Kind Philip has sent me some marvellous onyx & diamond links as a birthday present; how that man does spoil me & I'm amused to hear of the P.M.'s [*Lloyd George's*] efforts to get you to stay with him!! Naughty old man I say sweetie & how wise of you not to go; but I know how much you impressed him!!

Christ! I've only got 10 minutes to change for a dinner so must beat it, mon amour; how hopeless it is I always seem to be interrupted nowadays!! F–ck!!

16th July (5.00 P.M.), At sea, Adelaide to Hobart

Gud! how I curse myself for not having finished this endless screed last night & to have left it at Adelaide to catch a mail in 2 days' time!! . . . but you know how much I loathe not finishing a letter properly (I'm a vewy thorough little boy) & they told me I would have plenty of time in the ship this afternoon before we sailed & as I didn't turn in till 5.00 A.M. I didn't worry & I just wasn't capable!!

It was disgraceful sweetie but after the usual midnight supper party in Archie's room the Admiral & I sat up & talked to Grace for over 3 hrs so that I'm quite 'gaga' for want of sleep . . .

You'll think me quite mad for talking so much about old 'Mamma' Grace Weigall, though she really has been a kind of mamma (not 'mummie', Fredie darling!!) to me the last 4 days & she has cheered me up so much . . .

She really is a sweet old woman . . . she does know that we are great great friends angel & she also realises how much you've brought me out, & that I shouldn't have been any use if it wasn't for YOU!! . . .

I enclose a divine letter she thrust into my hand when we parted . . . it was sweet of her to write it, wasn't it!! [*She wrote glowingly of the Prince's magnetism encircling the world; of his being a ray of sunshine; of his power over the hearts and heads of his fellow creatures; she signed herself 'your bewildered, devoted & humble fat friend! Grace W.'.*]

Of course, she & Archie are the ideal kind of people to send out to govern a state . . . they are really doing marvellous work for the Empire

& their energy is amazing & they've set me a wonderful example of keenness which is going to help me a lot . . .

Only 2 more states to visit now though I don't think I've ever told you that I'm substituting a week in the 'back blocks' or interior of New South Wales for my visit to late German New Guinea; the bloody press have been hinting that I'm too soft to be able to rough it on a real up-country station, which I've not had a chance of doing yet so that I'm just going to show them that I can!!

But apart from that I ought to see that very important side of Australian life & it will be of far more value than seeing a crowd of revolting black savages who don't yet know whether they are British or Hun & care less!! . . . [*Australia had annexed German New Guinea during the war; in 1920, she was mandated to govern the former German colony.*]

17th July (10.30 P.M.)

I haven't been quite such a lazy little boy beloved as you might suppose as I've been worried by everybody on various business matters till I've almost gone mad & the Admiral & I have had to be vewy tactful with Grigg over several little items re the programme that have occurred lately . . .

I only hope the Admiral & I will be able to keep off a row with him before we get back to England, though it's really becoming more & more of an effort!! . . .

The Admiral has already been in chasing me off to bed so that I really think I had better go . . .

18th July (9.00 P.M.)

. . . I've lost my voice, not quite as bad as February last year but too bad to be able to speak though that's a relief. I'm such a wreck really it's quite pathetic & 'entre nous' I never really feel well nowadays though je t'emprie not a word as I tell everybody I'm merely tired; it's my nerves that have really cracked up from overstrain . . . but nerves affect everything, particularly one's tummy . . .

YOUR David.

Letter No 19
Government House, Hobart, Tasmania
20th July 1920 (1.00 A.M.)

My vewy vewy own sweet beloved darling one,

This is a bad 'come down' after Adelaide as you may imagine, angel; still the Allardyces aren't as bad as all that: the 'Weegles' have spoilt me re governors & their wives!! . . .

My voice has quite collapsed beloved anyway as regards speaking, though that is a great relief & gets me off a speech I'm due to 'hand out' at a lunch today. I tried to address the diggers when I landed but my voice broke down & I'm now croaking like an old frog!! . . .

The 4 days' programme here isn't really vewy strenuous, merely irritating, & old Sir John Allardyce [*actually Sir William*] helps all he can; considering he's an old Colonial Office official who hasn't spent a year all told in England during 50 years' service in various small crown colonies, I think he's amazingly up to date & understanding!! . . .

Nice people these Tasmanians, but naturally on the dull side as it's all so out of the way . . .

What dull rot I'm writing tonight my Fredie . . . still it's such a joy just prattling on to you about nothing at all . . .

22nd July (11.00 P.M.), H.M.S. RENOWN, Hobart

What a relief & almost a joy it is to get back to this marvellous old ship my sweetie . . . We've had the Allardyces & a few other officials to dinner tonight but got rid of them all before 10.00, thank God, as I really am terribly exhausted & they all say (even the Admiral & the newspapers!!) that I look ill, though I really don't feel at all ill only rather more worn out than usual (I was worn out before I even landed in Australia; N.Z. did me in) & extra depressed on account of my rotten voice!!

But I'll get it back on this trip all right beloved if only it's fine & calm & really go to bed early as I've promised Newport my doctor I will. So I mustn't write much more tonight, though what I think of turning in before midnight.

I'm a hopeless case I'm afraid mon amour & I do need you so so badly to chase me into bed with a big big stick . . . I won't live long without TOI to look after me . . . you've done it so efficiently for over a year now & you know how hopeless about everything I am!! Who is going to chase me to the dentist for instance if TOI doesn't? Personne, & that would be the answer to most questions re me if I hadn't got YOU!! . . .

Oh!! my little Fredie (try to imagine you are listening to David being more pathetic than he's ever been before) . . . the small domestic details that I mention are so so trivial as compared to the really big things you do for me (help & advice & comfort etc. etc.) & you must must continue to do for me if I am to 'carry on'!! . . .

At this time, the press were reporting back the strain the Prince was under; before he lost his voice, he was rambling in his speeches, and appeared to be close to a complete breakdown. The King was initially unsympathetic, but when additional reports reached him via Lloyd George, from Weigall and others, he began to be alarmed.

23rd July (5.00 P.M.), At sea

I feel ever so much better after a peaceful slack day at sea sweetie . . . and my voice is returning with the help of a patent inhaler. Although I'm completely & permanently worn out angel it's amazing how quickly I partially recover if I'm given even the smallest chance & can escape all crowds for a day or two & I only wish this was a longer trip instead of merely a 2 day trip as alas we reach Sydney on Sunday morning, when we land at once & leave by train for Queensland & I'm in for the worst & roughest & hardest 3 weeks of the whole trip!! . . .

Queensland is the most bolshie state of all & besides 4 or 5 strenuous days in Brisbane I've got ½ dozen stunting in the train doing up to 8 small places in one day, which would be bad enough if I was fresh but it's heart-breaking in my present state!!

I had yet another cable from Philip last night saying that what he cabled to Perth (about his thinking he would be able to fix things up re India) holds good, which is really very encouraging, isn't it, sweetheart. But I'm so intrigued to know how he's done it & how the P.M. is tackling H.M.? Oh! if only they would postpone India which becomes more & more of a nightmare each day; it's absolute madness sending me there this year beloved & such a d——d shame on me . . .

Queensland Government Railway (In the train at a siding), (South of Brisbane)
26th July 1920

My own precious beloved little sweetheart,

. . . We anchored in our old billet in Sydney harbour about 10.30
A.M. yesterday & landed in plain clothes & 'plus ou moins' unofficially,
though quite a bunch of people lined our route to the station & the
railway track through the suburbs . . . We are on our way up to
Brisbane . . . where alas I've got to go through just one more state entry
& procession though thank Gud! it's absolutely the very last one of all!!

Of course all may go well in Brisbane but somehow I'm full of
apprehensions as we'll be up against the bolshies properly & the acting
premier [*the Hon. J.A. Fihelly*], who met us at the state boundary this
morning, is the foulest & most infamous looking cut-throat Irish R.C.
that I've ever seen!! Of course the element up here is more Sinn Fein
than bolshie, really, but anyway whatever it is I don't like it at all!!

I'll be oh! so glad when tomorrow's pompous drive is over as these
stunts are always a rough indication of the public feeling towards — —
well, whatever it is that your little David represents . . .

We all feel rather like trapped animals up here as we are surrounded
by Sinn Feiners (all the Queensland officials are S.F.s) & so have to be
terribly careful what we say about anything; of course we may have the
wind up unnecessarily but I don't think so . . .

27th July (11.30 P.M.), Parliament Buildings, Brisbane

Just a few lines before I turn in sweetie to tell you that this Sinn Fein or
Bolshie (or whatever you like to call it) city has welcomed me just as
enthusiastically & kindly as all the other state capitals & I feel very grateful
to all these people for helping me out & showing that anyway for the next
few years Australia can't become a R.C. republic, which is apparently the
ulterior aim of quite a large section of the Australian Irish . . .

Oh! my beloved Fredie, the Admiral has just been in to show me a
cable from H.M. saying – you'll never guess – that he's postponed my
visit to India a whole year!! Oh!! sweetheart what a huge joy & relief
this marvellous news is to your little David, though you know how

that ghastly trip hung over him like an ever increasing inky black cloud & that the letters and the word INDIA grew in size each day!

If only H.M. had done this even a fortnight ago what a different man I should have been & oh! how much more pep I could have put into the stunting, worn out as I am!! I feel a new man already, only a few minutes after getting the cable so much has the news bucked me up; oh! & it's your birthday tomorrow mon amour & I feel this news is part of my birthday present to you . . .

Good old Philip; I bet I owe more to him than to anyone else for this postponement & how grateful I am to him!! Oh! it's all so so wonderful sweetie, just think of it, a whole year in the Old Country & near YOU my beloved little angel . . .

To think that instead of spending the best part of another whole years as a performing animal I'll be able to lead a man's life again, for I do feel so much like a turn in a circus sometimes during these tours . . .

But you've never read such an inane pompous cable as H.M. has sent, darling, which reads like an official proclamation; how it shows up his attitude towards me bringing in such balls as 'on the advice of my ministers'!! If only he knew how utterly ridiculous he is & how little I think of him or his ministers & still less of their — — advice!!

But the whole thing is that India is off, my precious one & that WE'll be together as much as WE like for the next year so that nothing else matters!! Oh! Oh! how I want you tonight mon amour to share my joy at this marvellous news . . .

29th July (2.00 A.M.)

We've been to another 'ball' tonight, semi-pompous, given by ½ dozen of the leading girls of Brisbane, though it was very boring & I can't think why I stayed there till 12.00 as I was tired . . .

It's been hard stunting . . . 4 hrs at the Queensland agricultural show (including a revolting lunch) . . . a civic garden party . . . & a trip to the Queensland 'Anzac Hostel' where all the permanently disabled men in the state are housed & medically looked after for life!!

There is an 'Anzac Hostel' in each state, run by the Commonwealth repatriation department, & I've been to them all & it's so sad & pathetic to see these poor fellows who can never recover!! They are mostly paralysed cases due to spinal wounds, a few double amputations & sundry queer cases of rheumatism etc., though they are amazingly cheery despite this ghastly fate!! I can't think why I dwell on this sordid subject sweetie but my visits to those sad establishments impress me yet depress me!

I've been working at a foul speech ever since I got back so that I'm just about dead now & I've got to start stunting again at 10.00 A.M. But I'm no longer so worn out mentally as the word India no longer haunts me . . .

I've been thinking so so fervently about you all day mon amour but particularly today or rather yesterday being your birthday, though you know I always ridicule that sort of thing!! But my sweetheart, 28th July will always be one of the greatest anniversaries for David as it commemorates the beginning of FREDIE his all all & everything . . .

31st July (1.00 A.M.)

We are off to a bush station for the weekend to stay with some people called Bell who we know & hope to ride the whole time & get fit. It ought to be quite fun if it's fine though the moon looks bad tonight & I fear the worst!! . . .

God keep you for your vewy vewy own devoted adoring little David.

Letter No 21
Coochin Coochin, Boonah, Queensland
1st August 1920 (1.00 A.M.)

My vewy Vewy own darling beloved

We really have no luck as it's been pouring 'jugs of blood' all day & is still & the country is in a fearful mess & we had a terrible drive out from Boonah, the railway terminus, 15 miles in a 2-seater driven by Bert Bell, one of the 3 sons, though we were better off than the bigger cars!! . . .

We didn't reach here much before 6.00 P.M. but it was all right when we did; the Bell family are really a charming bunch of people & very kind consisting of a dear old widow mother, 3 daughters (all plain & aged [gap] & 3 sons (2 of whom are ex-R.A.F. squadron commanders) &

1 daughter-in-law (wife of the civilian son & as dull as her husband!!).

I'm afraid we've been dancing to a gramophone & ragging ever since dinner sweetie which is why I'm so idiotically late again but they are all such a cheery crowd & they just wouldn't let us go to bed . . .

This is a perfect little bungalow 'homestead' full of souvenirs from the Old Country as old Mrs Bell & the girls were over there most of the war & so are quite fairly up to date, which helps a lot!! It seems quite funny to be staying at a private house with private people & such a relief after no alternative but the 'Renown', the train, or a Government House!!!! . . . I've got such a nice comfy little room where TOI et MOI could be oh! so so happy!!

(11.30 P.M.)

It's been a marvellous bright warm day beloved & we've all been out working the cattle from 10.00 A.M. till 5.00 P.M. which means at least 6 hrs riding as we called a halt for a picnic lunch for an hour!! . . .

I feel terribly well & much fitter tonight & am enjoying this life & long for a week here instead of only a weekend . . . I'm quite pleased with myself angel as I think they are rather impressed with my riding (how I do swank) . . .

How you would love the life here; anyway you would have loved today & your absence was the only complaint!! TOI et MOI could be oh! so so happy on a Queensland station as I've already said we could be on my ranch in Canada!! And it annoyed me riding with those girls today when it could so easily have been my Fredie & ought to have been HER!!

Oh! I've had some real brainwaves as a result of all the riding & open air sweetie; one is to cut out Sidney Greville & ask the Admiral to replace him which job he's accepted . . . as he's anyway going to leave the service he's delighted; of course I've no doubt H.M. will object but it won't be of any use as I'm absolutely determined . . . [*Sidney Greville was Treasurer of the Duchy of Cornwall and the Prince's Comptroller, with whom the Prince had stayed after his fever in July 1919.*]

I'm going to cut out Claud as well & tell him he must look for another job!! You know I've never liked him & you don't either & that lad irritates me & gets on my nerves more than I can say; besides he can't ride.

And then I'm going to say goodbye to Grigg for good & all when I get back although I know that behind my back my family are asking him to take up the permanent job of private secretary to me!! I just couldn't be more furious at this fresh effort on the part of my family to run me, beloved one, though it only gives me extra strength to fight them as I'm so looking forward to doing!!

Curiously enough Godfrey is going to be my Private Secretary!! It will be such a relief to collect only the people I want & start off again with a clean slate. Of course this is all extra secret sweetie . . . I'm sure you'll be pleased with David for his brainwaves, Fredie darling, & his determination to carry them out . . .

I'm just dropping off to sleep after all that . . . we'll be riding all day tomorrow again & they have early hours here . . .

2nd August (6.00 P.M.)

Just a scrawl before we leave Coochin . . . we've had another marvellous day's riding 'cutting out' cattle . . . that is picking out the fattest bullocks from a mob . . . they are put through a 'dip' to kill the 'young visitors' (as you call them angel) before they are driven down to the railhead . . .

We've got a desperate day in the train tomorrow . . . I've got to address 3,000 diggers in a wool-shed; so they are keeping me at it right up to the very end; no slacking allowed. It's dinner time so must stop now sweetie; à demain & bless you.

3rd August (6.00 P.M.), In the train to Brisbane

This is one of the worst days we've struck my Fredie but I'm not worrying & am so so happy with 2 more letters . . .

We've been station stunting all day & I've yet the 3,000 diggers & a — — party to face in Brisbane so I won't be far from death tomorrow . . . But do I care about that or anything else in the world with 2 such sweet divine & marvellous Fredie letters in my pocket saying all all the things I most want to hear . . . that you are tired of life without me . . . I've forgotten all about No 8 letter now, anyway till we meet, & you must forget all I wrote in answer to it . . .

4th August (3.00 A.M.)

Well, I'm still just alive sweetheart, despite the hour; the train got in about 9.00 P.M. & I drove straight to the Diggers' smoking concert in the wool-shed & rather excelled myself in my few words to them & wasn't nervous despite the 3,000 of them & several hundreds of them nicely 'shot away' too!! They were quite enthusiastic angel but not too wuf wiv me when I walked round all their tables . . .

We leave this city for good at 11.00 A.M. but have an hour's back-chat with heaps of nasty old men with long beards full of cheese to go through with first . . .

(11.30 P.M.), In the train at a siding near Towoomba (Q)

. . . Nothing has been more marvellous the whole trip, beloved, than the sending off Brisbane gave us this morning . . .

I'm not really in a fit state (No! I'm stone sober angel) to write any more . . . I'm going through hell with indigestion . . . I'm so part worn out now that it's only natural that my tummy should be too, same as everything else!!

Christ! how I prattle on to YOU about my rotten self . . .

Your devoted adoring little David.

Towoomba (Q)
4th August 1920 (6.00 P.M.)

Fredie darling precious beloved,

I'm not numbering this as it isn't a proper letter . . . I'm at a hotel here for ½ hr before a civic dinner so it's a case of real rush & no time to get my proper diary letter out to seal it up!! . . .

What a perfectly mad scrawl this is & there's such a perfectly good letter waiting for you in the train!! Oh! f— f— f— f—!!

So Duddie has gone dippy on Mary Pickford [*the actress who had married Douglas Fairbanks in 1919, and who, with Charlie Chaplin, set up United Artists*]!! Oh! my Gawd but there's no accounting for tastes!! Je deviens de plus en plus furieux que tu es sa femme mon amour; it's all wrong & an insult to you & foul for you. Mais ça suffit if I haven't written too much!! . . .

They say I must go down to this perishing dinner so I must stop now Fredie darling . . . How I'm thinking of you down at Lympne with the babies sweetie & long & long to spend August & September with you there!! Aren't you going up to Dunrobin? . . .

This little note carries all all your David's love et baisers & he ever whispers FREDIE VENUS.

In the early morning of 7 August, the Prince incurred the displeasure of the people of Gilgandra by not getting up to meet them. They 'counted him out', i.e. starting at one and counting to ten, which was a custom that was used to silence unpopular speakers. The Prince, fast asleep, was unaware of this problem, but, having been made aware of it, on his return through Gilgandra on 9 August, he was so popular that they 'counted him back in again'.

Letter No 22
Wingadee sheep station, Coonamble N.S.W.
7th August 1920 (10.00 P.M.)

Fredie darling precious beloved,

This wouldn't be such a bad spot if our hosts weren't such a bum crowd!! It's a station owned by the A. & N.Z. Land Company & we are staying with the Company's manager here, Feehan by name; I've just escaped from one of the worst dinner parties of my life: never have I found conversation harder to make . . .

We rode the 30 miles here through the bush with a relay of horses & a picnic ½ way, as well as a drinkie at a bush pub we were asked to stop at!! And it was a most priceless cavalcade my sweetie as some of our servants & such like were mounted & as each complained that his horse pulled I stood by to relieve them (swank), though of course they didn't pull at all really.

However we fetched up here safely & after shaking hands with all the diggers of the neighbourhood & their families I was taken to see the 'wool shed' where the shearing is done, though we are a whole month too early to watch the work in progress . . .

They've had terrible floods here last month & lost 5 to 6 thousand sheep, drowned or died of exhaustion!! One could hardly believe it till one passes lots of dead sheep as we did today . . . and this on top of 2 whole years of drought!! It's very bad luck on these station owners who have naturally lost thousands of pounds . . . they have to work really hard for every quid they make; station life is very strenuous indeed though I would love about a month of it . . .

I'm such a tired little David tonight & have had real bad indigestion & painies the last 2 days though I feel very fit & well after the riding . . .

8th August 9.30 P.M.

I've ridden for 5 hours today . . . this afternoon we all went out kangaroo hunting with long dogs & one gave us quite a good gallop as it's fairly open country, though we ran into some 'emus' (an inferior type of ostrich) & so switched off to them & killed 3!! I also chased a fox & 2 of the dogs chased & killed a kangaroo on their own, though we weren't in at the kill!! A very poor form of sport & I refuse to call it hunting, though we had a good ride & covered 20 miles easy!! . . .

It's marvellous getting all this hard riding . . . though thank Gawd we quit this station tomorrow as our hosts are too too sordid for words & the whole outfit has brought the 'blight' to us all. We've never felt so 'blue' or so bored, though we'll be all right as soon as we get clear of this family, who are very civilised, very genteel middle class people, who are the most irritating of all types, don't you think, sweetie? We've had to lunch with them as well as dine with them again & each meal gets worse!! What a contrast to Coochin . . .

9th August (11.00 P.M.) In the train in N.S.W.

A very uneventful day sweetie . . . we left Wingadee so as to reach the racecourse by 2.00 P.M. & we stayed till after the last race . . . The Coonamble races are famed for the heat & crookedness of all concerned & so I wasn't surprised at losing every quid (£15 in all) that I put on, though it was maddening!! . . .

I'm afraid we'll never get quit of all the federal & state officials & hangers on though how wild they make me . . . They are quite useless now & are merely out for a joy ride in the 'Royal Train', getting blotto each night on the principle that the government is paying & that if the

Government says 'Have a good time', then have a bloody good
time!! . . . But I'm horrified to find that I've used up the whole sheet
on all this 'balls' . . .

10th August (11.30 P.M.) Canonbar Station, Miowera (N.S.W.)

A very superior spot to Wingadee, Fredie darling, & a far pleasanter
atmosphere as this is a very luxurious homestead & we are staying with
nice people & 'du monde' more like the Bells which is a relief!!

This is one of many stations owned by Goldsborough Mort & Co &
Niall the chairman is really our host though this is the manager's house
(McLeod) & he & his wife are very nice & real good stamps of
Australians & their son is a good chap & rides well. [*The Prince accused
his father of judging people's character too much by their shooting ability; he
himself was certainly influenced by riding ability.*]

Niall's son is staying here with his wife; he was in a dragoon
regiment & taken prisoner at Cambrai & his wife might almost be
called a 'bit' by some people!! So it isn't all so sordid here as at the last
hole!! . . .

We went through the shearing shed on our way to the house where a
team of 15 cut-throats were at work & we spent 1 hr with them
watching them & talking to them. A real rough crowd, sweetie, &
fairly Bolshie as they trek round from station to station doing piece
work; they get 5d. for every sheep they do & the average is 130 a day,
so that is not exactly a low wage, though most of them booze away
every quid they make . . . [*Mountbatten's figures are very different from the
Prince's, suggesting that the shearers received 14 shillings per hundred, and
that a good target was 200 per day. As a rough guide, prices have risen by at
least 25 times since 1920.*]

Old J.M. Niall is one of the richest men in Australia so that it
doesn't hurt him at all to make a great splash for us out here by hiring
the head waiter & chef of the Hotel Australia, Sydney, as well as the
leading Sydney jazz pianist to play after dinner. But he's overdone it all
hopelessly angel & it rather nauseates me, particularly the vast amount
of food, & my indigestion is getting worse & I'm going through the
completest hell with it tonight & have suffered tortures all day!!

However the only thing to do is starve, not that that's any worry to me though it makes a 2 hr dinner such as we had tonight all the more trying. Oh! why must it always be the P. of W. sweetie instead of just plain David sometimes?

A fat lot of good it's been trying to show people out here for nearly 3 months that I'm only human & abhor any form of blatant advertisement of opulence of which this is one of the worst!! However it's all so terribly well-meant sweetie that perhaps I'm being hard on old Niall . . . but it all irritates me none the less & then this — — tummy trouble does depress me so!! However Newport has given me some patent soda dope tonight so I must hope for the best!! Bonne nuit mon amour & bless you.

11th August (6.30 P.M.)

We've just got in from a 50 mile ride into the bush, beloved, where we did some kangaroo hunting with long dogs & killed 5 though it's just about the mouldiest & tamest form of sport I've ever struck!! The unfortunate 'Roos' as they call them never get a chance & the bush was too thick to be able to gallop . . . the Admiral & I chucked it in disgust

Chatting with the Canonbar sheep-shearers.

after the 3rd kill but Dickie chased on & thought it marvellous & asked me how it compared to hunting in the Old Country!! Poor lad!! . . .

Old Niall had a fleet of cars out groaning with costly food for a 'picnic lunch' which developed into an enormous repast complete with Sydney waiters, which quite spoilt the day for me particularly as I couldn't face more than a biscuit!!

For once I was furious & had a row all by myself angel as of course I couldn't have one with any of the party, who were all tucking in & enjoying the priceless 'viands'!!

What I think of food just now & to add insult to injury I've shortly got to sit down to another vast dinner & there are some fearful rumours of some women having been asked to come in to dance at 9.00 P.M. Christ is the only suitable ejaculation . . .

12th August (2.00 A.M.)

I don't deserve a scrap of sympathy Fredie darling for sitting up in this idiotic way & it's not because I've been dancing or sitting out although 10 ham faced females did roll in at 9.00 P.M. As practically all the male guests (real tough bushmen) got toxi I stayed up to see them shove off in their cars loaded with women & it really was worth it, angel; it's been a real eye-opener to the atmosphere of bush & station life, which is after all what I'm supposed to be trying to get a hold of this week!! . . .

(11.30 P.M.), In the train to Sydney

We've just left Miowera & so the 'back block' trip is over; I'm quite sorry in a way or rather I only wish I could have spent more of the 3 months in Australia at stations in the bush . . .

This afternoon I rode 6 races & won them all which pleased me because I wasn't always riding the fastest horse, though of course I could give away two stone . . . Oh! I'm just crazy about riding races & am more determined than ever to get a chaser & ride in point to points next Spring . . .

I ran the mile from the house to the train siding with young Les McLeod, though he couldn't complete the course!! I beat him in two riding races this afternoon so I gave him a chance of beating me on his feet . . .Christ! what swank darling!! [*The Prince does not mention that the actual result was a dead heat with Mountbatten.*] . . .

13th August (11.00 P.M.)

. . . I'm late because I've had all the train staff to say goodbye to which is always a big proposition!!

3 more letters from Philip & then one from little Sheilie which was so sweet of her to write considering I've not written to her at all . . . I'm looking forward to seeing Mollee Little again tomorrow night when we are giving a tiny party in the ship & I expect she'll have lots of news of Sheilie!! Bertie sends another pompous yarn which infuriates me explaining how he's been too busy to see anything of the '2 Do's'; what I think of that boy & I'm more disappointed in him than ever.

And then I think we'll find the Weigalls at Sydney as the G.G. has asked them to stay at Admiralty House the 5 days we are there . . . it's so marvellous to think the whole programme is over now & that we'll be quite free private citizens more or less!!

The more I think of it the more amazed I am that I've been able to go through with this last 4 months. Christ only knows how we've done it as it seems more of a superhuman task the more one looks back!!

I'll start a new letter in the ship tomorrow . . . so au revoir . . . please forgive such a rotten dull screed but I'm so so tired after this hard week though it's done me lots of good & I'm vewy fit. David is quite a hard little boy now.

All all my love & baisers are yours sweetheart   Your David

Only 2 months more to wait till our sacred reunion . . .

> *Letter No 23*
> *H.M.S. RENOWN, Sydney*
> *15th August 1920 (1.30 A.M.)*

Fredie my vewy vewy own precious darling beloved

. . . We went out to the races at Randwick this afternoon (a special meeting they had organised for me sweetheart) . . . I saw Mrs Chisholm

& Mollee Little in the grandstand & had a yarn with them I need hardly add mostly about Sheilie!! Mrs C. is a sweet woman & I've planned to have another yarn with her & I was glad to see Mollee again & she's been on board for a slight private dinner & jazz party I've given tonight angel!! . . .

So anyway I'll turn in now . . . I've never been so hopelessly dead tired as I am now angel & I'm afraid this week isn't going to help me recover as there are jazz parties for us every night!! . . .

16th August (2.00 A.M.)

We've been to a small party at the house of a very rich old woman (Miss Walker); it's a very luxurious house complete with squash court, swimming bath etc. & we went up about teatime & had a game before dinner after which we danced & it developed into God's own rag, though Mollee (who was one of the party) & I weren't in ragging mood & wanted to discuss Sheilie & serious matters!! [*The Mountbatten diary records the Prince being actively involved in the horseplay, which ended only when a valuable oriental carpet was soaked with water.*]

So the result was that we both got vewy depressed sweetie & so did Dickie & so the 3 of us spent the last hour yarning on the staircase till we nearly dozed off!! I think Dickie is rather smitten with Moll, though he doesn't often get her to himself as she is really my little 'bit' or rather friend, as I've only got one 'bit' my Fredie & so couldn't have another . . .

The result is that we've become a 'trio', though Moll is 2 months older than me so that Dickie is the 'baby', though as I've often told you darling a vewy grown up one & he & I have become more inseparable than ever now so that we always hunt in couples & I don't enjoy anything without him on this trip . . .

Moll . . . is just crazy to meet you & I'm sure you would love her Fredie darling as she has so much in her that is of our atmosphere & ideas or rather I should say those of our little 'set', meaning Sheilie, Poots, etc. etc.!! Dickie & I monopolise her at parties here & the Admiral & Godfrey & Joey have also danced with her, though it's so typical of that bloody Claud & Dudley North never to have even asked her to!! . . .

18th August (2.00 A.M.)

. . . This afternoon Mollee asked Dickie & I to tea with her family but
we took her for a drive in the city in a car first & I drove the car angel,
a Crossley, & strange to say I didn't crash though I've only once driven
a car since I left England & never a Crossley before!!

But we laughed a lot; Moll's family aren't very exciting but quite
nice, though luckily Mrs Chisholm was there too which helped!! . . .
Then another but smaller party . . . though somehow I couldn't be 'full
out' or put any pep into the party as honestly honestly I just don't
enjoy any party wherever it is sans TOI . . . your absence ruins
everything for me which is rather inconvenient sometimes, particularly
when one is host & doesn't want to have an undertaker's expression,
which I must have had all this evening!! . . .

What you must think of me leading this mad life in Sydney; still I
suppose it's a kind of reaction after having been official for so many
months . . .

19th August (10.00 P.M.), At sea

Oh! how sad & disappointed I am . . . oh! the pain of it my beloved
again, no Fredie letter. What can have happened . . .

I called on the Governor General & Lady Helen Ferguson at
Admiralty House to say 'good bye-ee' before we sailed at noon, though
we took quite a party out with us as far as 'the Heads', where we
anchored at 1.00 P.M. to wait for the mail . . . there was Grace & Archie
& then of course Mollee Little & 8 or 9 other girls, all bits belonging to
& asked for by various members of the staff & ships' officers & they
lunched on board & didn't leave the ship till about 5.00 P.M.

We danced for 1 hr after lunch & then everyone took his bit into his
cabin, except for me angel, who only took Mollee for a final talk as she
isn't my bit at all!! I've got a terrible haunting feeling that all I've said
about Moll & seeing so much of her these last 5 days might make you
thulky, sweetie (though I like you to be thulky) but if only you
understand that I merely look on her as a second edition of Sheilie &
that I've made great friends with her & taken special trouble with her
merely because she is your greatest friend's greatest friend!!

I'm also quite fond of her for herself Fredie darling just as I'm fond of

Sheilie & Poots 'mais c'est tout'!! But for YOU I shouldn't probably have got to know Sheilie & the same is the case with Moll; & although we may have got ourselves talked about a little in Sydney beloved everyone knows it's because of 'Sheila Chisholm' & consequently because of Fredie!! This is no kind of apology mon amour because I have such an absolutely clear conscience about it all; the only thing I fear is giving you a false impression of it all though I don't think I have really!!

Moll & I had a final yarn about Sheilie who I'm afraid I'm going to miss by a whole month as she sails in the middle of September [*the Loughboroughs had decided to try to save their marriage by spending a year in Australia, with Loughie supposedly removed from the temptations of gambling and alcohol*] . . . she & Moll have written to each other every mail since 1915. Ours was quite a pathetic little parting at 5.00 P.M. as Moll is the only woman I've got to know at all well on this trip . . . as a matter of fact I think Mollee is rather fond of Roy Chisholm, Sheilie's youngest brother, a nice fellow & good-looking & he's certainly fond of her. [*They were married soon afterwards, despite Roy being annoyed by the amount of time she had spent dancing with the Prince.*]

But enough about Mollee, angel; she shoved off with the rest of the women & we sailed at 9.00 P.M. as soon as the aviators who brought the mail shoved off . . .

20th August (11.00 P.M.)

Although I didn't turn out till about noon sweetheart I don't yet feel terribly rested . . .

I don't think I've yet told you beloved what I think of the news that the old Duke of Connaught is going to India instead of me, though of course you are sure to have known it before it was official!!

Personally I'm sorry they aren't sending Bertie so as to give him a chance of working on his own & breaking right away from Buckhouse as I've been able to do!! And then India is easier to cope with than a dominion & so it would be letting him down lightly his first trip!! However that obviously isn't to be angel & I suppose they thought it was a good excuse to get the old Duke out of England for the winter; his doctors send him down to the Riviera early each Winter on account of the permanent bronchial cough he has though he hates going.

Now Fredie darling you will remember my telling you that I've made up my mind that Claud has got to quit; well I crashed with him & told him so this afternoon though I was vewy tactful & polite but firm & the interview couldn't have been more peaceful or satisfactory!!

He agreed that as we are in no way kindred spirits it just wasn't a scrap of use his remaining on as equerry to me!! We have remained quite good friends & it's eased the situation & cleared the air . . . I suggested his going to India with the Duke though he doesn't seem to freeze on to that idea much . . . Of course I'll have to help him all I can to get another job . . . I don't at all want the Lord Claud hanging round St J's P. for 3 months.

Of course Claud couldn't have been more of the courtier this afternoon & agreed with all I said though I haven't the least doubt that behind my back he's telling anyone in the ship he thinks will listen to him that I've behaved like a perfect — 4 letters & have treated him badly & he'll certainly do so to all his snobbish friends in London!!

But what do I care what he thinks or says or tells people as I know I'm in the right as regards the interests of the P. of W. to which job I'm anyway sticking for the present, though as we've both of us TOI et MOI so often said, it's just about the most difficult & trying & complex job on Earth!!

And that's why you must stick to me forever sweetie as my greatest friend & confidante which you can do without doing yourself or your sweet babies any harm whatsoever; do please please say you will my Fredie or I'll never never be able to carry on!! . . .

You see we are now coming to the end of another chapter in my life angel & it's the last chapter under the 'old régime'; by that I mean before I've had it all out with my father & we've come to a proper & clear understanding about everything, though I've only my own rotten self to blame that the 'old régime' has lasted so long which is far too long.

Of course we'll have several marvellous talks before I crash at Buckhouse as I shall want you to help me & supply me with ammunition for that great battle . . .

Claud Hamilton remained in royal service, becoming Equerry to George V and, after the King's death, Comptroller and Treasurer in Queen Mary's Household. He was replaced as Equerry to the Prince by the Hon. Bruce Ogilvy.

21st August (10.00 P.M.)

... But sweetheart to continue my yarn of last night!! I've besides everything else to look out for a new equerry when I get back ... I would be so grateful beloved if you could help me by suggesting a name or two or anyway of thinking of someone suitable!! Of course old Reggie would really be ideal for me & is longing to quit Buckhouse as you know, though his health would never stand the racket of life with me, I'm afraid, or rather I should say that bullet in his lung, not his health!!

I really want a chap younger than me & a cavalry man for preference as it's time I gave the cavalry a chance, having always had guardsmen. But anyway he must be able to ride & ride well angel & know all about horses & horse mastership too ...

Oh! by the way I don't think I've yet congratulated you on selling poor dear old No 1, Cumberland Terrace for £10,000! [*Freda had bought the house in 1919 for under £4,000.*] What an amazingly clever woman you are sweetie & I'm so so glad you've made so much out of it though for personal & romantic reasons I just loathe to think of that divine house which was so so much yours & only & entirely yours beloved being lived in by anyone else!! I hate it!! ...

I feel as if I've been away for years ... & we haven't met for 166 days!! Still I've just looked at & opened your sacred little locket (the one containing your precious hair), it's such a huge comfort my sweetheart ...

Oh! bless you bless you for ever & ever & God keep you for me (& that for ever & ever too) my little Fredie to whom her vewy vewy own little David is always instinctively whispering Venus Venus Venus Venus Venus Venus.

Letter No 24
24th August (1.00 A.M.), Suva, Fiji

Fredie precious darling beloved à moi

... We changed into really rough clothes & motored out to the outskirts of Suva, where there were some horses for us & we rode 8 miles into the interior along rough tracks ... we hardly ever went out

of a walk, the track being so rough . . . I set off to walk back to
Government House, much to the local people's amazement as it was
over 10 miles & it was somewhat of a strain as I haven't walked for
ages . . .

When I got back to Govt. Ho. Dickie & I threw ourselves into a vast
tiled bath (plenty of room for two!!) where we lay in cool water till
dinner which, accompanied by a couple of cocktails, revived me!! . . .

We sail at 7.00 A.M. & as I'm going to turn out & be on the bridge
when we leave harbour I'm going to bed right now sweetie!!

(10.00 P.M.), At sea

. . . This evening we've had quite a good film though you would have
blindfolded me angel had you been down below with me as there was
quite an attractive bit in the leading woman's part!! . . .

Second 24th August (10.00 P.M.)

Perhaps you'll remember my telling you that we missed out a whole
day on the outward trip when we crossed 180th meridian; well now on
the homeward trip we have to add in an extra day to counteract that
queer calculation, though it's all too complicated for me to
understand!! As if one wanted an extra day of this tropical heat . . .

25th August (6.30 P.M.)

We've had a vewy trying day ashore at Apia, Samoa, anyway trying to
me, sweetie, who just loathes natives & native stunts!! . . . I was driven
off to a kind of park where several thousand natives had been collected,
a few hundred of them curiously dolled up, who performed queer
dances & made still queerer noises . . . I had to sit there for 3 solid
hours watching all that balls till I nearly went mad & still more nearly
went to sleep & I also had to sit down to a nauseating feast which was a
vast amount of revolting looking native foods spread out on the floor of
a hut & everything reeked of coconut oil which these filthy Samoans
smear over their naked bodies!! It really was a case of 'Eee!', beloved, as
denoting pain, anyway it was pain to me!!

When I finally escaped at 3.00 P.M. the Administrator [*Colonel R.W.*

Tate] drove me up to his official residence which is Robert Louis Stevenson's house or bungalow where the great writer died 26 years ago & he's buried at the top of a hill close by which needless to say I strafed up to, sweetheart; not to see the grave, though I did just walk round it when I got to the top, but merely for the exercise!! They told me it would be ¾ hr before I was down again, but changing into flannels I was down in ½ hr . . .

We motored back to the town pier & I dashed in to the British Club for 5 minutes as they asked me to 'come in & have one' though they had all had several too many & so were quite 'shot away' & the President was in the worst state of the bunch!! Disgusting!! . . .

We are now heading straight for Honolulu . . .

26th August (1 1.00 P.M.)

Eee! but it's hot now sweetie . . . I've started asking the ship's officers aft to dinner again & have 4 or 5 each night which is quite a good thing to do & makes a change for me!! . . .

I'm still terribly restless angel & that is really my worst trouble. I find it so hard to sit down & concentrate on anything (except writing to you my beloved) & this heat doesn't exactly help me in this respect!! I can't even read much & invariably drop off to sleep when I do; so I don't really just know how I spend my days at sea though I do know I waste a fearful amount of time!! Venus. D.

27th August (10.00 P.M.)

We recrossed 'The Line' again today . . . it's good to feel I'm even in the same hemisphere as YOU again my beloved . . .

28th August (10.00 P.M.)

A little more breeze today so perhaps a shade cooler . . .

I've had a long yarn with Dickie this evening (not that we aren't always having long yarns) & we discussed life vewy seriously!! Of course you know he thinks he's very much in love with Audrey James & has lots of great friends who each give him different advice on the subject each time they write!!

He's so funny about it all sweetie though he takes it all so so seriously in his baby way (though he's only a baby in the matter of his love affairs) & he's always asking my advice, angel, which invariably is not to think of marrying till he's years & years older, particularly as he's a very able & keen young naval officer & crazy about the service in which I think he's got quite a big future & he'll make a name if he's lucky!!

As regards Audrey I tell him that I only just know her by sight from having seen her at 2 or 3 dances in London but that I'll have a look at her when I get back!! Do you know her sweetie? . . . [*Audrey James soon decided against marrying Mountbatten. In 1923, after her marriage to a wealthy cotton magnate called Coats, the Prince had a brief affair with her. Her husband was not amused.*]

I'm so worried sometimes because Dickie isn't popular with the staff as a whole & simply because they are jealous of his being my greatest friend & confidant instead of any of them!! . . . Of course he is 10 years younger than the youngest of them, though they are an exceptionally intolerant crowd & really neither he nor I care a damn what they think of us beloved!! But it's what they'll say when we get back & I don't want my 'little brother' Dickie badly spoken of at home!! . . . I'm so fond of that boy & he means so much to me when I'm away from TOI, far more than Bertie ever has or ever will . . .

MOANA HOTEL, HONOLULU, 30th August (6.30 P.M.)

. . . A mail was brought on board which at last contained a Fredie letter & I'm so so happy & comforted with it although I think you were feeling rather sad when you wrote it on 21st July . . . of course you hadn't received my famous letter in answer to No 8 when you wrote so I'm looking forward to 2 or 3 far happier ones at Acapulco or Trinidad . . .

We won't discuss India any more as it's such a back number now, though my bloody father has written me such a foul letter on the subject which will infuriate you when I give it you to read beloved!! Christ what I think of that man he really is the limit; in fact he's not a man at all & oh! how I utterly despise him & I'll show him how I do when I get back!! I guess I'll make him feel real sorry for being so unfair & unjust about me, who after all is only working for him (or rather what people are led to believe he represents) & so I feel he might be just a little grateful . . .

I didn't land till 1.00 P.M. . . . I had a good though sweltering game of golf after which I came to this hotel . . . I've just been surf bathing & got on better than last April though it's hard exercise & too strenuous on top of 18 holes of golf in a temperature of well over 80 degrees F . . .

I think I did congratulate you on making a clear £6,000 on your house transaction Fredie . . . how sweet of you to say our house in referring to No 1 Cumberland Terrace . . .

Must stop now for dinner though it's too hot to eat . . . I believe they dance after dinner & then it's the right thing to bathe by moonlight so I may be rather late to bed . . .

31st August

Yes, I was late to bed sweetie as we all danced till midnight & then bathed . . .

We sail at 6.00 P.M. tomorrow & I must now tell you that we are due to reach Portsmouth & London on Monday 11th October on which day I pray I'll be able to see you & will go quite mad if I can't!!

(2.00 A.M.)

As I was scribbling before dinner the Admiral told me I was gaining nothing by leaving this letter behind in Honolulu as the mail from Panama will get home quicker!! So I cut out trying to finish it . . .

The dancing wasn't as good as last night & I got let in for a nightmare dance with a completely toxy woman who had been dining tête-à-tête with one of our officers in his cabin on board & say this ship isn't exactly dry!!!!

Christ I was furious, as you may well imagine, my sweetie, & I could have killed the beta when she called me 'darling' & said I was stiff & formal when I refused to kiss her after she had asked me to!! She capped it all by saying I was afraid to!! . . . I was really quite sorry for the poor woman getting into that state & not knowing how much she was giving herself away!! . . .

The mosquitos are real bad here & the Admiral & I slept very bum last night as we got devoured!! Sorry for breaking into this d—d 'Yank' again sweetie but it's oh! so catching & I just caan't help it!! . . .

Au revoir et à bientot Fredie darling beloved . . . your vewy vewy own devoted adoring little amoureux, your David.

Letter No 25
H.M.S. 'Renown' at sea, Honolulu to Acapulco
1st September 1920

Fredie darling precious beloved little sweetheart

Well, here we are at sea again angel . . . on our way to Acapulco (Mexico) to oil . . . though I hear it's the laast place on Gawd's earth!! . . .

To return to my doings today our last day in Hawaii . . . the Admiral & I were taken off to the polo ground & stables by one Dillingham, a very rich man & a fine player who runs the polo on the island which is very high class . . . we knocked a ball about for 1 hr though I couldn't do it at all darling & had quite a wow wiv myself . . . but having just glanced at the latest picture papers which arrived by the last mail & seen nothing else almost but snaps of Harry playing in 1st class matches I'm naturally a little jealous . . .

By the way Harry & polo remind me that the King of Spain was in London in July beloved; I wonder if he rejoined the 'barrage' of which he elected himself a member last year? . . .

Poor old Dickie is rather ill tonight with real bad sunburn & he's got a touch of the sun too which has brought on fever!! But it's his own silly fault for overdoing the bathing; he was in the water 4 hrs the 1st afternoon, 8 hrs yesterday & 6 hrs today & lying full length on surfboards most of the time!!

I never bathed later than 9 A.M. or before about 5 P.M. & took care to keep my body underwater the whole time except when actually trying to surf, though that only lasts a matter of seconds really!! The poor boy is naturally in great pain tonight though there are several others in the ship as bad if not worse!! . . .

2nd September (1 0.00 A.M.)

I've had another bad day with indigestion sweetie; I didn't tell you I
was bad yesterday & I'm in such pain tonight . . .

It's naturally hot & I've been sprawling round looking at all the new
picture papers, though they infuriate me & disgust me angel with all
their silly 'society snaps' & futile & idiotic texts & columns!! Of course
sometimes people are let down by the Sketch & Tatler who publish
their photos without permission, but as often as not the snaps one sees
are posed for or anyway the people know they are being snapped & just
couldn't be more delighted!!

However I suppose that if I found a little snap of my Fredie, instead
of taking exception to the paper I would thoroughly approve, though I
know you loathe 'being in' those silly rags and as we've so often agreed
they are the worst inciters of Bolshevism, though I suppose we should
miss them if we hadn't got them to look at!!

4th September (1 0.00 P.M.)

It's always 10.00 P.M. isn't it? but then you see one gets into a sort of
fixed routine at sea & I always reserve my only little pleasure of the 24
hrs writing to my little Fredie till after dinner & as we always have 4 or
5 or 6 of the officers in I can't send them away till now!! . . .

Dickie's sunburnt legs are a bad sight & I spent a sordid half hour
this evening pricking his blisters with a needle though it didn't hurt
him!!

5th September (1 1.00 P.M.)

Sunday again . . . it's heating up again as I predicted & everyone is
peevish . . .

There's been a slight trouble tonight angel which has depressed me
as I've indirectly been the cause of getting a snotty [*midshipman*] into
trouble; one of them plays the 'jazz traps' very well & as I've got a small
set & am quite keen I sent for him from the gunroom to give me a
lesson!!

It seems that it was someone's birthday & so they had been 'hitting
it up' at dinner & though I didn't actually notice it myself the poor

brute was slightly shot away & was caught out by both the Admiral &
the captain when they came in later!! He's had his leave & 'wine bill'
stopped for the rest of the trip so that he won't be able to land again
till we get to Portsmouth, though perhaps going dry for a month won't
do him any harm!! But it's all rather an unfortunate incident & though
of course I'm in no way to blame yet but for my asking him up he
would never have been caught out, though he was a fool to come up if
he was only even just un tout tout petit peu toxy!! . . .

6th September (1 0.00 P.M.)

. . . Dickie is ever so much better & he's been able to have a good yarn
with the sub lieut. of the gunroom about that incident of the snotty
last night & what all the others are thinking & saying about it; it's a
relief to me to know that they don't bring my name into it at all,
sweetheart, which was the only thing I dreaded!! It would be terrible to
become unpopular with or get a bad name in the gunroom wouldn't it,
mon amour? . . .

   . . . Think sometimes of your lonely little David who loves you loves
you & adores YOU.

Letter No 26
H.M.S. 'Renown', At sea, Acapulco to Panama
9th September 1920 (1 0.00 P.M.)

My vewy vewy own precious beloved little Fredie,

   It's been a disastrous 24 hrs sweetie as you'll see!! We anchored in
Acapulco Bay & the first news that greeted us was that a stoker had
'pipped it' during the morning watch as a result of heat stroke, though
I am told he had twice had 'D.T.s'.

   So that was a bad start, wasn't it, angel, & then about 9.00 A.M. our
consul brought a mail on board but oh! the pain of it (you can guess
the worst now), no Fredie letter, though it wasn't a fat mail!!

   I got 2 letters from Philip, who gives me just a scrap of news of TOI
& Bertie also mentions your name & promises to keep you well
informed of all my movements: very gracious of him, isn't it, angel . . .

   I landed with Godfrey, Joey & Dickie for a walk; we nosed around

My vewy vewy own precious darling beloved,

. . . It's been a free day for me except for tonight when we gave a party on board 'Renown' . . . there was to have been dancing on board, but there was a torrential tropical shower which made that impossible so that it was something of a fiasco & too depressing for words my beloved!!

Trinidad 17.9.20.

Talking to negro returned men.

Fulfilling one of the last public duties of the tour.

the queer dirty little dago town & then 'hiked it' away into the hills for
2 or 3 miles . . . quite interesting to have landed just once in Mexico
though of course Acapulco isn't really much more than a village,
though the bay makes a fine harbour & it's one of the oldest Spanish
settlements. [*At that time, Acapulco had a population of about 5,000; the
town had been completely wrecked by an earthquake in 1909.*]

   But the people are too revolting for words, sweetheart, super dagoes
& some of them are quite black as a result of Spaniards inter-breeding
with the Indians; & of course they only talk Spanish so that I couldn't
make myself understood even in my bad Italian, though Godfrey
speaks Spanish fluently & so was able to help us buy a few queer
souvenirs such as 'sombreros' (those huge Mexican straw hats) etc. . . .

   We weighed & steamed out the bay at 5.00. When we got outside
we stopped the ship & buried the stoker who died this morning,
holding a funeral service on the fo'c'sle & tipping the body (sewn up in
canvas with a weight at its feet) overboard!! Rather impressive but
terribly sordid, though of course the men revel in all that . . .

11th September (11.30 P.M.)

I've got that rotten indigestion again tonight sweetie which besides
being vewy painful is rather a blow as I hoped so much I was cured
having gone a whole week without it!! . . .

12th September (9.00 P.M.)

'Painy' all gone angel & I'm feeling quite well again & oh! so so excited
at the news that there are 3 bags of mails waiting for us at Panama in
the morning!! . . .

   It's such a perfect & comforting thought that this is probably the last
letter that I'll be able to write to you mon amour; the next time we
communicate will be 'de vive voix'!! It's going to be so interesting
sweetie to see which of us has changed the most in 'on top' ideas; our
deep down thoughts & feelings we both know will never never change
a scrap . . .

   All all my ever increasing love . . . your David.

But we've all got the blues tonight as Godfrey & Joey are both sick (poisoned I think) & poor little 'Digger' (the wallaby) I was so keen to get home anyway for you to see, died while we were at dinner, also poisoned!! Some filthy grass or plant he must have eaten when he escaped into the bush for an hour this morning & we are all quite upset & shall miss him terribly on the ship!! He was such a sweet little animal & it's so tragic that he should have pegged out only 3 weeks from England! . . .

But I really must stop now my precious beloved, au revoir just once again my sweetie & please please take care of yourself & don't forget the little note to York House for me to find on 11th October, or better still give it to Bertie the day before to bring down to Portsmouth as he's going to meet me there!!

Oh! yes my little Fredie that's a marvellous brainwave & please please do that for your vewy vewy own devoted & adoring little amoureux your little David.

Bless you bless you & God keep my sweet divine lovely blessed one & only little sweetheart my little Fredie Wedie for ME!! All all my great great love VENUS David.

This is the last letter of the Prince's tour. Mountbatten records that they travelled over 45,000 miles by sea and land, visiting 208 places in the 210 days of the trip. The *Renown* had consumed nearly 36,000 tons of oil.

England

❧

1920–1

Pitsford Hall, Northampton
[The home of George Drummond, Master of the Pytchley Hunt.]
22nd December 1920

Fredie darling beloved à moi,

What a divine little talk we had this evening, didn't we, sweetheart, & all you said & told has made me happier than ever. How your devoted adoring little parpee [*puppy*] loves you loves you sweetie & how divine of you not to have gone on to that party at the 'Embassy' [*Club*] last night which shows that you wanted to make him happy as you know how he loathes your going to parties without him, though I'm so distressed to hear you've had that bloody indigestion again . . .

And then sending [*cuff*]links to Sandringham for me to choose, mon amour; how you are spoiling me & I'll get my head turned soon!! . . .

I've no news for you as I told you on the phone that I didn't have much of a day with the Pytchley, though lots of jumping & I kept up all right . . .

What a bore Philip is getting huffy because I didn't say goodbye to him, though it's our fault or perhaps more mine for having got into this state of daily communication with him!! We must try to somewhat loosen the ropes which with he has bound himself so tightly to us when we return after the New Year, though of course we'll keep in with him & make use of him to a certain extent!!

I like a little of Philip very much but not too much & I know you feel the same angel & it's 'too much' now!! . . .

How I wonder what you & Hannah [*Philip's cousin and hostess, married to David Gubbay, head of the David Sassoon firm*] had to say about me this afternoon; I hope no secrets as that wouldn't be at all kind, would it? You must tell me darling. How I'm looking forward to a Fredie letter tomorrow morning, just aching for one & I know one is on its way though the posts are so bad up here & I might have to wait another 24 hrs. Anyway I'll go to bed sweetheart & not finish till the morning in case you ask me anything in the letter if it does arrive.

Bless you bless you my vewy vewy own precious darling beloved little Fredie et bonne nuit et dors bien; your little parpee loves you loves you mon amour; your David's burning love (though also very tender love) is all all all all yours darling of my heart my Fredie.

Pitsford Hall, Northampton
23rd December 1920

Darling beloved little Fredie,

I'm just mad that I haven't been able to talk to you tonight sweetheart though they told me at Lamcote that you aren't arriving till tomorrow!!

No doubt you have told me of delaying your departure from London in that letter which I haven't got yet & I've rung up 3992 but can't get a reply, though that doesn't exactly surprise me at 11.00 P.M. But I'm very disappointed my beloved as you know I loathe not being able to talk to you on the phone each day when we are separated!! . . .

I'm a little bit peevish tonight because I took it properly today & have a stiff & aching left shoulder & arm though I'm d—d lucky not to have broken a collar bone, not that that is very serious!! I wouldn't mind if I could talk to TOI but as I can't well F— F—!!

Where on earth can you be this evening; oh! how I hate not knowing, sweetheart!! I hope to God not at a party with that bloody

Michael, that would be too much & I could murder him if you are, though perhaps I'm being hard on you!! But you must please forgive me angel as you know I'm peevish!!

I had a rotten day as far as hunting is concerned though it's been a very tiring day with lots of lepping but that is very good practice for me & it's done me worlds of good!! I was riding 2 horses that I really couldn't hold & one of them bolted with me twice, though only the length of a field each time.

Mais ça suffit sweetie as I'm boring you but your little 'parpee' likes to tell you everything oh! if only I was going to Lamcote tomorrow instead of to Sandringham; what I think of Xmas though please think of your David if you go to church on Xmas morning as I will only think of my Fredie when I go & pray for US & our happiness!! . . .

Good night & bless you my sweetheart; this is quite a silly letter but I'm not quite normal tonight.

> *York Cottage, Sandringham*
> *24th December 1920 (7.30 P.M.)*

Fredie darling darling beloved à moi

What perfectly divine links, my sweetheart, & I've chosen the plainer ones with diamonds in the centre & love them not only because you gave them to me but for themselves!! They go so well with my blue shirts & will look marvellous in 'boiled' cuffs too. Thank you thank you for them Fredie darling & bless you for being so so sweet to your little parpee who loves you loves you . . .

Christ it's bloody here & I'm so depressed mon amour & oh! how lonely & I feel quite a stranger here somehow & I'm not appreciated at all. I know I'm not though why should I be angel when I've absolutely nothing in common with the rest of my family & have really drifted away from them altogether. But I'm not grousing & don't care a f— whether I'm appreciated or not, though it's rather boring & makes our separation harder to bear than ever.

Old Reggie is about the only one who greeted me with a shadow of warmth today & I'm glad he is here!! But I've only been here a few hours darling so one can't get the atmosphere at once; there's been a kind of Xmas tree stunt this evening though a gloomier family

The Prince personalised his official Christmas card of 1920 for Freda.

gathering couldn't possibly be imagined!! I only hope you are doing better sweetie.

Post just off sweetie so à demain soir . . . bless you bless you mon amour I love you love you & only think of TOI & only look forward to 5th January. Ever your very very own devoted adoring little parpee your David.

Left arm very stiff & aching & the toss has shaken me a little though I'll be all right again tomorrow.

York Cottage, Sandringham
25th December 1920 (7.30 P.M.)

My very very own precious beloved one,

Only a little letter this evening my sweetheart as I hope to talk to you in a few moments & I'm struggling with a vast heap of Xmas cards though it's an unequal contest . . .

I went to church this morning & perhaps you did too sweetheart & I hope it was about 11.00 to 12.00 as then perhaps we prayed for each other at the same moment, which is rather a divine thought, isn't it, angel?

I rode this afternoon & my arm is much better & I've quite recovered from the toss, though it shook me up a lot. What a rush it is this evening & if I don't stop soon I'll miss the post & then I'll go mad. But I'll be able to tell you everything on the phone though I can't say I love you love you madly & desperately darling on the phone so I write it now though you know that so well now!!

Bless you my precious little Fredie darling toujours ton petit David.

York Cottage, Sandringham
26th December 1920 (6.30 P.M.)

Fredie darling darling beloved,

It was very very kind to be woken up with 2 letters from Lamcote this morning; bless you bless you for yours my sweetheart & of course it's not selfish but divine of you to say you don't want me to be quite happy without TOI!!

It's such a sweet little thing for you to have said & it makes me purr with love sweetie though you know it isn't necessary for you to say you don't want me to be quite happy sans TOI as you know how lonely & bored I am & then miserable on top though oh!! so so happy deep down mon amour because I know you love me!!

Please thank little Vera for her little letter; how happy she must be to have you at Lamcote & how happy you are making her darling; I'm very very envious of her just now she's getting far more than her share of you even though it is Xmas time!! Very hard on me sweetheart though Dieu merci ce n'est pas pour longtemps & I suppose I mustn't grudge her you as she doesn't get you very often.

I'm so ashamed of that foul little scrawl last night though you can't think what a rush it was & it was better than nothing. I've had a vast quantity of cards & letters which it's good propaganda to answer & I'm about square now through sitting up writing till 2.00 A.M.

I managed to put a scrap of pep into last night's Xmas party chez ma grand-mere & with the help of 4 glasses of port I made an effort to cultivate the spirit of the season & make a bit of noise & I even brought myself to dance with ma tante Maud of Norway, who is dance mad though 'no bonne' & we only had a gramophone.

I was dragged to church again this morning though I think church 2 days running is overdoing it & bad for one!! I must confess to being un peu désappointé that you didn't go yesterday my Fredie darling as I was imagining your precious beloved little self sitting or kneeling down at the same time as your little parpee was. And I prayed oh! so fervently for TOI et MOI & our future happiness mon amour & concentrated as you would say!! And I imagined you concentrating too angel, not that you weren't, although not actually in church!!

How I'm wondering whether that bloody Michael is worrying TOI from Wilton chérie? Please oh! please don't let him go over to see you & if he does please refuse to see him, or let him into the house & don't dance much with him if you meet him at parties or hunt balls!!

I just can't bear it any more angel & I just loathe to think of him messing around anywhere near you let alone to know it, though you promised sweetie!! It's funny but do you know Michael & I have not exchanged even Xmas cards; I wonder why? . . .

I love my links & thank you thank you again for them; you are far too sweet to me beloved et tu me gates though please go on spoiling me by loving me my Fredie!! You know that's all I want or ask for & it's all that keeps me alive & makes life worth living.

Bless you bless you again for your last letter & please always remember that whenever you think of your little parpee your David who loves you loves you so so madly & desperately that he is thinking of TOI!

A ce soir au telephone et à demain on paper!!!! But oh how I want you want you my beloved little Fredie.

York Cottage, Sandringham
27th December 1920 (7.00 P.M.)

My precious beloved little Fredie

Just back from hunting sweetheart & I haven't had a toss, not that we really did very much although we've had a certain amount of jumping!! Of course I'm terribly spoilt as I'm used to the marvellous grass country of Northampton & Leicester & the clean fences & I didn't jump a fence today that gave me a proper feel!! . . .

Oh! & Fredie darling who should I run into at the meet but Lady Coke who had come over with a bunch from Holkham!! And the little bitch made a dead set at me during the few moments I was in the house for a drink!! Christ! how I loathe that woman & she didn't get any change out of me!! . . .

I'm delighted to hear that Michael isn't worrying you too much & that he is going to Stockholm on Saturday!! I couldn't think of a better place for him angel except that it's not far enough away. Australia or N.Z. would be better or even the South Pole . . .

I enclose a letter that may amuse you darling; old Reggie Esher really is rather sweet suggesting that I should give you the tartan if I don't want it though I must have a look at it first!! [*The 2nd Viscount Esher – he spelled his name 'Regy' – wrote from his house in Callander offering the Prince some of his locally made tartan; he suggested that should he not like it, to give it away, only 'in the family. Mine I mean!' Freda was the daughter-in-law of Esher's sister, Violet, previously mentioned*].

I haven't had time to work out all those distances yet, Nottingham from here & on to London, as I've been out all day, but I will tomorrow or even after dinner. They've just come for the letters so goodnight my very very own precious darling beloved little Fredie all all your devoted adoring little parpee David's love is yours yours my sweetheart!!

York Cottage, Sandringham
28th December 1920 (7.00 P.M.)

Fredie darling precious beloved,

No luck on the phone up to now this evening though I'm to ring up again at 7.45. But you did tell me between 5.30 & 6 didn't you sweetie?

I'm so happy today with 2 letters from TOI & such divine letters & bless you & thank you for them angel!! I've been shooting today though I didn't enjoy it much & was so bored & I couldn't hit much though 'ce n'est pas mon métier', is it darling!!

I've got to go & dine chez ma grand-mere again tonight ce qui est assomant [*'wearisome': by now Queen Alexandra was almost totally deaf, which made socialising with her very difficult*] but dinner parties seem to do the poor old woman good so I suppose it's a kind act to go & my mamma & Mary are dining too. To think that I've got another whole week of this ghastly existence sans TOI to stick out Fredie darling it's a great strain & I'm already so terribly peeved & irritable & can hardly bring myself to be pleasant. Christ! how fed up I am with our long & useless & futile & unnatural separation.

Godfrey sent me the enclosed about Philip this morning which is a very unnecessary thing to have written & which I naturally entirely disregard!! But I send it as it will amuse you though it's foul & not at all true. [*'The enclosed' is a scurrilous cutting containing derogatory and anti-Semitic comments about the Prince's friendship with Sir Philip Sassoon.*] . . .

Bless you again for my 2 divine letters which are everything to me with our talks.

Ever your little parpee, David.

York Cottage, Sandringham
29th December 1920 (7.30 P.M.)

Fredie my darling precious beloved,

I've only got ½ hr to write & I've got oh! so much to tell you sweetie. First of all bless you bless you for 2 such divine darling letters that arrived at teatime. I haven't been able to write before because there's been a tenants' & servants' Xmas tree stunt this evening which has meant a lot of hard work for your poor little parpee distributing presents & crackers & Christ knows what!!

But Fredie darling I'm just livid & wild about that bloody snap in the Daily Mirror in which that —— —— little bitch Lady Coke is to be seen standing in front of me! A thousand curses on her, though as you can see (I've cut it out & enclose it in case you haven't seen it though I bet you have) I'm not apparently in the least bit conscious of her presence!!

Blast her for running up to Toria (who was on my right) at the moment the man snapped; just my luck, angel, though I warned you she might be in a snap. I'm so angry about it that I can hardly write on the subject & I'm unhappy about it too, though what you say about it

The Prince of Wales and Queen Maud of Norway (on horseback) with Queen Mary at the meet at Tittleshall, Norfolk.

The Prince's vitriolically annotated cutting of the Daily Mirror *picture. Why he turned against Lady Coke so savagely has never been established.*

not mattering a scrap between TOI et MOI relieves me enormously sweetheart, though you have every right to be angwy with your parpee for not watching out better & not moving away. However we'll talk about it on the phone after dinner.

I hope you aren't too tired after the ball last night & that you didn't enjoy it; how was Burghie & was that bloody Michael there? I loathed today's shoot as I couldn't hit anything & it was raining!! . . .

Oh! how I'm looking forward to next Wednesday my beloved. The Admiral & Godfrey have been worrying me on the phone so my time for writing has been cut terribly short though I'll be talking to you soon & I'll write again before I go to bed angel.

I love you love you love you mon amour my precious darling beloved little Fredie

your v. v. own little   David.

York Cottage, Sandringham
29th December 1920 (11.30 P.M.)

Fredie my darling precious beloved,

What an unsatisfactory talk we've just had sweetheart, though the line was rotten & there were people in the room your end. What a pity they can't mend the other & more private apparatus at Lamcote!! However thank Gawd I've been able to talk to my Fredie just a little bit as I'm feeling so mouldy & lonely tonight & loving her loving her so so madly!! . . .

I hope to God you'll be in by 7.45 which will be about my last chance to ring you before midnight as I've got to go to a bloody 'servants' party' with my mamma after dinner tomorrow night which will keep me out to au moins minuit I'm afraid my beloved.

Christ how late you were last night though I'm so glad you didn't enjoy the 'ball'; I shan't stay long at the Hunt Ball next Tuesday 4th January, no not your little parpee sans TOI!! Bless you for having enfin got my ring returned & for wearing it again; I just loathed seeing Philip's there instead & please don't wear his any more angel & above all not Michael's, it was a ring he gave you for Xmas, wasn't it, sweetie!! David wouldn't care for that at all!! . . .

I'm such a tired & lonely & fed-up little parpee now that I'm going to bed, my beloved; it's a truly devastating existence here & thank God this time next week we'll be together again sweetheart. This separation gets worse every day & night till I nearly go mad sometimes, particularly when we can't have a proper talk as we couldn't tonight & I'm very very peeved just now.

You see Reggie is the only man here who appreciates TOI & to whom I care to vaguely discuss TOI with & he goes on Saturday. But I like old Reggie & have got to know him far better this last week & we've made great friends, though not too great friends. You know what I mean, though what I like about him is that he thinks so much of TOI!! So long as it's not Michael I adore hearing men saying divine things about TOI my Fredie & to be able to discuss you vaguely!!

But to bed & so bonne nuit my precious darling beloved little angel. I love you love you far far more than ever.

30th December (6.30 P.M.)

I'm sad this evening as I've had no Fredie letter, c'est agaçant
[*irritating*] particularly as I know you've written.

I was shooting a little better today though that's not saying vewy
much though I wasn't quite so bored!! but I must confess to looking
forward to hunting again tomorrow with the West Norfolk & it's their
best country too & we are taking Mary out parce que 'ses periodes sont
passées'!!

How is the smoking going, Fredie my darling? I'm such a good
little parpee as I've only smoked 4 cigarettes up to now today & only
4 tiny wee pipes & one cigar. Aren't you pleased with your David
knowing what an inveterate smoker he is & I'm really feeling better
for it.

What I think of this bloody stunt tonight, though it will be better
than the Hunt Ball. I'm just dreading that, though promise I won't
dance with Lady Coke even if she asks me to!!

Mon amour this will probably be the last letter that you'll get from
me in 1920 so with all all my loving good wishes for your happiness &
ours in the New Year 1921 I ask you Fredie darling to forget all that
you wrote to me in that famous No 8 letter to Australia. Cut it all out
entirely for good & all at midnight tomorrow angel when your little
parpee David will be thinking of his precious beloved little Fredie &
praying so fervently for OUR happiness!!

Sweetheart please 'concentrate'; you said the other day that if you
'concentrate' on anything it always comes off. We don't want anything
awful to happen to old Duddie but please concentrate mon amour &
I've so often told you that I know one day we'll be far happier than we
are even now!! But that's not 'stop press' is it my beloved?

It's not that I've any doubt you've forgotten all about No 8 letter
months ago only I think perhaps you'll like to read this from me just
now angel & I want to make quite quite sure that it really dies with
1920!! It's cruel we can't see the New Year in together my beloved as I
always feel it's rather a solemn & thrilling moment & means something
that Xmas never does.

Perhaps I could try & ring you up about midnight tomorrow so that
we could be talking at the moment or as near it as possible; that would

be rather kind, wouldn't it, Fredie darling, kind for both of us . . .

A plus tard or any way à demain though I don't at all care to say the latter. Bless you bless you . . . & God keep you for your little David.

York Cottage, Sandringham
31st December 1920 (7.30 P.M.)

Fredie my darling darling beloved

Bless you for a little letter of 29th received this morning sweetie; we only got back from hunting at 6.00 so it's been a fearful rush this evening & I've only time for a short little scrawl. We had quite fun today as we were on the move all day & there was plenty of jumping though it poured 'jugs of blood' the whole time & it was more swimming than hunting & the going was terribly heavy . . .

Last night's servants' stunt was very grim though I did my duty darling & danced with all the ugliest house-maids etc. that I could find which I think went down well. That winds up the Xmas 'festivities' thank God & how I've loathed them all.

Post just off so goodnight Fredie my darling darling precious beloved little angel à bientot au telephone & again all all my wishes for 1921!! I love you love you sweetheart.

Ever your little parpee, David.

York Cottage, Sandringham
1st January 1921 (7.30 P.M.)

My precious darling beloved little Fredie,

No time for a long letter again sweetheart as I've only been in 1 hr from beagling & had to soak in a bath as I was drenched & cold & dead beat!! . . .

Two such divine letters from TOI this morning Fredie my beloved . . . how you comfort me about the snap of Lady Coke; of course it didn't really worry me angel as it was all so futile though I was enraged at appearing in a snap with that bitch in a newspaper so as everyone could see!! Blast her!! If I happen to appear with any woman in a purely private & unofficial way it must only be with TOI mon amour.

I'm sorry old Reggie has gone; he is a great companion to me here & is such fun to talk to!! He & I have had many real good laughs & we split our sides. Philip returns tonight & has asked me to ring after dinner so I think I will!! I'll ring you about 7.45 though hope I'll be able to talk to you again later as last night.

What a good little talk we had didn't we my Fredie? though I'm fed up with phoning & want to see TOI and kiss TOI & talk to TOI properly as we've now only 3 more days to wait my beloved!!

Must stop à bientot & bless you bless you sweetheart for loving me!! You'll never know how much I love you love you love you my precious darling little Fredie. Tous tous mes baisers except one for each of the babies. Ever your your little parpee David.

York Cottage, Sandringham
2nd January 1921 (7.00 P.M.)

Fredie my darling darling beloved,

It was so sweet of you to come down & talk to me this morning & you made me so happy & I didn't mind church so much, though I'll miss our talk this evening terribly much, angel!! . . .

Of course I quite understand how tricky it is with your father sweetheart as I have to suffer under just such a father myself, though I'm disappointed I can't go to Lamcote & lunch with your mamma & see Vera when picking you up. But that's a brilliant idea about Northampton Fredie darling & you must let me know all about the train when we talk after dinner tomorrow. One arriving Northampton about 2.00 P.M. would be a good time & I could have some cold lunch in the car for you & we could stop on the road to eat it, couldn't we? But you will see & any time that suits you suits me sweetheart though don't forget I am 3 hrs from Northampton!!

It is marvellous to think I am going to see TOI again so soon Fredie my precious darling beloved & your little 'parpee' is just whining & yapping & wagging his tail with joy & excitement; the next 2 days will drag terribly though hunting will help tomorrow along.

My mamma is going to the Hunt Ball on Tuesday but I've told her she mustn't stay late & must order her car for 11.00 P.M. . . .

I had a long talk to Hannah this evening who seems in good shape & was delighted to get your love!! As regards Sargent she's going to find out when he's actually sailing for U.S.A. because if it's not till end of January it's worth waiting till Philip has gone to the continent, which he apparently does on 12th!! I think she advises well!! . . . [*The Prince and Freda were planning to have their pictures painted by John Singer Sargent, whose 1923 portrait of Sir Philip Sassoon is in the Tate gallery.*]

A demain soir, your little parpee loves you loves you loves you more than he could ever say. Your little

David.

> *York Cottage, Sandringham*
> *3rd January 1921 (7.30 P.M.)*

Fredie my darling precious beloved

It's absolutely rotten & mouldy not having had a letter again today . . . voilà over 48 hrs since your last which is vewy sad for your poor little parpee.

We had quite a decent slow hunt this morning but did nothing this afternoon so it hasn't been much of a day though the weather was perfect & bright & warm & it was quite pleasant riding about.

Reggie came over from Holkham to hunt as he managed to get a mount & was attended by a vast crowd of women who are staying there & the little bitch was amongst them at the meet, though all she got was the most formal of 'good mornings' as I 'princed by' on a very fresh horse that I couldn't hold!

Christ! You would have laughed if you could have seen it all happen Fredie darling; first the attempt to give me the 'glad eye' & then her face of disgust when she realised I hadn't the slightest intention of stopping to talk to her. I enjoyed it a lot sweetheart & you missed a good turn!!

I expect there'll be some 'ogling' at the hunt ball tomorrow night; if only TOI was going to be there so as we could dance perfectly . . . But oh! for Wednesday darling, d–mn everything else, & I'm so longing to hear about the train at Northampton.

I've just been talking to Philip on the phone & he says Sargent has booked his passage for Wednesday 19th January. Philip goes abroad 12th January just a week before so perhaps we could both of us fit in sittings that week so as not to be worried by Philip!! But we shall see; anyway I haven't written to Sargent yet . . .

The young duke [*Bertie*] has been seedy today; overdid it running on Saturday I think, & his tummy has gone wrong; that bad operation he had in December 1917 [*actually November: for a stomach ulcer*] has weakened it a lot & he evidently mustn't run. I think my family blame me a little for taking him, but after all that's not my affair & he's 25 & ought to know what he can or can't do if anybody does!! And he ran well, though you'll be pleased to hear that your little 'Parpee' has established quite a reputation for himself in Norfolk as regards his running powers . . .

Now I must go & soak in a bath Fredie darling so à bientot au téléphone when you'll be able to tell me a lot. I love you love you so darling precious beloved little sweetheart à moi.

Your devoted & your adoring little parpee your David loves you loves you angel.

St James', SW
12.1.21 (3.00 A.M.)

Fredie my precious darling beloved,

What I think of leaving TOI in a few hours my sweetheart & not seeing TOI till Thursday evening, though it's my fault, I know, angel, & not very kind of me rushing away again. But you know I look on it all as stunting & work sweetie & I'm so keen to win anyway just one point-to-point race this spring, which I feel I could do given a little luck & if I take a little trouble!! And my incentive is that I know my Fredie would be extra pleased with her little 'parpee' if he did win one wouldn't she? Yes, she would!!

And bless you bless you for making life so happy for 'parpee' this last week; I don't think we've ever seen so much of each other in such a few days as we have since I picked you up at Peterborough. How extra sweet & divine you've been to me mon amour & all the petting I've had!! I'm a very very happy little 'parpee', in fact quite a spoilt little parpee but the petting isn't wasted!!

And tonight's party has been so divine for me too angel & we did dance well, didn't we, though I've got so much room for improvement. What a perfect idea the weekend at Lamcote is only we must keep it very quiet & informal or rather private as one might say. But I think it would be such a good little stunt re your family & such good propaganda with your father!!

Duddie does come in useful sometimes, doesn't he, though not tonight my beloved when I do want you so so terribly much & it's hard on us that we couldn't have been alone at [*number*] 65!! Not very kind when we were loving so so much tonight & then we both got quite tired suddenly at the same moment like two little children & we wanted to go to sleep in each other's arms!! But don't forget what I wrote for the New Year sweetheart; it's absolutely inconceivable that it won't happen some day.

I'm so hoping that you'll perhaps ring me but anyway we'll talk at 9.20 Fredie my darling darling precious beloved & it's à jeudi soir!!

Please don't be too nice to Michael.

Blessings blessings from your ever devoted adoring little 'parpee' David who loves you loves you.

So sad & lonely on top.

The collection of letters ends here.

EPILOGUE

George V died in January 1936, having stated with great prescience to Stanley Baldwin, the Prime Minister, that his eldest son would ruin himself within twelve months.

Queen Mary survived until after the death of George VI, and died in March 1953.

In early 1923, **Prince Albert**, Duke of York, was engaged to Elizabeth Bowes Lyon. He married her in April the same year. After the abdication in 1936, he became George VI; he died in 1952.

Prince George, Duke of Kent, was killed in 1942, when the aircraft in which he was travelling to Iceland crashed.

Prince Henry, Duke of Gloucester, lived until 1974.

Sheila, Lady Loughborough, was divorced in 1926. In 1928 she married Sir John Milbanke, known both as 'Buffles' and 'The Boxing Baronet', who died in 1947. Finally, in 1954, she was married again, to Prince Dimitri Obolensky. She died in 1969.

Lord Loughborough died in 1929, after a fall from a building in London; the inquest verdict was suicide.

Rosemary Leveson-Gower, who had married Lord Ednam, had a life beset by tragedy. Her brother, Alastair, died aged thirty of malaria in 1921 on a trip to Africa. In 1929, her seven-year-old son was killed by a lorry after losing control of his fairy-cycle. Less than a year later she was herself killed in a plane crash while returning from a weekend in Le Touquet.

Poots and Noel Francis's marriage ended in divorce; she later married Humphrey Butler, Prince George's Equerry. They were guests on the infamous *Nahlin* cruise with King Edward VIII and Mrs Simpson during the summer of 1936.

Dickie Mountbatten became engaged to Edwina Ashley, granddaughter and heiress of Edwardian financier Sir Ernest Cassel, during his tour of India with the Prince in February 1922. His extraordinary life and career is well documented. He was assassinated by the IRA in 1979.

Joey Legh and Sarah Shaughnessy were married in November 1920, with both 'The Boy' and 'Dirty Dick' in attendance. In 1930, they escaped the air crash which killed Rosemary Leveson-Gower, because of Sarah's fear of flying: concerned by the wind which had arisen, she persuaded Joey to accompany her home by sea. Joey continued in royal service, serving the Prince as King, and following him briefly into exile before joining the staff of George VI. He died from emphysema in 1955, and Sarah died a few hours later from cancer.

Claud Hamilton married Mrs Violet Newall in 1933, and also remained in royal service throughout his career. He died in 1975.

Joan Mulholland remarried, in 1922, the same 'Frederick Rudolph, 10th Earl of Cavan' who had commanded the Prince in Italy.

Philip Sassoon's career took him to the Air Ministry and, later, he became First Commissioner of Works in Neville Chamberlain's administration. In June 1939, a throat infection spread to his lungs, and he died at his Park Lane house, aged only fifty.

Reggie Seymour married Winifred Boyd-Rochfort in 1922; she died in 1925. His second wife was Lady Katherine Hamilton, daughter of the 3rd Duke of Abercorn (niece of the Lord Claud), whom he married in 1930. He continued as George V's Equerry, and, after the King's death, served in the same role for Queen Mary. He was created KCVO (Knight Commander of the Royal Victorian Order) in 1935 and died in 1938.

The Prince fulfilled his ambition to take part in both point-to-points and steeplechases, winning several, over the next few years. He also continued to hunt, until, after more than his share of falls and his father's severe illness in 1928, he bowed to pressure to give up riding.

His postponed trip to India took place in 1921–2, and proved difficult; the problems of his previous tours – depression, exhaustion and staff difficulties (even Halsey threatened to resign) – were still present, and were exacerbated by both political problems and the fact that he thought the tour was a waste of time, as it appeared to be achieving nothing. The Viceroy, Lord Reading, however, pronounced the visit a remarkable success.

The Prince's relationship with Freda continued until 1934, although, as time passed and the Prince's tours continued, her friendship with Michael Herbert intensified, and when there was talk of a divorce from Duddie in 1922, the Prince feared that she would marry him.

Although the divorce rumours subsided for the time being, her feelings for the Prince were never as strong again, and she again used the excuse of her children's reputation for seeing less of him. Despite his numerous affairs, and hers, she still retained an extraordinary hold over him. He continued to write copiously to her, and 2,000 further letters exist, from which extracts have been quoted in Philip Ziegler's biography *King Edward VIII*.

Although Wallis Simpson initially stole the affections of the Prince from his then mistress, Lady Furness, Freda did not last long either. In early 1934, she was wholly preoccupied for several months with the illness of her elder daughter. When the trouble was past, she telephoned York House, and, to the operator's extreme embarrassment, had to be told that instructions had been given that she was not to be put through.

In this cowardly and cruel fashion, without the courage to end it personally, the Prince terminated the sixteen-year relationship, and his affair with Mrs Simpson took over his life.

He finally succeeded his father in 1936, as King Edward VIII. He abdicated the same year, making his famous radio broadcast to the nation on 11 December, and married Mrs Simpson in 1937. He was created Duke of Windsor, and lived most of the rest of his life in exile in France. He died in Paris in May 1972.

Freda's marriage was dissolved in 1932, and in 1937 she married the Marques de Casa Maury, though this marriage, too, was dissolved, in 1954. She continued with her interest in interior design, buying, renovating and selling properties.

She remained remarkably discreet about her relationship with the Prince, and died in 1983, aged eighty-eight.

BIBLIOGRAPHY

Asquith, Lady Cynthia, *Diaries 1915–1918*, Hutchinson, 1968

Bradford, Sarah, *King George VI*, Weidenfeld & Nicolson, 1989

Bryan III, J. & Murphy, Charles, *The Windsor Story*, William Morrow, 1979

Donaldson, Frances, *Edward VIII*, Weidenfeld & Nicolson, 1974

Duff, David, *Queen Mary*, Collins, 1985

George, Duke of Sutherland, *Looking Back*, Odhams Press, 1957

HRH The Duke of Windsor, *A King's Story*, Cassell, 1951

Jackson, Stanley, *The Sassoons – Portrait of a Dynasty*, Heinemann, 1968

Kinross, Lord, *The Windsor Years*, Collins, 1967

Liversidge, Douglas, *The Mountbattens*, Arthur Barker, 1978

Morgan, Janet, *Edwina Mountbatten*, Collins, 1991

Princess Dimitri (Lady Loughborough), *Waltzing Matilda*, unpublished. By kind permission of the Earl of Rosslyn

Rose, Kenneth, *King George V*, Weidenfeld & Nicolson, 1983

Rose, Kenneth, *Kings, Queens & Courtiers*, Weidenfeld & Nicolson, 1985

Shaughnessy, Alfred (ed.), *Sarah: The Letters and Diaries of a Courtier's Wife, 1906–1936*, Peter Owen, 1989

Stuart, Denis, *Dear Duchess – Millicent, Duchess of Sutherland*, Gollancz, 1982

Taylor, A.J.P., *English History 1914–1945*, Oxford University Press, 1965

Toland, John, *No Man's Land*, Eyre Methuen, 1980

Winter, Denis, *Haig's Command*, Viking, 1991

Winter, J.M., *The Experience of World War I*, Macmillan, 1988

Ziegler, Philip, *Diana Cooper*, Hamish Hamilton, 1981

Ziegler, Philip (ed.), *The Diaries of Lord Louis Mountbatten*, Collins, 1987

Ziegler, Philip, *King Edward VIII*, Collins, 1990

Ziegler, Philip, *Mountbatten*, Collins, 1985

INDEX